First World War

and Army of Occupation

War Diary

France, Belgium and Germany

33 DIVISION
Headquarters, Branches and Services
Royal Army Ordnance Corps
Deputy Assistant Director Ordnance Services
7 November 1915 - 30 April 1919

WO95/2412/1

The Naval & Military Press Ltd
www.nmarchive.com
Published in association with The National Archives

Published by

The Naval & Military Press Ltd

Unit 10 Ridgewood Industrial Park,

Uckfield, East Sussex,

TN22 5QE England

Tel: +44 (0) 1825 749494

www.naval-military-press.com

www.nmarchive.com

This diary has been reprinted in facsimile from the original. Any imperfections are inevitably reproduced and the quality may fall short of modern type and cartographic standards.

Contents

Document type	Place/Title	Date From	Date To
Heading	WO95/2412/1		
Heading	33rd Division Divl Troops Dep. Asst. Dir. Ord. Serv. Nov 1915-Apr 1919		
Heading	D.A.D.O.S. 33rd Div. Vols I And II Nov 15 Apr 19		
War Diary	Bulford	07/11/1915	07/11/1915
War Diary	Fochester Boulogne	08/11/1915	09/11/1915
War Diary	Bethune	11/11/1915	13/11/1915
War Diary	Morbecque	14/11/1915	22/11/1915
War Diary	Busnes	23/11/1915	01/12/1915
War Diary	Bethune	02/12/1915	12/12/1915
War Diary	Busnes	13/12/1915	21/12/1915
War Diary	Busnes	02/12/1915	09/12/1915
War Diary	Bethune	30/12/1915	30/12/1915
Heading	D.A.D.O.S. 33rd Div Vol 3 Jan		
War Diary	Bethune	01/01/1916	10/01/1916
War Diary	Bethune	01/01/1916	20/01/1916
War Diary	Bethune	01/01/1916	30/01/1916
Heading	D.A.D.O.S. 33rd Division Vol IV		
War Diary	Bethune	01/02/1916	10/02/1916
War Diary	Bethune	01/02/1916	14/02/1916
War Diary	Bethune	05/02/1916	20/02/1916
War Diary	Bethune	01/02/1916	09/02/1916
Heading	D.A.D.O.S. 33 Div Vol 5		
War Diary	Bethune	01/03/1916	10/03/1916
War Diary	Bethune	01/03/1916	16/03/1916
War Diary	Bethune	07/03/1916	20/03/1916
War Diary	Bethune	01/03/1916	30/03/1916
War Diary	Bethune	01/03/1916	31/07/1916
War Diary	Treux	02/08/1916	12/08/1916
War Diary	E.II Central	13/08/1916	18/08/1916
War Diary	E.II Central Map 57D	18/08/1916	23/08/1916
War Diary	E.II Central	23/08/1916	31/08/1916
War Diary	Villars-Bocage	01/09/1916	01/09/1916
War Diary	Bernaville	02/09/1916	03/09/1916
War Diary	Tinques	04/09/1916	08/09/1916
War Diary	L'Arbret	09/09/1916	10/09/1916
War Diary	P.A.S	11/09/1916	13/09/1916
War Diary	P.A.S H.23.B.1.7	14/04/1916	15/05/1916
War Diary	Gaudiempre P.A.S	16/06/1916	21/09/1916
War Diary	Gaudiempre	21/09/1916	21/09/1916
War Diary	Henu	22/09/1916	29/09/1916
War Diary	Doullens	30/09/1916	19/10/1916
War Diary	Corbie	19/10/1916	20/10/1916
War Diary	Treux	21/10/1916	22/10/1916
War Diary	Happy Valley F.27 C Central	22/10/1916	23/10/1916
War Diary	F.27 Central	24/10/1916	25/10/1916
War Diary	Happy Valley F.27.C Central	25/10/1916	25/10/1916
War Diary	A.13.D.5.3	26/10/1916	31/10/1916
War Diary	Plateau	01/11/1916	08/11/1916
War Diary	Hallencourt	10/11/1916	06/12/1916

War Diary	Bray Sur Somme	07/12/1916	26/12/1916
War Diary	Long	27/12/1916	31/12/1916
War Diary	Long Back Area	01/01/1917	14/01/1917
War Diary	Long	15/01/1917	18/01/1917
War Diary	Bray Sur Somme	19/01/1917	07/03/1917
War Diary	Corbie	08/03/1917	31/03/1917
War Diary	Corbie Sur Somme	01/04/1917	02/04/1917
War Diary	Beauval	03/04/1917	04/04/1917
War Diary	Lucheux	05/05/1917	06/05/1917
War Diary	Saulty	07/04/1917	12/04/1917
War Diary	Stone Boisleux-Au-Mont Office Saulty	13/04/1917	13/04/1917
War Diary	Stone Boisleux-Au-Mont Office Blaireville (D.W.H.Q)	14/04/1917	14/04/1917
War Diary	Stone Boisleux-Au-Mont Office Hamelincourt	15/04/1917	25/04/1917
War Diary	Stone Boisleux-Au-Mont Office Admford	26/04/1917	11/05/1917
War Diary	Hamelincourt	12/05/1917	31/05/1917
War Diary	Adinfer Wood	01/06/1917	18/06/1917
War Diary	Hamelincourt	19/06/1917	30/06/1917
War Diary	Officer Stone-Boisleux-Au-Mont	01/07/1917	03/07/1917
War Diary	Cavillon	04/07/1917	31/07/1917
War Diary	La Panne Plage Belgium La Panne Ville	01/08/1917	04/08/1917
War Diary	La Panne Plage La Panne Ville	05/08/1917	18/08/1917
War Diary	Coxyde Bains Office Stone La Panne Ville	19/08/1917	20/08/1917
War Diary	Coxyde Bains La Panne Ville	21/08/1917	28/08/1917
War Diary	La Panne Plage La Panne Ville	29/08/1917	29/08/1917
War Diary	Officer La Panne Plage Stone La Panne Ville	30/08/1917	31/08/1917
War Diary	Eperlecques	01/09/1917	15/09/1917
War Diary	Westoutre	16/09/1917	24/09/1917
War Diary	Dezin Camp M.12.C.6.3 Sheet 28	25/09/1917	27/09/1917
War Diary	Blaringhem	28/09/1917	04/10/1917
War Diary	Wizernes	05/10/1917	05/10/1917
War Diary	Bailleul	06/10/1917	09/10/1917
War Diary	S.17.C.7.1 Sheet 28	10/10/1917	12/10/1917
War Diary	S.17.C.7.1	13/10/1917	15/10/1917
War Diary	Ravelsberg	16/10/1917	28/10/1917
War Diary	Ravelsberg S.17.C.7.1 Sheet 28	29/10/1917	16/11/1917
War Diary	Ravelsberg	17/11/1917	17/11/1917
War Diary	Brandhoek H.7.C Central Sheet 28	18/11/1917	05/12/1917
War Diary	H7.C Central Sheet 28	06/12/1917	12/12/1917
War Diary	Steenvoorde	13/12/1917	31/12/1917
Miscellaneous	No 33 Div Supply Cue		
War Diary	Steenvoorde	01/01/1918	03/01/1918
War Diary	Brandhoek H.7.C.6.7 Sheet 28	04/01/1918	13/01/1918
War Diary	Brandhoek	14/01/1918	22/01/1918
War Diary	Brandhoek H.7.C.6.7 Sheet 28	23/01/1918	28/01/1918
War Diary	Wizernes	29/01/1918	22/02/1918
War Diary	Brandhoek H.7.C.6.7 Sheet 28	23/02/1918	17/03/1918
War Diary	Brandhoek H.7.C.6.7	18/02/1918	20/02/1918
War Diary	Brandhoek H.7.C.6.7 Sheet 28	21/02/1918	22/02/1918
War Diary	Brandhoek	23/03/1918	26/03/1918
War Diary	Brandhoek H.7.C.6.7 Sheet 28	27/03/1918	06/04/1918
War Diary	Hauteville	06/04/1918	11/04/1918
War Diary	Caestre Station	11/04/1918	12/04/1918
War Diary	Stone Office Godewaersvelde R.7.A.2.1 Sheet 27	12/04/1918	14/04/1918
War Diary	Stone Office Godewaersvelde R.7.A.2.1 Sheet 27 Office R.14.B.8.4 Sheet 27	14/04/1918	15/04/1918
War Diary	Godewaersvelde R.7.A.2.1 Sheet 27	15/04/1918	15/04/1918

War Diary	Abeele L.25.D.8.0 Sheet 27	16/04/1918	20/04/1918
War Diary	Trois Rois O.26.A.9.8 Sheet 27	20/04/1918	30/04/1918
War Diary	Trois Rois	01/05/1918	01/05/1918
War Diary	Blaringhem	02/05/1918	02/05/1918
War Diary	Winnezeele J.11.C.4.5 Sheet 27	03/05/1918	04/05/1918
War Diary	J.11.C.4.5	04/05/1918	05/05/1918
War Diary	J.11.C.4.5 Sheet 27	06/05/1918	15/05/1918
War Diary	J.11.C.4.5	16/05/1918	19/05/1918
War Diary	J.11.C.4.5 Sheet 27	19/05/1918	14/06/1918
War Diary	J.11.C.4.5	14/06/1918	16/06/1918
War Diary	J.11.C.4.5 Sheet 27	17/06/1918	30/06/1918
War Diary	J.11.C.4.5	01/07/1918	02/07/1918
War Diary	Stone F.17.C.5.0 Office F22 Central	03/07/1918	08/07/1918
War Diary	Stone F.17.C.5.0 Office F.22 Central Sheet 27	09/07/1918	10/07/1918
War Diary	Stone F.17.C.5.0 Office F.22 Central	11/07/1918	30/07/1918
War Diary	Stone F.17.C.5.0 Office F.22 Central Sheet 27	31/07/1918	31/07/1918
War Diary	Office F.22 Cent Stone F.17.C.5.0	01/08/1918	12/08/1918
War Diary	Stone F.17.C.5.0	13/08/1918	13/08/1918
War Diary	Office F.22 Cent.	14/08/1918	17/08/1918
War Diary	Officer F.22 Cent Stone F.17.C.5.0	18/08/1918	19/08/1918
War Diary	Officer Stone Eperlecques	20/08/1918	27/08/1918
War Diary	Saulty	28/08/1918	02/09/1918
War Diary	Lucheux	03/09/1918	14/09/1918
War Diary	Stone Beaulencourt Office Les Boeuf	15/09/1918	15/09/1918
War Diary	Beaulencourt Les Boeufs	16/09/1918	16/09/1918
War Diary	Office 0.34.C.5.9 (Sheet 57.C) Stone Beaulencourt	17/09/1918	17/09/1918
War Diary	Office 0.34.C.5.9 Stone 0.34.D.1.9	18/09/1918	24/09/1918
War Diary	Office Le Mesnil Stone 0.35.D.1.9	25/09/1918	28/09/1918
War Diary	Office Stone Equancourt	29/09/1918	30/09/1918
War Diary	Equancourt	01/10/1918	10/10/1918
War Diary	Clary	11/10/1918	23/10/1918
War Diary	Forest	24/10/1918	24/10/1918
War Diary	Office Troisvilles Stone Clary	25/10/1918	31/10/1918
War Diary	Troisvilles	01/11/1918	04/11/1918
War Diary	Office-Forest Stone-Troisvilles	05/11/1918	05/11/1918
War Diary	Office Sarbaras Stone Troisville	06/11/1918	06/11/1918
War Diary	Office-Sarbaras Stone Troisvilles	07/11/1918	11/11/1918
War Diary	Office-Sarbaras Stone	12/11/1918	12/11/1918
War Diary	Englefontaine	13/11/1918	15/11/1918
War Diary	Office Beulainmont Stone	16/11/1918	16/11/1918
War Diary	Englefontaine	17/11/1918	17/11/1918
War Diary	Office Montigny Stone 0.18.B.4.3	17/11/1918	30/11/1918
War Diary	Office Selvigny Stone 0.18.B.4.3 Sheet	01/12/1918	05/12/1918
War Diary	Office Selvigny Stone 0.18.B.4.3	06/12/1918	10/12/1918
War Diary	Hornoy Somme	11/12/1918	25/12/1918
War Diary	Hornoy	26/12/1918	29/12/1918
War Diary	Hornoy Somme	30/12/1918	31/12/1918
Heading	33rd Division "G" War Diary Of January		
War Diary	Hornoy	01/01/1919	14/01/1919
War Diary	Andainville	14/01/1919	31/01/1919
War Diary	Andainville Somme	01/02/1919	18/02/1919
War Diary	Andainville	19/02/1919	22/02/1919
War Diary	Andainville Somme	23/02/1919	25/02/1919
War Diary	Andainville	26/02/1919	28/02/1919
War Diary	Andainville (Somme)	01/03/1919	03/03/1919
War Diary	Andainville	04/03/1919	31/03/1919

War Diary	Andainville (Somme)	01/04/1919	10/04/1919
War Diary	Blangy	11/04/1919	30/04/1919

33RD DIVISION
DIVL TROOPS

DEP.ASST DIR. ORD.SERV.

NOV 1915-APR 1919

D.A.D.O.S. 33rd Div:
Vols I and II

121
7809

Nov 15
1
Apr 19

Instructions regarding War Diaries and Intelligence Summaries are contained in F. S. Regs. Part II. and the Staff Manual respectively. Title Pages will be prepared in manuscript.

33rd Dvn
DADOS

WAR DIARY
or
INTELLIGENCE SUMMARY
(Erase heading not required.)

Army Form C. 2118

November, 1915

Place	Date	Hour	Summary of Events and Information	Remarks and references to Appendices
Bulford	7		Received instructions to proceed to Folkestone for embarkation for service in France	
Folkestone / Boulogne	8		Embarked / Disembarked	
	9			
Bethune	10–13		Attached to 2nd Division for instruction	
	14			
	15		Routine Duties — Notification received from Army HQ (OS 8/82, 14/11/15) that supplies of the Bipod mountings for machine guns Lewis	
	16		(referred to in WO letter 79/7881 (a 3) d/ 4/10/15. p 4. available for issue -	
	17			
Morbecque	18		A wagon limbered G.S. (2 horsed) in complete turn-out for 18th RF wired for to replace one destroyed	
	19		Indent wire submitted for Special articles of winter clothing & hypo helmets (at Rly Crossing	
	20		First Bulk wire to Ordnance Base	
	21		Brigades asked to report as to satisfactoriness or otherwise of tin water bottle	
	22		Bulk requirements wired for.	
	23		Bulk requirements wired for. 4 Motor lorries reported for permanent duty	
Busnes	24		General Note — Special winter clothing being received and issued to units — Do —	
	25		" 99 Inf Bde, No 3 Co Train, and 100 Fd Ambce to 2nd Dvn. 19 Inf Bde, No 26 Co Train[×] & 19 Fd Amb	
	26		(from 2nd Dvn. 28th Dvl Train joined.	
	⁝		Bulk requirements wired for, also 13,338 steel helmets.	

1875 Wt. W593/826 1,000,000 4/15 J.B.C. & A. A.D.S.S./Forms/C. 2118.

× Became No 3 Co 33rd Dvl Train

Instructions regarding War Diaries and Intelligence Summaries are contained in F. S. Regs., Part II. and the Staff Manual respectively. Title Pages will be prepared in manuscript.

33rd Dn
DADOS

WAR DIARY
or
INTELLIGENCE SUMMARY
(Erase heading not required.)

Nov 1915 Contd.

Army Form C. 2118

Place	Date	Hour	Summary of Events and Information	Remarks and references to Appendices
	27		Unsatisfactory reports received from Brigades re tin water bottles & forwarded (to Dvl Head Qrs.	
Busnes	28	Routine Duties	General Note — Special Articles of winter clothing being received and issued to units	
	29		Bulk requirements wired for, also 6000 of each shirts socks drawers vests and (towels for Dvl Laundry	
	30		— Do — also for magazines to complete to 64 per Lewis Gun, and periscopes No 14 (14) for R.A. 54th Dn and (2 each) 98th and 100th Inf Bdes. also for "Covers breech rifle (6000) vide G.R.O. 1165.	

[signature] Major
DADOS
33rd Dn
30/12/15

Instructions regarding War Diaries and Intelligence Summaries are contained in F. S. Regs., Part II. and the Staff Manual respectively. The Pages will be prepared in manuscript.

Army Form C. 2118

WAR DIARY
or
INTELLIGENCE SUMMARY

(Erase heading not required.)

D.A.D.O.S. 3rd Div

December 1915

Place	Date	Hour	Summary of Events and Information	Remarks and references to Appendices
BUSNES	1			
	2		Office 8 Rue de Sadi Carnot, Store Rue L'egalité. 226th Fd Co RE to 11th Fd Co RE from 2nd Div	
	3	Routine duties	Certain trench stores including 57 Hampton periscopes taken over from 7th Div. 400 braziers demanded from Base. No 1, 9 & 10 TM Batteries from 7th Div. Steps taken to illumine inadequately lighted billets.	
	4			
	5			
	6		50 bales of flannel shirts taken over from Ordnance Railhead. New Scale of anti-gas helmets viz (2 in possession and 1 in reserve promulgated	
BETHUNE	7			
	8			
	9	Routine duties	13th Essex Regt & 17th Middx Regt to 2nd Div. Issues of periscopes Box No 9, Vigilant Sniperscopes and pendulum sights to new army units	
	10		Indent wire for 20 Lewis guns for regular units to replace Vickers or Maxims withdrawn for (Machine gun Co	
	11		300 Tarpaulin arrived for CRE	
	12		54th Div Artillery to 1st Corps Troops.	
	13			
BUSNES	14		Issued magazines for Lewis guns to complete to 64 per gun	
	15		Issue of 100 Howell Protectors for trial. 1st Rl. W. Surrey and 2nd Worcester Regts (joined from 2nd Div.	

1875 Wt. W593/826 1,000,000 4/15 J.B.C. & A. A.D.S.S./Forms/C. 2118.

Instructions regarding War Diaries and Intelligence Summaries are contained in F. S. Regs., Part II. and the Staff Manual respectively. Title Pages will be prepared in manuscript.

33rd Dvn
D.A.D.O.S.

WAR DIARY
or
INTELLIGENCE SUMMARY

(Erase heading not required.)

December 1915.

Army Form C. 2118

Place	Date	Hour	Summary of Events and Information	Remarks and references to Appendices
	16		33rd Dvl Artillery joined from England	
	17	Routine duties	ORDNANCE No. Date 33rd DIVISION	
	18			
	19			
	20			
	21			
BUSNES	2		5000 pairs of socks demanded as Reserve – Urgent supply of No 14 periscopes for infantry Brigades 20 Lewis guns for regular battalions arrived 1st and 10th T.M. (Batteries to 12th Dvn.	
	3			
	4		4 Trench Mortars issued to 100th Inf Bde from workshops	
	5		2 more Trench Mortars to 100 I.B from workshops. Issue of disappearing mountings for Machine guns to 2nd A&SH; 2/RWF, 1st and 5th Scottish	
	6		Communicated with O.C. 1st Corps Troops re 3000 pairs of trousers and 3000 pairs	
	7		(of puttees to be held as a reserve under O.S. 14/139.	
	8			
	9		1st T.M Battery from 12th Dvn 15th T.M Battery from 2nd Dvn.	
BETHUNE	30		Moving into billets at Bethune	
	1		General Note Exceptionally busy throughout the month. Heavy consignments of stores and clothing arriving practically daily from the Base. A second blanket issued to all troops during the month not in permanent billets	

[signature] A. E. Stables

1875 Wt. W593/826 1,000,000 4/15 J.B.C. & A. A.D.S.S./Forms/C. 2118.

D.A.D.O. 33rd Div:
Vol: 3

Army Form C. 2118

Instructions regarding War Diaries and Intelligence Summaries are contained in F. S. Regs., Part II. and the Staff Manual respectively. Title Pages will be prepared in manuscript.

Jany 1916

WAR DIARY
or
INTELLIGENCE SUMMARY

(Erase heading not required.)

DADOS 33rd Dvn.

Place	Date	~~Hour~~	Summary of Events and Information	Remarks and references to Appendices
BETHUNE	1	ROUTINE DUTIES	Hastened supply of 1456 Magazines for Lewis guns due from Base	
	2		5 Periscopes No 9 issued to 98th Inf. Bde to replace Casualties	
	3		1 Machine gun damaged by enemy fire to Havre in truck 22595	
	4		Magazines for Lewis guns received and issued to units. 2 motor lorries broke down. 4 Machine guns received on loan from 2nd Dvn for 100th IB	
	5		Stage 1 of gas helmet re-equipment reported complete.	
	6		25 pairs of ankle boots under Complaint received from 98th Inf. Bde and returned to Base for transmission to RACD	
	7		7 Salvus sets demanded from Base to complete Dvl Allotment of 50.	
	8		Nothing of importance	
	9		— Do —	
	10		New Mob Table received for HQ Dvl Art. 3 telescopic rifles each issued to 18th, 19th, 20th and 21st RF, 16th Middx & 16th KRRC	
	1		Railhead Bethune. T/Lt. C S Mulhem from Calais for duty. Pte Beuford to Hosp. (Sick)	
	2		Lt Wooding AOD reported on boot inspection duty. 48 Mats protecting QF Spring case QF 13 and 18 pdr received from Base for RA	
	3		Specimen copies of revised bulk sheets received and supplies demanded from Base.	
	4		Lt Wooding AOD left. New Mob Tables received for Inf. & Pio bns & DAC.	(WA)
	5		Nothing of importance	
	6		— Do —	

Army Form C. 2118

WAR DIARY
or
INTELLIGENCE SUMMARY
(Erase heading not required.)

Instructions regarding War Diaries and Intelligence Summaries are contained in F. S. Regs., Part II. and the Staff Manual respectively. Title Pages will be prepared in manuscript.

Jany 1916

DADOS 33rd Divn

Place	Date	Hour	Summary of Events and Information	Remarks and references to Appendices
BETHUNE	17	ROUTINE DUTIES	Expert in repair of gum boots reported for duty and commenced a tour of units for instructional purposes.	
	8			
	9		Nothing of importance	
	20		– Do –	
	1		– Do –	
	2		– Do –	
	3		Expert in repair of gum boots left to 2nd Divn.	
	4		Short drawers issued on Med. Cert. to 2nd Argyll & Sutherland Highlanders	
	5		5000 'P' tube anti-gas helmets demanded as Dvl. Reserve in lieu of hypo	
	6		Nothing of importance	
	7		Notification received that 50 C.S.L. would be shortly issued to Divn as a reserve for use in event of evacuation of Bethune caused by severe shelling	
	8		Nothing of importance	
	9		No transport available. Appropriated for other Dvl purposes	
	30		Transport released. Bombers Knobkerries issued to infantry Brigades and 18th Middlesex Regt.	
	1		52 C.S.L. tents supplied to RA to supplement billeting accommodation	

[signature] Major
DADOS
33rd Divn

1875 Wt. W593/826 1,000,000 4/15 J.B.C. & A. A.D.S.S./Forms/C. 2118.

G. A. G. O. S

33rd Division

Vol IV

Instructions regarding War Diaries and Intelligence Summaries are contained in F. S. Regs., Part II. and the Staff Manual respectively. Title Pages will be prepared in manuscript.

33rd Divn
DADOS

WAR DIARY
or
INTELLIGENCE SUMMARY

(Erase heading not required.)

Feb 1916

Army Form C. 2118

Place	Date FEB 1916	Hour	Summary of Events and Information	Remarks and references to Appendices
BÉTHUNE	1	Routine Duties	1600 Hypo Anti-gas helmets returned to Base	
	2		1 3.7 Trench Mortar demanded for A/19 LTM Battery The first of the 2 additional bicycles in lieu of horses issued to RA Batteries	
	3			
	4		R Beeford from Hospital } Issues of PH helmets to infantry battalions.	
	5			
	6		Dvl Armourers' Shop opened	
	7			
	8			
	9		2 Vickers Machine guns (1 for 1st Middx Regt, 1 for 2nd A&SH) demanded to replace 2 destroyed by hostile fire	
	10		4 Light Trench Mortars demanded for A100 T.M. Battery to replace ones.	
	1			
	2			
	3		The second of the 2 additional bicycles in lieu of horses issued to RA Batteries	

1875 Wt. W593/826 1,000,000 4/15 J.B.C. & A. A.D.S.S./Forms/C. 2118.

Instructions regarding War Diaries and Intelligence Summaries are contained in F. S. Regs., Part II. and the Staff Manual respectively. Title Pages will be prepared in manuscript.

3rd Divn
D.A.D.O.S.

WAR DIARY
or
INTELLIGENCE SUMMARY
(Erase heading not required.)

Feb 1916

Army Form C. 2118

Place	FEB Date 1916	Hour	Summary of Events and Information	Remarks and references to Appendices
~ BÉTHUNE ~	14	Duties	An attachment for use with No 14 periscope issued to 19th Inf Bde 2 Machine Guns received from Base and issued 1 each to 1st Middx and 2nd A&SH	
	5			
	6		1 95-mm light Trench Mortar demanded for A 98 L.T.M. Battery to replace [illegible].	
	7			
	8		a/S Conductor Watts proceeded on leave. 5 Maxim Machine Guns held by 100 Bde on loan from 2nd Divn returned & despatched to Base	
	9		1st T M Battery to 12th Divn. 62nd T.M. Battery from 12th Divn 767 Fur Waistcoats despatched to Base for cleaning.	
	20		4 Maxim Machine Guns returned by 1/5 Scottish Rifles and despatched to Base	
	1		Demanded 8000 P H anti gas helmets to complete Divn to 1 per officer and man	
	2	Routine	1/6 Scottish Rifles joined 51st Divn Scale of Heliographs reduced - RA Hd Qrs 2 to Nil. Reg Inf Bns 6 to 4	
	3			
	4		208 Magazines to complete 1/6 Scottish Rifles to 64 per Lewis Gun demanded from Base	
	5		100 White suits issued for patrol duty in the snow. (50 to 98th and 50 to 100th Bde)	
	2		4th Kings L'pool Regt from 19th Divn. 16th Middx Regt and 18 R.F. to G.H.Q. a/S.C. Watts from leave. Issue of haversacks to 1 Squad N.I.H in replacement of satchels	
	7		4th Suffolk Regt from 15th Divn. 19th R.F. to G.H.Q. 4 Lewis Guns demanded from Base for 4/L'pool Regt.	
	8		8050 P.H Anti-gas helmets received from Base. 1 set of Math. scales authorised for pioneer battalion	
	9		21st R.F. to G.H.Q.	

[illegible signature]
Major DADOS
2-3-16

1875 Wt. W593/826 1,000,000 4/15 J.B.C. & A. A.D.S.S./Forms/C. 2118.

Instructions regarding War Diaries and Intelligence Summaries are contained in F. S. Regs., Part II. and the Staff Manual respectively. Title Pages will be prepared in manuscript.

DADOS
33rd Dvn

WAR DIARY
or
INTELLIGENCE SUMMARY

(Erase heading not required.)

March
1916

Army Form C. 2118

Place	Date	Hour	Summary of Events and Information	Remarks and references to Appendices
Bethune	1		Division posted to 11th Corps	
	2		Demanded an 18-pdr gun & carriage for A Battery, 156 Bde RFA to replace unser[illegible] by [illegible] fire	
	3			
	4		18-pdr gun and Carriage issued to A Battery 156 Bde RFA	
	5		4 Lewis guns received from Base & issued to 1/4 Suffolk Regt.	
	6		Demanded an 18-pdr gun for C Battery 166 to replace condemned by IOM	
	7		Issued 3 pontoon wagons to 11th Fd Co RE and 1 Limbered G.S. wagon to 1/5 Scottish Rifles	
	8		1 60-pdr gun issued to 23rd Heavy Battery RGA 208 Magazines for Lewis guns issued to 1/6 Scottish Rifles	
	9		Demanded 1 Lewis gun for 1/Cameronians to replace 1 destroyed by [illegible] fire	
	10		Issued 18 pdr gun to C Battery 166 Bde RFA. 4 Lewis guns received from Base & issued to 4th L'pool Regt.	
	1		1 Lewis gun for 1st Cameronians received from Base & issued to Unit	
	2			
	3			
	4			
	5		4 Maxims released by 1/4 Suffolk & 4 Vickers by 4th L'pools despatched to Base Major A Gray to 5th Corps Troops. Lt C.S. Mulkern assumed duties of DADOS	

1875 Wt. W593/826 1,000,000 4/15 J.B.C. & A. A.D.S.S./Forms/C. 2118.

Instructions regarding War Diaries and Intelligence Summaries are contained in F. S. Regs., Part II. and the Staff Manual respectively. Title Pages will be prepared in manuscript.

Army Form C. 2118

WAR DIARY
or
INTELLIGENCE SUMMARY
(Erase heading not required.)

DADOS
33rd Divn

March
1916

Place	Date	Hour	Summary of Events and Information	Remarks and references to Appendices
Bethune	16		1st floor of building occupied as Store collapsed 2nd satchel per officer and man demanded	
	7		20,000 p.h. Anti-gas helmets per officer & man demanded from Base	
	8			
	9		1 Limbered Wagon RE received from Base & issued to 18 Mx Regt	
	20		14,000 p.h. helmets received from Base	
	1			
	2			
	3		6000 p.h. helmets received from Base. 9th M.G. Squadron attached from 1st Cavalry Divn	
	4		4 Muzzle pivoting Mtgs received from Base	
	5		Demanded 2 addl Lewis guns for each Inf Bn to complete to 2 per Bn	
	6		8 Muzzle pivoting Mtgs received from Base	
	7		1 Travelling Kitchen for 16 KRRC received from Base & issued	
	8		227th Field Co RE from 39th Divn for training Bicycles demanded for RA HQ (2) & each RA Bde (HQ) (2) to replace horses	
	9			
	30			
	1		a/S Cond. Hire proceeded on leave	

[signature] Lieut
DADOS
33rd Divn

1875 Wt. W593/826 1,000,000 4/15 J.B.C. & A. A.D.S.S./Forms/C. 2118.

Instructions regarding War Diaries and Intelligence Summaries are contained in F. S. Regs., Part II. and the Staff Manual respectively. Title Pages will be prepared in manuscript.

WAR DIARY
or
INTELLIGENCE SUMMARY
(Erase heading not required.)

Army Form C. 2118

33rd DW DADOS 33rd DW ? Vol 2 APRIL 1916.

Place	Date	Hour	Summary of Events and Information	Remarks and references to Appendices
	1		24 Protractors semi circular 8" special to Calais	
	2		1 Limbered wagon issued to 2nd R W Fus.	
	3		Wired for 9 Adapters for muzzle pivot mountings	
	4			
	5			
	6		7 West Bomb Throwers received from 19th Divn and issued 19th I Bde 4 100th Bde 3	
	7		300 part worn blankets for gas proofing dug outs wired for by 11th Field Coy RE	
	8		Imprest Balance fixed at 500 F. A S/C Hill returned off leave	
	9		1 Travelling Kitchen issued to 1/6 Scottish Rifles	
	10		Inspection of D.A.C. + Train Vehicles. 4 3" Stokes mortars issued to 98/2 TMB.	
	11		Demand to ADOS for 42 Handcarts for Trench Mortar Batteries	
	12			
	13		20000 Helmets P.H demanded as a Divisional Reserve.	
	14		Wired for 1 3.7" mortar for 100/1 TMB to replace one condemned by I.O.M.	
	15		Jerkins + Drum waistcoats returned by units. 4 2" mortars received for X/33 TMB.	
	16		4 1½" mortars to Base. 1995 Helmets P.H.G + 1774 Box respirators demanded from Base	
	17		11 Protractors Semi Circular 8" special to Base	
	18			

1875 Wt. W593/826 1,000,000 4/15 J.B.C. & A. A.D.S.S./Forms/C. 2118.

Instructions regarding War Diaries and Intelligence Summaries are contained in F. S. Regs., Part II. and the Staff Manual respectively. Title Pages will be prepared in manuscript.

WAR DIARY
or
INTELLIGENCE SUMMARY
(Erase heading not required.)

Army Form C. 2118

APRIL 1916

Place	Date	Hour	Summary of Events and Information	Remarks and references to Appendices
	19		1 Bed complete demanded for 2/33 TMB 2". also 2 Breech mechanisms for 100/1 TMB 3.7"	
	20		Pte Benford to Hospital	
	21			
	22		3587 A S/Con Neal arrived for duty from 1st Cav. Divn	
	23			
	24			
	25		O/395 SC Pollard left for duty at Calais	
	26		Gas over town & trenches. Big rush for helmets to replace. DADMS ordered	
	27		that CRA, CRE & 86.0 Bdgs should render bulk indents to replace those "U"	
	28		98th & 100th Bdge M.G. Coys joined Divn from England	
	29			
	30		4 1½" mortars evacuated by 2/33 to Base.	
			D.A.G. 3rd Echelon. Base.	
			[signature] Lieut DADOS 33rd Divn	

1875 Wt. W593/826 1,000,000 4/15 J.B.C. & A. A.D.S.S./Forms/C. 2118.

SECRET

D.A.D.O.S.
33rd Division.

DADOS

Army Form C. 2118

MAY 1916

Instructions regarding War Diaries and Intelligence Summaries are contained in F. S. Regs., Part II. and the Staff Manual respectively. Title Pages will be prepared in manuscript.

WAR DIARY
or
INTELLIGENCE SUMMARY
(Erase heading not required.)

Vol 7

Place	Date	Hour	Summary of Events and Information	Remarks and references to Appendices
	1			
	2			
	3			
	4		Gas Expert appointed for Divn. 17900 P.H helmets recd (Reserve)	
	5		2 West Bomb throwers handed over to 35th Divn	
	6			
	7			
	8		2100 P.H helmets received completing 20000 held as Divl Reserve.	
	9		22 Vermorel Sprayers allotted for issue to Field Ambulances	
	10			
	11		New Vickers Gun demanded by 98th M.G. Coy. to replace one "U"	
	12		350 Steel helmets to go to Calais every 4 days for painting + sanding	
	13		Mr Mulkern starts on leave to England	
	14		New Vickers Gun demanded by 19th M G Coy. Maxim Gun received for 98th B M G Coy	
	14 15		350 Helmets steel to Calais for painting	

1875 Wt. W593/826 1,000,000 4/15 J.B.C. & A. A.D.S.S./Forms/C. 2118.

Instructions regarding War Diaries and Intelligence Summaries are contained in F. S. Regs., Part II. and the Staff Manual respectively. Title Pages will be prepared in manuscript.

D.A.D.O.S
33rd Division

WAR DIARY
or
INTELLIGENCE SUMMARY

(Erase heading not required.)

Army Form C. 2118

MAY 1916

Place	Date	Hour	Summary of Events and Information	Remarks and references to Appendices
	16		Bell air Gun sent to 1st Army Mob. Work Shops for repair. Retd same day	
	17		4 Lewis Guns of 16th KRRC to Armourers Shops for overhaul	
	18		Sent 350 Helmets Steel to Calais for Sanding. Maxim recd for 19th M.G. Coy	
	19		Dial Sight No 7 demanded by "B" Bty 166th Bdge RFA to replace one destroyed	
	20			
	21			
	22		2 West Bomb Throwers handed over to 39th Divn	
	23		Mr Mulkerns returned off leave. Lewis Gun demanded by 4th L'pools to replace one destroyed by shell fire.	
	24		2 3" Stoke mortars received and handed over to 100/2 TMB.	
	25		Received magazines for Lewis Guns to complete to 64 per gun in Division. Lewis Gun received for 4th Liverpools. One 18pdr gun demanded by "A Bty". 166th Bdge R.F.A. Brigade Ammtn Columns taken from Brigades and formed into Echelon "A" of D.A.C.	
	26		3 4.5" Howitzer Batteries of 167th Bdge split up, one each into 3 18pdr Brigades	
	27		All units report complete with 64 magazines per Lewis Gun	
	28		2 3" Stoke mortars recd + handed over to 100/2 TMB. One 18pdr QF recd for 166th Bdge RFA	
	29		9th H.L.I. joined into 100th Brigade from L of C.	
	30		6th Scottish Rifles struck off 100th Bdge. Received 500 Helmets P.H.G. for R.A.	

D.A.G. 3rd Echelon
BASE

C. Mulkerns
Lieut
D.A.D.O.S.

1875 Wt. W593/826 1,000,000 4/15 J.B.C. & A. A.D.S.S./Forms/C. 2118.

SECRET

D.A.D.O.S.
33rd DIVISION

JUNE 1916

Army Form C. 2118

WAR DIARY
or
INTELLIGENCE SUMMARY
(Erase heading not required.)

Instructions regarding War Diaries and Intelligence Summaries are contained in F. S. Regs., Part II. and the Staff Manual respectively. Title Pages will be prepared in manuscript.

June 1916.

DADOS 33rd Div

Vol 8

Place	Date	Hour	Summary of Events and Information	Remarks and references to Appendices
BETHUNE	1.		1st Blanket to be returned to Railhead. 134 Helmets steel handed over to 2/5. Warwicks.	
	2.			
	3.			
	4			
	5.		Wired for Maxim Gun for 19. Bde M.G. Coy. Wired for 100 Latrine Buckets by order of D.A.D.M.S.	
	6.		Bellairs Gun repaired & returned from Heavy Mob. Workshop. Wired for 2 cylinders gas for 20th R.F.	
	6.		4 Lewis guns ex 6th. Scottish to Calais.	
	8.		Maxim gun for 19th Bde MG Coy received. 1 3.7 Mortar issued to 100/1 T.M.B. from those returned by 19/2 + 98/2. T.M.B.	
	10.		1 Cylinder wired for, for 1st Queens. No 7 Dial Sight wired for, for A Battery 156 Bde R.F.A.	
	9.		360. Rifles returned to Base, surplus by reorganization of R.A.	
	12.		1 Maxim from 19th Bde. M.G. Coy. to Calais. 3 Grenades dummy stick & disc German pattern also 5 Stands for firing rifle grenades handed over to 33rd 35th, 39th, & 61st Divisions.	
	14.		Time advanced by 1 hour. 360 box respirators received.	

1875 Wt. W593/826 1,000,000 4/15 J.B.C. & A. A.D.S.S./Forms/C. 2118.

SECRET

D.A.D.O.S. 33rd DIVISION

Instructions regarding War Diaries and Intelligence Summaries are contained in F. S. Regs., Part II. and the Staff Manual respectively. Title Pages will be prepared in manuscript.

WAR DIARY
or
INTELLIGENCE SUMMARY
(Erase heading not required.)

JUNE 1916.

Army Form C. 2118

Place	Date	Hour	Summary of Events and Information	Remarks and references to Appendices
BETHUNE	15.		All stores demanded from Calais now. Return of Capes Mack. by all units except Cyclists	
	16.		480 Box Respirators received. 50 Flapper Fans received.	
	17.		4 3" Stokes Mortars issued to 100th T.M.B.	
	18.		800 Box Respirators received.	
	19.		650. Waistcoat Pattern Grenade carriers received.	
	20.			
	21.		12 Clinometers Field returned by Infantry Battalion.	
	22.		48 Box Respirators received.	
	23.		V/33. Heavy. T.M.B. joined.	
	24.		Spare dial sights No. 7. hastened for issue to R.F.A.	
	25			
	26.		11 Shields Body for protection of bombers. received.	
	27.		26 Lewis Guns demanded making 6 per Battn. Authority O.S.10. 1/1315/3 27.6.16.	
	28.		5000 Breech covers. Authority for local purchase asked for.	
	29.		74. Hot Food Containers withdrawn & sent to Base.	

C. M. Walker Lieut
D.A.D.O.S.

1875 Wt. W593/826 1,000,000 4/15 J.B.C. & A. A.D.S.S./Forms/C. 2118.

D.A.G. 3rd Echelon, Base.

SECRET

D.A.D.O.S. **WAR DIARY** or **INTELLIGENCE SUMMARY** 33rd Division

(*Erase heading not required.*)

Army Form C. 2118

33 July 31st 1916. Vol 9

1st Sheet

DADOS 33 Div

Instructions regarding War Diaries and Intelligence Summaries are contained in F. S. Regs., Part II. and the Staff Manual respectively. Title Pages will be prepared in manuscript.

Place	Date	Hour	Summary of Events and Information	Remarks and references to Appendices
BETHUNE	1/7/16		Body of Lewis Gun demanded by 20th Fusiliers. One 2" Trench Mortar demanded by Z/33 T.M Battery	
	2/7/16		16 Lewis guns demanded for issue to make to 8 per Battalion (authority Tel QB/9899 Ord Com. d/d 1/7/16 16 Lewis guns received from Base making issue up to 6 per Battalion. 20 Revolvers received for issue to Raiding parties. One 2" Mortar received for issue to Z/33 TMB	
	4/7/16		Lieut Stretton AOD and servant Pte Peake AOC reported for temporary duty with 33rd Division	
	5/7/16		8 Clinometers returned by 100th M.G. Coy.	
	6/7/16		Indent for 4 9.45 mortars for V/33 T.M.B. cancelled by 1st Army. reason stated that these mortars will be allotted as they become available	
	7/7/16		Wagon G.S for 254 Tunnelling Coy in exchange for limbered wagon authority OMG/Q/2294/2 d/d 3/7/16	
	8/7/16		Left Bethune for destination unknown	
	9/7/16		Arrived at Belloy-sur-Somme.	
	11/7/16		Arrived at Corbie	
	12/7/16		Arrived at Treux.	
	13/7/16		20 Lewis guns received making a total of 8 per Battalion. Issued handcarts for Lewis Guns at rate of 1X per Battalion. 1st Middlesex indent for a Officers mess cart.	
	14/7/16		Body of 18pdr. of Amm wagon demanded by B/162 Bde R.F.A Wagon G.S complete turnout demanded for 38 D Div Train to replace one destroyed	
	15/7/16		2 Carts water demanded for 1st Queens to replace 2 destroyed	
	16/7/16		Arrived at Meaulte. 1 Wagon G.S complete turnout required for 38 D Div Train 1 Cart Officers mess demanded for 166 Bde R.F.A. 3 Vickers guns demanded for 100th Bde M.G. Coy. all destroyed by shell fire	
	17/7/16		1 Carriage Amb for 19 F.A demanded to replace one destroyed.	
	18/7/16		1 Cart water for 99th F.A. 1 Wagon G.S for 5th Scottish. 1 Wagon Pontoon for 11th Field Coy. 1 Lewis Gun for 4th Suffolks. 1 Cart Water for 222 Field Coy. demanded. all destroyed by enemy shell fire 3 Vickers guns for 100 Bde M.G. Coy received.	
	19/7/16		2 Lewis Guns for 1st Queens 1 Wagon Pontoon and 1 Water Cart for 222 Field Coy. R.E. 2 Lewis Guns for 4th Suffolks. 1 Officers mess Cart. all to replace similar stores to meet casualties by shell fire 1 Lewis Gun for 4th Suffolks received	
	20/7/16		1 Body of wagon 18pdr for 33rd D.A.C. demanded. to replace one destroyed. Arrived at Albert.	

1875 Wt. W593/826 1,000,000 4/15 J.B.C. & A. A.D.S.S./Forms/C. 2118.

SECRET.

2nd Sheet.

Instructions regarding War Diaries and Intelligence Summaries are contained in F. S. Regs., Part II. and the Staff Manual respectively. Title Pages will be prepared in manuscript.

WAR DIARY
or
INTELLIGENCE SUMMARY
(Erase heading not required.)

Army Form C. 2118

July 1916

33rd Division

Place	Date	Hour	Summary of Events and Information	Remarks and references to Appendices
	21/7/16		3 Lewis Guns for 2 R W Fus. 5 mountings tripod, one hind portion limbered wagon demanded to replace others destroyed. 2 Lewis Guns for 1st Queens received. 5000 Suits [illegible] for men coming out of line	
	22/7/16		Wagon telephone for 162 Bde R F A. Lewis Guns 5 Scottish 2. 2nd Cameronians 2. 2nd A & S. 2 1st Middlesex 1. Cart water for 19th F A. Cart water for B/162 & 1 for D/162 Brigade R F A demanded to replace similar stores destroyed by shell fire. 1 Cart Water for 222 Field Coy. 1 Wagon limbered to 5th Scottish. 1 Kitchen Travelling for 1st Queens received.	
	23/7/16		3 Lewis Guns for 2nd R W Fus. received. Arrived at [illegible].	
	24/7/16		Lewis Guns – 1st Cameronians 1. 5 Scottish 4. 20th Fus. 6. 4th Suffolks 1. 4th King 1. 1st Middlesex 1. Vickers Gun 1 for 19th M G Coy. Cart Water for 101 F A. All demanded to replace similar stores destroyed by hostile shell fire	
	25/7/16		2 Lewis Guns for 9th H L I. 3 Lewis Guns for 16th KRR's. 1 Wagon G S for B Echelon D A C. 1 Water Cart for 1st Middlesex. 1 18 pdr QF gun for A/162 Bde RFA. All required to replace similar items destroyed by shell fire. Lewis Guns demanded on 22/7/16 received.	
	26/7/16		Travelling Kitchen demanded for 2nd R W Fus to replace one destroyed. 1 Vickers gun received for 19th M G Coy.	
	27/7/16		17 Pistols Very demanded to replace similar number destroyed or lost. 18 pdr QF gun for A/162 received. Lewis Guns demanded on 25/7/16 received.	
	28/7/16		Dial Sight No 7 required for A/162 Bde RFA to replace one blown away.	
	29/7/16		Body of Amm Wagon QF 18 pdr required by B/156 Bde R F A.	
	30/7/16		1 QF 4.5 Howitzer required by D/162 to replace one destroyed, also one Wagon Amm QF 4.5.	
	31/7/16		Wagon Amm QF 4.5 required by D/166 to replace one destroyed. Howitzer QF 4.5 for D/162 received. Limber 18 pdr QF and Dial Sight No 7 required to replace similar destroyed by A/162 Bde RFA.	

[signature]
Lieut
DADOS
33rd Div.

1875 Wt. W593/826 1,000,000 4/15 J.B.C. & A. A.D.S.S./Forms/C. 2118.

SECRET

August 1916.

Army Form C. 2118

WAR DIARY or INTELLIGENCE SUMMARY

(Erase heading not required.)

33rd Division

D.A.D.O.S.

Vol 10

Instructions regarding War Diaries and Intelligence Summaries are contained in F. S. Regs., Part II. and the Staff Manual respectively. Title Pages will be prepared in manuscript.

Place	Date	Hour	Summary of Events and Information	Remarks and references to Appendices
TREUX	2/8/16		9 Vickers machine Guns demanded to replace maxims for machine Gun Coys. 1 Cart Water demanded for A/156 Bde RFA to replace one condemned by I.O.M	
			1 Cart Cooks demanded for 98th M.G. Coy to replace one condemned by I.O.M	
	3/8/16		1 Cart Officers Mess demanded by B/167 to replace one condemned by I.O.M.	
	4/8/16		1 QF Limbered 4.5 wagon received for D/162 Bde RFA	
	5/8/16		1 Carriage QF 18pdr required by C/156 Bde RFA to replace one destroyed by shell fire. One 18pdr QF gun demanded by B/167 Bde RFA to replace one condemned, badly scored. 9 Vickers Machine Guns received making the 3 Machine Gun Coys complete with 16 Vickers each	
	6/8/16		15000 Safety pins for Smoke helmets demanded from Base. One Carriage field QF 18pdr received for C/156 Bde RFA	

[signature] for Lieut D.A.D.O.S

1875 Wt. W593/826 1,000,000 4/15 J.B.C. & A. A.D.S.S./Forms/C. 2118.

Instructions regarding War Diaries and Intelligence Summaries are contained in F. S. Regs., Part II. and the Staff Manual respectively. Title Pages will be prepared in manuscript.

WAR DIARY
or
INTELLIGENCE SUMMARY
(Erase heading not required.)

Army Form C. 2118

Place	Date	Hour	Summary of Events and Information	Remarks and references to Appendices
TREUX	7/8/16		Lieut. C.S. Mackson A.O.D. relinquished the duties of D.A.D.O.S. & proceeded to H.Q. 4th Army for duty with D.D.O.S. Lieut. A.M.E. Bravan, A.O.D. assumed the duties of D.A.D.O.S.	
			Refilling point for all units – VIVIER MILL – ALBERT road (southern portion) at 6pm daily. 18pdr carriage received for C/156 Bde. I.O.M. No17 workshop asked for it to be handed over to him for fitting of gun then in shop. Visited No17 shops re this matter.	
			Principal Bulk stores received – 1664 Canvas Carriers for Lewis Gun Magazines i.e. 128 per Bn – total authorised. 182 P.H.G. Helmets & 182 Box Respirators to complete scale for last two Lewis guns (7 & 8)	
			31 Steel Helmets collected from Salvage Dump.	
	8/8/16		95 Steel Helmets collected from Railhead. Issued these together with 31 collected 7/8/16 to 100th Bde. Arranged collection of as many wire cutters (all patterns), Lewis Gun Magazines, Very Pistols, Steel Helmets & Bomb Buckets as possible from Salvage & Railhead. Replied to letter from D.D.O.S. thro A.D.O.S. asking for report on improvised Braziers issued last winter. No complaints were received.	
			Refilling point same as on 7/8/16 & until further notice.	
			Visited Heavy Mobile shops re Spares for 2" Trench Mortars X, Y & Z/33. Trench Mortar Hand carts, 10 still required to complete scale. Notified A.D.O.S. 15th Corps during visit. 18pdr gun, piece only, received for A/167 & handed over to I.O.M.	

1875 Wt. W593/826 1,000,000 4/15 J.B.C. & A. A.D.S.S./Forms/C. 2118.

Army Form C. 2118

WAR DIARY
or
INTELLIGENCE SUMMARY
(Erase heading not required.)

Instructions regarding War Diaries and Intelligence Summaries are contained in F. S. Regs., Part II. and the Staff Manual respectively. Title Pages will be prepared in manuscript.

Place	Date	Hour	Summary of Events and Information	Remarks and references to Appendices
TREUX	8/8/16		No 17 workshop for fitting to carriage. Handed over surplus Shovels & Picks to No 6 R.E. Park. Sent surplus S.D. Clothing & Boots to Base. Visited "Q" in morning & evening. Visited Corps dumps for Salvaged stores.	
	9/8/16		Visited Heavy Mobile Shops re 2" T.M spares & arranged for all available on indents submitted to be issued to us. Scheme for washing underclothing of the Brigade coming out of the line in abeyance for present. Arrangements made with 15th Corps to supply the necessary stock of underclothing to start the scheme. Visited "Q" re Steel Helmets + vigilant periscopes, Box Respirators etc. for 98th Bde. Issued 30 to latter Bde. Small surplus of trousers, jackets & puttees as well as underclothing retained in anticipation of ~~large~~ increased demand of 100th Bde on coming into rest next week. Artillery H.Q notified that underclothing & pantaloons required for equipping 2 Bdes in rest would be supplied on demand from surplus. Demanded 150 Box Respirators to meet replacements & to complete scale of Div. Signal Coy. Lewis Gun Magazines received to complete to scale for 6 guns per Battalion & to meet all replacements.	

1875 Wt. W593/826 1,000,000 4/15 I.R.C. & A. A.D.S.S./Forms/C. 2118.

Army Form C. 2118

Instructions regarding War Diaries and Intelligence Summaries are contained in F. S. Regs., Part II. and the Staff Manual respectively. Title Pages will be prepared in manuscript.

WAR DIARY
or
INTELLIGENCE SUMMARY
(Erase heading not required.)

Place	Date	Hour	Summary of Events and Information	Remarks and references to Appendices
TREUX	10/8/16		Collected 150 Steel Helmets from Salvage Dump. Issued 210 to 19th Bde on instruction from 'D'. Drew 250 Steel Helmets from O.O. XV Corps Troops. All springs Running out 18 pdr. on receipt from Base to go to Corps Workshops. D.A.C. to demand as usual to keep Batteries supplied but no springs will be issued to D.A.C. for Batteries. Notified C.R.A. of latter. 'D' arranged for C.R.E. to supply all paint required by 19th Bde for Camouflage purposes. Issued 24 disinfecting sprayers for cleansing dugouts to C.R.A. & Infty Bdes; also 24 Mk V wire cutters to 100th Bde, from reserve collected. Visited Amiens for Local purchase. Visited 'D' in evening. 1 Large Telescope & 7 Small drawn from O.O. XV Corps Troops & issued to 100th Bde. for Infty Observation Post. To be handed to relieving Bde & finally to D.A.D.O.S. 'D' putting up question of Badges & Titles for re-inforcements of [illegible] regiments [illegible]	
	11/8/16		Issued 130 Steel Helmets to 162 Bde R.F.A. 2" T.M. Spares drawn as far as available at Heavy Mobile Workshops & issued. Spares not available, demanded from Heavy Mobile. Visited A.D.O.S., Railhead for Salvage, and No 17 Workshops. Arranged with DOM for him to wire units when to collect guns fitted in his shops from guns or carriages received & handed over to him either by me (in case of piece) & unit in case of carriage.	

1875 Wt. W593/826 1,000,000 4/15 J.B.C. & A. A.D.S.S./Forms/C. 2118.

Instructions regarding War Diaries and Intelligence Summaries are contained in F. S. Regs., Part II. and the Staff Manual respectively. Title Pages will be prepared in manuscript.

WAR DIARY
or
INTELLIGENCE SUMMARY
(Erase heading not required.)

Army Form C. 2118

Place	Date	Hour	Summary of Events and Information	Remarks and references to Appendices
TREUX	11/8/16		D/162 deficient of small number of parts, including No 7 Dial Sight & Carrier to enable 4.5" How received in 1st instant to be put into action. Majority of parts & spares demanded already supplied by Base. Have asked outstanding demands by wire! Tried to get a Carrier No 7 & Dial Sight from Shops. Former not available so of no use to draw & issue latter. Battery can strip Dial Sight & Carrier from another of their own Hows. undergoing repair in shops till Base supply a carrier & Heavy Mobile issue Dial Sight from Army pool on D.D.O.S. authority. Visited A.D.O.S. 3 Vermorel Sprayers required by 100th Bde. Can only be issued to replace losses or damaged. Collected 329 Steel Helmets from Salvage dump & arranged issue of 400 to 19th Bde. ~~[illegible]~~	
	12/8/16		Visited Amiens for Local Purchases. Arranged for new place near Div H.Q for office & dump. Present position too far from H.Q although convenient as regards space & position with regard to Railhead & Refilling point (midway between). Visited 15th Corps workshops to try & get a carrier for D/162. None available except as stated in above (11/8/16). Wired Battery to	

1875 Wt. W593/826 1,000,000 4/15 J.B.C. & A. A.D.S.S./Forms/C. 2118.

Instructions regarding War Diaries and Intelligence Summaries are contained in F. S. Regs., Part II. and the Staff Manual respectively. Title Pages will be prepared in manuscript.

WAR DIARY
or
INTELLIGENCE SUMMARY
(Erase heading not required.)

Army Form C. 2118

Place	Date	Hour	Summary of Events and Information	Remarks and references to Appendices
TREUX	12/8/16		take action as stated above. 100th Bde wired for 36 Vermorel sprayers to replace lost & damaged by shell fire. Demanded 30 (includes previous demand of 3) by wire. Further 200 Steel Helmets to be issued to 19th Bde to complete them. Then start on R.A. & issue up to 1000.	(issue arranged)
E. 11 Central	13/8/16		List of Trench Stores required by the Division being made by 'Q'. To be submitted to ADOS through D.A.D.O.S. Visited Corbie for L.P. Collected 150 Steel Helmets from Railhead. Moved office & dump to Divl HQ E. 11. Central Map 57D. Left reserve of Anti-gas appliances, wirecutters, Bomb Buckets, Lewis Gun Magazines & some surplus clothing, not at present reqd for issue but may be urgently required by Bde on coming out of line into rest, a the closed store at TREUX. Obtained 2 men from Divl Coy to guard store.	
"	14/8/16		Muslin urgently required by units for protection of food from flies. 200 yds received from Base. Purchased 100 yds to meet increased demands. To Amiens for L.P. Purchased extra soap urgently reqd by 100th Bde for washing clothes on coming into rest; also more muslin to meet further demands.	
"	15/8/16		Refilling time altered to 11.30 am. Same place as before. Not sufficient time to split up Bulk from Railhead & send to refilling point same day, arranged to send same to refilling point the next day but that stores can be taken to refilling point same day as received	

1875 Wt. W593/826 1,000,000 4/15 J.B.C. & A. A.D.S.S./Forms/C. 2118.

Instructions regarding War Diaries and Intelligence Summaries are contained in F. S. Regs., Part II. and the Staff Manual respectively. Title Pages will be prepared in manuscript.

WAR DIARY
or
INTELLIGENCE SUMMARY
(Erase heading not required.)

Army Form C. 2118

Place	Date	Hour	Summary of Events and Information	Remarks and references to Appendices
E. 11 Central	15/8/16		Fly traps in great demand by Divn & Bde H.Q. all other units supplied previously from Base. Issued 50 Steel Helmets to 2nd A & S Highlanders urgently reqd for re-inforcements, also 20 to C.R.A. Visited Heavy Mobile Workshop re 2" Mortar & Bed for Z/33. DDOS 4th Army authority for issue obtained as mortar & bed to be replaced were totally destroyed & could not be brought in to shops for exchange. Saw A.D.O.S. - latter requires information as to number of Lewis gun handcarts in possession of the Divn. Wired Bdes & Pioneers for this information as some units have a surplus & some are deficient. Visited IOM XV Corps Shops re repair of water carts for two Battalions. Arranged with him to exchange one cart for a serviceable one immediately so that unit should not be without one cart at least. The other unit to send in one cart at a time. Wired units to this effect. Pontoon Bipartite of 220th Fld Coy beyond local repair due to road accident. Wired unit to send in to IOM for inspection & repair if possible or to ask I.O.M to come & inspect pontoon.	
	16/8/16		To Amiens for L.P. more muslin & fly traps purchased to meet urgent demands. 2" Mortar & Bed issued to Z/33. One Lewis gun received from Abbeville & issued to 2nd A & S. Highlanders to replace one damaged by shell fire. A Dial Sight No 7 required by A/166 to replace damaged one. Wired Heavy Mobile Workshop to issue one in exchange. Wired Battery to send in damaged one.	None available at XV Corps Shops

1875 Wt. W593/826 1,000,000 4/15 J.B.C. & A. A.D.S.S./Forms/C. 2118.

Instructions regarding War Diaries and Intelligence Summaries are contained in F. S. Regs., Part II. and the Staff Manual respectively. Title Pages will be prepared in manuscript.

WAR DIARY
or
INTELLIGENCE SUMMARY
(Erase heading not required.)

Army Form C. 2118

Place	Date	Hour	Summary of Events and Information	Remarks and references to Appendices
	16.8.16		Demanded 400 old Blankets by wire – urgently required for doors of captured dug-outs. 250 Steel Helmets issued to 167 Bde under instructions from C.R.A. Reported 143 Lewis gun hand carts in possession of units to A.D.O.S. Arranged to withdraw surplus carts to issue to units who are deficient. Cancelling outstanding indents accordingly. Salvaged Lewis Gun Magazines to be issued in satisfaction of indents for replacements, provided all so issued are examined by the Armourer of the unit before being taken into use. Wrote all Infantry Bns accordingly. 250 Steel Helmets issued to 156th Bde R.F.A.	
	17.8.16		Visited Heavy Mobile Shops re Dial Sight for A/166 Bde. Wired A/166 to send damaged Sight to XV Corps Shops for inspection, also D/162 to send their damaged Dial Sight ^carrier^ to XV Corps Shops. Received 93 Steel Helmets & 376 Lewis Gun Magazines from Salvage. General office work.	
	18.8.16		Submitted draft for D.R.Os instructing units to return all Lewis Gun Handcarts surplus to scale of 12 per Bn, to me for issue to other units still deficient. Soap urgently required on opening Divl Baths at Nover Hill. Issued 125 lbs of surplus soap to O.C. Divl Baths. To Amiens for L.P. Bought Bass Brooms, & Scrubbing brushes required by Baths urgently. Demanded 1 cwt Hessian in anticipation of demands for Stoving material for Huts following G.O.C.s order	

1875 Wt. W593/826 1,000,000 4/15 J.B.C. & A. A.D.S.S./Forms/C. 2118.

Instructions regarding War Diaries and Intelligence Summaries are contained in F. S. Regs., Part II. and the Staff Manual respectively. Title Pages will be prepared in manuscript.

WAR DIARY
or
INTELLIGENCE SUMMARY
(Erase heading not required.)

Army Form C. 2118

Place	Date	Hour	Summary of Events and Information	Remarks and references to Appendices
F.11 Central Map 57D	18.8.16		Received list of Trench Stores estimated as required by the Division for Equipment of Trenches. Forwarded same to A.D.O.S.	
	19.8.16		Issued a No 7 Dial Sight & Carrier No 1 to D/162 Bde. Reported receipt to D.D.O.S. IV Army. Visited latter & also DOM XV Corps re Dial sights for D/162 & A/166. Demanded 3" Stokes Mortar Complete for 98th T.M.B. also 1 Lewis gun for 2nd A&S Highlanders. 5th Scottish Rifles reported deficient of an Officers Mess Cart. More demands for Fly-Traps & muslin. Visited Corps dump re T.M. hand carts & any other serviceable items also Railhead.	
"	20.8.16		Visited Staff Capt. 19th Bde. Found that 5th Scott. Rif. mess cart was not deficient but in a damaged condition due to wear. No shortage of any stores existing in the Brigade. Visited 'B' Echelon of 98th Bde but could not see Staff Capt. Saw T.O. of 2nd A&S Highlanders re three hind portions of travelling kitchens in Mecourt(?) Wood. Badly damaged beyond local repair & impossible to send them by road to DOM XV Corps. Instructed him to indent for 3 to replace 'V'. Visited S.C.R.A. re Dial Sights of A/166 & D/162. These must be sent in to DOM XV Corps for inspection before new ones can be issued or demanded from Base. Units previously wired to this effect. Asked Staff Capt to instruct them to do so at once. Also shewed him that complaint of 167 Bde RFA re underclothing was quite unfounded. Considerable issues had already been made from surplus & latest demand must	

1875 Wt. W593/826 1,000,000 4/15 J.B.C. & A. A.D.S.S./Forms/C. 2118.

Army Form C. 2118

Instructions regarding War Diaries and Intelligence Summaries are contained in F. S. Regs., Part II. and the Staff Manual respectively. Title Pages will be prepared in manuscript.

WAR DIARY
or
INTELLIGENCE SUMMARY
(Erase heading not required.)

Place	Date	Hour	Summary of Events and Information	Remarks and references to Appendices
	20.8.16		follow ordinary Bulk system & would be issued 21st instant. 4 50ft Tracing Tapes required urgently by 100th Bde for marking Trenches. Found C.R.E. had large amount of tracing tape & instructed unit to apply to him.	
	21.8.16		To Amiens for Local Purchases. Bought more Muslin & Fly traps. Received 1 Lewis Gun for 2nd A & S Highlanders & issued same also 1 3" T.M. complete for 98th T.M.B & issued same & had it delivered there. For washing dirty Clothes Bought Soap for Laundry at Amiens from proceeds at trench from Divl Baths.	
	22.8.16		Issued long handled & S.A. wire cutters to 100th & 19th Bde 'B' Echelon Delivered by car owing to them being urgently required in Front line. These wire cutters are to be returned to me on completion of the operations. 300 odd more Steel Helmets required to complete R.A. Issue to Infantry Bns for urgent demand for re-inforcements plentiful supply being obtained from Salvage & Railhead. Demanded 1 Lewis Gun for 2nd R. W. Fusiliers & 1 3" Mortar for 19th T. M. B.	
	23.8.16		Visited Amiens to pay for Soap purchased 21st instant & to see if Laundry had received correct quantity purchased. Visited A.D.O.S & Corps Workshops re Dial Sight. Asked Base if they could supply waterproof Muzzle Covers for Rifles instead of buying locally.	

1875 Wt. W593/826 1,000,000 4/15 J.B.C. & A. A.D.S.S./Forms/C. 2118.

Instructions regarding War Diaries and Intelligence Summaries are contained in F. S. Regs., Part II. and the Staff Manual respectively. Title Pages will be prepared in manuscript.

WAR DIARY
or
INTELLIGENCE SUMMARY
(Erase heading not required.)

Army Form C. 2118

Place	Date	Hour	Summary of Events and Information	Remarks and references to Appendices
E. 11. Central	23/8/16		Demanded 40 Vermorel Sprayers to replace losses + unserviceables. Required by R.A. 19th + 100th Bdes. Issued 250 Steel Helmets to 9th H.L.I. for Draft. Received tins 'Kaleo' for staining Tents. Notified units to draw requirement by D.R.O. Issued 432 Steel Helmets to R.A. units in completion.	
	24/8/16		Received No 7 Dial Sight for D/162. This is a spare sight, the spare having been issued from Base a few days previously + was mistaken for a replacement which was urgently required by the unit. Reported receipt of above to DDOS as spare + handed same into XV Corps shops for transfer to Army Pool. 120 Steel Helmets issued to 4th Suffolks. 12 Barrels '303' Vickers Gun demanded to replace 'U' Armd. Based to supply but asked unit for Armourers Certificate of condemnation. Visited D.C. RA re hastener for underclothing by 167th Bde + re another Dial Sight required by D/162. ~~[illegible]~~ unit had not sent 'U' one into shops for inspection as directed. Visited 100th Bde. H.Q.	
	25/8/16		Issued 200 Steel Helmets to H.Q. 98th Bde. Received 442 Caps for firing Mills No 23 Rifle Grenades. This completes 13 Bn to 34 each. To Corbie for Local Purchases. Received 1 Lewis Gun for 2nd R.W. Fusiliers + 1. 3" Mortar for 19th T.M.B. Rt a wire from ms demanding 5 Lewis Guns to replace others lost 'U' for 4th Suffolks, Ordnance Communications noted that in future numbers lost + numbers destroyed should be shewn separately. 18 pdr. Q.F. Gun received for B/167 + handed in to IOM XV Corps for fitting. Issued 99 Steel Helmets to 100th Bde.	

1875 Wt. W593/826 1,000,000 4/15 J.B.C. & A. A.D.S.S./Forms/C. 2118.

Instructions regarding War Diaries and Intelligence Summaries are contained in F. S. Regs., Part II. and the Staff Manual respectively. Title Pages will be prepared in manuscript.

WAR DIARY
or
INTELLIGENCE SUMMARY
(Erase heading not required.)

Army Form C. 2118

Place	Date	Hour	Summary of Events and Information	Remarks and references to Appendices
E. 11 Central	26.8.16		Visited Railhead & saw R.O.O. re notification of arrival of Vehicles. Letter from D.O.S. re revised giving orders of issue of No 74 Periscopes. Div H.Q. & T.M. Batteries included in this. All Salvus sets in possession of units to be withdrawn except from Mine Rescue Schools & Tunnelling Coys. None in possession of this Division. Additional Bags Tool Shoemakers filled authorised. 4 Secs of D.A.C. & Du Coys affected by this. Visited Heavy Mobile Workshops & arranged to buy repairable T.M. hand carts from Corps Salvage Dump for exchange for new ones. Ponton Bi-partite of 222 Field Coy R.E. sent to XV Corps Shops for inspection & repair. Very little damaged. Wired Unit to send in Carpenters to assist in repairs as Shops are very busy on guns, etc. 40 Vermorel Sprayers recd. 18 Middlesex (Pioneers) return 34 Cups No 23 Rifle grenades as not being reqd. Took into Stock to meet replacements. Demanded 18 pdr complete with Dial Sight & Carrier for B/162 to replace one totally destroyed.	
	27.8.16		Received 18 pdr gun for C/167 & sent to XV Corps Shops for fitting. Instructed D/162 to send their How reported to have broken springs R.O. to XV Corps Shops for repair. Springs cannot be issued to Batteries for fitting themselves. Visited A.D.O.S. Received 2 in Mortar with bed & traversing & elevating gear from Heavy Mobile Shops on authority of D.D.O.S. for Z. 33 T.M.B. Demand Lewis Gun for 1st Middlesex Regt	
	28.8.16		Saw A.A. & Q.M.G. re reply to observation of Financial adviser on purchase of Potato Cutting Machine for Harley St Soup Kitchen in 1st Army Area. Wired ADOS to arrange for return to XV Corps Shops of 'U' No 7 Dial Sight which D/162 handed over to H.Q. 167 Bde under orders from Div Arty instead of sending to Shops	[illegible]

Instructions regarding War Diaries and Intelligence Summaries are contained in F. S. Regs., Part II. and the Staff Manual respectively. Title Pages will be prepared in manuscript.

WAR DIARY
or
INTELLIGENCE SUMMARY
(Erase heading not required.)

Army Form C. 2118

Place	Date	Hour	Summary of Events and Information	Remarks and references to Appendices
E 11 Central	29.8.16		Asked ADOS if Pioneer Bn & 3 Field Coys of the New Zealand Divn attached to the Division for rations & in this Divl Area should be administered by me for Ordnance stores as these four units are very urgently in need of stores not being able to obtain any from their own Division owing to distance. Authority obtained from ADOS to DOS. Usual move orders issued & indents accepted from units. Boots required especially. Units attached to Divn troops. The Queen's Regt are in possession of a Lewis Gun which can only be fitted with a copper gas cylinder, supplied with it. This cylinder is not interchangeable with the other Steel Cylinders. Unit indented for a spare copper cylinder to meet emergencies should the one in the gun become 'U'. Spare received & issued & C.O.O. Havre informed of circumstances & asked if gun itself should be returned for examination. Recd 1 Lewis Gun for 11th Middlesex. Units submitting large demands for underclothing to provide a change for troops. This should be obtained from Divl Baths & only demands to replace unserviceable underclothing should be submitted. Re 12 Vickers M.G. Barrels demanded by 100th M.G. Coy – these received to-day. Unit has not yet brought armourers certificate of condemnation – instructed therefore to send in Barrels for examination by an Armourer at my Store. This done & only 7 found unserviceable. Wrote Staff Capt 100th Bde re this matter	

1875 Wt. W593/826 1,000,000 4/15 J.B.C. & A. A.D.S.S./Forms/C. 2118.

Instructions regarding War Diaries and Intelligence Summaries are contained in F. S. Regs., Part II. and the Staff Manual respectively. Title Pages will be prepared in manuscript.

WAR DIARY
or
INTELLIGENCE SUMMARY
(Erase heading not required.)

Army Form C. 2118

Place	Date	Hour	Summary of Events and Information	Remarks and references to Appendices
E 11. Central	30.8.16		Divn moving into rest area. 100th Bde moves to Ribemont. Other Bdes come out of line & move to E.12.a. Refilling point at Albert-Vecquemont Mill Road 5 and as before. R.A. at 11 am other units 8. a.m. Wired Base to suspend issues till further notice. Boots & accoutrements, oil, grease etc cannot be stopped. Ensured 1st Sept being clear day. Received 3 in. Mortar for 100th T.M.B. Units cannot take stores while moving hence it is better to stop issues altogether for a day except to Artillery who are remaining in line & will be transferred to 24th Divn for all purposes. 98th Bde instructed by 'Q' to return the 1 Large Telescope & 6 small issued to them for Infantry Observation Posts, to DADOS on leaving line. Instructed by 'Q' to move store & office to Villers-Bocage on 1st September. H.Q. Divn moves there 31st instant	
	31.8.16		Issued surplus shirts & [illegible] Boots which cannot be delivered to units of Divn owing to moving, to New Zealand Pioneers & 3 Field Coys who have submitted urgent demands for them. These 4 units will be transferred to 24th Divn relieving us 1st Sept. Issued move orders to all concerned transferring 33rd Divn Artillery complete & 4 N.Z. units as above to 24th Divn for administration.	

31/8/16 [illegible] Lieut. DADOS 33rd Div.

1875 Wt. W593/826 1,000,000 4/15 J.B.C. & A. A.D.S.S./Forms/C. 2118.

DADOS

September 1916

Army Form C. 2118

VOL 11

Instructions regarding War Diaries and Intelligence Summaries are contained in F. S. Regs., Part II. and the Staff Manual respectively. Title Pages will be prepared in manuscript.

WAR DIARY
or
~~INTELLIGENCE~~ SUMMARY
(Erase heading not required.)

SECRET

Place	Date	Hour	Summary of Events and Information	Remarks and references to Appendices
VILLARS-BOCAGE	1/9/16		Moved to VILLARS-BOCAGE. – leaving reserve of Smoke Helmets etc to be cleared ~~at~~ next day from TREUX. Left Sergt. Webb and Pte Benford, Clerk & Storeman respectively with D.A.D.O.S 24th Divn to assist in administration of 33rd Div Arty. Handed over all outstanding Indents & Balance sheets of latter units & of N.Z. units to D.A.D.O.S 24th Divn. Visited A.D.O.S XV Corps re the handing over of any T.M. Hand Carts, Telescopes for Infantry Observation Posts to XV Corps on Division leaving that formation – also action to be taken re Clerk & Storeman left behind on instructions of A.D.O.S should Divl Arty leave 24th Divn. Wired R.T.O ALBERT to re-consign trucks for me to next Railhead i.e. ST RICQUIER.	
BERNAVILLE	2/9/16		Cleared Store at TREUX, sending lorries with Smoke helmets etc direct to next stopping place of Div H.Q. i.e. to BERNAVILLE. All lorries had to make two journeys to clear store completely. Wrote A.D.O.S. reporting no T.M. Hand Carts were in possession that had been made by 4th Army Shops hence none would be left behind by Division. Moved in afternoon & evening to BERNAVILLE.	
	3/9/16		Visited Railhead ST RICQUIER & asked R.T.O to re-consign any trucks received for me to Railhead TINQUES (final RAILHEAD of Divn in rest area) – also arranged ~~to~~ to load two trucks with all my reserve stores for reconsignment to TINQUES. Obtained two trucks from R.T.O and loaded same with all latter stores. Arranged with 'Q' office to move straight to TINQUES & open office & store there, clearing reconsigned trucks arriving at TINQUES & be ready to issue to Divn on arrival in final billeting area on [illegible] instant.	

1875 Wt. W593/826 1,000,000 4/15 J.B.C. & A. A.D.S.S./Forms/C. 2118.

Instructions regarding War Diaries and Intelligence Summaries are contained in F. S. Regs., Part II. and the Staff Manual respectively. Title Pages will be prepared in manuscript.

WAR DIARY
or
INTELLIGENCE SUMMARY
(Erase heading not required.)

Army Form C. 2118

Place	Date	Hour	Summary of Events and Information	Remarks and references to Appendices
BERNAVILLE	3/9/16		Received 3 - 3in Mortars for 98th T.M.B. ~~[illegible]~~ Delivered by lorry from ABBEVILLE. Arranged with Signals re messages, letters etc to be sent to TINQUES to-morrow through 17th Corps Signals	
TINQUES	4/9/16		Loaded lorries with all remaining stores, office furniture, kits + Detachment Camp equipment + travelled all afternoon to TINQUES. Saw Town Major + obtained store, office + billets. Arranged with Signals, 17th Corps to send D.R. three times daily to office to deliver + collect wires, letters, etc., wired R.T.O.s at two intermediate Railheads of Divn to reconsign any trucks received for me to TINQUES. Now in 3rd Army + administered by 17th Corps	
TINQUES	5/9/16		Wire received from Calais stating Base changed + outstanding demands transferred from HAVRE, and asking for statements as to position of P.H.G. Helmets and Bicycles in lieu of Horses. Sent these lists by next D.R.L.S giving list of units administered by me. Arranged to wire Calais when prepared to receive stores from them. Cart. W.T for 1st Middlesex Regt reported at Mericourt Station - wired R.O.O to reconsign same to TINQUES. The two Trucks containing my reserve Helmets + other Stores arrived Railhead.	
	6/9/16		Cleared latter Trucks + placed Smoke-Helmets, Steel Helmets etc in Store.	

1875 Wt. W593/826 1,000,000 4/15 J.B.C. & A. A.D.S.S./Forms/C. 2118.

Instructions regarding War Diaries and Intelligence Summaries are contained in F. S. Regs., Part II. and the Staff Manual respectively. Title Pages will be prepared in manuscript.

WAR DIARY
or
INTELLIGENCE SUMMARY
(Erase heading not required.)

Army Form C. 2118

Place	Date	Hour	Summary of Events and Information	Remarks and references to Appendices
TINQUES	6.9.16		Wired Base Calais of preparedness to receive stores - cancellation of outstanding demands not necessary. Received memo from DDOS 4th Army advising move of 33rd Divn less Artillery & giving instructions as to transference of demands. No notification of final location of Div HQ received.	
" "	7/9/16		Cleared Railhead of a truck of general stores, horseshoes and clothing. 15 3 days issues together. Prepared stores for issue to units on their arrival. Visited ADOS 17th Corps & was informed 33rd Divn had left 17th for 7th Corps. Visited Div HQ & confirmed this. Owing to this further move units would be unable to draw stores for at least three days. Loaded up portion of Anti-gas Helmets, Steel Helmets & Reserve Stores in two trucks at Railhead & reconsigned them to 7th Corps Railhead to be there on 9th instant. Arranged to carry about half the Reserve of Anti-gas Helmets, together with stores split up for issue, on lorries. Each Bde W.O. given a lorry for his own stores to avoid confusion. Pte Amor. A.O.C arrived for duty as Divl Troops Storeman vice Pte Master A.O.C. sent to Havre for duty.	
" "	8/9/16		Sent all surplus stores i.e. Horseshoes & picketing gear for the 33rd Divl Artillery to Base as it was useless to reconsign them by Rail owing to further move of Artillery from 24th Divn to another Division. Impossible to deliver by lorry owing to great distances to be covered. New Railhead on 9th Saulty - L'Arbret.	

1875 Wt. W593/826 1,000,000 4/15 J.B.C. & A. A.D.S.S./Forms/C. 2118.

Instructions regarding War Diaries and Intelligence Summaries are contained in F. S. Regs., Part II. and the Staff Manual respectively. Title Pages will be prepared in manuscript.

WAR DIARY
or
INTELLIGENCE SUMMARY
(Erase heading not required.)

Army Form C. 2118

Place	Date	Hour	Summary of Events and Information	Remarks and references to Appendices
TINQUES	8/9/16		Went over to L'Arbret with one lorry of Smoke helmets. Saw Town Major & fixed up good Store & offices. Dumped Helmets in the Store.	
L'ARBRET	9/9/16		Moved to L'Arbret with four lorries. Arranged Stores ready for issue to Units on 10th instant. Visited ADOS 7th Corps & received information as regards system of Bulk book keeping Salvage, Armourers, Pattee & Shoemakers Shops. List of returns required & correspondence affecting this Divn in Ordnance matter received from A.D.O.S. 100th Bde ~~required~~ Steel Helmets & P.H. Gas Helmets urgently on taking over portion of new front. These are available & can be drawn at once. Sent for Sergt Webb reported as being left stranded at E 11 central Map 52D with all 33rd Artillery indents & some stores. 7th Division moved 33rd Artillery as a whole to 33rd Divn, leaving the above N.C.O with all indents.	
" "	10/9/16		Both Bases confused over Bulk demands for 33rd Artillery as these had been sent down by 24th, 7th & 33rd Division within one week. Ascertained that 33rd Divn Artillery had proceeded direct to 3rd Army 6th Corps from 4th Army 15 Corps. Hence their move to 33rd Divn only a paper one. On advice of ADOS 7 Corp	

1875 Wt. W593/826 1,000,000 4/15 J.B.C. & A. A.D.S.S./Forms/C. 2118.

Instructions regarding War Diaries and Intelligence Summaries are contained in F. S. Regs., Part II. and the Staff Manual respectively. Title Pages will be prepared in manuscript.

WAR DIARY
or
INTELLIGENCE SUMMARY
(Erase heading not required.)

Army Form C. 2118

Place	Date	Hour	Summary of Events and Information	Remarks and references to Appendices
L'Arbret	10/9/16		I cancelled all demands put down by these Divns to avoid confusion & advised D.A.D.O.S. 12 Divn of action taken. He is now making provision for all stores for the Artillery passed to him by VI Corps. All outstanding Indents forwarded to him. Arranged to move Store & office to Divl. H.Q. at Pas on 11th instant. All stores re-consigned from TINQUES received & offloaded – also heavy load of stores direct from Base. Practically all units called at L'Arbret to draw stores.	
PAS	11/9/16		Moved office & proportion of remaining stores, Reserve helmets etc to PAS. Refused store allotted to me by Camp Commandant 7th Corps as quite unsuitable. An Emergency store opened on open ground between PAS & Henu at	C 23.b.1.7.
			Submitted several drafts for D.R.O.s on Demands, returning of unserviceable stores by units, Salvage etc in accordance with 3rd Army system with regard to these matters. Greater check must be kept on units in interest of economy. Demanded 80 extra Camp kettles for 4 Bns of 19th Bde going into line & therefore unable to use their Travelling kitchens	

Instructions regarding War Diaries and Intelligence Summaries are contained in F. S. Regs., Part II. and the Staff Manual respectively. Title Pages will be prepared in manuscript.

WAR DIARY
or
INTELLIGENCE SUMMARY
(Erase heading not required.)

Army Form C. 2118

Place	Date	Hour	Summary of Events and Information	Remarks and references to Appendices
PHS	11.9.16		Saw ADOS re demands for Trench & Billet Stores. Requirements to be submitted to Corps taking into account Stores taken over in Trenches & all Billet stores in charge of Town Majors	
PHS	12.9.16		Cleared several days stores from Railhead. Sent a lorry load of stores to D.A.D.O.S. 12th Div for 33rd Div Artillery attached to him. Received balance of 12,000 P.H.G. Gas Helmets & was able to complete all outstanding demands of units in the Division. ~~Div~~ 30 C.S.L. Tents issued to me by 7th Corps for the Div. Issued to Town Major Humbercamps (15) and 213 Fd Coy (15) on instructions from ~~Div~~ Div H.Q.	
" "	13.9.16		D.D.O.S. 3rd Army visited offices in morning. Saw A.D.O.S. re demand in this Army for 2 in T. Mortars on Dial Sights. No pools maintained all demands for replacement to be sent to Base in ordinary way. Saw Q re personnel for Armourers, Bootmakers & Pattee [?] Shop. The following units received from VI Corps Troops for administration:- 9th Heavy Battery (4.7") 2/1 N. Midland R.G.A., 2/1 Lowland R.G.A. All Rifles fitted with Telescopic sights to be sent by Base direct to O.O. 3rd Army Troops No 2	

Instructions regarding War Diaries and Intelligence Summaries are contained in F. S. Regs., Part II. and the Staff Manual respectively. Title Pages will be prepared in manuscript.

WAR DIARY
or
INTELLIGENCE SUMMARY
(Erase heading not required.)

Army Form C. 2118.

Place	Date	Hour	Summary of Events and Information	Remarks and references to Appendices
			instead of to D.D.O.S. of the Div. Consequently all future Indents should be endorsed to that effect & O.O. 3rd Army Tps should be notified of number and date of Indent, unit & numbers of rifles demanded.	
PAS +C.23 b.1.7	14.4.16		Large quantity of stores issued to units from store in open. P.H. helmets withdrawn in replacement by P.H.G gradually being returned in the cases in which the P.H.G were packed. Submitted further drafts to S.R.O. re signing of Indents by O.C. returning old stores, packing of P.H. helmets for return.	
"	15.5.16		Went out with D.A.A. & Q.M.G. to choose a suitable store & shops found an empty house in SAUDIEMPRE for the store and a blacksmiths shop in same village which could be used as an Armourers shop. Visited Heavy Mobile Workshops in DOULLENS to obtain two charged air cylinders for Strombos horns in possession of 19th Bde. Took in two empty cylinders. All outstanding demands for Lewis Gun Hand carts cancelled by Base as no further issues are to be made to 1st 2nd & 3rd Armies. Arranged with G for H.Q. Section of Salvage Coy to work near my stores & sort out all returned Ordnance under my instructions	
SAUDIEMPRE +PAS	16.6.16		Moved Store to SAUDIEMPRE, Office remaining at PAS. Allotted Salvage party a space in the yard for sorting & packing & issued written instructions to the Corporal in charge as to disposal & packing of returned Ordnance.	

1875 Wt. W593/826 1,000,000 4/15 J.B.C. & A. A.D.S.S./Forms/C. 2118.

Instructions regarding War Diaries and Intelligence Summaries are contained in F. S. Regs., Part II. and the Staff Manual respectively. Title Pages will be prepared in manuscript.

WAR DIARY
or
INTELLIGENCE SUMMARY
(Erase heading not required.)

Army Form C. 2118

Place	Date	Hour	Summary of Events and Information	Remarks and references to Appendices
GAUDIEMPRE & PAS	17.9.16		Demanded 5000 ~~socks~~ worsted as a reserve to be always maintained for emergencies. All units asked to submit demand for number of Ball cages required for hubs of their Lewis Gun hand carts & also to render a statement of number of serviceable carts in possession to enable sets of tools to be demanded in Bulk. Submitted indent for equipment of Armourers Shop after consultation with Arm S/Sgt Milne who is taking charge of the shop.	
" "	18.9.16		Visited 100th Bde H.Q. & saw Staff Captain on various matters. Proceeded to 19th Bde H.Q. & saw Staff Captain re demands by Battalions for underclothing to replace dirty but not necessarily unserviceable. This cannot be done. Units must arrange to wash their underclothing regimentally or it must be washed at a Laundry under Divisional arrangements. Only demands to replace actually unserviceable can be passed. Proceeded to 98th Bde H.Q. & saw Staff Captain on several small points. 33rd Divl Artillery rejoined from 12th Div.	
"	19.9.16		All surplus stores on re-organization of 33rd Divl Artillery when with 12 Divn returned to me by 'B' Echelon. Includes several range-finders, angle of sight instruments, telephones & No 14 Periscopes. The vehicles rendered surplus, which should have been completely turned out but were not, were sent to Railhead to be held by R.O.O. until their disposal was determined by DDOS &T.	

1875 Wt. W593/826 1,000,000 4/15 J.B.C. & A. A.D.S.S./Forms/C. 2118.

Instructions regarding War Diaries and Intelligence Summaries are contained in F. S. Regs., Part II. and the Staff Manual respectively. Title Pages will be prepared in manuscript.

WAR DIARY
or
INTELLIGENCE SUMMARY

(Erase heading not required.)

Army Form C. 2118

Place	Date	Hour	Summary of Events and Information	Remarks and references to Appendices
GAUDIEMPRE + PAS	20/9/16		Checked Artillery Indents received from 12th Div with Base summaries. As 167th Bde had become extinct owing to absorption into 156 + 162 Bdes (now 6 gun Batteries); also C/166 had been absorbed into A + B/166 (now 6 gun Batteries) all outstanding indents for these units had been cancelled by Base. Any stores on hand sent to Base with Vouchers. Asked DADOS 3rd Army if advisable to cancel all outstanding artillery indents seeing that on re-organization each Battery had become a six-gun in lieu of a four-gun Battery + the scale of equipment would therefore be different. He gave me choice of cancelling if I considered Battery QMS's were insufficiently trained + would therefore be likely to duplicate demands + cause great confusion, or of allowing indents to stand + submit draft to CRA for inclusion in R.A. Orders instructing all Batteries to exercise care in future demands so as to allow for equipment already due to them on Indent. Decided to allow indents to remain without Cancellation. Urgent Bulk demands sent to Base for stores for all Artillery units.	
" "	21.9.16		Drew 13,500 Blankets from O.O. 3rd Army Troops No 2 at Frevent by means of 12 lorries obtained from 7th Corps. This number completes the Division to scale of 1 Blanket per man, allowance having been made for 3000 which will shortly be available from O.O. 7th Corps Troops. Took over store of DADOS 17th Div at Henu who was gradually moving out. Stacked Blankets as received in one portion of store + in a marquee	

1875 Wt. W593/826 1,000,000 4/15 J.B.C. & A. A.D.S.S./Forms/C. 2118.

Instructions regarding War Diaries and Intelligence Summaries are contained in F. S. Regs., Part II. and the Staff Manual respectively. Title Pages will be prepared in manuscript.

WAR DIARY
or
INTELLIGENCE SUMMARY
(Erase heading not required.)

Army Form C. 2118

Place	Date	Hour	Summary of Events and Information	Remarks and references to Appendices
~~[illegible]~~ GAUDIEMPRE.			Placed a W.O. in charge of them for issuing purposes & instructed all units to draw on 22nd instant without fail. Moved Armourers with all tools, kit & building material to Henu to take over 17th Div Armourers shop & get to work as soon as possible.	
HENU	22.9.16		Moved Office ~~[illegible]~~ from PAS to HENU with Div H.Q. also moved store from GAUDIEMPRE to HENU, leaving Anti-gas Helmets till the next day on account of transport difficulties. Blankets being drawn continuously all day & mostly issued by end of the day. No sign yet of consignment of 3000 to complete from O.O. 7th Corps Troops. Found large quantity of salvaged stores left in dumps by 17th Div. Instructed by Corps to clear same away as soon as possible.	
	~~22.9~~			
" "	23.9.16		Authority given for demands to be submitted for certain items of winter Clothing i.e. Bands body, vests & drawers woollen. Winter Scale of Clothing comes into force on 15th October 1916. Started Bootmakers & Tailors shop in HENU. Plenty of repairable boots for former & patterns for latter available from Salvage. The tools demanded for Armourers for Bicycle repairs received from Base. Output of repaired bicycles greatly increased by added facilities.	

Instructions regarding War Diaries and Intelligence Summaries are contained in F. S. Regs., Part II. and the Staff Manual respectively. Title Pages will be prepared in manuscript.

WAR DIARY
or
INTELLIGENCE SUMMARY
(Erase heading not required.)

Army Form C. 2118

Place	Date	Hour	Summary of Events and Information	Remarks and references to Appendices
HENU	23.9.16		156th Bde R.F.A. moved to 35th Divn; 162, 166, Bdes, 'A' Echelon D.A.C and H.Q Coy Divl Train moved again to 72nd Divn. Medium & Heavy T.M. Bs & 'B' Echelon of D.A.C remaining with 33rd Divn. Took over administration of various Heavy Artillery units, A.T. Coy R.E., Tunnelling Coy, etc from 17th Divn on relieving latter. Arranged to send all stores for artillery units to appropriate	
" "	24.9.16		Divns as above, on receipt each day. All bombers shields issued to Bdes a few days previously being returned to me again, together with those shields taken over from Bdes 17th Divn. These shields are Corps Stores & must be handed in to 007th Corps Troops on Division leaving. Census required of number of huts in Divl area, including those taken over from 17th Divn & those issued direct to this Divn by Corps. No huts are to be taken away. DADMS dealing with this matter in conjunction with myself as I have record of numbers received from Corps & returned to Corps from my stores. Returned 300 long Handled wire cutters to R.E. Park. These include 200 returned to me by 100th Bde being Corps Stores.	

1875 Wt. W593/826 1,000,000 4/15 J.B.C. & A. A.D.S.S./Forms/C. 2118.

Instructions regarding War Diaries and Intelligence Summaries are contained in F. S. Regs., Part II. and the Staff Manual respectively. Title Pages will be prepared in manuscript.

WAR DIARY
or
INTELLIGENCE SUMMARY
(Erase heading not required.)

Army Form C. 2118

Place	Date	Hour	Summary of Events and Information	Remarks and references to Appendices
HENU	25.9.16		General routine work. Visited ADOS + DDOS at Saulty. 480 blankets drawn from OO 7th Corps Troops as part of the 3000 due to us. Issued this number to complete one unit. Six Tailors doing good work repairing puttees. Bootmakers Shop requires extra personnel owing to quantity repairable boots received from Salvage. Some difficulty in obtaining more Bootmakers. Sent 2 Dial Sights, received from 33rd Divl RA on leaving this Division, to DADOS 37th Divn as 33rd Artillery in re-organisation & exchanges of guns with 37th Divn had apparently borrowed these Sights from latter. Units drawing stores in good time from Store. Salvage dumps ~~almost~~ being cleared.	
" "	26.9.16		Sent a lorry load of repairable wheels to Heavy Mobile workshops. This is correct procedure in this Army. Obtained two new wheels, urgently required, in exchange. Was informed that HQ Coy 33 Divl Train were urgently in need of wheels No 200 + 200A. This unit now with 12th Divn. Visited Hvy workshop myself + asked OOM to reserve as many such number of possible for this unit. Wired 12th Divn to arrange collection	

1875 Wt. W593/826 1,000,000 4/15 J.B.C. & A. A.D.S.S./Forms/C. 2118.

Instructions regarding War Diaries and Intelligence Summaries are contained in F. S. Regs., Part II. and the Staff Manual respectively. Title Pages will be prepared in manuscript.

WAR DIARY
or
INTELLIGENCE SUMMARY
(Erase heading not required.)

Army Form C. 2118

Place	Date	Hour	Summary of Events and Information	Remarks and references to Appendices
HENU.	26.9.16.		Demanded lever breech mechanism 60pdr for 2/1 Lowland RGA on IOMs condemnation.	
" "	27.9.16.		General routine work. Another consignment of 120 blankets drawn from OO 7th Corps Troops. Demanded 4.7" Q.F. (gun only) condemned by I.O.M. for premature in muzzle, for 9th Heavy Battery. Informed by 12th Divn that portion of our Artillery with them had been transferred to 14th Divn. location of store the same as before so delivery of stores by me not affected. Prepared to move on instructions from 'Q'.	
" "	28.9.16.		Move postponed ~~by~~ until 30th & then only to Doullens. Final destination of Divn not yet clear. One Brigade's still in line. Medium & Heavy T.M.B remaining in present area. 49th Divn has not taken over my store as originally arranged but are remaining in PAS. 48th Divn taking over our Divnl Area jointly with 49th & DADOS 48th Divn arranged to take over my store & supplies etc. on 30th instant.	

Army Form C. 2118

WAR DIARY
or
INTELLIGENCE SUMMARY
(Erase heading not required.)

Instructions regarding War Diaries and Intelligence Summaries are contained in F. S. Regs., Part II. and the Staff Manual respectively. Title Pages will be prepared in manuscript.

Place	Date	Hour	Summary of Events and Information	Remarks and references to Appendices
HENU	28.9.16		wired Base to suspend issues till further notice owing to coming move. 19th & 100th Bdes already moving & consequently very little stores drawn by their units. 98th Bde still drawing as before. The last consignments of Bulk from Base should be oil & grease etc arriving tomorrow & Horseshoes on 30th. These two latter could not be suspended as our Artillery with 35th & 14th Divns were in urgent need of them.	
" "	29.9.16		General routine work. Visited Doullens with Camp Commandant & arranged Store & office there. Warned Armourers to pack up ready for moving & made arrangements for moving stores of 2 Bdes & Divl Tps also office to Doullens first thing on 30th. 98th Bde Stores & smoke helmets & shops to remain for second journey of lorries. Issues to 98th Bde units proceeded as usual. Could not ascertain to what formation to move the attached units. Divn. could not inform me definitely. However I had all outstanding indents collected together ready for handing over	

Instructions regarding War Diaries and Intelligence Summaries are contained in F. S. Regs., Part II. and the Staff Manual respectively. Title Pages will be prepared in manuscript.

WAR DIARY
or
INTELLIGENCE SUMMARY
(Erase heading not required.)

Army Form C. 2118

Place	Date	Hour	Summary of Events and Information	Remarks and references to Appendices
BOULLENS	30.9.16		Moved stores & office as arranged to Doullens. Found office chosen for me there not available so had to find another. Fixed up store satisfactorily, but had to leave finding suitable shops till later owing to difficulty in accomodation & consequent time req'd in hunting for shops. Left one days accumulation of Salvage at Henu in charge of Salvage officer with instructions to have it all sorted, together with any more which might be dumped, ready for collection by lorry. Wired R.T.O at new Railhead, BOUQUEMAISON to hold over three trucks for me until 1/10/16 as I could not clear owing to moving.	

30/9/16.

[signature] Lieut
DADOS
33rd Div

1875 Wt. W593/826 1,000,000 4/15 J.B.C. & A. A.D.S.S./Forms/C. 2118.

DADOS 33rd Div.

WAR DIARY
or
INTELLIGENCE SUMMARY
(Erase heading not required.)

October 1916

WO 95/12 (?)

SECRET

Army Form C. 2118

Instructions regarding War Diaries and Intelligence Summaries are contained in F. S. Regs., Part II. and the Staff Manual respectively. Title Pages will be prepared in manuscript.

Place	Date	Hour	Summary of Events and Information	Remarks and references to Appendices
DOULLENS	1/10/16		Started Armourers + Bootmakers shops. Reconsigned Horseshoes for 33rd Divl Arty direct from BOUQUEMAISON to 35th Div (156 Bde units) + 14th Div (162, 166 Bde units) as distance was too great for lorries to take them to DADOS's of 35th + 14th Div. Loaded other Bulk + detail stores, already in store, for the Div Arty in these lorries for reconsignment, thus despatching all stores for Arty which had been demanded on my Bulk issues. Received 26 Lewis Guns + 532 Magazines. This completes Bns to 10 guns + to half scale 15 32 Magazines for these last two guns. Demanded Hyposcopes, balance of magazines etc to complete the two extra guns. Receipt reported to DDOS + ADOS. Visited ADOS re transfer of Attached Corps Troop units to 49th Divn. New system of Bulk Book-keeping started to-day, with current demand + last week's issues all be shewn.	
"	2.10.16		Visited IOM 7th Corps re watercart + Travelling Kitchen of Pioneers. He would not condemn but arranged to repair at once if sent to him immediately. Warned unit accordingly. Collected balance of 2400 Blankets from OO. 3 A.T.No 2 + stores for issue to units not already in possession. Balance remaining after these issues to go to DADOS 49th for the Corps Troop units transferred to him. Arranged with DADOS 49th to receive from his store to X. Y + Z. T.M.Bs + Pioneers, all stores sent for them by me, to save transferring these units as they are only temporarily attached to 49th Div. Obtained Certificate of Condemnation for Wagon Limb. R.E. of 33rd Div Signal Coy owing to the parts necessary for its repair 15 Pole Eyes, Limbers hooks etc not being sent up by Base although hastened repeatedly. Instructed unit to indent for a new wagon on this certificate. Opened Divl Tailors Shop. Quarterly Bulk return checked + despatched to ADOS with explanation of greatly varying monthly issues on account of continual changes in numbers of units	

Army Form C. 2118

Instructions regarding War Diaries and Intelligence Summaries are contained in F. S. Regs., Part II. and the Staff Manual respectively. Title Pages will be prepared in manuscript.

WAR DIARY
or
INTELLIGENCE SUMMARY
(Erase heading not required.)

Place	Date	Hour	Summary of Events and Information	Remarks and references to Appendices
DOULLENS			+ the changing situation arrangements the Divn being in action, or in rest. Sample of Steel Helmet cover, made in Tailor's Shop from unserviceable S.D. Jackets, submitted to SOC for approval & approved.	
	3.10.16		Sent 1000 Blankets to DADOS 49th Div for issue to units transferred to him. General Routine work. Started Salvage Dump & instructions previously issued by W.C.O.? hold good.	
	4.10.16		General routine work. Applied to HQ for DGO to inspect Div Reserve of Anti-gas Helmets as many cases had been damaged due to constant loading & offloading on various moves. It is thought a good many helmets have deteriorated in anti-gas properties due to exposure to air, rain etc. although broken cases when found had been nailed up as well as possible again. In accordance with 3rd Army Scheme for the overhaul, periodically of all Machine Guns in possession of units, asked DAQMG to arrange for the preparation of a programme for sending in the guns of one Bde at a time at the rate of 3 Lewis & 1 Vickers Gun per day to Divl Armourers Shop. 25 Sample of approved pattern of Steel Helmet Cover made in Tailor's Shop for distribution to units to enable them to make their own covers in accordance with CRO. Purchased a few Brooms, Lamps Hurricane & Scrubbing Brushes locally for 100th Bde Baths which are opening tomorrow morning. Wrote long report to ADOS criticising system in vogue of transferring stores & outstanding demands of Divl Artilleries when latter are transferred to other Divs especially when Artilleries move from one to another in quick succession.	

Army Form C. 2118

Instructions regarding War Diaries and Intelligence Summaries are contained in F. S. Regs., Part II. and the Staff Manual respectively. Title Pages will be prepared in manuscript.

WAR DIARY
or
INTELLIGENCE SUMMARY
(Erase heading not required.)

Place	Date	Hour	Summary of Events and Information	Remarks and references to Appendices
DOULLENS			Requested that a letter system be instituted as Bart. Artilleries have great difficulty in obtain Stores regularly if present system is rigidly adhered to. Authority received for demanding Horse-rugs on scale of 1 per Horse in Divn.	
	5.10.16		First issue of 1000 Steel Helmet covers made by Base off indents submitted for the whole Divn. If balance is received the necessity for units to make covers regimentally is obviated. Latter is desirable as there is [illegible] of units using serviceable service dress for this purpose, instead of really unserviceable clothing. Received 18 inner + 18 outer Spring R.O. to complete spares of 'B' Echelon D.A.C. These ordered by D.D.O.S. 3rd Army to be sent immediately to I.M. Workshops + instructions issued by him to Base + to all D.A.D.O.S.'s in the Army that all Springs R.O. are to go direct to I.M. Shops + none demanded by or issued to D.A.C.s. Visited D.D.O.S. re this matter.	
	6.10.16		Received 25 Lewis Gun hand carts for distribution. Ordered by D.D.O.S. 3rd Army. Obtained reports fr. Bdes + Pioneers of numbers of serviceable carts in possession + used this information as a basis for distribution. Issued so as to bring all units up to 12 serviceable hand carts each as far as possible. Wired units to collect direct from Railhead. Again discussed matter of issue of Covers or Paint for Steel Helmet with Q. A recent D.R.O. allows units to demand either Covers or Paint. G.O.C. wishes uniformity to obtain among Bdes or Bns i.e. the whole Bde or Bn must have either paint or covers but not both. This renders a large number of the Covers demanded from Base	

1875 Wt. W593/826 1,000,000 4/15 J.B.C. & A. A.D.S.S./Forms/C. 2118.

Instructions regarding War Diaries and Intelligence Summaries are contained in F. S. Regs., Part II. and the Staff Manual respectively. Title Pages will be prepared in manuscript.

WAR DIARY
or
INTELLIGENCE SUMMARY
(Erase heading not required.)

Army Form C. 2118

Place	Date	Hour	Summary of Events and Information	Remarks and references to Appendices
DOULLENS			Surplus as GOC 100th Bde has decided to have all helmets in his Bde painted & sanded.	
			On instructions from Q applied to ADOS for the issue of 2 Marquees & 100 hot food containers, the first for accomodation of Div. H.Q. on coming move into forward area where no houses or huts exist & second for taking hot food to trenches during coming operations.	
			3000 prs Socks received to complete Div Reserve as an equal number had been put into PAS laundry for immediate starting of same to enable units to obtain a clean change of underclothing as soon as possible.	
	7/10/16		Authority given by Corps to draw 1500 ~~wire~~ wire breakers & 100 L.H. wirecutters from 7th Corps R.S. Park (No 5). 100 L.H. Cutters at present in store from Salvage at various times. These wirecutters & Breakers are to be returned to me after use for return to Corps. Drawn 8th instant not being available to day. ~~Tents & Shelters drawn for S.O.~~ Trucks arriving very late at Railhead now. Lorry load of miscellaneous stores for 156th Bde ADA received from 35th Div. Found out that 156th Bde had been moved to 49th Div so sent lorry on to wagon lines of Bde with the stores to save time in delivery. Sent some SD Clothing received off my last Clothing Bulk for B/156 Bde to DADOS 49th Div for issue. All 33rd Div Arty now administered by 49th Div except T.M.B.s & 'B' Echelon DAC	

1875 Wt. W593/826 1,000,000 4/15 J.B.C. & A. A.D.S.S./Forms/C. 2118.

Army Form C. 2118

Instructions regarding War Diaries and Intelligence Summaries are contained in F. S. Regs., Part II. and the Staff Manual respectively. Title Pages will be prepared in manuscript.

WAR DIARY
or
INTELLIGENCE SUMMARY
(Erase heading not required.)

Place	Date	Hour	Summary of Events and Information	Remarks and references to Appendices
DOULLENS			Stores still being received from Base for Corps Troop units recently transferred to 49th Divn. Sent these in daily as received to DADOS 49th Divn. ADOS visited office in evening. Said balance of 32 Magazines for last two guns received should not have been demanded as the scale of magazines would shortly be reduced. Have nothing official about this so demand was submitted in accordance with existing instructions. Instructed by ADOS to arrange for carrying out of general instruction re Salvage etc in case of an advance in view of pending operations. Saw G in this matter & was told administrative orders were being issued & Salvage Coy formed to deal with collection & disposal of surplus & abandoned stores. Understand I am to remain at Doullens & take stores to refilling points when Division moves into the line as no accommodation exists in the new area for my stores and doubtful if the scheme will work in practice. Tarpaulins for Ammunition Dumps can be drawn from OO 3rd Army Troops in addition to those being sent up by Base for this purpose (20)	
	8/10/16		Arranged to draw huts & shelters allotted to Div by Corps for accommodation purposes, from OO 7 Corps Troops tomorrow & deliver to Town Majors direct. Visited DADOS 49th Div. is giving him assistance in form of a Sergt; a clerk & a Storeman for the administration of 3rd Div artillery now attached 49th [illegible]	

1875 Wt. W593/826 1,000,000 4/15 J.B.C. & A. A.D.S.S./Forms/C. 2118.

Instructions regarding War Diaries and Intelligence Summaries are contained in F. S. Regs., Part II. and the Staff Manual respectively. Title Pages will be prepared in manuscript.

WAR DIARY
or
INTELLIGENCE SUMMARY
(Erase heading not required.)

Army Form C. 2118

Place	Date	Hour	Summary of Events and Information	Remarks and references to Appendices
DOULLENS			arranged to send him the personnel provided 38 Div Arty came remaining with 49th Div for any length of time. Informed by ADOS this was so. Received instructions from Q to purchase necessary paint, tarps + brushes for the camouflaging of 20 WP covers for Ammunition Dumps. Tents + Shelters drawn for 00 3rd Corps Troops + taken to Beauvillers + Sailly au Bois. Answered complaint from No 3. Sec D.A.C re their inability to get horse-shoes, showing that shoes had been issued + receipt obtained which O.C. unit states were never received by them. Lack of all stores very serious with R.A. [illegible] Investigated the whole matter + asked ~~DADOS 49~~ Div to submit special + urgent bulk demands on Base to enable the Artillery to obtain their requirements, especially horseshoes as soon as possible. Wired 38th 14th Divs to send on any stores they had for 38th Div Artillery by lorry + not by rail, to avoid delay. Special barbed wire mats required for experimental purposes by 'G'. Bought khaki drill for outer cover + flock for stuffing same + had mat made up in Tailors shop. Moved X.Y + Z.V.T.M.Bs to 49th Div.	

1875 Wt. W593/826 1,000,000 4/15 J.B.C. & A. A.D.S.S./Forms/C. 2118.

Instructions regarding War Diaries and Intelligence Summaries are contained in F. S. Regs., Part II. and the Staff Manual respectively. Title Pages will be prepared in manuscript.

WAR DIARY
or
INTELLIGENCE SUMMARY
(Erase heading not required.)

Army Form C. 2118

Place	Date	Hour	Summary of Events and Information	Remarks and references to Appendices
DOULLENS	9/10/16		Bought paint, etc. & had 20 covers w.p. camouflaged for R.A. dumps. Visited Staff Capt 100th Bde & discussed question of supply of Boilers w.o. taps for Travelling Kitchens, Lewis Gun hand carts, Brake gear of Limb: G.S. Wagons, paint or covers for steel helmets of the Bde. G.O.C. Bde wants Paint for whole Bde. Issued 1000 Covers rec'd from Base to 19th Bde. Issued 1500 wire breakers and 200 L.H. wire cutters to 3 Bdes under distribution from 'Q'. Wrote A.D.O.S. asking if urgent action could be taken to obtain a supply of Boilers w.o. taps as outstanding demands were very heavy & hastening action on my part had produced no effect. Matter urgent if units have to rely on their Travelling Kitchens. 18 more Lewis Gun hand carts advised as despatched from Base. Asked 'Q' for distribution. Received instructions to purchase 50,000 metal hooks & eyes for sewing to Infantry Greatcoats to enable the flaps to be fastened back for purposes of attack. Tried Local Purchase in Doullens but could not obtain sufficient. C.R.A. 33rd Div reported lack of horse-shoes very serious. Ascertained from 35th & 14th Div that the shoes [illegible] reconsigned to them on 1/10/16 had been reconsigned to 49th Div for 33rd Div Arty. Visited D.A.D.O.S. 49th Div specially & investigated whole question of supply of Stores to Artillery preparing statement of outstanding demands on Base & numbers of all bulk items required to complete. Asked D.A.D.O.S. 49th Div to send special Bulk demands for horseshoes, no provision having been made by 35th & 14th Div the previous week owing to transference of the Artillery from them to 49th Div. Obtained 36 boxes of shoes from D.A.D.O.S. 48th Div as an emergency issue & also issued a few boxes of my own surplus shoes. Shoes arrived [illegible] A.M. 10th from 35th Div & were sent on to 49th Div by lorry. Sent Sergt Webb [illegible] & [illegible] to D.A.D.O.S. 49th to assist his staff	

(1875) Wt. W593/826 1,000,000 4/15 J.B.C. & A. A.D.S.S./Forms/C. 2118.

Instructions regarding War Diaries and Intelligence Summaries are contained in F. S. Regs., Part II. and the Staff Manual respectively. Title Pages will be prepared in manuscript.

WAR DIARY
or
INTELLIGENCE SUMMARY
(Erase heading not required.)

Army Form C. 2118

Place	Date	Hour	Summary of Events and Information	Remarks and references to Appendices
DOULLENS	10/10/16		Bought 40,000 Hooks & Eyes in Amiens. Balance of 32 Magazines for each of the last 36 guns issued received from Base. 18 Lewis Gun handcarts received at Railhead. Very difficult to obtain correct information as to number of serviceable handcarts in possession of Bns. Finally succeeded in making distribution which gave all units 12 serviceable carts each. Arranged for the unserviceable carts to be returned to my store. General office work	
	11/10/16		~~[illegible]~~ 130 Steel helmets urgently required. Wired ADOS for them. Sent out camouflaged covers to R.A. H.Q at Sailly-au-Bois. Barbed wire mat no good - too heavy & bulky. Wadding required for stuffing instead of flock. Question of supply of S.D. Greatcoats to officers brought up. Referred matter to Q who are submitting to Corps for Army approval. Wrote ADOS re supply of T.M. Handcarts, last instructions being that whole matter ~~of~~ supply was under consideration. Units hastening issue to complete establishment. Provision having been made for Pouches & Cases Belt for Machine gunners, of 1908 & 1914 pattern Equipment in ~~the~~ proportion according to mob table Equipment of units, 100 M.G. Coy urges supply of 1908 holsters although 1914 Equipment was provided for in this case. Base have already supplied 1908 holsters in full & 1914 pouches in full. No 1914 holsters available, wired base to send up 1908 holsters in lieu of 1914 for this unit. Drew 130 Steel Helmets from those collected by 007 Corps Troops. ADOS is arranging further supply from C.C.S. Indented on Base at same time for 500 urgently required for re-inforcements. 19th Bde units moving forward & therefore unable to draw stores from Doullens. Their stores must be sent to refilling points in future.	
	12/10/16		D.D.O.S. visited Store & office & checked expenditure from Bulk Books & examined 100 Bde Indents. Afterwards went round Shops with him. Tailors must turn out more puttees by not spending so much time in carefully repairing them	

1875 Wt. W593/826 1,000,000 4/15 J.B.C. & A. A.D.S.S./Forms/C. 2118.

Instructions regarding War Diaries and Intelligence Summaries are contained in F. S. Regs., Part II. and the Staff Manual respectively. Title Pages will be prepared in manuscript.

WAR DIARY

or

INTELLIGENCE SUMMARY

(Erase heading not required.)

Army Form C. 2118

Place	Date	Hour	Summary of Events and Information	Remarks and references to Appendices
DOULLENS			all holes to be cut away + short lengths of pulley so formed joined together. A sewing machine decided to be a necessity for increasing output. Visited DADOS 49 re position of supply of all stores to 38th Div Arty. Impressed on my Sergeant, who has charge of their indents, the necessity for carefully scrutinising all indents + bring all long-outstanding items especially gun-parts to notice of DADOS 49th Div for hastening action. ADOS asked if there was any shortage of hay nets experienced by me. Informed him that none had been received for three weeks + were urgently required. He reports great shortage of them generally. ADOS states no further issues of T.M. hand carts would be made yet. Good quantity of 1914 Equipment collected + sorted at Salvage Dump + found fit for issue. This will reduce next Bde demand to nil. Submitted draft for DRO withdrawing all L.G. hand carts in excess of 12 per Bn. All returned should be in an unserviceable condition as every Bn should now only be in possession of 12 serviceable carts.	
" "	13.10.16		Saw 'Q' re personnel for sorting returned Ordnance at my Salvage Dump as under new Salvage scheme these are withdrawn to Salvage Coy. Visited Amiens for L.P. of material for Salvage Armlets + other Tailors materials + tools. 500 Steel Helmets received from Base. This will enable all outstanding demands to be met + will leave a balance to meet further current demands. Bought, after great difficulties, several sheets of specially compressed wadding - very light, tough + soft for	Special mat

1875 Wt. W593/826 1,000,000 4/15 J.B.C. & A. A.D.S.S./Forms/C. 2118.

Instructions regarding War Diaries and Intelligence Summaries are contained in F. S. Regs., Part II. and the Staff Manual respectively. Title Pages will be prepared in manuscript.

WAR DIARY
or
INTELLIGENCE SUMMARY
(Erase heading not required.)

Army Form C. 2118

Place	Date	Hour	Summary of Events and Information	Remarks and references to Appendices
DOULLENS	14/10/16		17 damaged Lewis Gun Hand carts received from units at my store: all have wheel or tyre troubles. Saw 100th Bde [illegible] on all Steel Helmets in his Bde being painted khaki. Received instructions from 'Q' to buy sufficient paint at once. Div Gas Officer visited me with reference to latest instructions as to ~~[illegible]~~ inspection & disposal of salvaged anti-gas appliances. We inspected samples of them at Salvage Dump. Saw 'Q' re having a trained NCO from Gas School to take charge of any reserve of Gas Helmets. Reserve now only 5000 P.H. The surplus boxes are all being stencilled with the word UNUSED across them before despatch to Railhead. Arranged to hand over 2000 of my stock of P.H.G. Helmets to DADOS 17th Div as my present stock is too large. Submitted draft for D.R.O. calling for a report on numbers of Spanish Revolvers in possession of units preparatory to withdrawing the already faulty ones for inspection & condemnation & for ~~latter~~ later withdrawal & examination at the Armourer's Shop. All these revolvers are to be gradually replaced as they are ~~[illegible]~~ bad. Demanded 3,600 Capes Macintosh authorised for manufacture & obtained distribution of them from 'Q'. General office work. the whole Division	
" "	15.10.16		Visited DADOS 4th G.H.Q. again re position of supply of stores to 32nd Artillery. Went on to R.A. H.Q. & discussed the whole matter with Staff Captain. Great shortage at Bases & L. of C. Hay nets very urgently required. R.A. would like their equipment completed before 19th or 20th if possible. Brought whole question before [illegible]	
	16.10.16		14. Lewis Gun hand carts sent to Railhead after examination & removal of a few good wheels by Armourers, to make other handcarts serviceable. Again visited DADOS. 49th Div re our Artillery & then DADOS 4th G.H.Q. [illegible] provision for 400 Steel Helmets to complete to whole [illegible] officers & men. Visited [illegible] Corps. He cannot take in any more wheels for repair at present.	

1875 Wt. W593/826 1,000,000 4/15 J.B.C. & A. A.D.S.S./Forms/C. 2118.

Army Form C. 2118

WAR DIARY
or
INTELLIGENCE SUMMARY

(Erase heading not required.)

Instructions regarding War Diaries and Intelligence Summaries are contained in F. S. Regs., Part II. and the Staff Manual respectively. Title Pages will be prepared in manuscript.

Place	Date	Hour	Summary of Events and Information	Remarks and references to Appendices
DOULLENS			but if notified of vehicles requiring repair he can find out if Shops at Sovastre can take them as they have only Heavy gun work & no vehicle work at present. SI of A Section suggested Heavy Mobile Workshops could undertake repair of Baking Boilers W.O. Cops as they have Tinsmiths on their staff. Settled policy to be adopted in Tailors shop for the output of a thoroughly serviceable puttee with edges turned over & sewn to avoid future fraying & tearing, without waste of time in ~~fancy~~ fancy repairs. All holes in the puttee before repair to be cut out & the ends so formed to be joined up again. Balance of surplus P.H. Helmets sent to Base. 5000 now remain as reserve. Submitted draft for DRO instructing units requiring covers for steel helmets to complete, to indent for them at once.	
	17.10.16		Informed proposed offensive on this Front will not take place & that preparation made for the provision of Tarpaulins for Ammn Dumps (47 already in area + store) Tentage, hot food containers (120 expected from Base) should stop. All wirebreakers & wirecutters, tentage & Tarpaulins issued to the Div to be sent into me for return to Corps or handed over in the area to relieving Divn. Warned of move of the Divn within 48 hours to unknown destination by Q. Cancelled all issues from Calais Base till further notice as a precaution. Very few units were able to call at Store owing to the packing up & departure of their transport. Only small quantity of stores, however remain in store. Informed that 33rd Div Arty are moving from 49th Div to XIII Corps Troops. Visited DADOS 49 & asked him to ensure that all stores be received for them after they have left, are sent on to ~~O.O. XIII Corps~~ by lorry to avoid any delay. Tarpaulins & tents ~~[illegible]~~ in store at present to be sent to O.O. 7th Corps Troops tomorrow.	

1875 Wt. W593/826 1,000,000 4/15 J.B.C. & A. A.D.S.S./Forms/C. 2118.

Army Form C. 2118

Instructions regarding War Diaries and Intelligence Summaries are contained in F. S. Regs., Part II. and the Staff Manual respectively. Title Pages will be prepared in manuscript.

WAR DIARY
or
INTELLIGENCE SUMMARY
(Erase heading not required.)

Place	Date	Hour	Summary of Events and Information	Remarks and references to Appendices
DOULLENS	18.10.16		Armourers, Bootmakers & Tailors shops packing up ready to move. Of course to send any stores on hand to refilling points as units would not be able to accept them. Arranged to leave Sergt Webb & Ptes Connor & Benford with DADOS 49th Div until 33rd RA actually leave them, when I will give instructions as to their movements of this personnel. Saw ADOS on various matters to be settled before leaving Corps area. Informed him hot food containers not now required by the Div. He will get 3rd Army to cancel them. Prepared to move on 19th to Corbie. Railhead Corbie. Wired ADOS numbers of trucks at BOUQUEMAISON which I could not clear owing to moving & requested they be reconsigned to new Railhead. This arranged later in day by DDOS 3rd Army who informed me of action taken & asked if I had cancelled issues from Calais till further notice. Informed him I had done so. Informed me he is arranging ~~Calais~~, Havre & Rouen to commence issues to me in 4th Army area on receipt of notification from me. & wired Calais to transfer outstanding demands. Everything now ready for moving.	
	19.10.16		Moved with 3 lorry loads to Corbie, leaving Armourers, Shoemakers & some heavy stores behind for later journey. Found 20th Div had not cleared their stores fr DADOS store in Corbie. However found office clear & sufficient space for my stores was made by carefully stacking up of their stores. They will clear balance of their stores in morning without fail. Reported my arrival & position of store to ADOS 14th Corps on phone. He advised me to continue issues from Bases although we may only stay here eight hours. Received large packet of letters & circulars, giving instructions for Ordnance Services with 4th Army, from ADOS. A good many of these letters were received by me on previous	

1875 Wt. W593/826 1,000,000 4/15 J.B.C. & A. A.D.S.S./Forms/C. 2118.

Instructions regarding War Diaries and Intelligence Summaries are contained in F. S. Regs., Part II. and the Staff Manual respectively. Title Pages will be prepared in manuscript.

WAR DIARY
or
INTELLIGENCE SUMMARY
(Erase heading not required.)

Army Form C. 2118

Place	Date	Hour	Summary of Events and Information	Remarks and references to Appendices
CORBIE.	19.10.16		Stay in 4th Army area. Latest instructions are – rendition of certificate of receipt & cancellation of outstanding indents monthly, – keeping of unofficial reserves of Shorts, Cells Electric 'S', Torches, Buffer oil, Flannelette, etc. – wired Bases to continue issues & sent list of units administered by me to Base & to ADOS.	
	Do.		Reported position of supply of Lewis Gun Handcarts, No 14 periscope. T.M handcarts Lewis Guns, Vickers Guns, Magazines. R.O springs in possession of DAC	
	20.10.16		Sent 3 lorries back to DOULLENS to clear balance of stores & shops if possible. Lorries returned with Armourers but could not bring Shoemakers Shop. Broken down limb portion Kitchen travelling at Villers Bocage. Asked 'Q' to send a lorry to collect it & bring to me for inspection as IOM's shop is too far away at Mametz. Vehicle brought in in evening. Found it had a broken axle & other damage to wheels. Sent it to Railhead & demanded replacement from D.D.O.S. 4th Army (who can allot any surplus vehicles there may be in Army) Informed A.D.O.S. of action taken in circumstances of workshop too far away & he agreed to it. Several S.S. wagons of 'B' Echelon in bad state of repair. Instructed OC to send in to 14th Corps Shops at Mametz at first opportunity & meanwhile to purchase timber for the temporary repair of them by his wheelers. No reconsigned trucks from BOUQUEMAISON yet received.	
TREUX	21.10.16		Moved to TREUX. Lorries brought Armourers shop, personnel & reserves of Anti gas helmets, socks, boot brackets etc. Sent lorries back to clear CORBIE & bring office gear along as soon as possible. Advised of 3 trucks to be cleared from CORBIE. Two contain 24 Lewis gun handcarts. Returned these to Base as latest	

Instructions regarding War Diaries and Intelligence Summaries are contained in F. S. Regs., Part II. and the Staff Manual respectively. Title Pages will be prepared in manuscript.

WAR DIARY
or
INTELLIGENCE SUMMARY
(Erase heading not required.)

Army Form C. 2118

Place	Date	Hour	Summary of Events and Information	Remarks and references to Appendices
TREUX.			authority only allows 12 Handcarts per Bde + as these are already in possession the 24 handcarts just received are surplus. Reported the return of them to A.D.O.S. No magazines will need to be returned as a good many are deficient from original scale of 64 per gun now reduced to 48 per gun. Visited R.T.O. + tried to induce him to reconsign the truck direct to new Railhead. He states it would cause great delay in receipt as it would have to be sent to Romescamps. Decided to clear truck on return to store sent two lorries to Corbie to clear. Submitted demands for Jerkins, gloves, undercoats fur by urgent wire to Rouen + hastened issue of horse-rugs. Impossible to make accurate provision as many units have not submitted their requirements. Submitted an approximate demand but a supplementary one will have to be submitted later. Hastened the underclothing already demanded on 9th + hastened on 13th.	
	22.10.16		Moved to Happy Valley Railhead position. Div H.Q. being at Citadel. A.O.C. personnel + stores of 6th Div Arty + Guards Div Arty are at Happy valley as left by D.A.D.O.S 6th Div on moving. Am now administering 6th + Guards Div Artillery. A W.O. + two men left by 6th Div and a Sergeant and two men left by Guards Div. Applied to A.D.O.S. for some Covers + a Marquee very urgently required for forming a store. The two Marquees left with 6th + Guards Stores are only large enough to contain them. ADOS wired that a Marquee could be drawn from DOS 14th Corps + some Trench Shelters from OO 14th Corps Troops. Am still in difficulties for covering as armourers require the Marquee. Railhead now Edgehill.	

Army Form C. 2118

WAR DIARY
or
INTELLIGENCE SUMMARY
(Erase heading not required.)

Instructions regarding War Diaries and Intelligence Summaries are contained in F. S. Regs., Part II. and the Staff Manual respectively. Title Pages will be prepared in manuscript.

Place	Date	Hour	Summary of Events and Information	Remarks and references to Appendices
HAPPY VALLEY F 27. Central	22.10.16		Established office at Div H.Q. the Citadel. Ground at Happy Valley getting very soft & difficult for lorries. Sent 2 lorries to clear from EDGE HILL & remainder back to TREUX for shops & remaining stores. Several journeys will have to be made to clear. Units have difficulty in drawing from store so stores will have to be sent to refilling points. This is difficult owing to congested state of roads & shortage of lorries (one to Treux & one to collect Marquee covers etc. 96 Sets of G.S. Packs [illegible] to be taken over at 3 pm from 4th Div D.A.D.O.S. Found these sets in great state of confusion, just as returned by units of 4th Div. With great difficulty sorted out 96 sets by my own staff & issued 30 sets to each Bde & 6 sets to Pioneers. Several component parts missing as taken over. Issued 750 Blue & White armbands for runners & White Calico for Battalion Signalling to Aeroplanes.	
" "	23.10.16		Div moving forward into line to-morrow. Position of my ~~[illegible]~~ rest store notified by Div H.Q. as A 21a central by Plateau Railway. Went up to try & find suitable spot (4th Div reported they had partially constructed a wooden frame & lorry standings. From map reference given could not find this spot nor any place suitable for a store ~~[illegible]~~ owing to mud congested traffic & absence of suitable standings for lorries. Reported this to Q & asked if correct position could be given me to enable me to find it. Another map reference	

Instructions regarding War Diaries and Intelligence Summaries are contained in F. S. Regs., Part II. and the Staff Manual respectively. Title Pages will be prepared in manuscript.

WAR DIARY
or
INTELLIGENCE SUMMARY

(Erase heading not required.)

Army Form C. 2118

Place	Date	Hour	Summary of Events and Information	Remarks and references to Appendices
F.27. Central	24.10.16 ~~24.10.16~~		given me ~~but still could not find the place~~. Arranged to go up again & instructed Armourers to load up their shop on lorry & set out ~~[illegible]~~ to meet me at new Dump when chosen. Waited several hours by ~~refilling point~~ Plateau Railhead for this lorry but it did not arrive. However ~~no~~ suitable place could be found within the limits of the area bounded by Bray–Maricourt road, Maricourt road & Carnoy–Montauban road. Reported this to 'Q'. Railhead now Plateau. 6th & Guards have a lorry each so they can go to Railhead & extract all stores for their units, splitting up Bulk with my representative & load ~~the~~ stores on to their own lorries thus avoiding any confusion of stores. All indents for Artillery units are kept by the AOC representatives. I arrange for all guns & vehicles required & sign all indents which, however are registered by them & bear 6th & Guards Div numbers. Three bulk wires sent nightly so as to keep demands of 35th Div units, Guards Artillery & 6th Div Artillery all separate to avoid confusion on receipt & for record purposes.	
	~~25.10.16~~			
	25.10.16.		Div have moved forward, Div HQ being in two portions advanced & Rear. My store still at Happy Valley until suitable place found to move to, to-morrow. Car left permanently with me while detached from Div H.Q. to enable me to keep in touch ~~communication~~ with Railhead Corps & Rear Div H.Q. A.D.O.S. wired me in morning correct Map reference of Dump left by 4th Div	

Instructions regarding War Diaries and Intelligence Summaries are contained in F. S. Regs., Part II. and the Staff Manual respectively. Title Pages will be prepared in manuscript.

WAR DIARY
or
INTELLIGENCE SUMMARY
(Erase heading not required.)

Army Form C. 2118

Place	Date	Hour	Summary of Events and Information	Remarks and references to Appendices
HAPPY VALLEY F.27 Central	25.10.16		went up & found same to be most suitable place although very muddy, arranged to move there first thing in morning. Sent stores to common refilling point by Plateau Railhead & experienced difficulty in getting units to take it. Very difficult place for issues to be made from lorries owing to very congested state of traffic & lack of suitable lorry standing.	
A.13.d.5.3	26.10.16.		Loaded up 2 lorries with office gear, covers W.P. & necessary stores for starting dump & sent them off to new dump, remaining lorries to refilling point. On arrival at new dump proceeded to put covers on wooden framework & pitched tents! Ground very soft & wet. On return of lorries from refilling point sent them to clear Railhead. Left Armourers till later at Plateau together with some stores not required at once. ~~For~~ Standings used for 3 lorries & require re-inforcing. Asked Q to wire all Bdes & Div Troop Units position of my store & instructions to draw from there regularly. Minden Post (8th Div Signals) will take our messages & DRs from Rear HQ call several times daily. My Chief Clerk S/Cdr Neal went on leave in evening.	
	27.10.16		Cleared Armourers with Marquee & brought them to A13d 5.3 (new store) pitched marquee & started shop going. Sent a lorry to Happy Valley & clear salvage from there & take to	

Instructions regarding War Diaries and Intelligence Summaries are contained in F. S. Regs., Part II. and the Staff Manual respectively. Title Pages will be prepared in manuscript.

WAR DIARY
or
INTELLIGENCE SUMMARY
(Erase heading not required.)

Army Form C. 2118

Place	Date	Hour	Summary of Events and Information	Remarks and references to Appendices
A13 d.5.3			Grovetown Railhead. Salvage cannot be returned to Plateau at present. This lorry brought back from Happy valley the wire breakers & wirecutters, bombers shields which have been collected from units & are to be returned to 007 Corps troops & No 5 RE Park 7th Corps as soon as full numbers received.	
	28.10.16		Winter clothing beginning to arrive at Railhead as advised. Trucks from Paris ~~very late in arriving some~~ advised as being despatched with horse-rugs, undercoats, fur, jerkins. 'Q' have been hastening issue of Jerkins to Divs. Urgent wires sent to Rouen hastening issue. Rouen wired back not available but would give this Div priority of issue on next consignment expected in a day. ADOS took matter up with them & notified me that 9000 would be sent off tomorrow. Horse-rugs (1573) received direct from HAVRE. Issued them to units as fast as received from Railhead. ~~Great~~ Experienced difficulty in clearing Railhead owing to quantity of stores, shortage of lorries & fatigue party. Trucks must be cleared by 6 pm or earlier each evening & train does not arrive till noon. Owing to traffic congestion lorries are held up in getting to & from Railhead. However managed to clear Railhead each day	

Army Form C. 2118

Instructions regarding War Diaries and Intelligence Summaries are contained in F. S. Regs., Part II. and the Staff Manual respectively. Title Pages will be prepared in manuscript.

WAR DIARY
or
INTELLIGENCE SUMMARY
(Erase heading not required.)

Place	Date	Hour	Summary of Events and Information	Remarks and references to Appendices
A.13.d.5.3			accomodation now becoming serious question owing to large amount of winter clothing arriving daily. applied to RE for timber & trench boards & to ASCs for Covers & Saleable Kettle goods to be protected from weather. General office work	
	29.10.16		2450 of Second Blanket per man arrived Railhead. Cleared with lorries & wired 'Q' for distribution. These could not be given at once so had to keep lorries loaded all night as there was no accomodation for them to store & it was desirable to issue them out straight away to Units. Base wired if I could accept two trucks Blanket per day. Replied could not do so at present as no accomodation existed & did not understand why these were being sent up as no authority had yet been issued for drawing 2nd Blanket. Found out from ADOS these Blankets were being issued in advance & that authority would be issued later. wired 'Q' if I should accept any ~~[illegible]~~ more of 2nd Blanket & asked if accomodation was available to store them on receipt. No reply received so wired Base to send up on receipt of wire from me when accomodation existed. Brought lack of accomodation to notice of ADOS. Units cannot accept	

1875 Wt. W593/826 1,000,000 4/15 J.B.C. & A. A.D.S.S./Forms/C. 2118.

Instructions regarding War Diaries and Intelligence Summaries are contained in F. S. Regs., Part II. and the Staff Manual respectively. Title Pages will be prepared in manuscript.

WAR DIARY
or
INTELLIGENCE SUMMARY
(Erase heading not required.)

Army Form C. 2118

Place	Date	Hour	Summary of Events and Information	Remarks and references to Appendices
A.13.d.5.3			2nd Blanket at present, being in action, except 19th Bde + 98th to whom the 2450 just received are to be issued. 2 Bns each. Tried to do this by lorry but only one lorry load (19th Bde) could be delivered owing to traffic regulations. ~~[illegible]~~ ~~[illegible]~~. Issued balance to 19th Bde units on application to my store, this being only means of getting rid of them quickly + satisfying urgent demands of these units. 98th Bde would have had the second half if [illegible] had been provided by Div. H.Q. as requested at first.	HT
	30/10/16		Several condemnations of guns of 6th + Guards Artillery received from IOM 14th Corps. Guns wired for immediately. Also a good many vehicles condemned by IOM on inspection + reported by units as being unserviceable. In latter cases wired them to take to IOM or in the case of a Pontoon wagon of 11th Field Coy which could not be moved wired unit to effect temporary repairs + take to IOM or to 1st IOM to inspect it where it was. 6th + Guards Div. Artillery urgent supply of winter clothing. Delay caused in both cases by [illegible] + Gds Divs passing on lists of winter clothing for re-demand by me as [illegible]	

1875 Wt. W593/826 1,000,000 4/15 J.B.C. & A. A.D.S.S./Forms/C. 2118.

Army Form C. 2118

Instructions regarding War Diaries and Intelligence Summaries are contained in F. S. Regs., Part II. and the Staff Manual respectively. Title Pages will be prepared in manuscript.

WAR DIARY
or
INTELLIGENCE SUMMARY

(Erase heading not required.)

Place	Date	Hour	Summary of Events and Information	Remarks and references to Appendices
AB.d 5.3			to their changes of Bases these demands had been cancelled. Explained this to Staff Captains of each Div Artillery. Sent in lists of outstanding demands for Triggers urgently required by D.A.C.s. Return of Springs Ro. 18pdr issued during previous week & numbers on demand ahead of week for both Artilleries reported to ADOS. This is required weekly & 24 inner & 24 outer must always be on demand for each D.A.C. to ensure supply of springs to I.O.M. as all in excess of 12 of each are handed over by DACs to him.	
	31.10.16		Gloves & bands body received off winter clothing demand submitted on 21st. 20 hot food containers received for Div from Corps Troops. Issued 10 each to 19th & 98th Bde. 13th Corps wired asking for proportion of our sniper stores to be diverted to our Div Arty in XIII Corps as none were available with Corps Troops for them. Wired Base to divert 10 off our demand for 60. Instructed W.O. i/c 6th Div Arty & Sergt i/c Guards Div Arty to revise their outstanding indents over 1 month old & see which could be cancelled preparing lists accordingly to be in my office by 5th. Instructed my own W.O. similarly. This return is required on 6th by ADOS.	

1875 Wt. W593/826 1,000,000 4/15 J.B.C. & A. A.D.S.S./Forms/C. 2118.

Instructions regarding War Diaries and Intelligence Summaries are contained in F. S. Regs., Part II. and the Staff Manual respectively. Title Pages will be prepared in manuscript.

WAR DIARY
or
INTELLIGENCE SUMMARY
(Erase heading not required.)

Army Form C. 2118

Place	Date	Hour	Summary of Events and Information	Remarks and references to Appendices
A.13d5.3	31.10.16		2prs Traces were short urgently required owing to bad state of roads. 'O' wired Corps for authority for issue of these in addition to the 2prs per Bn authorised by GRO 1444. Reported to ADOS latter had all been issued to units who had demanded them. Question of outstanding demands for Boilers W.C. tops brought up by Base & ADOS & large demands from this Div commented upon. ADOS forwarded list for review & cancellation if possible.	

[signature] Lieut
D.A.D.O.S.
33rd Div

1875 Wt. W593/826 1,000,000 4/15 I.B.C. & A. A.D.S.S./Forms/C. 2118.

Army Form C. 2118.

Instructions regarding War Diaries and Intelligence Summaries are contained in F. S. Regs., Part II. and the Staff Manual respectively. Title Pages will be prepared in manuscript.

WAR DIARY
or
INTELLIGENCE SUMMARY

(Erase heading not required.)

D.A.D.O.S
33rd DIVISION.
Vol 13
SECRET

10th Sheet.

Place	Date	Hour	Summary of Events and Information	Remarks and references to Appendices
PLATEAU.	1/11/16		Limbered RE wagon for 33rd Div! Signals arrived and unit notified	
			Cart water tank for 75th B'de R.G.A — " —	
			18 pdr gun and carriage for 111th Bty 24th Brigade — " — at MERICOURT — " —	
	2/11/16		Wired Base for 5000 Socks to replace Division Reserve. Wired Rouen for an extra 2000 Jerkins to complete Infantry	
	3/11/16		Sent supplementary indent to Base for Winter clothing.	
			Wired Base for 2 Lewis Guns for 1st Cameronians to replace 2 condemned	
			19th Brigade require 3000 PH and 2000 PHG gas helmets to replace similar number rendered unserviceable through being saturated with rain	
			Demanded 7000 Gas helmets P.H. for replacement of P.H and P.H.G.	
			1 Lewis gun issued to 1st Middlesex and 1 to 1st Cameronians to replace 2 rendered unserviceable, these 2 guns were made serviceable by armourers from Salvage stock	
	4/11/16		Demanded 1 wagon limbered RE and 1 wagon pontoon without boat for 222nd Field Coy RE to replace similar vehicles condemned by I.O.M.	
			Asked 33rd Q to arrange for transport of Blankets direct from Plateau to units owing to congestion of stores consequent of arrival of winter clothing	
			Demanded 5 Lewis Guns for 9th H.L.I. to replace 5 lost in action	

2449 Wt. W14957/M90 750,000 1/16 J.B.C. & A. Forms/C.2118/12.

Instructions regarding War Diaries and Intelligence Summaries are contained in F. S. Regs., Part II. and the Staff Manual respectively. Title Pages will be prepared in manuscript.

WAR DIARY
or
INTELLIGENCE SUMMARY
(Erase heading not required.)

Army Form C. 2118.

33rd Division D.A.D.O.S.

SECRET

2nd Page

Place	Date	Hour	Summary of Events and Information	Remarks and references to Appendices
PLATEAU	4/11/16		Requested use of 2 15th Corps lorries to cope with large amount of stores coming to hand. Braziers. Winter Clothing. Smoke helmets etc	
	5/11/16		3 Lewis Guns demanded for 1st Cameronians arrived and issued.	
			Demanded 12000 Blankets from Base. 2 Blankets per man	
			Demanded 1 Cart Officers Mess for 87th Bty R.F.A also 1 Wagon Limbered GS	
			Demanded 1 Cart Water Tank for 112th Bty R.F.A	
	6/11/16		Units wired to send in Spanish make Revolvers for inspection of Armourer	
	7/11/16		Demanded GS limbered wagon complete for. 111th Bty R.F.A to replace one unserviceable	
			Demanded 1 Cart water tank for 112th Bty R.F.A to replace one beyond repair	
			Demanded 1 Cart Officers mess for 87th Bty R.F.A — — — —	
			5 Lewis Guns received to day for 9th H.L.I and issued	
			One Ambulance wagon demanded for 99th F.A to replace one unserviceable	
	8/11/16		Transferred 6th Div. & Guards Div. Arty to 6th Division	
HALLINCOURT	10/11/16		Transferred 11th, 212th & 222nd Field Coys and 18th Middlesex from 33rd Div. to 29th Div.	
			Hind portion GS limbered wagon demanded for 1st Queens to replace one destroyed shell fire	
	12/11/16		2 Hind portions K.T. and 1 Cart Officers mess demanded for 4th Liverpools, others destroyed by shell fire	
	13/11/16		Urgent wire sent to Base for 300 pairs boots for 5th Scottish.	
	14/11/16		Asked 15th Corps for 2 loop hole plates and 2 Stands rifle grenade for 100th Bde.	
			1 Lewis Gun for 2nd R Welsh & 3 for 2nd Worcesters demanded to replace others destroyed	

2449 Wt. W14957/M90 750,000 1/16 J.B.C. & A. Forms/C.2118/12.

Instructions regarding War Diaries and Intelligence Summaries are contained in F. S. Regs., Part II. and the Staff Manual respectively. Title Pages will be prepared in manuscript.

WAR DIARY
or
INTELLIGENCE SUMMARY
(Erase heading not required.)

33rd Division
DADOS

Army Form C. 2118.

SECRET

3rd Sheet

Place	Date	Hour	Summary of Events and Information	Remarks and references to Appendices
HALLENCOURT	14/11/16		arranged with DADOS 29th to send stores for 33rd unit attached to him half way ie to	
	15/11/16		212th Field Coy moved back to me	
	16/11/16		Urgent wire sent to Base for 230 Rugs horse	
	17/11/16		1 Lewis Gun for 2nd RWFus and 3 for 2nd Worcester received and issued	
			15th Corps asked if it would be possible for Battalion to be clothed entirely with Leather Jerkins instead of a mixture of Jerkins - Fur Coats	
			Indent sent down for 300 Braziers.	
			Application for Stores for Divisional Rest Area. 500 Lamps Hurricane. 790 Tubs washing. 470 Brooms Bass and 349 Tubs Urine. to 15th Corps.	
	19/11/16		30 Stoves heating. 10 Lamps hanging 10 Standing demanded for Divl Rest Station	
			300 Steel helmets demanded	
	20/11/16		Fore portion GS limbered wagon required for 1st Middlesex.	
	20/11/16		Suggested to 98th Brigade that all Vickers & Lewis Guns be sent into Divl Armourers Shop for overhaul and any necessary repairs so that guns may be in good order when Division moves up again.	
	21/11/16		1 Lewis Gun demanded for 4th Liverpool to replace one condemned	
			1 Wagon Amb. for 99th FA at Railhead HANGEST.	
	22/11/16		Received programme of repair to Vehicles from 1 OM. & Ord Depot. and informed units accordingly	

2449 Wt. W14957/M90 750,000 1/16 J.B.C. & A. Forms/C.2118/12.

Instructions regarding War Diaries and Intelligence Summaries are contained in F. S. Regs., Part II. and the Staff Manual respectively. Title Pages will be prepared in manuscript.

WAR DIARY
or
INTELLIGENCE SUMMARY
(Erase heading not required.)

Army Form C. 2118.

33rd Division
D.A.D.O.S.

SECRET

4th Sheet

Place	Date	Hour	Summary of Events and Information	Remarks and references to Appendices
HALLENCOURT	22/11/16		One Lewis Gun issued to 5th Scottish from guns recovered from Salvage	
	23/11/16		10000 Helmets P.86 demanded from Base to replace a similar number in Division damaged by rain.	
			All 33rd Divisional Arty returned to 33rd Div. from 13th Corps Troops	
	25/11/16		I.O.M. 14th Corps Workshops hastened to supply any vehicles he might have in shops which were left in repair there when Div. was in 14th Corps	
	26/11/16		15th Corps asked if Amn Sub Park should not be ordnanced by Corps Troops	
			11th and 222nd Field Coys RE and 18th Middlesex rejoin Div. from 29th Div.	
			Amn Sub Park moved to 15th Corps Troops.	
	28/11/16		4.5" Howitzer of 162 Bde R.F.A. sent into Workshops at RIBEMONT for repairs.	
	29/11/16		1 Cart Officers mess for H.Q. 162 Bde demanded.	
			Wired I.O.M. No 8 Ord Depot if he had any wheels No 300 2nd Class C owing to vehicles being in such a bad state.	
	30/11/16		219 Sheets ground & 460 Blankets demanded for 18th Middlesex owing to unit having to hand them over to Town Major Montauban.	

7/12/16.

[illegible] Wheal
Capt
for D.A.D.O.S.
33rd Div.

2449 Wt. W14957/M90 750,000 1/16 J.B.C. & A. Forms/C.2118/12.

1st Sheet

33

Instructions regarding War Diaries and Intelligence Summaries are contained in F. S. Regs., Part II. and the Staff Manual respectively. Title Pages will be prepared in manuscript.

WAR DIARY
or
INTELLIGENCE SUMMARY
(Erase heading not required.)

Army Form C. 2118

D.A.D.O.S.
33rd DIVISION.

SECRET

Vol 14

Place	Date	Hour	Summary of Events and Information	Remarks and references to Appendices
HALLENCOURT.	1/12/16		Demanded 2 Hind portions Kitchen Travelling for 20th Fus. to replace 2 abandoned.	
	-"-		Division moving into forward Area shortly. All units hastening supply of wagon parts.	
	-"-		D.A.Q.M.G. reports paint supplied for helmets steel is too light.	
	2/12/16		Suspended issues from Bases in view of early move. One Wagon Ambulance	
	-"-		demanded for 19th F.A. to replace one condemned by I.O.M.	
	-"-		Cancelled supply from Base of Back Area Billet Stores. Buckets Latrine, Brooms bass	
	-"-		Demanded 10000 pairs Socks to be sent up to Forward Area Railhead. (Bel-air)	
	4/12/16		Informed Bases now prepared to receive stores. Put stores on rail.	
	6/12/16		Moved Personnel and Shops to Bray sur Somme.	
BRAY sur SOMME.	7/12/16		Found 11 wagons stores awaiting us at Railhead Bel-Air. Demanded Hind Portion K.T.	
	-"-		for 1st Queens to replace one abandoned. Wagon Amb for 19th F.A. at Railhead and	
	-"-		unit informed by wire. 2 Hind portions K.T arrived at Railhead for 20th Bns and	
	-"-		unit informed by wire. 3 Maltese Carts for 33rd Div! Signals in place of pack	
	-"-		animals arrived and taken away by unit. Hastened supply of magazines Lewis	
	-"-		Gun outstanding. Received 50 Stoves Soyers. 400 Latrine Buckets and 240 Kettles	
	-"-		Camp for Billet stores.	
	8/12/16		Demanded Hind portion K.T. for 1st Midds + 4th Suffolks to replace 2 abandoned.	
	-"-		Drew from 15th Corps Troops 2990 pairs Gum boots being first consignment of 10,000	
	-"-		Drew 100 Tents C.S.L from 15th Corps Troops, also received Hot food containers, Braziers.	
	10/12/16		33rd Divisional School transferred to 8th Division.	

1875 Wt. W593/826 1,000,000 4/15 J.B.C. & A. A.D.S.S./Forms/C. 2118.

Instructions regarding War Diaries and Intelligence Summaries are contained in F. S. Regs., Part II. and the Staff Manual respectively. Title Pages will be prepared in manuscript.

2nd Sheet

WAR DIARY
or
INTELLIGENCE SUMMARY
(Erase heading not required.)

33rd DIVISION
D.A.D.O.S.

SECRET

Army Form C. 2118

Place	Date	Hour	Summary of Events and Information	Remarks and references to Appendices
BRAY SUR SOMME	11/12/16		One hind portion K.T arrived for 4th Suffolks and unit wired to draw.	
	"		One hind portion K.T ... ... 1st Middlesex	
	"		One hind portion K.T ... ... 1st Queens	
	"		Asked O.O. 8th Division to take over a small quantity Area Stores left at HALLENCOURT.	
	"		Demanded 1500 Blankets for issue to reinforcements who are arriving without	
	12/12/16		166th Brigade and Batteries moved from 33rd Divn to 8th Division. Issued 400	
	...		Carriers Ammn 18 pdr for pack animals to 33rd C.R.A. Received 8 Chaff cutting	
	"		machines from 4th Army thro Base. Demanded one ~~[illegible]~~ wagon Amn 18pdr for A/162 to	
	"		replace one lost in the mud.	
	13/12/16		4 Rifle Batteries (3 Rifles) received from 15th Corps. 2 issued to 98th Bde + 2 to 100th Bde.	
	"		Received a further 1250 Capes macintosh from Corps for distribution. Water proof ration	
	"		bags hastened from Base. Demanded 500 Jerkins for men coming up country without.	
	14/12/16		Y/33 H.T.M.B and No 3 Sec 30th D.A.C. transferred to 8th Division. 178th + 181st Brigades	
	"		~~[illegible]~~ RFA. Head Qrs D.AC Nos 1, 2 & 3 Sec DAC of 40th Division temporarily transferred to 33rd	
	16/12/16		Demanded one Water Cart for B/162 to replace one unserviceable.	
	"		Boilers without taps urgently required and Base urged to expedite supply	
	17/12/16		Demanded one 18pdr Carriage Amn for No 1 Sec D.A.C (33rd)	
	18/12/16		One 18 pdr wagon Amn arrived for A/162. unit notified of arrival. One Wagon	
	"		limbered RE demanded for 212 Field Coy to replace one destroyed by shell fire.	
	"		Demanded 2 Hind portions K.T for 9th H.L.I to replace 2 unserviceable through all boilers being unserviceable & not available at Base	

1875 Wt. W593/826 1,000,000 4/15 J.B.C. & A. A.D.S.S./Forms/C. 2118.

3rd Sheet

Instructions regarding War Diaries and Intelligence Summaries are contained in F. S. Regs., Part II. and the Staff Manual respectively. Title Pages will be prepared in manuscript.

WAR DIARY
or
INTELLIGENCE SUMMARY
(Erase heading not required.)

33rd Division
D.A.D.O.S.

Army Form C. 2118

SECRET

Place	Date	Hour	Summary of Events and Information	Remarks and references to Appendices
BRAY SUR SOMME	19/12/16		1 Cart Officers mess demanded for D/156 to replace one beyond local repair. Demanded 1000 Jerkins for reinforcements. Sent urgent hastener for Taps + Wrenches for "B" Echelon 33rd D.A.C owing to appearance of frost. Had Detachment A.O.C up for medical inspection for classification A-B. result all except 2 were placed in Catagory "A" Two best specimens placed in "B".	[illegible]
	20/12/16		Demanded 250 Dry Batteries for Electric torches, also hastened outstandings. supply very slow from Base and unable to purchase locally. moved X Y + Z TMB to 8th Division. Had V/33 HTMB retransferred to 33rd Demanded 5000 P.H Helmets to keep up Divisional Reserve.	[illegible]
	21/12/16		Received 24 Lewis Guns from Base. This makes all Battalions in Division in possession of 12 Guns with exception of 15th Middlesex (Pioneers) who have 8. Demanded 2000 Blankets for reinforcements. One 18pdr Ammn Wagon arrived for No 1 Sec 33rd D.A.C. unit informed. One water cart arrived for B/162 Bde RFA	[illegible]
	22/12/16		One Cart Officers mess demanded for H.Q. 156 Bde R.F.A. 69 Hot food containers received from 15th Corps	[illegible]
	23/12/16		Received 64 sets pack saddlery from 15th Corps - Demanded one pontoon Wagon for 11th Field Coy RE to replace one condemned by I.O.M.	[illegible]
	24/12/16		~~Exchange of 33rd Supply Col Lorries for 21st notified as taking place on 27th O.C 33 D.S.C wired me to arrange exchange of 4 G.S. lorries [illegible] with [illegible] 8th Div in most convenient way~~	
	25/12/16		2 Hind portions K1 arrived at Mericourt for 9th H.L.I. Cart Officers mess received for D/156 Bde R.F.A.	[illegible]

1875 Wt. W593/826 1,000,000 4/15 L.B.C. & A. A.D.S.S./Forms/C. 2118.

4th Sheet

Instructions regarding War Diaries and Intelligence Summaries are contained in F. S. Regs., Part II. and the Staff Manual respectively. Title Pages will be prepared in manuscript.

WAR DIARY
or
INTELLIGENCE SUMMARY
(Erase heading not required.)

33rd Division
D.A.D.O.S.

Army Form C. 2118

SECRET

Place	Date	Hour	Summary of Events and Information	Remarks and references to Appendices
BRAY sur SOMME	26/12/16		Officers mess Cart for H.Q 156 Bde RFA arrived. Several cases of Mange breaking out. Animals isolated and horse rugs + dippers urgently demanded. One RE limbered wagon for 212 Field Coy RE arrives and unit informed. Railhead moved to HANGEST from 28th inclusive. 162nd and 181st Brigades RFA moved to 40th Divn also No 1 + 2 Sec 33rd DAC and Nos 2 + 3 Sec 40th D.A.C. Packed up ready for departure in morning.	[initials]
LONG	27/12/16		Moved Personnel + Stores to LONG. Large quantity of all stores expected from Base + reconsignment owing to moves + units heavy demands for re-equipment.	to moves + units heavy demands for re-equipment [initials]
	28/12/16		Demanded one hind portion K.T. for 1st Queens. 33rd Bde R.G.A. 134 + 135th Batteries RFA D/32 Brigade 4.5 moved from 4th Division to 33rd Div for administration.	
	29/12/16		33rd Brigade RFA. 32nd 33rd 36th + 55th Batteries R.F.A. + No 2 Sec 8th DAC moved from 4th Division to 33rd Division. One 18pdr Carriage demanded for 36th Battery of 33rd Bde R.F.A. to replace one damaged by hostile shell fire.	[initials]
	30/12/16		4th 8th 40th 33rd + 15th Corps Divl schools of Instruction moved to 33rd Division. 2 Wagons Amb. demanded for 99th F.A. to replace 2 beyond local repair. 2 Hind portions of KT for 9th H.L.I which came up to MERICOURT were put on rail + reconsigned to HANGEST owing to distance. Applied to 15th Corps asking if Works Battalion could not be administered by 40th Division. replied Yes.	[initials]
	31/12/16		Demanded hind portion KT for 4th Kings Liverpools to replace one abandoned. Sent 3 lorry loads of Stores to 40th Division. for units that had recently been administered by 33rd Divn	[initials]

H. Qrs 33rd Division

[signature] Lieut DADOS

1875 Wt. W593/826 1,000,000 4/15 J.B.C. & A. A.D.S.S./Forms/C. 2118.

— 33rd DIVISION —

Instructions regarding War Diaries and Intelligence Summaries are contained in F. S. Regs., Part II. and the Staff Manual respectively. Title Pages will be prepared in manuscript.

WAR DIARY
or
INTELLIGENCE SUMMARY
(Erase heading not required.)

D.A.D.O.S.

SECRET

JANUARY 1917. 1st Sheet

Vol 15

Army Form C. 2118.

Place	Date	Hour	Summary of Events and Information	Remarks and references to Appendices
LONG — Back Area	1/1/17		Demanded Kitchen Travelling hind portion for 2nd A&S which had to be abandoned on line of march.	
	3/1/17		Received one 18 pdr gun for A/86 Bty of 33rd Bde. This gun was wired for to replace one badly scored and condemned by I.O.M 15th Corps	
	"		One 18 pdr carriage received at Railhead for 36th Bty 33rd Bde.	
	5/1/17		Wired CRA to arrange to collect stores which were accumulating & causing congestion in my dumps. Demanded a Wagon Ambulance for 101st B.A to replace one condemned by I.O.M.	
	6/1/17		Demanded Travelling Kitchen complete for 2nd RWF to replace one abandoned on line of march.	
	7/1/17		Demanded 6 range finders to complete 3 MG Corps to 4 each. One Cart Officers mess received for 27th Bty 33rd Bde. RFA. One body KT received for 4th Liverpools. 2 Wagons Amb. received for 99th F.A. 5 Hand carts Lewis Gun received for 20th Fusiliers. Instructed 2nd A&S to send in Lewis guns that had not been overhauled to Armourer Shop.	
	8/1/17	Inspected Divl Transport	Demanded rear portion of a limbered wagon for 4th Suffolks, one unserviceable. Demanded Cart Officers mess for B/156 to replace one abandoned. Demanded Cart Water for 33rd Bty 38th Bde RFA. Inspected transport of C.R.E. 33rd Divn.	
	9/1/17		Field forge with anvil and base allowed by G.R.O. letter to Infty & Arty Bdes. 100th Infty Bde doesn't want one.	

2449 Wt. W14957/M90 750,000 1/16 J.B.C. & A. Forms/C.2118/12.

Continued

7 A.D.O.S. 33rd DIVISION

Instructions regarding War Diaries and Intelligence Summaries are contained in F. S. Regs., Part II. and the Staff Manual respectively. Title Pages will be prepared in manuscript.

WAR DIARY
or
INTELLIGENCE SUMMARY
(Erase heading not required.)

SECRET.

Army Form C. 2118.

2nd Sheet

Place	Date	Hour	Summary of Events and Information	Remarks and references to Appendices
LONG [illegible]	11/1/17	Inspected Divl Transport	Ordered Machine Guns of 100th M.G. Coy in for general overhaul	
			Demanded Water Cart for A/156 to replace one condemned by I.O.M.	
			Demanded 9 Carts hand Lewis Gun for 1st Cameronians for replacement	
			Demanded 1 Cart Officers mess for 1st Middx to replace one stolen	
			Demanded Rear portion wagon limbered GS for 222nd F.C. for replacement	
			Extra Lewis Gun allowed for Divl Schools making 3. 33rd Divl decide	
			that extra gun is not required so do not draw one	
			One Lewis Gun recd for 8th Divl School and one for 40th Divl School	
			Wagon Amb arrived at Railhead for 101st Field Amb.	
			Cart Officers mess arrived " " B/156 RFA	
			Hind portion wagon limbered " for 4th Suffolks	
			Kitchen travelling complete arrived for 2nd Worcesters	
			Hind portion KT arrived for 2nd A. & S.	
	12/1/17		Demanded 4 Carts hand Lewis Gun for 2nd A&S for replacement	
			2nd Worcester instructed to send in Lewis Guns for overhaul by Armourers	
			178th Bde RFA transferred from 33rd to 40th Divn	
	13/1/17		Demanded one GS wagon limbered for 9th HLI for replacement	
			Demanded 2000 Shirts from Rouen for keeping up stock in Divl Laundry	
	14/1/17		Demanded Water Cart for B Echelon DAC to replace one condemned	
			Suspended all issues from Base in view of early move up to front area	
	~~15/1/17~~		~~[illegible]~~	

2449 Wt. W14957/M90 750,000 1/16 J.B.C. & A. Forms/C.2118/12.

D.A.D.O.S. 33rd DIVISION

Instructions regarding War Diaries and Intelligence Summaries are contained in F. S. Regs., Part II. and the Staff Manual respectively. Title pages will be prepared in manuscript.

WAR DIARY
or
INTELLIGENCE SUMMARY.
(Erase heading not required.)

SECRET

3rd A Sheet

Army Form C. 2118.

Place	Date	Hour	Summary of Events and Information	Remarks and references to Appendices
	15/1/17		Made all necessary arrangements for a barge to be detailed to convey stores to Front area	
	16/1/17		Collected Area stores from No 6 area and had several	
	"		interviews with Q + Corps as to quantity and description of stores likely to be required in Front area	
	17/1/17		Made arrangements for part of personnel with one lorry to proceed to Bray on morning of 18th for the purpose of opening dump as early as possible	
			27th Bty 32nd Brigade indented for a new Observation Wagon but 4th Army ruled that tho the Battery had been issued with this vehicle previous to coming over seas that a new one could not be issued as vehicle did not form part of a Battery Transport.	

A5834 Wt. W4973/M687 750,000 8/16 D. D. & L. Ltd. Forms/C.2118/13.

D.A.D.O.S.
33rd Division

Instructions regarding War Diaries and Intelligence Summaries are contained in F. S. Regs., Part II. and the Staff Manual respectively. Title Pages will be prepared in manuscript.

WAR DIARY
or
INTELLIGENCE SUMMARY
(Erase heading not required.)

SECRET
3rd SHEET

Army Form C. 2118.

Place	Date	Hour	Summary of Events and Information	Remarks and references to Appendices
LONG	17/1/17		30th Brigade RFA re transferred to 4th Division	
	18/1/17		Demanded one Lewis Gun for 4th Suffolks to replace one condemned	
			Moved A/26 formerly A/166 Bty RFA to 3rd Corps from 33rd Div	
BRAY SUR SOMME	19/1/17		Moved No 3 Coy 33rd Train to No 8 Ord Depot owing to epidemic among horses	
	"		and unit being isolated in Back area. Moved Dump from Long to	
	"		Bray sur Somme. Used a barge from I.W.T to move bulk of stores etc	
	20/1/17		Moved all Divisional Schools attached i.e. 4th 8th 40th 33rd & 15th Corps Hqrs	
			to 8th Div who passed them on to 48th. 48th moved up from Back Area	
			same day and would not accept them so 8th had to keep them	
			pending a decision as to disposal of Schools from 4th Army.	
			Demanded 198 Stretcher Trench to complete units to scale as laid down	
			in GRO 1180. Received a Lewis Gun for 4th Suffolks. Demanded	
			sight dial No 7 for several Batteries of Arty who state that these stores	
			were deficient on taking over guns of other Batteries. Raised question	
			generally how this should happen as Arty are invariably deficient	
			of stores of all nature when transferred from one Division to another	
	21/1/17		One QF Shield 4·5 demanded for 58th Bty R.F.A to replace one deficient	
			when taken over from D/5 Battery RFA. Water Cart demanded for	
			4th Liverpools to replace one condemned by I.O.M. Demanded	
			400 Latrine Buckets & 100 Mud Scrapers to furnish new area.	
			One Cart Officers Mess received for 18th Middlesex	
	22/1/17		Demanded One Cart Maltese for 2nd Worcesters to replace one condemned.	

2449 Wt. W14957/M90 750,000 1/16 J.B.C. & A. Forms/C.2118/12.

D.D.O.S.
33rd Division

Instructions regarding War Diaries and Intelligence Summaries are contained in F. S. Regs., Part II. and the Staff Manual respectively. Title Pages will be prepared in manuscript.

WAR DIARY
or
INTELLIGENCE SUMMARY
(Erase heading not required.)

SECRET

Army Form C. 2118.

4th SHEET.

Place	Date	Hour	Summary of Events and Information	Remarks and references to Appendices
Somme	26/1/17		~~[illegible]~~ 2 3" Stokes mortars demanded for 19th T.M.B. to replace 2 lost from regimental transport. One Cart Officers Mess complete with harness demanded for [illegible] 156th Bde to replace similar store stolen from Transport Lines.	
	27/1/17		14th Bde R.F.A. moved from 33rd Division to 15th Corps Troops. One water cart received for 9th H.L.I. 5000 Socks 3000 Vests and 1000 Drawers Woollen demanded for Divisional Exchange. 2 3" Stokes mortars received for 19th T.M.B. 30000 Small Box Respirators in 3 sizes (1 [illegible] (2) [illegible] (4)) demanded for Divn. One cart tool R.E. and One wagon limbered R.E. required by 212 Field Coy to replace similar articles destroyed by shell fire.	
Sur	28/1/17		Demanded 1000 Blankets for issue to re-inforcements coming up without.	
Bray	29/1/17		One Lewis Gun required by 4th Suffolks to replace one destroyed by shell fire. One Vickers gun demanded for 98th M.G. Coy to replace one beyond local repair. G.H.Q. letter published authorizing withdrawal of Lewis Gun hand cart which will be replaced by G.S. Limbered wagons as they become available. For the present Battalions have enough transport for the 12 guns in possession, but 6 handcarts are allowed to be retained in case 4 extra guns are issued before Limbers are available.	
	31/1/17		One G.S. wagon complete demanded for No 2 Coy A.S.C. to replace one destroyed by bomb. One 18 pdr gun (gun only) demanded for 36th Bty to replace one condemned for scoring.	

2449 Wt. W14957/M90 750,000 1/16 J.B.C. & A. Forms/C.2118/12.

D.A.D.O.S.
33rd DIVISION

Instructions regarding War Diaries and Intelligence Summaries are contained in F. S. Regs., Part II. and the Staff Manual respectively. Title Pages will be prepared in manuscript.

WAR DIARY
or
INTELLIGENCE SUMMARY
(Erase heading not required.)

SECRET

Army Form C. 2118.

5th and last Sheet

Place	Date	Hour	Summary of Events and Information	Remarks and references to Appendices
Bray sur Somme	31/1/17		One Lewis gun made serviceable from Salvage and issued to 5th Scottish R. to replace one condemned. Wagon limbered GS required by 2nd A&S to replace one destroyed by shell fire. 600 Gum boots short received for Supply Col – "B" Echelon D.A.C.	
	[illegible]		Collected area stores from No 6 area and had several interviews with O – Corps regarding quantity + description of area stores required for Forward Area	
	[illegible]		Left Dump with part of personnel to open new Dump at Bray, remainder staying behind to load up barge + follow on next day.	

To
33rd Div.

[signature] Lieut
D.A.D.O.S.
4.2.1917.

2449 Wt. W14957/M90 750,000 1/16 J.B.C. & A. Forms/C.2118/12.

Instructions regarding War Diaries and Intelligence Summaries are contained in F. S. Regs., Part II. and the Staff Manual respectively. Title Pages will be prepared in manuscript.

WAR DIARY
or
INTELLIGENCE SUMMARY

(Erase heading not required.)

Army Form C. 2118.

SECRET

D.A.D.O.S.
33rd Division

Vol 16

Place	Date	Hour	Summary of Events and Information	Remarks and references to Appendices
BRAY sur SOMME	1/2/17		One Lewis Gun for 4th Suffolks and One Vickers Gun for 98th Machine Gun Coy received to-day. 30 Vermorel Sprayers wired for from Base for 19th Brigade whilst in line. First consignment of Small Box Respirators received to-day.	
	2/2/17		Corps asked for extra 1000 yds white calico for gun tracks. Replied not available	
	3/2/17		One Water Cart demanded for 4th Suffolks.	
	4/2/17		Permission of Corps asked for Local Purchase of 1305 metres calico. 50 Vermorel Sprayers demanded by wire from Base for front line. One Lewis Gun demanded for 2nd RW Fus, to replace one destroyed by shell fire. One Wagon limbered GS demanded for 212 Field Coy to replace one condemned. One Lewis Gun demanded for 1st Cameronians to replace one destroyed by shell fire.	
	5/2/17		10,000 Cutlasses hastened on Base. One Lewis Gun demanded for 2nd Worcesters to replace one destroyed by shell fire.	
	6/2/17		Large demand for under clothing put down on Base on account of bad condition of men in front line who require complete changes when coming out to rest. One Lewis Gun received for 2nd RW Fus.	
	7/2/17		33rd Supply Column moved from 33rd Divn to 15th Corps Troops for administration. One Lewis Gun received for 1st Cameronians. One Lewis Gun received for 2nd Worcesters. Demanded 34 Lewis Guns from Base to complete all units except Pioneers with 14 each.	

2449 Wt. W14957/M90 750,000 1/16 J.B.C. & A. Forms/C.2118/12.

2 Sheet

WAR DIARY
or
INTELLIGENCE SUMMARY
(Erase heading not required.)

SECRET
D.A.D.O.S.
33rd DIVISION

Army Form C. 2118.

Instructions regarding War Diaries and Intelligence Summaries are contained in F. S. Regs., Part II. and the Staff Manual respectively. Title Pages will be prepared in manuscript.

Place	Date	Hour	Summary of Events and Information	Remarks and references to Appendices
BRAY sur SOMME	8/3/17		Small Box Respirators issued prior to Sept. 16 called in.	
	10/3/17		Demand put down on Base for 1500 Capes mackintosh. 2 Directors No 4	
	-"-		surplus on re-organization of Arty, taken to Artillery School.	
	11/3/17		One Officers mess Cart demanded for C/156 Bde RFA to replace one	
	-"-		condemned as being beyond local repair. 100 Sets Dent bottoms	
	-"-		received from 15th Corps Troops and issued to D.M. Suzanne. One	
	-"-		Cart Water Tank demanded for No 4 Coy Train A.S.C. to replace	
	-"-		one condemned.	
	12/3/17		One Cart Water Tank demanded for D/156 33rd Bde to replace one condemned.	
	-"-		Asked ADOS if No 3 Sec 33rd D.A.C. were still to be considered a separate	
	-"-		unit as indents were still being received from 3 Sect. 3 Stokes Mortars	
	-"-		demanded for 100th T.M.B. to replace 3 condemned. One Lewis Gun	
	-"-		demanded for 2nd Worcesters to replace one rendered unserviceable by shell fire.	
	13/3/17		34 Lewis Guns received from Base, this consignment makes all Battalions	
	-"-		except Pioneers in possession of 14 Lewis Guns. Demanded 2500	
	-"-		Smoke Helmets PH to complete Divisional Reserve.	
	14/3/17		One G.S. wagon handed over to No 2 Coy Train to replace one condemned.	
	16/3/17		One Tool Cart R.E. demanded for 11th Field Coy R.E. to replace one	
	-"-		destroyed by shell fire. One Lewis Gun demanded for 1st Queens to replace	
	-"-		one condemned by armourer. One Water Cart received for 4th Liverpools. One	
	-"-		wagon limbered received for 9th H.L.I. Limber of a R.E. wagon received for	
	-"-		222nd F. Coy. Water Cart received for 33rd Bty 33rd Bde R.F.A. Vehicles have been	
	-"-		held up by Base for nearly a fortnight owing to congestion on railway	

2449 Wt. W14957/M90 750,000 1/16 J.B.C. & A. Forms/C.2118/12.

3rd Sheet

Instructions regarding War Diaries and Intelligence Summaries are contained in F. S. Regs., Part II. and the Staff Manual respectively. Title Pages will be prepared in manuscript.

WAR DIARY
or
INTELLIGENCE SUMMARY
(Erase heading not required.)

SECRET

D.A.D.O.S.
33rd DIVISION

Army Form C. 2118.

Place	Date	Hour	Summary of Events and Information	Remarks and references to Appendices
BRAY SUR SOMME	16/3/17		One Lewis Gun received for 2nd Worcesters. 3 Stokes Mortars received for 100 T.M. Bty.	
	17/3/17		2 G.S. wagons limbered complete demanded for B Echelon to replace others condemned.	
	19/3/17		34 Lewis Guns received from Base. This makes all Battalions in possession of 16 Lewis Guns except 18th Middlesex (Pioneers) who have 8.	
	19/3/17		One Lewis Gun received for 1st Queens.	
	-"-		86 and Coy 166th Bde (late 8th 156th Bde) moved from 33rd Divn to No. 8 Ord Depot for administration	
	20/3/17		2 Wagons G.S. limbered required for "B" Echelon to replace 2 condemned. One Cart Officers mess each for 86 D/156 + C/156 Bde at Railhead. One water cart each for 4th Suffolks, 55th Bty 33rd Bde R.F.A. + No. 4 Coy Train A.S.C. at Railhead. One hind portion of G.S. limber for 2nd A. + S. at Railhead. One Cart Maltese for 2nd Worcesters at Railhead. One wagon limbered complete for 212 F. Coy R.E. at Railhead. One wagon limber 18 pdr for 32nd Bty 33rd Bde at Railhead. This glut of vehicles is caused by traffic being congested and Base not having suitable trucks available to load vehicles on.	
	21/3/17		Divisional School for some reason or the other are not in possession of Lewis Guns for instructional purposes neither do they require them.	
	22/3/17		100th Bde badly require 100 No 18 Periscopes. Reply sent that as each Battalion in Divn should have 80 that probably number required could be obtained without any further supply from Base. 3 Coy Train return to 33rd Divn from No. 8 Ord Depot, to whom they were temporarily attached whilst animals had mange etc.	

2449 Wt. W14957/M90 750,000 1/16 J.B.C. & A. Forms/C.2118/12.

4th Sheet

Instructions regarding War Diaries and Intelligence Summaries are contained in F. S. Regs., Part II. and the Staff Manual respectively. Title Pages will be prepared in manuscript.

WAR DIARY
or
INTELLIGENCE SUMMARY
(Erase heading not required.)

SECRET

Army Form C. 2118.

D.A.D.O.S.
33rd DIVISION.

Place	Date	Hour	Summary of Events and Information	Remarks and references to Appendices
BRAY SUR SOMME	23/2/17		11 Wagons Limbered G S complete Transport demanded on Base. These wagons are for transport of Lewis Guns by Battalion in place of Handcarts Lewis Gun which have been called in and sent to Base. 1280 Paillasses received from Base and issued to Camp 19. All issues on Bases suspended today to avoid congestion at Railhead consequent on Thaw precaution.	
	24/2/17		Suspension of Issues on Bases cancelled.	
	25/2/17		Wired to 98th Bde requesting Staff Officer to give necessary instructions to have guns which have been overhauled ~~[illegible]~~ removed from Armourers Shop.	
	26/2/17		Demanded 70 eyelet pliers, which it is proposed to issue with Bags Sharpeners filled. One Vickers gun demanded for 19th M. G. Coy.	
	27/2/17		Received 140 Chests M G for use with Lewis Guns when in Limbers	
	28/2/17		One Vickers Gun received for 19th M.G. Coy. Wired Corps that 1300 Gloves MT ASC would be required if issue was made to Transport Drivers in place of woollen gloves. 2 Dial Sights No 7 surplus to requirements sent to Base. Also quantity of stores which have become surplus on re-organization of Arty. from No 3 Sec. D.A.C. who have become absorbed in Nos 1 & 2 Sections. Thaw precautions still on.	

[signature] Lieut
D.A.D.O.S.
Midnight 28/2/17

2449 Wt. W14957/M90 750,000 1/16 J.B.C. & A. Forms/C.2118/12.

1st Sheet

Instructions regarding War Diaries and Intelligence Summaries are contained in F. S. Regs., Part II. and the Staff Manual respectively. Title Pages will be prepared in manuscript.

WAR DIARY
or
INTELLIGENCE SUMMARY
(Erase heading not required.)

Army Form C. 2118.

SECRET

7.A.7.O.S.
33rd DIVISION

Vol 17

Place	Date	Hour	Summary of Events and Information	Remarks and references to Appendices
BRAY sur SOMME	1/3/17		One body RE limbered demanded for 212th Field Coy RE.	
	2/3/17		4th Army have a quantity of fittings for Limbers for Machine Guns available and desire to know how many are required	
	3/3/17		Demanded one Lewis Gun for 4th Suffolks to replace one rendered unserviceable by hostile shell fire. Division completely equipped with small Box Respirators	
	4/3/17		4th Army require to know probable requirements of Bags ration waterproof for the ensuing 3 months. Not possible to be given as the exigencies of the campaign cannot be foreseen for next 3 months	
	5/3/17		One Water cart demanded for B/156 to replace one condemned. 100 Brooms Bass demanded for use in Billets, horse lines, etc. Suspended all issues from Base Rouen in view of imminent move to rest area	
	6/3/17		Received one Lewis Gun from Base for 4th Suffolks, One RE Tool cart and One Limbered wagon RE received for 11th Field Coy RE	
	7/3/17		Removed suspension of issues from Bases. Moved 33rd Arty RGA to 8th Division, made all necessary arrangements to move Store & Office from Bray to Corbie on 8th.	

2449 Wt. W14957/M90 750,000 1/16 J.B.C. & A. Forms/C.2118/12.

2nd Sheet

Instructions regarding War Diaries and Intelligence Summaries are contained in F. S. Regs., Part II. and the Staff Manual respectively. Title Pages will be prepared in manuscript.

WAR DIARY
or.
INTELLIGENCE SUMMARY
(Erase heading not required.)

SECRET

D.A.D.O.S.
33rd DIVISION.

Army Form C. 2118.

Place	Date	Hour	Summary of Events and Information	Remarks and references to Appendices
CORBIE	8/3/17		Moved into new Store at Corbie. Demanded one 18pdr gun without carriage or breech mechanism for C/162 Bde R.F.A to replace one condemned for scoring	
	9/3/17		Sent general hasteners to Base Ordnance which embraced all technical stores, such as M.G. Parts, Wagon Parts, wheels, Binoculars, Compasses etc etc. This was done in order to equip the Division up to establishment as soon as possible, as in view of forthcoming operations, it is essential all units be completely equipped. 4th Army called for a report as to suitability of material at present being used in the construction of Nose Bags + general consensus of opinion was that material was quite good if used with care + consideration.	
	10/3/17		Made request to ADOS 15th Corps to be supplied with mechanical means for fighting fire. Question of increasing provisional issue of Rangefinders to Infantry from 2 to 6 raised by D.O.S. Special hastener sent to Base Ordnance to expedite delivery of 11 G.S. Limbered wagons to this Division to complete L.G. Transport. Received 3000 cartridges dummy for drill purposes. Demanded one No 7 Dial Sight for A/162 Bde RFA	[signature]

2449 Wt. W14957/M90 750,000 1/16 J.B.C. & A. Forms/C.2118/12.

3rd Sheet

Instructions regarding War Diaries and Intelligence Summaries are contained in F. S. Regs., Part II. and the Staff Manual respectively. Title Pages will be prepared in manuscript.

WAR DIARY
or
INTELLIGENCE SUMMARY
(Erase heading not required.)

SECRET

D.A.D.O.S
33rd DIVISION.

Army Form C. 2118.

Place	Date	Hour	Summary of Events and Information	Remarks and references to Appendices
CORBIE	11/3/17		One 18pdr gun received for C/162 Bde RFA. Demanded one Officers Mess Cart for 20th Bns to replace one condemned. Received 2000 paillasse (in further part of demand for 10000). 700 issued to CRA + 1300 to 98th Bde	
"	12/3/17		Made application to ADOS 15th Corps for supply of 17000 sets of under-clothing, owing to inability of laundry to supply, to complete 2 sets per man. ADOS replied "not available"	
"	13/3/17		Demanded 17000 sets of underclothing from Rouen by priority wire, to complete one spare set to be carried in pack. Reported demand to D.D.O.S 4th Army for necessary transport arrangement, D.D.O.S. refused to take action until AA & QMG explained the great necessity for the demand.	
"	14/3/17		Demanded Body portion of K.T. for 2nd RWFus. Demanded 900 goggles anti-gas to replace issues and to complete reserve.	
"	15/3/17		Received One mess cart for 20th RFus. Requested 4th Army to expedite supply of 11 Limbered Wagons for transport of L.G. Asked Base to cancel demand for 17000 sets underclothing as DDOS had arranged supply of smaller number of washed sets from 4th Army Laundry. One water cart received for B/156 Bde RFA. One RE Limbered wagon received for 212 Field Coy RE	
"	16/3/17		Sent indent to Base for reserve supplies of Oil Lub. [illegible], Flannelette, Boots as such items are likely to be needed at short notice, in event of a general advance.	[signature]

2449 Wt. W14957/M90 750,000 1/16 J.B.C. & A. Forms/C.2118/12.

4th Sheet

Instructions regarding War Diaries and Intelligence Summaries are contained in F. S. Regs., Part II. and the Staff Manual respectively. Title Pages will be prepared in manuscript.

WAR DIARY
or
INTELLIGENCE SUMMARY
(Erase heading not required.)

SECRET

Army Form C. 2118.

D.A.D.O.S.
33rd DIVISION.

Place	Date	Hour	Summary of Events and Information	Remarks and references to Appendices
CORBIE	17/3/17		11th Field Coy RE report 2 pontoons waterlogged and otherwise unserviceable. Wired I.O.M to inspect and report as to probable condemnation + replacement. These pontoons were subsequently condemned + replaced. Received One body K.T for 1st Middlesex. One Water cart for 11th Field Coy RE, both these vehicles were repaired by I.O.M at Hangest + put on rail by him as Divn had moved + railhead was at Bel. Air.	
	18/3/17		Urgent hasteners sent to Base for Lamps + Batteries electric. Bicycles allowed in lieu of horses for Senior Chaplains, C of E + Non Conformist. Auth. AG D/1989/5 19/12/16	
	19/3/17		Suggestions called for by 4th Army as to reducing numbers of nails issued for Horse shoes. General opinion was that numbers were only sufficient for efficiency	
	20/3/17		Demanded 2 pontoons bi-partite for 11th Field Coy RE to replace 2 condemned	
	21/3/17		Received one Lewis Gun for 1st Cameronians.	
	22/3/17		Made application to draw puttees from 15th Corps Troops, owing to RA personnel being partly fitted with ankle boots + FS boot being bad for long marches.	
	23/3/17		Base again urgently requested to meet outstanding demands for wagon parts and Lewis Mac Gun parts.	

5th Sheet

Instructions regarding War Diaries and Intelligence Summaries are contained in F. S. Regs., Part II. and the Staff Manual respectively. Title Pages will be prepared in manuscript.

WAR DIARY
or
INTELLIGENCE SUMMARY
(Erase heading not required.)

Army Form C. 2118.

SECRET

D.A.D.O.S. 33rd Division.

Place	Date	Hour	Summary of Events and Information	Remarks and references to Appendices
CORBIE	23/3/17		17000 sets of underclothing received from Base and necessary arrangements made to issue one complete set per man in Division. Sent up by Rouen in spite of cancellation owing to mislaying of my wire by Base.	
	24/3/17		Urgent wire sent to Base to re-equip 11th Field Coy RE who had practically all the Equipment carried on the man destroyed by fire at La Motte Brebière. These stores came up and were issued to unit without delay. Base treated this demand, which included Bulk as well as Detail stores as a Detail demand.	
	2?/3/17		33rd Divl Arty moved from 33rd Divn to 15th Divn, 6 hand carts for Light T.M.Btys demanded. New Mob Table for L.T.M.Bs which reduced hand carts from 16 to 8 received this day.	
	26/3/17		Received notification from 3rd Army that all 3rd Army were being supplied from Abancourt as from April 1st. As 4th Army are supplied from Abancourt no action is necessary. Visited DDOS 4th Army re handing in of Jerkins and Fur Coats by Division without the usual sorting & Boards of Survey owing to lack of time. This agreed to and instructions given to store them under directions of ADOS 15th Corps.	

[signature]

2449 Wt. W14957/M90 750,000 1/16 J.B.C. & A. Forms/C.2118/12.

6th Sheet

Instructions regarding War Diaries and Intelligence Summaries are contained in F. S. Regs., Part II. and the Staff Manual respectively. Title Pages will be prepared in manuscript.

WAR DIARY
or
INTELLIGENCE SUMMARY
(Erase heading not required.)

SECRET

Army Form C. 2118.

D.A.D.O.S. 33rd Divn

Place	Date	Hour	Summary of Events and Information	Remarks and references to Appendices
CORBIE	28/3/17		Visited ADOS 18th Corps & discussed Ordnance arrangements on arrival of Divn into 18th Corps i.e. special stores to be drawn etc. Authority obtained from ADOS 15th Corps to store Jerkins & Rain Coats at Corbie before moving. Divl guard to be left in charge.	
	29/3/17		One body K1 received for 2nd RWelsh. One Cart Water received for No 3 Coy Train. Wire demand sent to Base for Buckets carrying hand grenades for units who at last moment find that they have not got them. Also demand for 5 Bicycles for 98th Bde Signals who also at last moment found 5 were deficient from their Equipment. Reported these 2 demands to AA&QMG for action with formations concerned, as to why demands were so delayed. Purchased 14,000 metres of white tape to equip Platoons with about 60 metres each for trench planning under GS instruction. G.O.C.s authority obtained for this purchase of £25 worth of stores. Had sample bags for carrying rations and tools made up at Amiens. Rifles for firing grenades which have bulged barrels are being handed in and sent to Base. New pattern of rifle grenade permits of its being fired from a serviceable rifle. GS authority for drawing with special grenade rifles issued.	

2449 Wt. W14957/M90 750,000 1/16 J.B.C. & A. Forms/C.2118/12.

7th Sheet Last.

Instructions regarding War Diaries and Intelligence Summaries are contained in F. S. Regs., Part II. and the Staff Manual respectively. Title Pages will be prepared in manuscript.

WAR DIARY
or
INTELLIGENCE SUMMARY
(Erase heading not required.)

SECRET

Army Form C. 2118.

D.A.D.O.S.
33rd Division.

Place	Date	Hour	Summary of Events and Information	Remarks and references to Appendices
CORBIE	30/3/17		Issued 3 sample bags for carrying rations ~~equipment~~ tools etc to 100th Bde for experimental purposes in carrying intrenching tools. Ordered 248 bags to be ready by 4th inst – 200 for rations + 48 for tools	
	31/3/17		Return of Jerkins ~~Dur~~ Waistcoat for storage in Ordnance completed today, quite satisfactorily, all being properly bundled + all wet + damp garments labelled to distinguish them from dry + stored separately, under constant supervision of a Divl. Guard, owing to danger of heating + subsequent outbreak of fire. Stock of clean underclothing handed over to Army Laundries a 20th Divn from 33rd Clothing Exchge for use in their laundry. Final issue of Bulk Stores before moving received from Base to complete Division. Base have completed outstanding indents with the least possible delay and quantity of Stores received by Division during last 3 weeks constitutes a record.	

"G"
33rd Divl. H.Q.
1/4/17

[signature]
Lieut
DADOS
33rd Divn

2449 Wt. W14957/M90 750,000 1/16 J.B.C. & A. Forms/C.2118/12.

Instructions regarding War Diaries and Intelligence Summaries are contained in F. S. Regs., Part II. and the Staff Manual respectively. Title pages will be prepared in manuscript.

WAR DIARY or INTELLIGENCE SUMMARY.

(Erase heading not required.)

DADOS 33rd Divn

April 1917

Secret

Army Form C. 2118.

Place	Date	Hour	Summary of Events and Information	Remarks and references to Appendices
Corbie-sur-Somme	1/4/17		Made preparations for moving. Instructed by 'Q' to lend 2 of my lorries to them for formation of Amiens + area Stores dumps in 3rd Army area (18th Corps) ready for the Division on arrival there before going into action. Move will therefore have to be carried out on two lorries. This does not admit of any trucks being cleared at successive Railheads whilst on the move, + as units will also not be in a position to accept any quantity of stores + are now very well equipped no bulk demands will be submitted to Base till further notice + all issues remain suspended for the present. Made final arrangements with firm in Amiens for the date of supply of the 200 Canvas Halters + Tool Carriers ordered on 28th ultimo. The final lot will be ready for collection on 3rd inst.	
" "	3/4/17		Sent off two lorries to report to Ord. Officer (Major Batten) at 18th Corps HQ at Pas with personnel for loading, stacking, detonating ammunition + carpentering: also sent 700 wooden crates for petrol tins camp + pack saddles (supplied by CRE) in same lorries. The 175 sets Pack saddlery allotted to this Div by 3rd Army will be drawn by Major Batten with the 2 lorries. Sent off 2 lorries with all reserve Antigas appliances, Socks etc to next dump at Beauval. These lorries will return same day ready for moving office + remaining stores (all reserves) to Beauval.	
~~Beauval~~	4			
Beauval	3/4/17		Moved from Corbie to Beauval in two trips. 12 T.M. handcarts demanded by wire about a week before arrived at new Railhead Frechencourt. Asked RTO for these to be reconsigned but this could not be done in view of strict Traffic regulations. Arranged to collect 4/4/17 as [illegible]	

A5834 Wt. W4973/M687 750,000 8/16 D. D. & L. Ltd. Forms/C.2118/13.

Army Form C. 2118.

WAR DIARY
or
INTELLIGENCE SUMMARY.

(*Erase heading not required.*)

Instructions regarding War Diaries and Intelligence Summaries are contained in F. S. Regs., Part II. and the Staff Manual respectively. Title pages will be prepared in manuscript.

Place	Date	Hour	Summary of Events and Information	Remarks and references to Appendices
	3/4/17		at Beauval until 5th inst. also collected balance of Ration Carriers from Amiens. Delivered the 12 Hand carts to 2 T.M.Bs, direct by lorry in evening. Q. N. L. I. report deficiency of 6 Lewis Gun hand carts (1007/9") the number being handed into salvage by them in error before the receipt of the Limb. G.S. Wagon to replace them. Battalion prefer to be without them by General Staff issued instructions for them to be completed in view of forthcoming operations. Wired A.D.O.S. 18th Corps to ask if they could be obtained from any Div or Corps troops Dump. Corps replied "not available" ~~[illegible]~~ ~~[illegible]~~	
Beauval	4/4/17		Made efforts to obtain the 6 Hand carts from Railhead & Salvage Dumps but without success. "Q" arranged direct with D.D.O.S. 3rd Army for supply. Wired A.D.O.S. accordingly asking from what Dump the carts should be drawn. 300 yds white calico urgently required for provision of extra aircraft ground signals for Battalions. Wired A.D.O.S. if any available at Corps troops: Replied "none available" purchase. The small amount of Retail stores on hand issued to units at villages they passed through & dump moved. Reserves of Bulk maintained intact.	
Lucheux	5/5/17		Moved to Lucheux with 2 lorries. 4 loads Reserves & Shop Equipment left at Beauval to be collected & conveyed tomorrow direct to next store at Saulty. Arranged to make reduced issues of ~~Reserve~~ Bulk Horseshoes, Dubbin, grease, Boots etc from Reserve & demand on Base on usual days to replace issues & complete the Reserves which are larger than authorised Reserves to permit of regular issues of even quantities of stores as units are able to carry & dispose of on the march. The Div^l Train is also unable to accept any large quantity of stores for any units so of necessity the issues must be small & of only the most urgently needed stores.	
	6/5/17		~~Moved to~~ Remained at Lucheux one day beyond original programme. This enabled me to make issues as above to units. Visited L'Arbret near Saulty Railhead	

Instructions regarding War Diaries and Intelligence Summaries are contained in F. S. Regs., Part II. and the Staff Manual respectively. Title pages will be prepared in manuscript.

WAR DIARY
or
INTELLIGENCE SUMMARY.
(*Erase heading not required.*)

Army Form C. 2118.

Place	Date	Hour	Summary of Events and Information	Remarks and references to Appendices
Lucheux.	6/4/17		No stores or office accommodation available here. Went to Saulty village & saw Town Major who allotted me a very small store with a promise of an office & billets as accommodation also very scarce here. Lifted suspension of issues on both Bases as am now in a position to deal with usual programme of supply, being situated near Railhead & Divn remaining in area round about for some days. Moved 2 loads of of Reserves & Shop Equipment from Bedural to this store. Bulk stores required for issue to 19th Bde at Lucheux were brought back by the 2 lorries to Lucheux after offloading at Saulty. All Reserves & Equipment transferred to Saulty leaving only Office & Stores at Lucheux to be moved in one trip to Saulty tomorrow. The delay of 24 hours made this possible with only 2 lorries. Officers Mess Cart (Civilian pattern) of 2 R.W.F. left in unserviceable condition on road near Lucheux. Inspected cart & found it to be immobile & would have to be abandoned. Demanded new one to replace & notified D.D.O.S. of location of old cart for notification to A.D.O.S. & T. 3rd Army. Visited A.D.O.S. 18th Corps at Hauteville & discussed various points. Went to St Pol & saw D.G.O. re distribution of 50 tools detaching Container to S.B. Respirators. Gas N.C.O.s with units are capable of detaching & refitting new Boxes. Distribution given 20 per Bde & 15 to Div Gas School.	
	~~7/4/17~~			
Saulty	7/4/17		Moved to Saulty. Sent lorry to DUISANS to deliver remaining 33rd A. Defect Stores to D.A.D.O.S. 15th Divn who is now administering our R.A. On return journey 6 L.G. Hand Carts for H.L.I. were drawn from D.A.D.O.S. 3rd Divn on 3rd Army authority. Hand carts were issued same day direct to units. Arranged to send Stores daily to refilling points by lorry. Must keep in touch with Octrain S.S.O. for location & time of refilling as same are sometimes altered several times in a day to meet new situation caused by changes of train etc. Truck of Ordnance received from Base Havre, not seen due est. Issues being made	

A5834 Wt. W4973/M687 750,000 8/16 D. D. & L. Ltd. Forms/C.2118/13.

Instructions regarding War Diaries and Intelligence Summaries are contained in F. S. Regs., Part II. and the Staff Manual respectively. Title pages will be prepared in manuscript.

WAR DIARY
or
INTELLIGENCE SUMMARY.
(Erase heading not required.)

Army Form C. 2118.

Place	Date	Hour	Summary of Events and Information	Remarks and references to Appendices
Saulty	7/4/17		Controller issues to units & demands on Base in bulk ~~as~~ items. Still holds Divl H.Q. at Pommier. Kept in close touch with 'Q' daily as Div may move at anytime & so necessitate special supply arrangements. Hind portion of Travelling kitchen required by 5th Scottish to replace one damaged in axle but mobile. Arranged for unit to take to DOS after next move, for repair.	
" "	8/4/17		Visited ADOS 18th Corps, Div H.Q. & DOM Beaumetz re vehicles being brought in to him. He would not condemn hind portion of T.K. for 5th Scottish & could not repair it quickly. As it is absolutely necessary for Battalion to be complete in kitchens on move, this action causes obstruction. Demanded new H. Portion for unit by wire & instructed them to use old one till it became immobile & then to abandon & report location. One blanket per man being dumped at Bailleulval, Bailleulmont and Berles-au-Bois. Also underclothing on the man being exchanged for clean in the pack & the dirty dumped at above villages under a guard. Hind portion R.E. limber required by 212 Field Coy R.E. to replace one condemned by DOS. As before all the army all wheels required to be obtained from AOS Workshop as exchange for unserviceable. The return of 2nd blanket is due on 15th & ADOS said arrangements must be made for getting the dumped blankets to Railhead after [illegible]. This will be difficult if any offensive operations & move forward of Divn.	

A5834 Wt. W4973/M687 750,000 8/16 D. D. & L. Ltd. Forms/C.2118/13.

Instructions regarding War Diaries and Intelligence Summaries are contained in F. S. Regs., Part II. and the Staff Manual respectively. Title pages will be prepared in manuscript.

WAR DIARY
or
INTELLIGENCE SUMMARY.
(Erase heading not required.)

Army Form C. 2118.

Place	Date	Hour	Summary of Events and Information	Remarks and references to Appendices
SAULTY	9/4/17		Hastened all outstanding Grenade Carriers as there are important [illegible] in advance. D.A.C.s to hold their establishment of Springs &c as a reserve & not to make issues to Batteries without Army Authority. Stocks at workshops are maintained by D.D.O.S. of Army. All issues of Springs to Batteries are via Corps Workshops. All batteries of Field R.A in Corps are complete with 5 Ammn Carriers per gun.	
"	10/4/17		Issues of stores to units difficult owing to changes in time of refilling without notice. Frequently lorry has to deliver stores to each unit causing delay in other work owing to shortage of lorries available when required. With 2 lorries the work must necessarily be slower than with proper establishment of 4 lorries. 10 extra Water carts MK V allotted by Corps for ~~extra~~ increased water carrying during hot weather. These carts brought from Beaumetz to my Store Saulty complete with all Harness etc. Parked them outside store. Issues only to be made on authority of D.D.W. H.Q. Saw & re [illegible] a large quantity of which has not passed through my hands but drawn & issued direct by D.W. H.Q. Must ~~[illegible]~~ be informed of all transactions otherwise I cannot keep records up to date.	

A5834 Wt. W4973/M687 750,000 8/16 D. D. & L. Ltd. Forms/C.2118/13.

Instructions regarding War Diaries and Intelligence Summaries are contained in F. S. Regs., Part II. and the Staff Manual respectively. Title pages will be prepared in manuscript.

WAR DIARY
or
INTELLIGENCE SUMMARY.
(Erase heading not required.)

Army Form C. 2118.

Place	Date	Hour	Summary of Events and Information	Remarks and references to Appendices
Saulty	11/4/17		Visited Ordnance Gun Park, [illegible], to which indents for all parts of Guns, Machine Guns, Trench Mortars as detailed on lists supplied by Base Havre, have been extracted & cancelled simultaneously off demands at Base. All future demands for these items will be made in duplicate & 3 copies sent to Gun Park. Owing to shortage of parts of guns & M.G.s units must state in indents if parts are required to complete spares or "to keep guns in action". Issues of gun parts for latter reason will only be made by IOM of Corps Shops & these will be the only parts supplied for the present. Supply Officer 98th Bde refused to accept Ordnance for 98th Bde units at refilling point owing to uncertainty of the Train Coys seeing units for two or three days & also because all wagons were already fully loaded. The latter difficulty discussed with OC Train who laid it down that unless the quantity of stores delivered to refilling point daily for each unit was small (not more than 2 cwt) the Train Coys could not take it for fear of overloading.	
" "	12/4/17		Division transferred to 7th Corps. Spoke to ADOS 7th Corps on phone. Salvage work is taken up very strongly in this Corps & ADOS advised me of position of Main Dumps. 30th Div Arty transferred to me as 30th Div are being relieved by 33rd. Visited DADOS 30th re taking over. He will turn over all Bulk & detail he receives or has now on hand for 30th RA units to my Store [illegible].	

A5834 Wt. W4973/M687 750,000 8/16 D. D. & L. Ltd. Forms/C.2118/13.

Army Form C. 2118.

Instructions regarding War Diaries and Intelligence Summaries are contained in F. S. Regs., Part II. and the Staff Manual respectively. Title pages will be prepared in manuscript.

WAR DIARY
or
INTELLIGENCE SUMMARY.
(Erase heading not required.)

Place	Date	Hour	Summary of Events and Information	Remarks and references to Appendices
Saulty	12/4/17		We cannot give particulars of Billets in area we are taking over owing to continual changes of Town Majors & handing over of Billets. Moved 73 San Sec to XV Corps troops & received 33rd Supply Col from XV Corps troops. Visited new Railhead at Boisleux-au-mont.	
Store:- Boisleux-au-mont. Office Saulty	13/4/17		Sent 1 lorry with B de Loos & materials for constructing a temporary Store to Boisleux-au-mont Railhead & Store was constructed very near Railhead on side of main Road. 1 lorry sent to St Pol to draw huts for accomodation of Divl HQ at next HQ Blairville Quarry. Demanded a Column to send me my 2 lorries which were lent to Divn at beginning of month & returned to Column 10/4/17. Two trucks arrived Railhead one 48 hours late & the other 24. Impossible to clear these trucks without these lorries. Other 2 lorries with [illegible] not available for rest of day. R.T.O. agreed to hold over trucks containing stores urgently required if cleared first thing in morning. Remained forward to Div HQ at Blairville myself, office could not be moved from Saulty. Demanded G.S. Wagon for 212 Field Coy R.E. to replace one abandoned day move.	
Store:- Boisleux-au-mont. Office Blairville (Div HQ)	14/4/17		No lorries arrived although Sup Col & Q had been notified of shortage & inability to move or carry on issues & had arranged to supply the lorries which were being used for supply work. Trucks were returned to Regulating Station by R.T.O. Invest O.C. Regulating Station to reconsign to new Railhead. Demanded 18 pdr gun for C/150 condemned for scoring of bore. Moved office late in evening to Blairville	

Army Form C. 2118.

Instructions regarding War Diaries and Intelligence Summaries are contained in F. S. Regs., Part II. and the Staff Manual respectively. Title pages will be prepared in manuscript.

WAR DIARY
or
INTELLIGENCE SUMMARY.
(Erase heading not required.)

Place	Date	Hour	Summary of Events and Information	Remarks and references to Appendices
Store:- Boisleux-au-Mont. Office:- Hamelincourt	15/4/17		Moved office to Div H.Q. Hamelincourt. Store now ready to receive stores. Refilling point for all units adjoins store so units can easily draw from stores & delivery by lorry not needed. Normal system of Bulk supply resumed & reserves reduced to authorised scales. Instructions issued by D.A.G. to Brigades to send in 6 Armourers & 6 Shoemakers to me as personnel for Armourers & Shoemakers shop which will be opened as soon as material & tentage can be obtained for accomodation. Demanded ~~[illegible]~~ one Lewis Gun for 2nd R.W. Fusiliers to replace one destroyed by Shell fire. Head portion M.T. demanded for 1st Cameronians to replace one broken down on line of March.	
"	"			
"	16/4/17		Took up question of collection of Salvage & visited Shrapnel Corner Dump where I found about 1 lorry load of Ordnance ready for collection arranged to collect 17/4. Instructions issued to Salvage personnel i/c Salvage Dump adjoining my stores. General office work. 2 trucks sent to Regulating Station for Saulty on 14th arrived & were cleared to-day. Wrote A.D.O.S.	
"	17/4/17		8 Lewis & 1 Vickers gun salvaged by 4th Suffolks from Hindenburg Line. Took them into Armourers Shop for inspection & repair. Arranged with A.D.O.S. to notify him of all receipts of Machine Guns from Salvage giving the Nos. Repairable & Unserviceable separately. When a gun is issued from stock notify A.D.O.S. M.G. & not D.D.O.S. as well. If possible demands already at Gun Park for guns are to be interfered with by issues from stock in part completion & subsequent cancellation. This leads to confusion. Salvaged guns to be retained to meet future demands.	

A5834 Wt. W4973/M687 750,000 8/16 D. D. & L. Ltd. Forms/C.2118/13.

Instructions regarding War Diaries and Intelligence Summaries are contained in F. S. Regs., Part II. and the Staff Manual respectively. Title pages will be prepared in manuscript.

WAR DIARY
or
INTELLIGENCE SUMMARY.
(Erase heading not required.)

Army Form C. 2118.

Place	Date	Hour	Summary of Events and Information	Remarks and references to Appendices
~~Store:~~ Boisleux-au-mont. Office at Hamelincourt	17/4/17		Two light Spring wireless carts in possession of Signals + HQ RA withdrawn + despatched by Rail to OO XV Corps Troops under instructions from 15th Corps. 5000 sets less 3000 pr Socks demanded urgently from Base for starting Clothing Exchange + Laundry. Maltese Cart demanded for 2nd A+S Highlanders to replace one broken down on line of march.	
" "	18/4/17		Trusses + Tents Shelter + Tarpaulins urgently required by Divn for accommodation. Corps asked by Divn Q + allotments made. Tent bags collected by me + issued on distribution. Lewis Gun Magazines very short + as many as possible must be salvaged completed + re-issued if serviceable. Demands on Park must state if magazines are required. Nothing further notified as regards authority to draw the 18 pdr gun demanded for C/157 A FA Bde on 14th. Hastened DD Ordnance for reply. Was informed by memo that this gun had already been drawn by unit on 16th from Gun Park. The gun authority me to collect never received by me hence I could take no action. Notified receipt of this gun in usual way.	
" "	19/4/17		3 Lewis guns complete with Spares demanded for 1st Cameronians to replace 3 destroyed by Shell fire. 4 L.G. demanded for 20th R. Fus for same reason. 4 issued from Salved stock meanwhile. These 4 will be replaced by 4 received from Gun Park. On instructions from AD Ordnance 7th Corps moved 155th (Army) RFA Bde to 29th Divn. One Lewis Gun received from Gun Park for 2nd R W Fusiliers. General routine work. Shoemakers Shop now running [illegible] as HP Marquee received from Base provides sufficient accommodation together with Leather [illegible] collected [illegible]	

Army Form C. 2118.

Instructions regarding War Diaries and Intelligence Summaries are contained in F. S. Regs., Part II. and the Staff Manual respectively. Title pages will be prepared in manuscript.

WAR DIARY
or
INTELLIGENCE SUMMARY.

(Erase heading not required.)

Place	Date	Hour	Summary of Events and Information	Remarks and references to Appendices
Store Boulieux-au-mont Office Humbercourt	20/4/17		Took up question of Goggles Anti-gas with Div Gas Officer. Under CRO 783 every man with an S.B.R should also have a pair of Rubber Sponge Goggles. These replace the 8 pieces now in possession which the D.G.O states are of no use for protection against lachrymatory. List of Salvage Dumps with map references completed from information received from Bdes & from visits to them myself. Main Dumps in Back area Glevapont Corner near Bellacourt. Main Div^l Dumps (later over for 21st Div^n on relief) Boiry-St-Martin. 60 F.S. Lamps very urgently required for lighting tunnels & 24 underground dugs. Authority obtained to draw from O.O Corps Troops. Sent a lorry to collect but latter broke down going & remained ditched all night. ~~collected early in morning~~. Bde Wo's & Armourers instructed to make all possible use of Salvaged Stores - magazines & Spare parts for Lewis Guns very urgently required.	
" "	21/4/17		Collect the 60 F.S Lamps early in morning by car & delivered by car to 98th Bde Advanced H.Q on Henin - Croiselles Road. Visited subsidiary Salvage Dumps. Sent 500 S.B.R 10% 2, 80% 3, 10% 4 to 33rd Depot Bn at Beneville to enable reinforcements for the Div^n passing through the Depot to be fitted by the Gas Officer there. Demanded on Base to replace. Visited Doullens for R.P. Bought 82 Electric Torches for immediate issue for operations. 4 more Lewis Guns made serviceable from Salvage - Reported to A.D.O.S. All remaining L. G. Handcarts in possession of Bns now returned on receipt of Limb^d G.S. wagon. 50 Handcarts asked for now [illegible] [illegible] returned	
	22/4/17		Increased scale of issue of Bombers Sacks approved by Army Commander. Demanded 960 to complete to 128 per Bn. 1 & 1 per Bomber. Drafted instructions for the return of 2nd Blanket per man. This was due 15th this month under "Return of Winter Clothing" but 'Q' decided it was not possible to collect before 25th. Instructions will be dated accordingly. Each unit to [illegible] for preliminary survey so that final board of survey need only concern itself with the [illegible] probably unserviceable articles	

A5834 Wt. W4973/M687 750,000 8/16 D. D. & L. Ltd. Forms/C.2118/13.

Instructions regarding War Diaries and Intelligence Summaries are contained in F. S. Regs., Part II. and the Staff Manual respectively. Title pages will be prepared in manuscript.

WAR DIARY
or
INTELLIGENCE SUMMARY.

(Erase heading not required.)

Army Form C. 2118.

Place	Date	Hour	Summary of Events and Information	Remarks and references to Appendices
	23/4/17		one Body. K.T. demanded for 2nd Worcesters to replace one condemned. One G.S. wagon received for 21 [illegible] Coy. 1 Lewis Gun issued from stock to 1st Camerons to replace an additional casualty	
[illegible] Boisleux-au-Mont Office [illegible]	23/4/17		Collected 7 Lewis Guns complete with spares for Ord Gun Park - 3 from Cameronians 4 from 20th Fusiliers. Latter taken into stock to replace 4 issued to unit. 3 more guns salvaged & made serviceable & retained to meet future demands. Withdrawal of Hyposcopes from Battalions now completed. 25 only handed in. Remainder either lost, unserviceable or handed into Salvage from time to time.	
" "	24/4/17		Heavy casualties in Lewis Guns have occurred in recent fighting. 32 complete guns required as first estimate. Demanded 24 and issued 8 from stock to 4th Suffolks who lost 15 guns complete. 2 3" Stokes Mortars demanded for 98th T.M.B and 4 Vickers Guns for 98 M.G. Coy. Mortars demanded from Havre others from Gun Park. Could not give details of units requirement on first demand but obtained this information from Brigades & sent supplementary wires. All arrangements made for collecting 2nd blanket from units dumps by lorry, surveying & despatch to Base over several days according to allotment of trucks by D.O.O. Detailed estimation & programme of times of collection sent to all units.	
" "	25/4/17		Further casualties in Lewis Guns notified by 100th Bde & 19th as follows: 1st Queens require 11, 16 K.R.R.C. 7, 2nd R.W. Fus 3, 5th Scottish Rifles 3. As 5 of the first 24 demanded can be taken in satisfaction of these later demands, wired for 19 guns detail of units requirements. Question raised by 2nd Army as to why all spares are lost when a gun is lost. The supply of spares is very difficult & every effort must be made to preserve spare parts as far as possible & to collect as many as possible from salvage in forward area.	

Army Form C. 2118.

Instructions regarding War Diaries and Intelligence Summaries are contained in F. S. Regs., Part II. and the Staff Manual respectively. Title pages will be prepared in manuscript.

WAR DIARY
or
INTELLIGENCE SUMMARY.
(Erase heading not required.)

Place	Date	Hour	Summary of Events and Information	Remarks and references to Appendices
Stores – Boisleux-au-Mont Office Hamelincourt	25/4/17		One Vickers Gun salved, made serviceable & issued to 19th M.G. Coy to replace a casualty. Refitting of Divn being taken in hand at once as unit is now out of line & being relieved by 21st Divn. Saw as many Quartermasters as possible today & impressed on them the necessity of overhauling the equipment of their units at earliest possible date & indenting to complete establishment & replace "unserviceable" without delay to enable me to take immediate action & so obtain the stores required within the next week if possible. Obtained from them confirmation of demands for Lewis Guns & spares. A good many Lewis Gun Magazines have been salvaged & reissued. (about 350)	
Stores – Boisleux-au-Mont Office Adinfer.	26/4/17		Moved Office to ADINFER. All 2nd Blankets except those of 19th Bde stored at Bailleulval, collected by lorry & stacked near my Store at Boisleux-au-Mont. The unserviceable kept separate from the serviceable as conditioned by units & a careful record kept by my checker of numbers received & from which units. Stores must now be delivered by lorry to refilling point as units are too far back to draw. Arranged separate ordnance refilling point at convenient place in each Brigade area. Staff Capts of Bdes consulted on this matter & latter issued instruction to units to draw every other day accordingly. 100th Bde draw on 27th & every other day. 19 & 98 on 28th & every other day. This & Salvage avoid having all [illegible] out at refilling at once. 2 must be retained for Railhead [illegible]	

A5834. Wt. W4973/M687 750,000 8/16 D. D. & L. Ltd. Forms/C.2118/13.

Instructions regarding War Diaries and Intelligence Summaries are contained in F. S. Regs., Part II. and the Staff Manual respectively. Title pages will be prepared in manuscript.

WAR DIARY
or
INTELLIGENCE SUMMARY.
(Erase heading not required.)

Army Form C. 2118.

Place	Date	Hour	Summary of Events and Information	Remarks and references to Appendices
St. Ordnance Office – A. Dn. per	27/4/17		2 Stokes Mortars received for Base. Attended Board of Survey on Unserviceable Blankets & completed the survey in morning. About 8% found Unserviceable on total numbers returned. The 19 Lewis Guns of which full enquiries had been made before demanding, were issued for today. 43 Guns now outstanding. Units indents for technical stores (clothes, wire cutters, bomb buckets, binoculars & compasses) coming in well. Arranged with R.O.O. Saulty to allot one truck for Blankets being surveyed at Bailleulval & serviceable being sent to Railhead.	
" "	28/4/17		Went to Bailleulval with Board of Survey & found that the Blankets had not been sorted preliminarily by the 19 Bde in accordance with instructions of a week ago. Sorting parties had to be obtained & about 4000 Blankets inspected & surveyed. There was done just in time to enable a load of 2500 to be taken to Saulty in time to fill the truck allotted. The Balance of the Serviceable & also the Unserviceable in 10s were taken to my store & added to the General Dump for disposal to Base or Salvage.	
" "	29/4/17		Checked carefully all outstanding demands for Lewis Guns & spare parts & instructed Bde W.O.s to cancel those items which have been on demand over a month as these are probably all covered by later casualties where complete spare part bags have been lost & demanded to replace. Visit Salvage Dump. Reduced original demand	

A5834 Wt. W4973/M687 750,000 8/16 D. D. & L. Ltd. Forms/C.2118/13.

Instructions regarding War Diaries and Intelligence Summaries are contained in F. S. Regs., Part II. and the Staff Manual respectively. Title pages will be prepared in manuscript.

WAR DIARY
or
INTELLIGENCE SUMMARY.

(Erase heading not required.)

Army Form C. 2118.

Place	Date	Hour	Summary of Events and Information	Remarks and references to Appendices
[illegible] Boisleux-au-Mont [illegible]	29/4/17		of 24 Lewis Guns to 19 as a unit. 1st Middlesex with S/Capt 98th Bde found they had salvaged 5 guns of which they were originally deficient & had not reported this. They are now complete with exception of S.P. bags which demand was allowed to stand. After this all doubtful demands were investigated & confirmed. Maltese Cart arrived for 2nd A & SH. Body G.S. limbered arrived for 1st Cameronians & 20th Fusiliers. Collected 2000 suits SD Clothing from Ordnance Sun Park Grevent & split up in accordance with Bde summary in lieu of demands from Base.	
[illegible]	30/4/17		Instructions issued two days ago for the handing in of remaining items of winter clothing complied with & all items of 3 Bdes collected at refilling points except in case of 100th Bde who are moving today & have accordingly dumped their winter clothing at their late Bde Store for collection at same time as surplus greatcoats socks etc of casualties. Arranged to collect with extra lorry being supplied 1/5/17. 19 & 98th also moving on 1st May so no refilling will take place then. To avoid any delay all stores ready for issue including SD Clothing from Sun Park for refilling purposes, sent out by lorry to 19 & 98th & 100th late this evening. Refilling point on 2nd & onwards will be at Boisleux au Mont so no necessity to send out to units. Lorry sent to Sun Park to collect 38 Lewis & 4 Vickers Machine Guns complete. These will be available for issue 1/5/17 & will complete all Machine Guns in Div of establishment.	

[illegible] Capt.
33rd Div. DADOS

A5834 Wt. W4973/M687 750,000 8/16 D. D. & L. Ltd. Forms/C.2118/13.

Instructions regarding War Diaries and Intelligence Summaries are contained in F. S. Regs., Part II. and the Staff Manual respectively. Title pages will be prepared in manuscript.

WAR DIARY or INTELLIGENCE SUMMARY.

(Erase heading not required.)

DADOS 33rd Div. May 1917. SECRET Vol 19

Army Form C. 2118.

Place	Date	Hour	Summary of Events and Information	Remarks and references to Appendices
Store Boulincourt – au-mont. Office Adinfer	1/5/17.		Heavy Mobile Workshop are not accepting any more wheels for repair & numbers 'S' available for issue is very limited. Demands being submitted to Base in usual way. Informed by ADOS that only Lewis Gun parts required to keep guns in action will be supplied. No spares can be issued only to salvage. Visit Div Salvage Dump & gave NCO in charge a list of stores most urgently required & arranged to collect 2/5/17. Visited Doullens & Amiens for LP. Send urgent wire to Havre hastening all Technical stores such as wirecutters, Bomb Buckets, Bicycle, compasses in order to complete establishment of Div as soon as possible. One GS Wagon for 150 BAC demanded.	
"	2/5/17		Position of supply of 1½" Illuminating Pistols investigated. GS say 12 per Bde must be in possession as all SOS Signal cartridges are being supplied in 1½" & not 1". Only 9 in possession although 36 were in possession when Div was last in line (of 48 withdrawn from Infantry Bdes & issued to RA when leaving 4th Army, 36 were returned to Infantry Bdes). Issued 3 from Armourer's Shop (Salvaged) to 100th Bde. Demanded 3000 prs socks to enable deficiency on issue of 10,000 set underclothing to 3 Bdes to be made up. Other garments sufficient to meet requirements. This underclothing demanded under instructions of AA & QMG as Laundry at Camp had not started just prior to Div coming out of line. Underclothing taken off the man 8 ... Bdes at Bailleulval, Bailleulmont & ~~...~~ Bienvillers. To be collected & taken to Foden disinfector at Berles-au-Bois. Asked for 2 extra lorries for 2 days to accomplish this.	
"	3/5/17.		Demanded 18 Pistols 1½" by wire to complete to 12 per Brigade. All wire cutters outstanding very urgently required by units in case of sudden move into the line. Wired ADOS asking if number required to complete could be obtained at once from Gun Park to save delay. GS wagon arrived for No 2 Sec 30th DAC who were transferred to 30th Div some days ago	

A5834 Wt. W4973/M687 750,000 8/16 D. D. & L. Ltd. Forms/C.2118/13.

Instructions regarding War Diaries and Intelligence Summaries are contained in F. S. Regs., Part II. and the Staff Manual respectively. Title pages will be prepared in manuscript.

WAR DIARY
or
INTELLIGENCE SUMMARY.
(Erase heading not required.)

Army Form C. 2118.

Place	Date	Hour	Summary of Events and Information	Remarks and references to Appendices
Store Bouleux-au-Mont [illegible] Officer [illegible]	3/5/17		1st Cameronians complaining that they cannot obtain Bulk & Default Store demanded. [illegible] & found [illegible] Bulk demands were too late for last weeks issue but in time for inclusion in this weeks. Default [illegible] mostly Lewis Gun Parts which are not being issued as spares but only to [illegible] guns in action. Units Guns are all ready for action & they have a good quantity of spares. Saw [illegible] Q. M & Armourer & explained these points. In view of urgency, collected all serviceable shovels & picks from Salvage Dump to satisfy units demands to replace all their entrenching tools which they handed over when last in line. Also issued Boots from Surplus & Shoemakers Shop & horseshoes from surplus in my Store & [illegible] 21st [illegible] & completed SD Clothing from surpluses. This is the only units whose demands were late.	
"	4/5/17		Visited Store & found out number of wirecutters & [illegible] carriers received from Base this morning & numbers still outstanding after receipts were taken into account. 100 MKV & 000 SA not [illegible] required after receipts from salvage accounted for. Saw [illegible] & he wired [illegible] and 3rd Army for authority to draw these wirecutters from G.P. Went on to Doullens for [illegible] & in order to obtain wirecutters without delay went on to Gun Park at [illegible]. On arrival found authority to issue had not arrived & could not get through on phone to [illegible] to ask if wirecutters could be drawn at once to save standing carriage. [illegible] Drew few small items of equipment of outstanding indents at Gun Park. Received weekly Salvage Statement for Salvage Officer & sent [illegible] to collect wire-cutters & entrenching tools urgently required. 3rd Army wired [illegible] authority for issue of wire cutters from Gun Park, Doullens [illegible]	

A5834 Wt. W4973/M687 750,000 8/16 D. D. & L. Ltd. Forms/C.2118/13.

Instructions regarding War Diaries and Intelligence Summaries are contained in F. S. Regs., Part II. and the Staff Manual respectively. Title pages will be prepared in manuscript.

WAR DIARY
or
INTELLIGENCE SUMMARY.
(Erase heading not required.)

Army Form C. 2118.

Place	Date	Hour	Summary of Events and Information	Remarks and references to Appendices
	4/5/17		Muslin will be ~~[illegible]~~ required for immediate issue on scale of about 20 yds per Battalion. Wired D.D.O.S. to say if this can be supplied from Base or if resort to be had to L.P. Received ADOS later today forbidding purchase of any Trolite Stores of French manufacture. This renders L.P. of Muslin impossible. Asked Havre to make issues of all technical Stores, [illegible] [illegible] [illegible] of 18 [illegible] [illegible] within 3 days as Div is likely to enter line again at end of that time.	
	5/5/17.		Authority given to draw 18 pdr gun & carriage for A/156 from Gun Park. Unit cannot collect with horses so arranged to collect by lorry tomorrow. Lorry sent to HMW to collect 6 of 200 wheels.	
	6/5/17		ADOS wires that Fly traps, Muslin & Sprayers should be obtained from nearest San. Sec. Informed "Q" that DDMS should demand on 56th San Sec. Lorry sent to Mesnil to collect 18 pdr & carriage from Gun Park & take to No. 9 Ord. Workshop for fitting into A.M. etc. Visited Stores in [illegible]. No trucks arrived today ~~[illegible]~~ Picketing Seacloths should arrive today by programme. Notified as arriving tomorrow. Gave orders for Salvage to be collected from Henencamps & La Couchie 7/5/17, as requested by D.D.O.S. Stores collected to be sorted at these dumps & conveyed direct to nearest R'head i.e. Saulty. 3rd Army wired instructing Divisions to submit indent for MK 2 Ammn limbers & wagons (18 pdr) to replace any MK. I without baskets in possession of attached R.A. Wired 150 Bde R.F.A. for requirements & no MK 2 required as no MK I are in possession. Reported to ADOS numbers of [illegible] [illegible] demanded by units, recovered by Salvage & received from Gun Park since operations in the Corps commenced 15 [illegible] 15th alt..	

A5834 Wt. W4973/M687 750,000 8/16 D. D. & L. Ltd. Forms/C.2118/13.

Instructions regarding War Diaries and Intelligence Summaries are contained in F. S. Regs., Part II. and the Staff Manual respectively. Title pages will be prepared in manuscript.

WAR DIARY
or
INTELLIGENCE SUMMARY.
(*Erase heading not required.*)

Army Form C. 2118.

Place	Date	Hour	Summary of Events and Information	Remarks and references to Appendices
Store Bouleux-au-Mont. Office Humbercamp	7/5/17		Lorry returned with 18 pdr gun from Gun Park. General Routine work. D.D.O.S. 3rd Army called in afternoon on [carriage] found me away at the time. Large proportion of outstanding technical Stores received from Base to-day. Outstanding [illegible] now quite small. Informed 'Q' accordingly. DDOS visited Store at Bouleux. The 100 Mud Scrapers received from Base on an very old indent dating from February in Somme area, not now required. D.D.O.S. ordered their delivery to nearest R.E. Park.	
" "	8/5/17		→ Spoke ADOS on phone re wire I sent to him yesterday hastening supply of [illegible] to 38th San Sec who had not received any from OO 7th Corps Troops. ADOS taking no action as hastening must be done through laid-down procedure. ie ADMS to San Sec. San Sec to OO Corps Troops & latter on Base. Informed 'Q' accordingly & asked ADMS to hasten. Notified OO 7th Corps Troops is holding a reserve of "Cups for firing Rifle Grenade" & very urgent demands for these should be submitted to ADOS. No more Salvaged Rifles found to be serviceable are to be sent to Base until further notice as they are all required for re-arming of RA Batteries to complete to authorised Mob table scale. About 100 serviceable Rifles in reserve at Armourers are available for this issue. A large number more can be put to stock after inspection & cleaning. 2 lorries sent to clear all Salvage at Humbercamp Village - where large quantity was reported to be by ADOS. Several loads collected & cleared to Saulty Railhead.	
" "	9/5/17.		Visited Store & saw ADOS. Inspected Corps Salvage Dump near R'head & also Ordnance Dumped by 33rd Salvage Coy close to Corps Salvage with intention of handing over to Corps Salvage Officer who is taking over operations. All Ordnance from Div Salvage Dump should be delivered to me for sorting & disposal. Head equipment, accoutrements, harness, Picks & Shovels & Boots in both dumps selected & collected by me	

A5834 Wt. W4973/M687 750,000 8/16 D. D. & L. Ltd. Forms/C.2118/13.

Instructions regarding War Diaries and Intelligence Summaries are contained in F. S. Regs., Part II. and the Staff Manual respectively. Title pages will be prepared in manuscript.

WAR DIARY
or
INTELLIGENCE SUMMARY.
(Erase heading not required.)

Army Form C. 2118.

Place	Date	Hour	Summary of Events and Information	Remarks and references to Appendices
	9/5/17		lorry & later to my Dump for re-issue. There is great shortage of wheels at Base & as many salvaged & returned wheels as possible are being sent to Base not H.M.W. CRO being published authorising the issue of rifles to Batteries of Artillery to complete to scale of 36 per Battery. At present 10 per Battery are in possession. This issue must be completed as soon as possible. AOC Corps orders received authorising appointment of Sergts Webb & Robb to a/Sub Condr & of Pte Firth to a/Sergeant. Issued Part II order accordingly. Wrote to 'Q' Harbouring Corps 'Q' for issue of muslin last night. ADOS gave authority for LP of 300 yds for immediate issue. 3rd ARO received later authorising San Sec in 3rd Army to hold Sprayers, Fly Traps & Muslin for issue to DWs as required.	
	10/5/17		General routine work. Wired ADOS 7 Corps for authority to draw 144 Caps for firing rifle Grenades from 007 Corps Tps as there are very urgently required to satisfy all outstanding demands of 100th Bde who are first Bde to go into action & are provided with No 23 grenades. 007 Corps troops holds a reserve of these caps for emergency. Authority given & caps drawn in evening will be issued 11/5/17.	
	11/5/17		Notice of move of HQ to Hamelincourt 12/5/17 received. Arranged for lorry to collect office gear, etc. & convey to new H.Q. Div relieves 21st Div in line. Went to Amiens in afternoon for LP. Purchased 330 yds muslin very urgently required for covering food & 6 Combined Hammers & Screwdrivers for issue to all Dumps. Issued to B Echelon for distribution. GS wagon recd fr 150th Bde AA & Q.	

A5834 Wt. W4973/M687 750,000 8/16 D. D. & L. Ltd. Forms/C.2118/13.

Instructions regarding War Diaries and Intelligence Summaries are contained in F. S. Regs., Part II. and the Staff Manual respectively. Title pages will be prepared in manuscript.

WAR DIARY
or
INTELLIGENCE SUMMARY.
(Erase heading not required.)

Army Form C. 2118.

Place	Date	Hour	Summary of Events and Information	Remarks and references to Appendices
Hamelincourt	12/5/17		Moved office from Adinfer Wood to Hamelincourt. Visited Store & gave distribution of Muslin. Instructed Salvage to collect 300 sets web Equipment for exchange for leather Equipment in possession of 2 R.W. Fus. All Salvage Corps are sending Web Equipment & any damp [illegible] washable [illegible] to be done. Queen's report body of one of their kitchens broken down on line of march. Wired them to give location to enable body to be collected & taken to [illegible] workshop. Under instruction of Corps Q. Corps Salvage Officer is retaining stocks of certain stores when in serviceable condition. These are for emergency issues.	
	13/5/17		Issued 200 sets of underclothing to 7th Corps Infantry School under instructions of A.D.O.S. A.D.M.S. informed me that he had given orders for all technical stores such as watches, Binoculars, Compasses etc to be taken off wounded men by Field Amb. and handed in by them to my store.	
	14/5/17		Went to Corps Head Qrs to attend conference with A.D.O.S and D.A.D.O.S. of Div[ns] in the Corps. Supply of underclothing gone into generally. A.D.O.S says a scheme is being started for all underclothing to be cleaned and issued to Divisions by Corps. Only clothing to replace actual unserviceable articles being made by Divisions	
	15/5/17		All outstanding indents for 150th Bde were hastened on Base. A.D.O.S requires to know number of Mark I wagons Amb. in possession of Arty with me. Sent reply "Nil", all Mark II.	[signature]

A5834 Wt. W4973/M687 750,000 8/16 D. D. & L. Ltd. Forms/C.2118/13.

Instructions regarding War Diaries and Intelligence Summaries are contained in F. S. Regs., Part II. and the Staff Manual respectively. Title pages will be prepared in manuscript.

WAR DIARY
or
INTELLIGENCE SUMMARY.

(Erase heading not required.)

Army Form C. 2118.

Place	Date	Hour	Summary of Events and Information	Remarks and references to Appendices
HAMELINCOURT	16/5/17		300 Brushes wire carding allowed per Divn under authority DOS. OS4 1395 d/d 12/5/17. and that number demanded on Base. ADOS wired to know number of rifles required to complete issue to Arty at full scale ie 36 per Bty. Replied sufficient in Divl Armourer Shop	
	17/5/17		293rd Bde AFA moved by 17th Divn to 33rd. OO 33rd Divl Arty was transferred from 12th Divn to 33rd Divn for Ordnance supplies. Drew 9 CSL Tents and 2 Store Tents from O.O. 7th Corps Troops. These are for use of Division for mobile accomodation.	
	18/5/17		One Lewis Gun demanded by 1st Middlesex and one issued from Divl Armourer Shop.	
	19/5/17		Demanded hind portion of a Limbered GS wagon for 3 Sec 33rd DAC to replace one destroyed by shell fire.	
	20/5/17		Hastened supply of Protractor MG on Base. These items are very badly needed by MG Coy.	
	21/5/17		500 Bars of soap deficient in Bonne Truck. Base wire they will send up in next truck.	
	22/5/17		Demanded hind portion K.T. for 9th HLI to replace one condemned by I.O.M. Demanded hind portion Limber for 9th HLI to replace one destroyed by shell fire. Issued a Water Cart from Divl reserve to 4th Suffolks and demanded one from Base to complete number held. Demanded 3 Lewis Guns for 5th Scottish Rifles to replace 3 destroyed by shell fire.	

A5834 Wt. W4973/M687 750,000 8/16 D. D. & L. Ltd. Forms/C.2118/13.

Instructions regarding War Diaries and Intelligence Summaries are contained in F. S. Regs., Part II. and the Staff Manual respectively. Title pages will be prepared in manuscript.

WAR DIARY
or
INTELLIGENCE SUMMARY.
(Erase heading not required.)

Army Form C. 2118.

Place	Date	Hour	Summary of Events and Information	Remarks and references to Appendices
— HAMELINCOURT —	23/5/16		Was informed by 7th Corps that it is not now necessary to prepare indents on Gun Park in duplicate. Wired to ADOS to find out if he had any later information as to destination of 150th Bde AOA	
	24/5/16		Received urgent wire to supply 6 1½" pistols to 19th Bde units. Issued 6 from Store. Demanded 13 Lewis Guns from 3rd Army Gun Park to replace losses & destroyed by shell fire.	
	27/5/16		moved 293rd Bde AOA from 33rd Divn to 17th Divn. Wired Division for location of dump and arranged to send all stores we had to Amas. Wired ADOS for instructions as to disposal of stores for 150th Bde AOA. received reply that information was being obtained and would be sent me in due course. Second portion Limbered GS wagon arrived for 3 Sec 33rd DAC. Wired to 3 Brigades to return Electric Signalling Lamps which had become surplus owing to introduction of Daylight Signalling Lamps.	
	30/5/17		Received 17000 Goggles rubber sponge from Base. Was informed by ADOS that 150th Bde had been moved to OO 9th Corps Troops. All work in connection with move of 150 Bde AOA has been carried out by 3rd Army. Wired 9th Corps Troops for map reference, received reply "WIPPENHOEK". All stores for 150th Bde AOA loaded up and consigned by rail to OO 9th Corps Troops.	[signature] Capt

A5834 Wt. W4973/M687 750,000 8/16 D. D. & L. Ltd. Forms/C.2118/13.

Instructions regarding War Diaries and Intelligence Summaries are contained in F. S. Regs., Part II. and the Staff Manual respectively. Title pages will be prepared in manuscript.

WAR DIARY
or
INTELLIGENCE SUMMARY.
(Erase heading not required.)

Army Form C. 2118.

Place	Date	Hour	Summary of Events and Information	Remarks and references to Appendices
HAMELINCOURT	27/6/17		Went by car to 3rd Army Gun Park and collected 5 Bags Spare part filled which were urgently required by units to put Lewis Guns into action.	
	28/6/17		Demanded 200 lbs cutch on Base as a large number of tents were being received without any colouring matter. Drew 235 Tents C.S.L. from O.O 7th Corps Troops. This number completes establishment of Division and includes 195 which are intended for use in forming Divisional Rest Camp.	
	29/6/17		Demanded 7 Lewis Guns and 5 Bags Spare part from Gun Park, these being required by units to replace losses in action.	
	30/6/17		Received wires from Army Corps calling for distribution of the 7 guns demanded on 29th. This information was given in my wires and reply sent to Army Corps accordingly. Drew a quantity of logwood stain from 7th Corps Troops also made issues of stain to units in possession of white tentage.	
	31/7/17		Sent down demand to Rouen for 5000 Socks for issue in replacement of worn out ones. Drew 7 Lewis Guns from Gun Park. Indented for 180 Periscopes Vigilant to replace losses in 100th Bde. Moved to Adinfer Wood. Divn moves to reserve area.	

A.W.E. Beavan Capt
DADOS
33rd Divn

A5834 Wt. W4973/M687 750,000 8/16 D. D. & L. Ltd. Forms/C.2118/13.

Instructions regarding War Diaries and Intelligence Summaries are contained in F. S. Regs., Part II. and the Staff Manual respectively. Title Pages will be prepared in manuscript.

WAR DIARY
or
INTELLIGENCE SUMMARY
(Erase heading not required.)

D.A.D.O.S. 33rd Div[n]

June 1917.

SECRET

Vol 20

Army Form C. 2118.

Place	Date	Hour	Summary of Events and Information	Remarks and references to Appendices
~~[illegible]~~ Adinfer Wood	1/6/17	—	Now Bdes are in reserve area distance to my store too great for horse transport. Arranged Bde refilling points accordingly with Staff Captains. 98th Bde remain in area close to Boisleux-au-Mont. Their units can therefore draw direct from my stores. Attached 18th Middlesex & 19th Field Amb to nearest Bde refilling point ~~to suit~~ to save their transport. Other units attend their own Bde refilling point. Demand 1 Lewis gun for 2nd Worcesters to replace one destroyed by shellfire in recent operations.	
" "	2/6/17		Discussed refitting question with "Q". Must be completed by 30th inst. G.O.C. has ordered all Steel Helmets to be freshly painted & sprinkled with Sawdust. Reviewed all outstanding demands & found only ~~few~~ two indents for 100th Bde units outstanding. Sawdust to be drawn from Canadian Forestry Corps at Courcelles-le-Comte. Sent special reminder for all important Technical Stores to C.O.O. Havre asking if all outstanding demands could be met within next fortnight.	
" "	3/6/17.		Demanded 3 cwt Paintsby wire. Collected sufficient sawdust for whole Divisions helmets. Cancelled indent outstanding for Tab & Button for sewing to greatcoats to enable flaps to be looped back. If these are fitted at this time of year most of the greatcoats will have been replaced by the Winter when the looping back is most required. Demand to be resubmitted in September. Drew Lewis Gun from Gun Park for 2nd Worcesters.	
"	4/6/17		The 2 Lamps Electric Signalling Field per Bn returned on issue of Lucas Signalling Lamps are required for 18th Corps Signalling School. Asked Signals to obtain 3rd Army authority as the G.R.O. orders the surplus Lamps to be returned to Base. 'Q' obtained this authority so 10 were handed over to O.C. Signal Coy. 8 extra Chaffcutters ~~allotted~~ as additional allotment off totals asked for in May. These machines are Army Stores, are must not be taken out of Army area on Div leaving latter.	

2449 Wt. W14957/M90 750,000 1/16 J.B.C. & A. Forms/C.2118/12.

Instructions regarding War Diaries and Intelligence Summaries are contained in F. S. Regs., Part II. and the Staff Manual respectively. Title Pages will be prepared in manuscript.

WAR DIARY
or
INTELLIGENCE SUMMARY

(Erase heading not required.)

Army Form C. 2118.

Place	Date	Hour	Summary of Events and Information	Remarks and references to Appendices
[illegible] (Wood)	5/6/17		Attended Conference at ADOS 7th Corps Office. DADOS of 14th, 18th, 50th, 21st Divn + OO 7th Corps Troops also attended. The scheme for supply of necessaries and small value thro' Divnl & EFC Canteen discussed & made quite clear by ADOS. Payment to be made by OC Canteens in similar manner to that laid down for issues of Ordnance Stores to Mess Officers on Payment vide GRO 498. Suggested that when attached units leave a Divn suddenly & the DADOS does not know to which formation they will be transferred he should send all outstanding indents direct to ADOS of the Corps who can communicate with Army & find out destination of moving units. This will avoid delay frequently caused by holding up indents by late formation whereas sufficient information is available at first. In order that the DADOS ~~[illegible]~~ receiving a new units from another formation may know what previous bulk issues have been made to them with a view to checking the new units demands the DADOS of the units late formation should send on a statement of the previous months (say) issues in the principle items of bulk to the new DADOS. The GRO laying down summer scale of clothing requires amendment as regards the instructions for issue of Cotton Drawers in replacement of Woollen Drawers as latter become "U". It is impossible for men to wear the latter during hot weather & there is no alternative but to replace the Woollen Drawers by Cotton even though the former may be serviceable. Various other matters discussed	

2449 Wt. W14957/M90 750,000 1/16 J.B.C. & A. Forms/C.2118/12.

Army Form C. 2118.

Instructions regarding War Diaries and Intelligence Summaries are contained in F. S. Regs., Part II. and the Staff Manual respectively. Title Pages will be prepared in manuscript.

WAR DIARY
or
INTELLIGENCE SUMMARY
(Erase heading not required.)

Place	Date	Hour	Summary of Events and Information	Remarks and references to Appendices
Adinfer Wood	5/6/17		including Gun Park scheme. Decided it ~~is~~ located too far back to be of any service as regards acceleration of issues in cases of urgency. I gave A.D.O.S. a paper giving my opinions & experience of various subjects of importance in Ordnance supply as far as the previous two months administration during heavy offensive action on part of the Division & suggesting desirable alterations with reasons for them.	
"	6/6/17		O.O. 1st Corps Troops ~~is~~ moving so his refitting stock of S.D. Clothing, Boots, puttees is available for issue to Division in reduction of their weekly demands on Base. Arranged with O.O. by ~~wire~~ & phone to take ~~S.D.~~ Boots, puttees & S.D. Clothing & wired totals required rather when requirements could be ascertained. This covers refitting of Division with Clothing.	
"	7/6/17		Great shortage of Service Colour Paint. Asked C.R.E. if any could be obtained from R.E. Park. Replied not available. A.D.O.S. 1st Corps suggested obtaining paint of various colours from Base & ~~ask~~ instruct units to paint camouflage effects on their vehicles in lieu of the Service Colour. This only feasible for R.A. units. Not desired by rest of Division. Hastened outstanding demand for S.C. Paint, specially. Decided D.A.D.O.S. of Divns must supply their Divnl Reinforcement Bns with the equipment & clothing required for drafts. This previously done by O.O. Corps Tps. Owing to distance of Depot Bn from Divn it will only be possible to send once a fortnight to them.	

2449 Wt. W14957/M90 750,000 1/16 J.B.C. & A. Forms/C.2118/12.

Instructions regarding War Diaries and Intelligence Summaries are contained in F. S. Regs., Part II. and the Staff Manual respectively. Title Pages will be prepared in manuscript.

WAR DIARY
or
INTELLIGENCE SUMMARY
(Erase heading not required.)

Army Form C. 2118.

Place	Date	Hour	Summary of Events and Information	Remarks and references to Appendices
A Hooper Wood	8/6/17		Supplied 00 7th Corps Troops with 150 serviceable Rifles & Bayonets from Armourer's shop under instructions from A.D.O.S. 7th Corps. 100 set aside for Depot Bn to be sent first opportunity. All attached R.A. units have been completed to new scale of 36 per Battery. Not now necessary to accumulate rifles. All surplus to 100 for reserve can be sent to Base. 3 cwt Steel Helmet paint received & issued on scale of 28 lbs per Bn. 3 cwt Stone Colour Paint also received as first issue off total outstanding. Marked up indents to this total & informed Base of indents completed or reduced. Saw Staff Capts of 3 Bdes. No complaints & equipment of all units satisfactory. Bde being completed most [illegible] demands [illegible] as result of [illegible]	
"	9/6/17		Demanded 1 Lewis Gun for 1st Queens to replace one condemned for wear by Armourer. This gun could not be repaired as all working parts were badly worn. 3 Chaff cutters advised as awaiting collection by me from 00 7th Corps Tps. This is first issue of allotment of 8 to this Div. Issued 1 per Brigade. Bdes detailing unit to which machine is to be issued.	
"	10/6/17		~~A further supply of Steel Helmet paint reqd. Demanded & cut by wire.~~ Reviewed 1st Middlesex (Pioneers) issues of S.D. clothing for last 3 months as it was thought this unit's demands have been excessive compared with other Bns. On comparison with the weekly average issue of an Infantry Bn it was found that the Pioneers average weekly issue was ~~only~~ greater in the same proportion as their strength is greater than that of the average Bn & taking into account the greater wear & tear of pioneer work this unit's demands are not excessive. Visited Gun Park at [illegible] & drew Lewis Gun for 1st Queens & also some L.G. parts required by 2nd A & S Highlanders to put a Lewis Gun in action.	

2449 Wt. W14957/M90 750,000 1/16 J.B.C. & A. Forms/C.2118/12.

Instructions regarding War Diaries and Intelligence Summaries are contained in F. S. Regs., Part II. and the Staff Manual respectively. Title Pages will be prepared in manuscript.

WAR DIARY
or
INTELLIGENCE SUMMARY
(Erase heading not required.)

Army Form C. 2118.

Place	Date	Hour	Summary of Events and Information	Remarks and references to Appendices
Adinfer Wood	11/6/17		Under instructions from 7th Corps all tentage in charge of 'C' Artillery Camp Hendecourt is to be taken over from 14th Divn by this Divn. Accordingly visited Town Major Hendecourt, checked all huts in 'C' Camp & gave receipt for 75 Tents. E.S.L. & 30 Trench Shelters. Copy of receipt sent to 7th Corps. Unable to obtain sufficient returned & salvage Boots for repair in Divl Shop. Wired 7th Corps for location of any Dumps where they could be obtained. Replied - none available anywhere. 'Q' issued an order that units must return all Boots beyond their own repair to enable Divl Shop to carry on. Obtained 200 yards more Butter Muslin from 7th Corps Troops. This quantity already issued to Corps San Sec administering this Divn but direct issue made owing to urgency of our requirements. Drew up programme for handing in 1st Blanket & same issued by 'Q' to all formations. Units allowed to retain 25% if desired.	
" "	12/6/17		32nd Divl Employment Coy now designated 230th Employment Coy. All concerned notified. Blankets received from one Brigade at refilling point to-day. Arrange for 5 Trucks at Railhead for despatch of all Blankets after conditioning & surveying. On reviewing outstanding indents for Lewis & Vickers Guns found a considerable number of old indents. As many of the guns for which components are outstanding have been lost & replaced by new guns it follows that these old demands should be cancelled. Cancelled all indents for Lewis gun parts both at Base & at Gun Park prior to 31st May in date. Cancelled all indents for Vickers Gun Parts prior to 15th May in date, the latter date being chosen in conformity with Gun Park scheme of consolidated demands on Base. Notified all units & action	

Army Form C. 2118.

Instructions regarding War Diaries and Intelligence Summaries are contained in F. S. Regs., Part II. and the Staff Manual respectively. Title Pages will be prepared in manuscript.

WAR DIARY
or
INTELLIGENCE SUMMARY
(Erase heading not required.)

Place	Date	Hour	Summary of Events and Information	Remarks and references to Appendices
			taken & instructed them to take careful stock of their present establishment & to indent to complete as soon as possible	
Ridufer Wood	13/6/17.		A further supply of paint for Steel Helmets required. Demanded 4 cwt by urgent wire. ~~Salvage mess tins with [illegible] [illegible] & [illegible]~~	
" "	14/6/17.		Visited Doullens for Local Purchase. Visited Staff Captain 100th Bde & discussed situation as regards supply of Ordnance to the Bde. Very few important items outstanding. Handed over to Chief Clerk who will act as D.A.D.O.S. when Capt Bearan is on leave.	
" "	15/6/17.		Capt. Bearan D.A.D.O.S proceeded on leave to England. Division going into line again on 20th inst. Situation as regards important technical stores required when in line reviewed with A.D.O.S.	
" "	16/6/17.		Made Local Purchase of 20 Electric Torches & issued to 19th Bde for raid. Hastened Steel helmet Paint from Base. also hastened 1" Very Pistols outstanding.	
" "	17/6/17.		General Routine work. Made further purchase of 9 Torches & 20 refills	
" "	18/6/17		General Routine work.	
Hamelincourt	19/6/17.		Divn moved into forward area. Store remains at Boisleux au-Mont. Moved office to Div HQ, Hamelincourt.	

2449 Wt. W14957/M90 750,000 1/16 J.B.C. & A. Forms/C.2118/12.

Instructions regarding War Diaries and Intelligence Summaries are contained in F. S. Regs., Part II. and the Staff Manual respectively. Title Pages will be prepared in manuscript.

WAR DIARY
or
INTELLIGENCE SUMMARY
(Erase heading not required.)

Army Form C. 2118.

Place	Date	Hour	Summary of Events and Information	Remarks and references to Appendices
Hamelincourt	20/6/17		Instructions received from Ordnance 3rd Army that in future all demands for stores in sections 14 to 18 less 16B for items of Havre supply would be sent to Calais Depot & all outstanding demands have been transferred. Also all demands for guns & carriages are to be sent to Calais & not to Gun Park. All outstanding demands transferred from Gun Park to Calais. Divn require 4 Anti-aircraft mountings for Lewis guns. 7th Corps asked to supply but none available. Matter taken up by "C" Office with 3rd Army H.Q.	
"	~~21/6/17~~			
	21/6/17.		Demanded 50 Electric Torches from Base. Local pattern torch being expensive & of very inferior ~~value~~ quality. Drew 1 Soyers Stove from O.O. 7th Corps Troops for Canteens for tea-making while Divn is in line.	
"	22/6/17.		33rd Div Arty less H.Q. RA (already with 33rd Divn) moved from 21st Divn to 33rd Divn. They were transferred to 21st Divn by 56th Divn on 20th inst on leaving 6th Corps area. Demanded 8, 1½ tons [illegible] to meet urgent demands	

2449 Wt. W14957/M90 750,000 1/16 J.B.C. & A. Forms/C.2118/12.

Army Form C. 2118.

WAR DIARY
or
INTELLIGENCE SUMMARY
(Erase heading not required.)

Instructions regarding War Diaries and Intelligence Summaries are contained in F. S. Regs., Part II. and the Staff Manual respectively. Title Pages will be prepared in manuscript.

Place	Date	Hour	Summary of Events and Information	Remarks and references to Appendices
Hamelincourt	23/6/17		R.A. indents reviewed with a view to checking if ~~all~~ provision had been made when in 6th Corps for various issues of special stores authorised by GROs & 3rd Army letters etc since 33rd RA left this Division.	
"	24/6/17		Bulk stores handed over & delivered to my store by 56th Div for 33rd RA units. No outstanding bulk demands transferred. Any further bulk for which 56th Divn have made provision will be sent to us when received by former Divn.	
"	25/6/17		General Routine Work.	
"	26/6/17		33rd RA not yet issued with Rupper Sponge Anti-gas goggles. ADOS having ordered the return of 2500 [illegible] surplus to our Divl requirements a fortnight earlier we have none available to meet the RA requirements namely 2500. Wired ADOS asking if these 2500 could be re drawn. Replied not now available. Demanded from Base.	
"	27/6/17		Notified by G move of Divn to Back area (Divl HQ Courcelles) would take place from 1st to 4th inst. My store to be moved on last named date. Accordingly suspended all issues from 3 Bases after 29th inst as I cannot receive stores after 1st at Railhead. All issues to units to close after 29th except to RA units who are remaining in forward area.	

2449 Wt. W14957/M90 750,000 1/16 J.B.C. & A. Forms/C.2118/12.

Instructions regarding War Diaries and Intelligence Summaries are contained in F. S. Regs., Part II. and the Staff Manual respectively. Title Pages will be prepared in manuscript.

WAR DIARY
or
INTELLIGENCE SUMMARY
(Erase heading not required.)

Army Form C. 2118.

Place	Date	Hour	Summary of Events and Information	Remarks and references to Appendices
Hanebeaut	28/7/16		Took stock of Reserves. - Antigas appliances - wire cutters, oil grease dubbin, flannelette, Torches, Yukon Packs, [illegible] - Bayonet fighting sacks & dummy grenades for training purposes in back area.	
			ADOS visited Store & ordered SA & 14" wirecutters to be returned to OO 7th Corps Troops before moving as these were allotted by 7th Corps originally for special operations. Asked for decision from AA & QMG before complying with this order. Yukon packs tried by Bdes but there is not sufficient time to properly test them before moving. They must therefore be taken to back area. 7th Corps issued instructions by CRO that DADOS OS of Divn are now responsible for all tentage records & an AOC representative must be present at all handing over or taking over of tentage.	
" "	29/7/16		Wrote RTO Bertleux asking for 2 Trucks to be allotted to me on 2nd Inst for loading up with all Stock & reserves not urgently required which I can not carry on my 4 lorries in addition to essential reserves & Officer Store Equipment, personnel etc. Sent 13 empty Strombos Horn Air Cylinders handed in by Bdes & DGO to me to 3rd Army Heavy Mobile Workshop & obtained 13 filled Cylinders in exchange which I handed over to DADOS 21st Divn who is taking over forward area to be vacated by 33rd Divn. Obtained Statement of tentage in possession of Divn from Q for purposes of return due on 30th to 7th Corps. After this all tentage will be issued through me & records kept by me of disposal. List of outstanding Guns (18 pdrs) to 33rd HA units passed to me by 56th DADOS via 21st DADOS shews 5 guns outstanding between 1 week & 1 fortnight. Wired Coolalas asking if any of these	

2449 Wt. W14957/M90 750,000 1/16 J.B.C. & A. Forms/C.2118/12.

Army Form C. 2118.

Instructions regarding War Diaries and Intelligence Summaries are contained in F. S. Regs., Part II. and the Staff Manual respectively. Title Pages will be prepared in manuscript.

WAR DIARY
or
INTELLIGENCE SUMMARY
(Erase heading not required.)

Place	Date	Hour	Summary of Events and Information	Remarks and references to Appendices
			had been issued by him. Replied - none yet issued. Informed Staff Capt. RA accordingly.	
Hamelincourt	30/6/17.		Transferred 33rd Div Arty including H.Q. RA & 'B' Echelon D.A.C. to DADOS 21st Divn & passed to him a statement of bulk already demanded & to be demanded by him. To avoid delay in issue to RA units arranged Base to transfer a certain proportion of Bulk already demanded by me (these demands including RA requirements) to DADOS 21st Divn & delete from my wire. This latter will be able to issue to 33rd RA units on usual days of issue. Arranged for 33rd RA units to continue to draw from me till 2nd inst to enable me to issue all RA stores in my store before moving to back area. Any stores received by me in back area for 33rd RA will be moved over to DADOS 21st Divn. Handed over all outstanding detail with list of guns still due to Batteries. Ordered Armourers & Shoemakers Shops to close down & pack up ready for loading in trucks on 2nd. Quantity of packsaddlery surplus to 175 sets to be reclaimed by 'B' Echelon DAC returned to me for handing over to O.O. 7th Corps Troops.	

A.W.S. Bevan Capt
DADOS 33rd Div

2449 Wt. W14957/M90 750,000 1/16 J.B.C. & A. Forms/C.2118/12.

Instructions regarding War Diaries and Intelligence Summaries are contained in F. S. Regs., Part II. and the Staff Manual respectively. Title Pages will be prepared in manuscript.

WAR DIARY
or
INTELLIGENCE SUMMARY
(Erase heading not required.)

D.A.D.O.S 53rd Div

SECRET.

July 1917

Vol 21

Army Form C. 2118.

Place	Date	Hour	Summary of Events and Information	Remarks and references to Appendices
Office & ~~Armentieres~~ Stores - Boisleux-au-mont.	1/7/17		Moved office ~~with Div H.Q.~~ to stores at Boisleux. Not worth while moving to Adinfer with Div H.Q. as latter move to Back Area on 3rd inst while office & stores do not move till 4th. D.A.D.O.S remains with Div H.Q. in order to be in touch with "Q" throughout the move. Sent surplus Packsaddlery (all sets incomplete) to O.O. 7th Corps Troops. A.D.O.S 7th Corps complained that Packsaddlery was not made up into sets but sent loose. Impossible to make any complete sets owing to number of deficiencies in components. Obtained authority from A.A. & Q.M.G. to send all SA & 12" Wirecutters back to 7th Corps. Yukon packs to be taken to back area & not sent to Base as not required by Division. G.O.C. wishes all units to paint their vehicles without delay. Wired Base to complete all outstanding demands (1400lbs) Paint S.C. by next truck.	
" "	2/7/17		Loaded 2 trucks at Railhead with all reserves, instructional Stores, & Marquees (except expendable reserves which may be required for immediate issue) Armourers & Shoemakers shops & had these trucks labelled to new 53rd Div's Railhead & despatched. They should arrive at final Railhead in back area on 5th. The Division will use an intermediate Railhead on 3rd & 4th but trucks should normally be retained at Regulating Station sufficient time to avoid arriving at the latter Railhead. Sent lorry to Saulty a brokendown travelling kitchen belonging to 2 A & S.H. & handed vehicle over to R.O.O. for despatch to Base. Demand body, W.T. to replace. [illegible] Obtained information from "Q" as to location of Tentages to be handed over to 48th Div & time the latter's representative would be available to take over. Sent an A.O.C. man to Monchy (19th Bde late H.Q.) to check handing over & to obtain a receipt. The remaining tentage at Basseux to be taken over by 48th Div on 3rd, arrange for A.O.C. man to attend at fixed hour. Reported quantities handed over to A.D.O.S 7th Corps.	

2449 Wt. W14957/M90 750,000 1/16 J.B.C. & A. Forms/C.2118/12.

Army Form C. 2118.

Instructions regarding War Diaries and Intelligence Summaries are contained in F. S. Regs., Part II. and the Staff Manual respectively. Title Pages will be prepared in manuscript.

WAR DIARY
or
INTELLIGENCE SUMMARY
(Erase heading not required.)

Place	Date	Hour	Summary of Events and Information	Remarks and references to Appendices
Office & Store Boisleux-au-Mont.	3/7/17.		Moved with Div H.Q. ('A' Echelon) to Villers Bocage. Store & office remain at Boisleux to-day & move direct to final Div H.Q. at Carillon on 4th. Sent 2 lorries to Div H.Q. for transporting packs of a Battalion to end of their first day's march. Lorries returned at 7 p.m. in evening all 4 lorries ready for road on morning of 4th. Sent a wire to R.O. Belle Eglise to reconsign any trucks arriving there for me as I cannot clear owing to move. Division now administered directly by 3rd Army – not being in any Corps. All returns to be sent to D.D.O.S. direct.	
Carillon	4/7/17.		Moved in advance of Div H.Q. to Carillon. Inspected office & store, arranged site for marquee for armourers shop & allotted portions of store to Bde W.O.s – Anti-gas reserves – Boot shop & Salvage & Reserve stores. All personnel with remaining stores, office equipment & reserves arrived by lorry 6 p.m. Armourers Marquee erected.	
" "	5/7/17.		Div H.Q. arrived at Carillon. No trucks at Railhead. R.T.O. at Railhead SALEUX asked to take up matter of non-arrival of the 2 trucks despatched from Boisleux with Romer lamps. Armourers & Shoemakers cannot commence work owing to non-arrival of their tools etc in these 2 trucks. General routine work in office & stores.	

2449 Wt. W14957/M90 750,000 1/16 J.B.C. & A. Forms/C.2118/12.

Army Form C. 2118.

Instructions regarding War Diaries and Intelligence Summaries are contained in F. S. Regs., Part II. and the Staff Manual respectively. Title Pages will be prepared in manuscript.

WAR DIARY
or
INTELLIGENCE SUMMARY
(Erase heading not required.)

Place	Date	Hour	Summary of Events and Information	Remarks and references to Appendices
Cavillon.	6/7/17.		Arranged programme for taking in Lewis & Vickers Guns for overhaul into Divl Armourers Shop, commencing with 19th Bde. First lot to be handed in on 7th. Programme arranged for 4 Lewis from each Bn throughout the Divn (except Pioneers) & 4 Vickers from each M.G. Coy. Ten guns (8 Lewis & 2 Vickers) can be taken in one day, overhauled & repaired & returned to units the next day by [illegible]. 750 lbs S.C. Paint recd from Base in response to hastener. Distribution made accordingly to all units with transport to enable all to commence painting at once. Arranged refilling points for 19th & 98th Bdes owing to their units being located a considerable distance from my store. 100th Bde units are comparatively close so can draw direct from my store. Refilling for 19th commences on 7th & continue on 9th, 11th & so on. – for 98th commences on 8th & continues 10th, 12th & so on. Ten ton Pickeling Gear oil & grease & horseshoes, also 43 wheels & large quantity of detail received. This large issue is due to issues being suspended from 30th ultimo till 4th inst at Base. The two tracks have not yet arrived. Wired Romescamps to trace & forward to my Railhead at once. Balance of approx 800 lbs of Service Colour paint is required at latest by 9th inst. Wired COO & arranged asking if [illegible] of this amount, completing all outstanding demand could be made to arrive 9th. COO replied none would be made [illegible].	Question of [illegible] taken up with Q. Arranged for 12 Sayers Stoves off Divl Scale of 60. 40% [illegible] & 50 Latrine buckets.

2349 Wt. W14957/M90 750,000 1/16 J.B.C. & A. Forms/C.2118/12.

Instructions regarding War Diaries and Intelligence Summaries are contained in F. S. Regs., Part II. and the Staff Manual respectively. Title Pages will be prepared in manuscript.

WAR DIARY
or
INTELLIGENCE SUMMARY
(Erase heading not required.)

Army Form C. 2118.

Place	Date	Hour	Summary of Events and Information	Remarks and references to Appendices
Carillon.	7/7/17.		collected 1 Lewis Gun for 5th Scottish from 3rd Army Gun Park No 1 who were just about to [illegible] 10 Tons Clothing & necessaries received from Rouen — includes 5000 shirts for Clothing Exchange. A truck per AM70 from Abbeville with 1400 Pt helmets. No sign of the two trucks yet. Delay is very serious as Armourers cannot commence overhaul of Machine guns etc. Received wire from No 8 Ord: Depot Abbeville that these trucks had arrived there & asking for disposal. Wired him to reconsign at once to Saleux. Visited RTO Amiens but no trace of the trucks there. Went on to Saleux & asked R.T.O to take up with Abbeville. Talked to R.T.O Romescamps on phone. He has not yet received the trucks from Abbeville but will forward them to Saleux immediately on receipt. Sent priority wire to Romescamps & Abbeville asking for information concerning these trucks & urging reconsignment. Notified by Abbeville trucks being reconsigned this evening. Delay due to no train being available for 2 days. General Routine work. Cancelled one German Machine Gun ordemand from Base as one has been allotted to the Div from 4th Corps School BOVES by 3rd Army.	[illegible] received after closing [illegible]. Pt helmets received
	8/7/17		Demanded one 3" Mortar for 150th T.M.B to replace one rendered unserviceable by shell fire & returned to salvage. In reply to wire from Q, 3rd Army wires that nearest Mobile Ordnance workshop for repair of vehicles of this Division is at Albert. As vehicles cannot be sent by road this distance I asked "Q" to apply to 3rd Army for authority to send vehicle by Rail to D.M.W. for repair & return to Divnl Railhead when repaired.	

2449 Wt. W14957/M90 750,000 1/16 J.B.C. & A. Forms/C.2118/12.

Instructions regarding War Diaries and Intelligence Summaries are contained in F. S. Regs., Part II. and the Staff Manual respectively. Title Pages will be prepared in manuscript.

WAR DIARY
or
INTELLIGENCE SUMMARY
(Erase heading not required.)

Army Form C. 2118.

Place	Date	Hour	Summary of Events and Information	Remarks and references to Appendices
			~~850 lbs paint received in completion of allotment~~ Distribution again made evenly	to all units in proportion to their transport. This makes 1500 lbs issued within 8 days.
Carillon	9/7/17		The 2 trucks containing reserves & Shop equipment received & offloaded. Armourers shop set up & work commenced on guns ~~found~~ requiring overhaul. All spares had previously been checked & deficiencies noted & condition of guns noted so that repairs could be commenced immediately the shop equipment arrived. Shoemakers shop opened. Prepared a statement of total issues of underclothing to Divn via Clothing Exchange & direct issues to units, since January 1st 1917 to date. This is required by A A & QMG to ascertain how many complete renewals of underclothing a/the man have been made during the period. Compared total issues with receipts of unserviceable returned to Base over same period. The difference between the two totals in each item should approximate to present stock in clothing exchange. This was found to be the case, so no losses have occurred, ~~&~~ & hence no waste. Received 50 latrine buckets + 12 Soyers Stoves from Base. Distribution obtained from "Q".	
	10/7/17		Hastened issue of 3000 Cartridge Dummy Drill urgently required for training purposes. Demanded a further 12,000 on 3rd Army authority obtained by "Q" & "G". Collected 2 Strong tents from COO Abbeville on loan to Divn for Horseshow. ... could not obtain any washing basins 3½ gall. from COO Abbeville for use at the Horse Show.	

Army Form C. 2118.

Instructions regarding War Diaries and Intelligence Summaries are contained in F. S. Regs., Part II. and the Staff Manual respectively. Title Pages will be prepared in manuscript.

WAR DIARY
or
INTELLIGENCE SUMMARY
(Erase heading not required.)

Place	Date	Hour	Summary of Events and Information	Remarks and references to Appendices
Carllon	11/7/17		One lot of Bayonet fighting gear received. 700 Sacks have been issued 300 are in store awaiting issue. Demanded another 400 to complete requirements. Base report no Cartridge Dummy Drill available at present. Informed "Q".	
	12/7/17.		General routine work.	
	13/7/17.		Collected a German Machine Gun from 4th Corps School at AUXI-S. Issued it complete with belt & belt box to 19th Bde on instructions from "Q". Bought Red, white & black paint 25 kilos of each sort for issue to Bde for Signboards, targets & gym methods. C.R.E. could not obtained from R.E. depot in back areas. Obtained sole authority for the purchase. "Q" order the withdrawal & return to Base of all thick woollen drawers & replacement by thin cotton owing to the weather conditions. Demanded 10,000 pr Cotton Drawers by wire. Also demanded 5000 Shirts & 5000 socks to maintain stock in clothing exchange.	
	14/7/17		Base sent large quantity of stores (horse-shoes &c) for 33rd Div Arty units in our truck instead of 21st Div truck. Reconsigned these stores at once to D.A.D.O.S. 21st Divn.	

2449 Wt. W14957/M90 750,000 1/16 J.B.C. & A. Forms/C.2118/12.

Army Form C. 2118.

Instructions regarding War Diaries and Intelligence Summaries are contained in F. S. Regs., Part II. and the Staff Manual respectively. Title Pages will be prepared in manuscript.

WAR DIARY
or
INTELLIGENCE SUMMARY

(Erase heading not required.)

Place	Date	Hour	Summary of Events and Information	Remarks and references to Appendices
Carillon.	14/7/17		Collected 14 Soyers stoves from Hun Dump at Bapaume on 3rd Army authority. Issued these to Brigades for forming baths for troops. Large number of wheels of all natures have been asked by [illegible] of units [illegible] demands during last week. 3 + 1 artificers with a small number of tools & equipment arrived by lorry from 3rd Army Heavy Mobile Workshop to form a local ordnance repair shop for vehicles owing to distance of Heavy Mobile shop from Div[l] area. Fixed up [illegible] for shop & instructed units to send in vehicles for repair. Arranged with Q to notify units direct when more vehicles could be taken in. Opened record book shewing unit, vehicle sent in, repairs required, when repairs commenced & when finished.	
	15/7/17		Wired A.O.W.W. asking if they could supply timber, rivets, wood plate etc. (in quantity required for repair of vehicles.) Replied that they could supply limited quantities. Sent lorry to Albert to collect lots of material required. Also sent an NCO from 20th [illegible] to be tested as an Armourer at A.H.Q. in accordance with instructions from O/C A.O.C. Records 3rd Echelon G.H.Q.	
	16/7/17.		General Routine work.	
	17/7/17		} Div[l] Horse Show held. Suspended all issues by order of Q for these days. Sent a party each day from Detachment & attached personnel to see the Show.	
	18/7/17			

Instructions regarding War Diaries and Intelligence Summaries are contained in F. S. Regs., Part II. and the Staff Manual respectively. Title Pages will be prepared in manuscript.

WAR DIARY
or
INTELLIGENCE SUMMARY
(Erase heading not required.)

Army Form C. 2118.

Place	Date	Hour	Summary of Events and Information	Remarks and references to Appendices
Cavillon	19/7/17		Visited Amiens for local purchase. 13 Soyer Stoves out of 14 issued, returned from Horse Show ground. Issued these to Bdes a scale of 4 per Bde extra to original allotment of first 12 stoves. Arranged with O.C. Train to collect five Stove tents from Show ground after checking for completeness & conveyance to Abbeville. 2 are to be returned to C.O.O. Abbeville & 3 to Australian General Hospital. No wheels sent in for repair by 98th Bde ~~also~~ although latter were warned on 18th to send in 2 wheels this morning. Owing to this there has been no work in the shop to-day & valuable time has been wasted. Reported this to 'Q' who warned Bde to send in wheels 20th inst without fail. The 3 wheels completed on 18th inst have been removed by units owning them.	
" "	20/7/17		Sent the five Stove tents by lorry to Abbeville. 5 wheels sent into shop by 2nd Worcesters & Pioneers, for repair. Owing to lack of material & screw cutting apparatus, artificers are unable to carry out necessary repairs to water carts [illegible] must take the parts requiring replacement to Ordnance Workshop at Abbeville tomorrow & get them to make the new ones.	

2449 Wt. W14957/M90 750,000 1/16 J.B.C. & A. Forms/C.2118/12.

Army Form C. 2118.

Instructions regarding War Diaries and Intelligence Summaries are contained in F. S. Regs., Part II. and the Staff Manual respectively. Title Pages will be prepared in manuscript.

WAR DIARY
or
INTELLIGENCE SUMMARY
(Erase heading not required.)

Place	Date	Hour	Summary of Events and Information	Remarks and references to Appendices
CAVILLON	21/7/17		list to Appendix & handed in to Ordnance components for repair in the Mobile workshops to be ready for collection 24th inst. 212 Field Coy moved north in advance of the Divn. "Q" inform me they have gone to XV Corps so wired ADOS 15th Corps for information as to which Division this Fd. Coy was attached. [illegible] 66th Divn. Moved next to 66th Div [illegible] way. There is time for overhauling arms & [illegible] & 4 Lewis per Battalion & M.G. Coy in one Brigade. Wired 19th Bde to arrange programme commencing today 2.30 pm & lasting till 25th inst when all guns taken to workshops have been repaired & returned to units.	
	22/7/17.		New M.G. Coy joined Div. to complete establishment of 4. No 248 from England. Issued usual move orders. Saw an officer of the Coy. & explained to him system of [illegible] scale etc also sent him a list of special stores with scale & authorities for demand & which he may not be in possession in which case I instructed him to submit indents accordingly. Numerous issues to Canteen & [illegible] notified for publication of this information in D.R.O.s [illegible] to 2nd Army for disposal of outstanding [illegible] 33rd Div [illegible]	
	23/7/17		[illegible]	

Instructions regarding War Diaries and Intelligence Summaries are contained in F. S. Regs., Part II. and the Staff Manual respectively. Title Pages will be prepared in manuscript.

WAR DIARY
or
INTELLIGENCE SUMMARY
(Erase heading not required.)

Army Form C. 2118.

Place	Date	Hour	Summary of Events and Information	Remarks and references to Appendices
	23/7/17.		Both Bases have despatched my stores in trucks for 21st & 50th Divs whom I wired latter for location of Dump or Railhead or to arrange me to collect stores by lorry.	
Candas	24/7/17.		Went to Abbeville ~~[illegible]~~ & collected the repaired watercart parts. This will enable 2 watercarts to be finished off. General Routine work. 21st Div wired 2 tons equipment recd for me. I wired 3rd Army HQ to direct my lorry in morning to return via 21st Div Dump & pick up this equipment. 50th Div wired stores not yet received. Lorry was sent to St Pol for tools or material for artificers & also for stores from Gun Park.	
	25/7/17.		→ General Routine work. Saw Q re preparations for moving North. Div commences to entrain on 31st inst. No stores at Railhead can be accepted after 29th inst till conclusion of move.	
	26/7/17		Suspended issues from 3 Bases, Havre, Rouen & Calais after 27th at Bases 29th at Railhead. Reviewed outstanding detail indents of 98th & 100th Brigades. Very few items outstanding – mainly wagon parts. Technical stores practically complete.	
	27/7/17.		Ord 3rd Army wired Bases & Gun Park to suspend issues from 28th inst & transfer all indents to Ord CALAIS. I am to notify latter when I am prepared to receive stores. Wired Gun Park asking if all available stores offering indents could be set aside for collection by me on 29th before moving as all M.G. parts are urgently required to complete unit equipment.	

2449 Wt. W14957/M90 750,000 1/16 J.B.C. & A. Forms/C.2118/12.

Instructions regarding War Diaries and Intelligence Summaries are contained in F. S. Regs., Part II. and the Staff Manual respectively. Title Pages will be prepared in manuscript.

WAR DIARY
or
INTELLIGENCE SUMMARY

(Erase heading not required.)

Army Form C. 2118.

Place	Date	Hour	Summary of Events and Information	Remarks and references to Appendices
~~[illegible]~~ Cardlin	28/7/17		Last refilling for 19th & 98th Bdes 29th inst. Fixed up special refilling 29th for 98th Bde at 2.30 p.m. Wired ~~[illegible]~~ 3 Brigades & Pioneers that last day for receiving Salvage would be 30th inst. Lamps to Machine Guns of 98th Bde received to-day will be ready for return at refilling point tomorrow.	
" "	29/7/17		Saw AA & QMG, who has just returned from reconnaisance of new area ~~[illegible]~~ between Dunkerque & Nieuport & obtained location of Div H.Q. & Brigade areas. Fixed up suitable Ordnance refilling points at 2 places. One for 19 & 98 Bde together & one for 100th Bde & Pioneers. My store, office & [illegible] will be at Div H.Q. at Rosendael near Dunkerque. Arranged to move with 4 lorries on 1st. Journey to be done in 1 day if possible. I move by car on 31st to make necessary arrangements before stores & personnel arrive on 1st. Visited [illegible] & ordered manufacture of 400 Black & Green armbands for all Sgts NCOs in Div. Will be paid for out of Canteen Funds. Saw RTO Saleux & arranged for a truck to be allotted to me for loading on 31st for consignment to new Railhead at Dunkerque	

2449 Wt. W14957/M90 750,000 1/16 J.B.C. & A. Forms/C.2118/12.

Instructions regarding War Diaries and Intelligence Summaries are contained in F. S. Regs., Part II. and the Staff Manual respectively. Title Pages will be prepared in manuscript.

WAR DIARY
or
INTELLIGENCE SUMMARY
(Erase heading not required.)

Army Form C. 2118.

Place	Date	Hour	Summary of Events and Information	Remarks and references to Appendices
Carillon	30/7/17		Made all arrangements for moving on 1st. Shoemakers & part of Salvage personnel to entrain with D.D.S. & Q on 31st to save space in my 4 lorries. All anti-gas reserves & [illegible] by lorry to avoid risk of delay in reclaiming them at other end. Arranged to load all surplus stores, [illegible] packs, stock & equipment of both Armourers & Shoemakers shop in truck morning of 31st. Two men being sent in truck as conveymen & to make enquiries in case of delay en route. Sent 5 Artificers with tools & surplus material back to 3rd Army H.Q. w. by lorry. Lorry also took 2 store tents to be delivered to O.O. 7th Corps troops on return journey. All stores awaiting issue at Sunpark to be collected. Sent an N.C.O. to Amiens to take stock of the Area (Ordnance) store collected & dumped at Detail Camp by 33rd Supply Column yesterday. Sent [illegible]	
"	31/7/17		Moved by car to Dunkerque. Truck loaded at Railhead as arranged & despatched to Dunkerque. 4 lorries loaded to-night ready for starting first thing on 1st.	

2449 Wt. W14957/M90 750,000 1/16 J.B.C. & A. Forms/C.2118/12.

D.A.D.O.S. 33rd Div. 31/7/17.

[illegible] Capt. D.A.D.O.S.

Army Form C. 2118.

22

SECRET

August 1917 D.A.D.O.S. 33rd Div.

WAR DIARY
or
INTELLIGENCE SUMMARY

(Erase heading not required.)

Instructions regarding War Diaries and Intelligence Summaries are contained in F. S. Regs., Part II, and the Staff Manual respectively. Title Pages will be prepared in manuscript.

Place	Date	Hour	Summary of Events and Information	Remarks and references to Appendices
La Panne Plags. Belgium La Panne Ville	1/8/17		Saw ADOS XV Corps re Area Stores to be issued to the Division in new area. Ammunition Carriers 18pdr & 4.5" have already been issued to 33rd Div Arty by 66th Div to whom they are attached. Div to be completed to 300 sets Packsaddlery (175 sets brought into Corps area from 3rd Army) 150 sets Texas Packs for Rations & 300 sets Water Tin Carriers. Area Commandants are responsible for Tentage in Corps area.	
			Railhead – Coudekerque Branch Dunkerque for next few days. Went to Dunkerque & left message with R.T.O. giving destination to which my 4 lorries were to proceed on arrival at Dunkerque. Saw Area Commandant as to my requirements for a Store, Shops etc. Was allotted the Concert Hall La Panne Ville which is large enough for Store, Armourers & Shoemakers Shops.	
"	2/8/17		4 Lorries with personnel etc arrived about 2 p.m. Store & Shops arranged & opened & billets for personnel. Wired Base to reopen issues. Only a portion of Units have yet arrived in the area.	
"	3/8/17		Went to Docks Station Dunkerque & found that the Truck loaded & despatched from Saleux on 31st ult. had arrived & was in the French yard. DADRT agreed to shunt it so as to be available for clearing by lorry in afternoon. 4 Lorries sent to clear 2 p.m. Arranged with R.O.O. Coudekerque to advise me daily of arrival of Trucks to avoid sending lorries 12 miles out & 12 miles back needlessly.	
"	4/8/17		Demanded 20,000 Extension Pieces for S.B. Respirators on 4th ARO recently published. ADOS notified me he has arranged for the manufacture of 900 special Sacks for 300 sets of Texas Packs being issued to 33rd & 32nd Divs (150 sets each) by Chef d'Intendance at Dunkerque. The necessary Canvas to be drawn by me from "French" R.E. Dump Coxyde & sent by lorry to Habillement & Campement 63 Rue Soubise Dunkerque as soon as possible. Owing to delay in the R.E. obtaining the Canvas this will have to be held up for a few days. Arranged Bde refilling as follows – 100th Bde at Skyvelde on every other even day 19th Bde at Bray Dunes every other odd day. 98th being in La Panne can draw direct. Same applies to Pioneers. ADOS notifies me 125 sets Packsaddlery are available at O.O. XV Corps Troops. The Horse Rugs & cordage for the Texas packs received from Base without indent.	

2449 Wt. W14957/M90 750,000 1/16 J.B.C. & A. Forms/C.2118/12.

Instructions regarding War Diaries and Intelligence Summaries are contained in F. S. Regs., Part II. and the Staff Manual respectively. Title Pages will be prepared in manuscript.

WAR DIARY
or
INTELLIGENCE SUMMARY

(Erase heading not required.)

Army Form C. 2118.

Place	Date	Hour	Summary of Events and Information	Remarks and references to Appendices
La Panne Plage / La Panne Ville	5/8/17		As 66th Div. Ordnance Store is [illegible] to mine it is more convenient to get my own Artillery re transferred to me from 66th Div than to send necessary personnel to assist 66th D.A.D.O.S as previously arranged. Asked A.D.O.S. asking if 33rd Divl Arty could be retransferred. He replied "Yes". 66th Div accordingly moved the whole formation back to me. Demanded 600 Latrine Buckets & 600 Washing Basins 3½ gallon as area stores – the number in the area not being sufficient for 4 Divisions. Fixed up a Salvage & Area Store Dumps near stores. Collected Hedging Stores from C.E. XV Corps, wire cutters, Yukon Packs, Pack saddlery S.S. etc. from O.O. XV Corps Troops. Drew 14 Chaffcutters from O.O. XV Corps Tps. 7 already in Possession of R.A & Divl Train. Asked Q for distribution.	Ropes head for water tin carriers.
" "	6/8/17		List of Local Purchases for as long a period as possible required by Army for information of French Intendance. Sent in a list since ~~January~~ August 1916 to A.D.O.S. This return will also be required monthly in future. 33rd Div Arty are deficient of 6 18 pdr Guns (piece only) & have been so for over two months as the Guns were not available while in 3rd Army area. Reported deficiencies by wire to A.D.O.S & hastened the outstanding indent at Calais. The sixth gun for B/156 was never demanded apparently by other Division to which R.A were attached at the time ~~of it~~. Found out from D.O.S. VI Corps that the gun was sentenced to be exchanged as having life of less than 1000 rounds. A.D.O.S informed me the Q.M.G's authority under which gun was sentenced. Demanded replacement quoting the authority which D.D.O.S queried. I have put matter in hands of A.D.O.S XV Corps who obtained the correct authority from Ordnance 3rd Army. All now in order. Rearranged A.O.C personnel to deal efficiently with the work, ~~and~~ as three are now on leave in England for 10 days.	

2449 Wt. W14957/M90 750,000 1/16 J.B.C. & A. Forms/C.2118/12.

Instructions regarding War Diaries and Intelligence Summaries are contained in F. S. Regs., Part II. and the Staff Manual respectively. Title Pages will be prepared in manuscript.

WAR DIARY
or
INTELLIGENCE SUMMARY

(Erase heading not required.)

Army Form C. 2118.

Place	Date	Hour	Summary of Events and Information	Remarks and references to Appendices
La Panne Plage La Panne Ville	7/8/17		Obtained distribution of Chaffcutters. A.D.O.S. is drawing up a list of Divnl requirements of Chaffcutters – 25 suggested: we have 21 at present. 300 sets wooden Water Tin Carriers being made for us at Heavy Mobile Workshop. Each set = 3 Carriers is 1 top + 1 bottom board to carry 4 – 2 gallon petrol tins or 5 new pattern Water Tins. Drew wirecutters of various patterns from O.O. 15th Corps Troops. Red calico for making rifle range flags urgently reqd. Wired Corps asking if any available. Replied – none – demand on Base – done. 100th Bde require special issue of 160 Rodolium Sights to 2nd Worcesters for use upon Rifle Grenades. Submitted for authority thro usual channels to DDOS. COO have instructed to issue to the 2nd Worcesters without indent soon as possible. Railhead changed to Adinkerke – Oosthoek from to-day.	
"	8/8/17		ADOS 15th Corps writes scheme adopted whereby all bicycles in the Divn are periodically sent to Armourers Shop for inspection, overhaul, registration & approval of Divnl Sign. Also all Rifles held as Divl 'Reserve' should be completed with oil bottles + pull through. A small reserve of SBRs (a proportion of each size) issued to units (number according to strength roughly) to be maintained by them & used only in cases of emergency where it was essential for a man to exchange his 'ir' SBR immediately owing to the dangerous Gas attacks in Nieuport Sector".	
"	9/8/17		Drilled six Tripod Mountings of 100th MG Coy + fitted depression stops in Armourers shop. Lorry sent to collect canvas for Rs dump Coxyde & delivered to Chef d'Intendance Dunkerque. Visited latter personally + arranged rate of manufacture + days of delivery with their officer. Attended with OC 33rd Divl Train a demonstration by OC 49th Divl Train on the assembly & use of the Texas pack sets. Each consist of 3 sacks closed at both ends with an opening in the middle, 1 horse rug + 1 saddle blanket to form a protecting pad on animals back, 40 feet 1½" Cordage for lashing + 1 ground-sheet for covering the pack when in use for protection against rain. Took notes of the method of using + capacity (50 complete rations per set	

Instructions regarding War Diaries and Intelligence Summaries are contained in F. S. Regs., Part II. and the Staff Manual respectively. Title Pages will be prepared in manuscript.

WAR DIARY
or
INTELLIGENCE SUMMARY

(Erase heading not required.)

Army Form C. 2118.

Place	Date	Hour	Summary of Events and Information	Remarks and references to Appendices
La Panne Plage.	10/8/17		Distribution of Latrine Buckets, washing Bowls & Chaffcutters proceeding. Spoke S.O. officer re question of relative numbers of S.B.R.s returned owing to exhaustion of containers as against defects due to other causes. The latter preponderate very largely. No need to increase reserve of containers. It would be advisable to temporarily increase stock of S.B.R.s to meet abnormally high demands in the area.	
La Panne Ville	11/8/17		Sent list of Local Purchases for July to A.D.O.S. for passing on to French Army. This brings all Divns in 1st Corps up to same level as regards dates up to which the return has been rendered. Reported 21 chaffcutters in possession of Divn to A.D.O.S. A.D.O.S. spoke A.A.&Q.M.G. on clothing exchange matters & pointed out that a record should be kept under our Divl system of providing men with clean underclothing, of the 2nd set of underclothing taken off reinforcements on joining the Divn. to bring them into line with rest of the Divn. as by this means a check can be kept on wastage which may arise through this not being carried out."	
" "	12/8/17.		Asked 98th Bde to arrange for Q.M.s to attend at my office, on a programme, to enable me to personally check their outstanding indents with them. A certificate that this has been done is required by A.D.O.S. monthly. Visited Dunkerque for Local Purchase. Special issue of 16 pendulum sights to 2nd Worcesters authorized by D.O.S. to be supplied by C.O.O. Havre. Received 18 pdr gun (recovery) from C/162. 1600 water tins received from Base. Final scale 3000 per Div.	

2449 Wt. W14957/M90 750,000 1/16 J.B.C. & A. Forms/C.2118/12.

Instructions regarding War Diaries and Intelligence Summaries are contained in F. S. Regs., Part II. and the Staff Manual respectively. Title Pages will be prepared in manuscript.

WAR DIARY
or
INTELLIGENCE SUMMARY

(Erase heading not required.)

Army Form C. 2118.

Place	Date	Hour	Summary of Events and Information	Remarks and references to Appendices
La Panne Plage. La Panne Ville.	13/8/17		Comparison of my record of issues & receipts of new & unserviceable underclothing respectively with Clothing Exchange transactions & present stock reveals a large shortage in latter. AA & QMG ordered both records to be carefully re-checked to avoid possibility of clerical error. No error found in my account. Losses obviously due to units not returning as many dirty articles as they have been issued with. Orders issued by AA & QMG to prevent this in future. Question of Bicycles for Belgian Interpreters now attached to Div raised. No extra horses or bicycle are allowed than at present authorized for the French Mission. Latter must lend to Belgian Mission in Belgian Area.	
"	14/8/17		21 Bicycles ~~to~~ to be issued to Divl Units in replacement of equal number of Draught horses to be withdrawn forthwith. Demanded the Bicycles under QMG authority. Issued instructions that the surplus set of Saddlery are to be returned to me for despatch to Base. Scheme submitted to 'Q' for taking in Bicycles from Divl units on a programme & approved. 6 per day can be inspected & repaired if necessary. Urgent wire received from ADOS asking for a return at once of Tents (1) Properly Hatched. (2) Painted etc (3) Not Stained at all. Information urgently required by Army H.Q. Wired all formations with tentage to ~~give~~ report above to me by wire as soon as possible. Divn moving into line & taking over from 32nd Divn on 18th inst. DADOS 20 visited forward area & informs me there are no anti-gas blankets for the dugouts protection. Hastened my outstanding demand for 200 submitted on 3rd inst.	

2449 Wt. W14957/M90 750,000 1/16 J.B.C. & A. Forms/C.2118/12.

Instructions regarding War Diaries and Intelligence Summaries are contained in F. S. Regs., Part II. and the Staff Manual respectively. Title Pages will be prepared in manuscript.

WAR DIARY
or
INTELLIGENCE SUMMARY

(Erase heading not required.)

Army Form C. 2118.

Place	Date	Hour	Summary of Events and Information	Remarks and references to Appendices
La Panne Plage. La Panne Ville	15/8/17		~~[illegible]~~ Saw Chief Clerk of D.A.D.O.S. 32nd Div in latter's absence on leave as to taking over from him on 18th. Decided not to move our respective stores but simply to exchange offices. I move to Coxyde Bains 32nd Div move to La Panne. Forward area is equipped with Area Stores. The 3 Tram Coys & supply refilling points will all be close together on the La Panne–Coxyde Road near Zeepanne Cross roads. Arrange to use their refilling point for Ordnance Refilling an hour later than supply refilling on all even dates – 97th & 98th; odd days 100th Bde even days. Received one 18 pdr gun for B/156 R.F.A. No1 Sec DAC report they are very short of horseshoes owing to move from 66th Div & carrying forward of demand to 33rd Div. Where change in bulk programme has resulted in any bulk demands not being supplied for several days after the usual date by old programme obtained a number of shoes of various sizes from 15th Corps Troops to meet the emergency.	
~~[illegible]~~ "	16/8/17		~~[illegible]~~ Visited supply refilling points & arranged times of Ord Refilling with S.Os. Saw Staff Captains of 3 Bdes & notified them date & time of refilling. Sent another pastener to Base for Adh-gas blankets asking for a reply as to when they may be expected & also requesting Base to send up serviceable blankets in lieu of "unserviceable" if latter not available in sufficient numbers. Div now hastening these blankets – very urgently required. ~~[illegible]~~ 24 Hurricane lamps urgently required by 19th Bde in line. Rang up ADOS & obtained authority to draw from 15th Corps Tps. Done & lamps delivered 18 B Sec DAC	

2449 Wt. W14957/M90 750,000 1/16 J.B.C. & A. Forms/C.2118/12.

Instructions regarding War Diaries and Intelligence Summaries are contained in F. S. Regs., Part II. and the Staff Manual respectively. Title Pages will be prepared in manuscript.

WAR DIARY
or
INTELLIGENCE SUMMARY

(Erase heading not required.)

Army Form C. 2118.

Place	Date	Hour	Summary of Events and Information	Remarks and references to Appendices
La Panne Bloge ville.	17/8/17		Drew 20 Holford Containers from DADOS 32nd Divn and issued them to 95th Bde for use in line. No reply received to my 2nd [illegible] to Base for anti-gas Blankets. Position very serious in event of enemy gas attack. Reported matter to A.D.O.S. XV Corps who advised sending a lorry direct to Base Calais to draw the Blankets and any [illegible] & sprayers were required for spraying the Blankets.	
	18/8/17		Lorry sent accordingly first thing in morning. Lorry returned about 7 pm delivered Blankets & sprayers direct to 'B' Echelon DAC for transport to line. Took over Anti-gas appliances in Store with DADOS 32nd Divn. ~~Moved office~~	
Coxyde Bains Office. Store :- La Panne ville.	19/8/17		Moved office to Coxyde Bains. Bdes moving up. Arranged special refilling for 100th at [illegible] Coy Train dump for to-day. Question of [illegible] [illegible] in area taken up. Div Arty have orders to [illegible] their [illegible] by 20th. Borrowed a Sayers stove and a wooden tub from DADOS 66th Divn & issued to DAC together with necessary quantities of [illegible] etc for [illegible] 40 [illegible]. Purchased 6 Brushes Sweeping & loaned to DAC pending arrival of those demanded from Base. Staff Capt will arrange for [illegible] to be properly done as per instructions issued by me.	
" "	20/8/17		66th DADOS drew SD Clothing urgently required by him & surplus with me. Wired him sizes & numbers available. Saw 'Q' re Post Mountings for Vickers & Lewis Guns AA Sights & Chronometers. 13th Corps completing as to above authorised scale which will shortly be [illegible]. Drew 45 more Lewis AA Sights for [illegible] Corps T[illegible] and 3 Belt Boxes for use with Vickers Guns. Informed DMGO & obtained distribution	

2449 Wt. W14957/M90 750,000 1/16 J.B.C. & A. Forms/C.2118/12.

WAR DIARY
or
INTELLIGENCE SUMMARY
(Erase heading not required.)

Instructions regarding War Diaries and Intelligence Summaries are contained in F. S. Regs., Part II. and the Staff Manual respectively. Title Pages will be prepared in manuscript.

Army Form C. 2118.

Place	Date	Hour	Summary of Events and Information	Remarks and references to Appendices
~~La [illegible]~~ ~~[illegible]~~ Coxyde Bains La Panne Plage	21/8/17		Received Corps RO ordering all [illegible] in Div¹ Area to be properly [illegible] at once according to instructions contained in the order. ADOS forwarded suggestions for ensuring this is done. [illegible] to [illegible], take them to a central spot & [illegible] them over a period of 7 days by a specially trained party, as he suggests. "Q" issued instructions to all formations to draw the necessary chemicals in solution form (to be prepared by me & put in tins) and the necessary tubs & brushes & to carry out [illegible] as per instructions reporting by 31st inst that this had been done. Issued 1 Lewis Gun to 1st Camerons from stock in Armourers shop made up from salvage to replace 1 destroyed by shell fire in line.	
" "	22/8/17		Purchased 6 oilskin suits for D.G.O. to enable him to carry out experiments in protecting men engaged in neutralizing mustard gas in shell holes with Chloride of Lime, from the effects of the gas on the skin. Large number of water tins taken over in a dump at Nieuport found to be damaged by Shrapnel. "Q" moved Corps for 1200 to replace. Corps authorized drawing of 800 from 32nd Div & 400 from 66th Div. Drew these & issued to B Sec D.A.C	
" "	23/8/17		An extra emergency Reserve of 1000 S.B. Respirators required in Nieuport dumps. "Q" have asked Corps for necessary authority. Meanwhile instructing me to send up two lots of 250 each (proportionate sizes) by B Sch D.A.C to Nieuport & [illegible] dumps. This done. Only 500 SBRs now in Reserve in my store to meet [illegible] to units. Sprayers [illegible] & [illegible] [illegible] regd. [illegible] from Base. Asked ADOS if I may purchase locally [illegible] necessary.	

2449 Wt. W14957/M90 750,000 1/16 J.B.C. & A. Forms/C.2118/12.

Instructions regarding War Diaries and Intelligence Summaries are contained in F. S. Regs., Part II. and the Staff Manual respectively. Title pages will be prepared in manuscript.

WAR DIARY
or
INTELLIGENCE SUMMARY.
(Erase heading not required.)

Army Form C. 2118.

Place	Date	Hour	Summary of Events and Information	Remarks and references to Appendices
Locyde Bans. Lalanne Pille	24/8/17.		Shortage of Haynets due to erroneous issues in part of Bans & also to delay caused by alteration in Bath programme. 1500 nets received today to complete outstanding demands. 70 Sprayers received. Distribution obtained from ADMS. Asked Staff Capt 190 Bde to arrange a programme for O.C.s to attend at my office at a rate of two per day for revising their outstanding indents with me. Staff Capt RA enquired about 18 pdr Correction Scales for his Batteries. These were indented for by me several months ago & issued to the RA [illegible] 8 or a 6th Corps but were apparently withdrawn again for some reasons. Instructed Staff Capt RA to forward indent to replace Scales withdrawn quoting the [illegible] under which originally issued.	
" "	25/8/17.		Vickers Gun demanded for 19th M.G. Coy. Salvaged & repaired gun issued to replace. New gun received afterwards but put into stock instead of the Salvaged Gun. Issued the gun from stock to 248th M.G. Coy to replace one destroyed. Saw D.G.O. re refusal of R.A. units to accept Containers to repair of S.B.R.s which had no other defect than an exhausted container. These units have no grounds for refusal as each Battery has a Gas NCO who is provided with the accessory tools for detaching container. Instructed Anti-gas Storeman accordingly. As A.D.O.S. informs me that S.O.C. 4th Army has decided that D.A.D.O.S. & [illegible] are personally responsible for [illegible] of tents when [illegible], I am making up standard solutions of [illegible] & Bichromate of Potash & issuing same in water [illegible] to units on scale of 1 tin of each per tent.	

A5834 Wt. W4973/M687 750,000 8/16 D. D. & L. Ltd. Forms/C.2118/13.

Instructions regarding War Diaries and Intelligence Summaries are contained in F. S. Regs., Part II. and the Staff Manual respectively. Title pages will be prepared in manuscript.

WAR DIARY
or
INTELLIGENCE SUMMARY.
(Erase heading not required.)

Army Form C. 2118.

Place	Date	Hour	Summary of Events and Information	Remarks and references to Appendices
			Also purchase wooden barrels cut them in half & made wooden tubs which are issued for mixing the hot water solution & Copper Sulphate before painting the tents. Brushes sweeping & whitewash received from Base & issued with the form of Solution. Full instructions for use issued to all units. Purchased 71 Flytraps - what obtainable at Dunkerque & made equitable distribution of outstanding demands.	
Coxyde Bains La Panne Ville	26/8/17		Issued 3 prs old trousers from Salvage & 4 Electric Torches to 98th Bde for a raid. Purchased 3 Direct scale for APM for preparing Signboards urgently required in Army area which is destitute of them at present. All Vickers Guns & Tripods of 100th M.G. Coy require overhaul. These have never been done (except 4 in Canteen area) owing to the late CO refusing to send them into armourers shop for inspection & overhaul. Consequently the whole lot are in a bad state. Saw the present O.C. & instructed him to send his guns in at rate of 4 per day. 3 guns out of first four found to have no serviceable Check levers & plates. Wired Base that these to put the guns in action. 2 MK IV Mountings also condemned as beyond local repair & replacements wired for.	
	27/8/17		Authority given by Q.M.G. for increase of our Dist Reserves of SBRs by 1000 to provide the 1000 in Nieuport for Emergency. Demanded by wire from Base. Authority given by SHQ for the Purchase of Firelites in Belgium. Reported position of supply of Fly traps & Butter Muslin to Corps for action with Base.	

A5834 Wt. W4973/M687 750,000 8/16 D. D. & L. Ltd. Forms/C.2118/13.

Instructions regarding War Diaries and Intelligence Summaries are contained in F. S. Regs., Part II. and the Staff Manual respectively. Title Pages will be prepared in manuscript.

WAR DIARY
or
INTELLIGENCE SUMMARY
(Erase heading not required.)

Army Form C. 2118.

Place	Date	Hour	Summary of Events and Information	Remarks and references to Appendices
			Letter received from ADOS XV Corps asking for my views on Divl A.O.C. establishment & if any reduction in A.O.C. personnel was possible. Later a wire received from ADOS asking how many 'A' category men below rank of Sergeant could be liberated for service with Infantry if replaced by suitable 'B' category men. Wired back 5 available, 3 Storemen & 2 Clerks. One more may be available if he is found to be category 'A' on his return from leave.	
Coxyde Bains La Panne ville	28/8/17		Received 6 Rifles with Tel Sights from 3rd Army Sniping School per A.M.T.O. This completes the Divl establishment of 4 per Bn except one for 1st Cameronians. Informed by 'Q' that Divn is moving at short notice – to La Panne temporarily & then elsewhere. Suspended issues from Bases at once with exception of vehicles, harness etc urgently required by 4 Coy Train to replace others damaged by shell fire on 26th & Lewis guns outstanding to 5th Scottish & 1st Cameronians. Wired Base to send these vehicles etc & guns up on 66th Divn track as we are using the same Railhead. Prepared lists of all Area & Corps Stores in possession of Divn shewing present distribution & indicating disposal on leaving. Sent list to 'Q' for decision as to disposal.	
La Panne Plage La Panne ville	29/8/17		Instructions received by 'Q' from Corps as to disposal of Packsaddlery, Yukon Packs, Texas Packs, water tin carriers, wire cutters, chaffcutters etc. All except 100 Yukon Packs to be returned to O.O. XV Corps Tps. Commenced collection of these Stores from 'B' Echelon DAC & delivery to O.O. XV Corps Tps. 'Q' have issued instructions for 3 Hall Brumo, 8 Pivot AA Mountings and 4 Clinometers to be handed in to me for delivery to O.O. XV Corps Troops.	

2449 Wt. W14957/M90 750,000 1/16 J.B.C. & A. Forms/C.2118/12.

Instructions regarding War Diaries and Intelligence Summaries are contained in F. S. Regs., Part II. and the Staff Manual respectively. Title Pages will be prepared in manuscript.

WAR DIARY
or
INTELLIGENCE SUMMARY
(Erase heading not required.)

Army Form C. 2118.

Place	Date	Hour	Summary of Events and Information	Remarks and references to Appendices
Office:- La Panne Plage. Store La Panne Ville.	30/8/17		Saw DADOS 32nd Div & informed him that remaining stocks of anti-gas appliances, 15 Pistols 1½" & balance of Mulching materials & implements would be handed over to him. He will collect from my store. Prepared typewritten list giving full detail of these stores & instructions for using the Mulch. Sent duty DRLS to DADOS 32nd Div. Warned all units who have not drawn remaining small quantities of stores from my dump to do so at once. As 100th Bde have moved some distance away arranged a refilling point with Staff Captain & delivered all remaining stores. Machine Guns repaired & bicycles ditto to 100th Bde units by lorry. Sent lorry out to 19th Bde in Synthe area (past Dunkerque) with all remaining stores including five Lewis Guns. Lorry collected one chaffcutter left by 100th Bde with Area Commandant at Ghyvelde & also delivered stores to Pioneers. Arranged with R.O.O. St Idesbalde for a truck to be loaded with my Anti-gas Reserves, Shops & equipment etc for consignment to new Railhead (probably St Omer) via Calais.	
Office La Panne Plage. Store La Panne Ville.	31/8/17.		→ Sent complete list shewing disposal of all area & corps stores to DADOS XV Corps. Loaded up the truck first thing in morning & dispatched it with 2 Conroy men to act as guards. Vehicles for 4 Coy Train also reconsigned as unit could not collect them before moving. Carried reserves of oil, flannelette, dubbin & horseshoes also Detail Stores for 4 Coy Train & necessary Armourer's Equipment to enable shop to be opened in our new area on lorries. All Salvage cleared to Railhead. Lorries loaded ready for moving off again [illegible]	

[illegible] Capt DADOS 35 Div

2449 Wt. W14957/M90 750,000 1/16 J.B.C. & A. Forms/C.2118/12.

Army Form C. 2118.

Instructions regarding War Diaries and Intelligence Summaries are contained in F. S. Regs., Part II. and the Staff Manual respectively. Title Pages will be prepared in manuscript.

WAR DIARY or ~~INTELLIGENCE SUMMARY~~

(Erase heading not required.)

SECRET

D.A.D.O.S. 33rd Division

September. 1917.

Vol 23

Place	Date	Hour	Summary of Events and Information	Remarks and references to Appendices
Eperlecques	1/9/17		Moved from La Panne on 4 lorries & opened store in Eperlecques. Good accomodation for shops. Opened Armourers & Boot Shop. Visited St OMER station, which is new Railhead from to-day. No Trucks in.	
" "	2/9/17		33rd Div Arty staying behind Div in 15th Corps until 3rd & are then moving direct to 10th Corps area. Similarly the 3 Field Coys & Pioneers. 212th Field Coy is still with 66th Div. Latter requested to move them back to me on 3rd inst. & to forward all stores received for unit to me. Div is now in 5th Corps which is administered by 5th Army. Communicated with ADOS 5th Corps re method of obtaining M.G.s & parts. Instructed for the present to transfer all outstanding indents to 5th Army Gun Park for supply. Reported position of store & office, particulars of DADOS workshops, list of units administered & armament to DDOS 5th Army & repeated to ADOS 5th Corps. Xth Corps are making provision for the battle stores we shall require when going into line in Xth Corps area.	
" "	3/9/17		Visited 5th Army Gun Park. They have a lorry service for delivering stores daily to DADOS in the Army. Asked G.P. to complete my indents as soon as possible to make good all deficiencies in units' equipment. Also visited Ordnance workshops allotted to us for vehicle repairs. Shop notified as Nos 24 + 29 but on arrival at Arneke found shop had been taken over by No 2 & 16 workshop who will carry out our repairs. Units can send vehicles in direct to I.O.M. as he is not busy. Wired Staff Capt 33rd Div Arty to arrange a refilling point for 33rd D.A. units as I have large quantity of bulk & detail stores for issue to them & would arrange to send it to this point by lorry.	

2449 Wt. W14957/M90 750,000 1/16 J.B.C. & A. Forms/C.2118/12.

Instructions regarding War Diaries and Intelligence Summaries are contained in F. S. Regs., Part II. and the Staff Manual respectively. Title Pages will be prepared in manuscript.

WAR DIARY
or
INTELLIGENCE SUMMARY
(Erase heading not required.)

Army Form C. 2118.

Place	Date	Hour	Summary of Events and Information	Remarks and references to Appendices
Esquelbecq	4/9/17		General Routine work. To secure economy in the issue of M.Gun parts & bicycle parts & accessories have decided on a scheme whereby all issues to units are made from Armourers Shop, if possible immediately indent is submitted. Units indents are then bulked & a D.A.D.O.S. indent sent to Base weekly to maintain the stock in Shop constant by exactly replacing issues from initial stock at Shop. Issued a circular to all formations setting forth this scheme in detail. Prepared DADOS indents for an initial stock of Lewis & Vickers parts & Bicycle parts & submitted same to Gun Park for the MGs parts & to Base for the cycle parts.	
"	5/9/17		Staff Capt 33rd Div Arty has arranged refilling for RA units at Reninghelst (Sheet 28) at 3pm on 6th inst. Wired him this will be convenient. All stores for R.A. (3 lorry loads) being sacked up & labelled ready for loading & easy issue at refilling point. No 3 Field Coys & Pioneers have been attached to 2nd 24th Div for administration. Issued necessary move orders and arranged to send lorry to DADOS 24th Div with stores for these 4 units on 6th.	
"	6/9/17		Lorries sent to RA refilling & to DADOS 24th Div. 10th Corps have transferred all 33rd Div Arty to 24th Div for Ordnance service. Notified 24th Div I would send a Sergeant & Storeman with 1 lorry & all outstanding stores for RA units to them on 8th inst. Saw QMS of 1st Cameronians & 20th Royal Fusiliers & revised indents with them	

2449 Wt. W14957/M90 750,000 1/16 J.B.C. & A. Forms/C.2118/12.

Instructions regarding War Diaries and Intelligence Summaries are contained in F. S. Regs., Part II. and the Staff Manual respectively. Title Pages will be prepared in manuscript.

WAR DIARY
or
INTELLIGENCE SUMMARY

(Erase heading not required.)

Army Form C. 2118.

Place	Date	Hour	Summary of Events and Information	Remarks and references to Appendices
Eperlecques	7/9/17		Visited 3 Brigade H.Qs & informed them how supply of outstanding & lime stood. The Slamet Clinometers [illegible] by 100th M.B have been received to complete the 3 L.T.M.B.s. Informed Bdes all Sniperscopes in possession (8 per Bn) to be returned to me. Only now allowed as Trench Stores for Bns in line to save units transport. Took up question of numbers of Vickers & Lewis Anti-Aircraft sights in possession also mountings & numbers required to complete. Lewis mounts seem to have been lost in last area or else handed over to other Divn without authority. Cannot trace to whom the original 22 were issued by XV Corps	
"	8/9/17		100th M.G. Coy want if possible to obtain Rotatable Traversing Dials for their Mk IV Tripod Mountings with the pointer on the right hand side of pin i.e. the 0° must be able to be arranged on right side. This question has already been put up to W.O. by 3rd Army. Put forward to ADOS Xth Corps giving a reference to the 3rd Army correspondence. Sufficient Kitchen [illegible] for 100 Tents in store to meet units requirements in this area, which should only be for their authorised tentage & not for area tentage in back area.	
"	9/9/17		Received notification of area & battle stores which were available for us to draw from 10th Corps Tps & 2nd Army Troops on entering 10th Corps area for operations.	

2449 Wt. W14957/M90 750,000 1/16 J.B.C. & A. Forms/C.2118/12.

Instructions regarding War Diaries and Intelligence Summaries are contained in F. S. Regs., Part II. and the Staff Manual respectively. Title Pages will be prepared in manuscript.

WAR DIARY
or
INTELLIGENCE SUMMARY

(Erase heading not required.)

Army Form C. 2118.

Place	Date	Hour	Summary of Events and Information	Remarks and references to Appendices
Eperlecques	10/9/17		General Routine work. 19th Corps have taken over the area from 5th Corps. Saw A.D.O.S. 19th Corps. He requires new list of returns. Programme for repair of bicycles been carried out in Armourers shop & will be completed by 12th inst.	
"	11/9/17		General Routine work.	
"	12/9/17		Visited A.D.O.S. 10th Corps re situation as regards Ordnance on Division leaving 10th Corps. Also visited D.D.O.S. 2nd Army & discussed points of interest to the Div. on so leaving 2nd Army especially re winter clothing as Div has put in special application for their winter clothing in our office	
"	13/9/17		General Routine Work. Capt. Cabitt 4th Suffolk Regiment reported to me fm H.Q. 98th Bde for short instruction in the main outlines of supply of Ordnance Stores in the field, the being part of Staff learners course of instruction as arranged by the General Staff.	
"	14/9/17		Shops. Closed in preparation for moving them to forward area (Westoutre) on 15th to enable my move to be completed on 16th inst.	
"	15/9/17		Loaded 2 lorries with Armourers & Bootshop equipment & sent them to Westoutre with a W.O. to take charge of Store & to take over 203 sets G.S. Pack saddlery being left at Store at Westoutre by D.A.D.O.S. 39th Divn for us. Lorries returned in evening ready for move of office & Stores on 16th. Collected the 5 Mk IV Tripods (Vickers) belonging to 100th M.G. Coy from No 2 & 6 workshops anew as latter could not repair the defective crosshead etc. The Dials	

Instructions regarding War Diaries and Intelligence Summaries are contained in F. S. Regs., Part II. and the Staff Manual respectively. Title Pages will be prepared in manuscript.

WAR DIARY
or
INTELLIGENCE SUMMARY
(Erase heading not required.)

Army Form C. 2118.

Place	Date	Hour	Summary of Events and Information	Remarks and references to Appendices
			Elevating & traversing fitted to these tripods have to be taken off them before sending the defective tripods to Base. 5 New Tripods less Dial S+T demanded by wire. Cleared remaining salvage (3 loads) to Railhead with the 3 lorry.	
Westoutre.	16/9/17		Loaded 3 lorries with office kit, Bde Ords office, as much stores as possible & cookhouse. Left anti-gas appliances & salvage personnel, kitbags etc. to be collected later in day. Opened Stores officer shops in Westoutre. Collected balance left at Esperlecques in evening, lorries were loaded overnight & left for Westoutre at 4 a.m. arriving Westoutre 8.30 am.	
"	17/9/17		Visited Railhead Bailleul. No trucks in. Brigades are in Northern area. Arranged refills for 19 & 98 on 19th at their respective Bde H.Qs & for 100 Bde on 18th inst at their Bde H.Q. Staff Capt. agree & have notified units to attend.	
"	18/9/17		Visited DADOS 23rd Div to whom my artillery, 3 Field Coys & Pioneers are now attached. Found very little bulk or detail stores had been received while my artillery were with 2?? Div and 23rd Div owing to delay in receipt of trucks from Base. Bulk demands for all my units attached to these Divs in turn have been kept separate to enable Base to divert to correct Div on transfers taking place. Arranged with DADOS 23 Div to take back my units & arranged for my personnel in my division to me at Westoutre forthwith. Notified the units concerned	

2449 Wt. W14957/M90 750,000 1/16 J.B.C. & A. Forms/C.2118/12.

WAR DIARY
or
INTELLIGENCE SUMMARY.
(Erase heading not required.)

Army Form C. 2118.

Instructions regarding War Diaries and Intelligence Summaries are contained in F. S. Regs., Part II. and the Staff Manual respectively. Title pages will be prepared in manuscript.

Place	Date	Hour	Summary of Events and Information	Remarks and references to Appendices
			to draw from me forthwith. ~~[illegible]~~	
Westoutre	19/9/17.		Drew all area & battle stores allotted from OO 2nd Army Tps & some from OO 10th Corps Troops. Notified 'Q' they are awaiting distribution. Question of supply of Ration carriers & Crates water tin for packsaddlery taken up. 200 Paillasses for use as Ration carriers (improvised) allotted by ADOS & drawn. 30 prs Crates water tin also allotted. Divl Carpenters Shop is making 50 prs of Divl pattern. Purchased the necessary cordage for the ropes required for these crates & obtained ADOS covering approval purchase being over £5. Sent lorries over to 23rd Ordnance Store & drew all available battle & [illegible] stores which have arrived for my RA Field Coys & Pioneers. Special Railhead for Ordnance store only opened at Ouderdom "A". Instructions issued by Corps that [illegible] must check contents of trucks themselves as the Railhead representative stops at supply Rhead to deal with old ordnance.	
"	20/9/17		40 ~~[illegible]~~ prs Crates water tin allotted in addition to [illegible]. Drew these & reported to 'Q'. Latter require another 30 prs to complete to 100 prs from Corps. Wired ADOS for these. Sent ~~[illegible]~~ area & battle stores to Brigades under distribution from 'Q' & handed over balance to 'B' Echelon DAC to be held at Main Divl Ammn Dumps as reserve. 100 Yukon packs distributed & another 150 drawn from Corps. Another 100 are required. Wired ADOS	

A5834 Wt. W4973/M687 750,000 8/16 D. D. & L. Ltd. Forms/C.2118/13.

Instructions regarding War Diaries and Intelligence Summaries are contained in F. S. Regs., Part II. and the Staff Manual respectively. Title pages will be prepared in manuscript.

WAR DIARY
or
INTELLIGENCE SUMMARY.
(Erase heading not required.)

Army Form C. 2118.

Place	Date	Hour	Summary of Events and Information	Remarks and references to Appendices
			10th Corps for these. Latter instructed me to draw from 41st Div. Base. N.B. The first 100 Yukon Packs carried by the further Div. were deficient of the 10 yds of cordage for lashing per pack; also the 100 drawn for 41st Div. were in same condition. As these packs were required for use within 48 hours, Local Purchase had to be resorted to to the extent of 1000 yds. Cordage sufficient for 100 packs has been demanded by wire from Base. Vickers & Lewis A.A. sights & mountings has lended. Informed that 3rd Army were providing & indents at Base have been cancelled.	
Westoutre	21/9/17		Bdes moved into Westoutre area preparatory to taking over in line from 23rd Div. on 24th. Reviewed situation as regards supply of all essential equipment. Div. practically complete. Base have duplicated a whole week's supply of bulk owing to non-compliance by them of "Instructions to O.O.s in the Field" re the re-demanding of bulk stores not received on correct day. Reported all particulars to A.D.O.S. & returned surpluses to Base. 19th Bde find all their Battalions are short of cardigans which should have been maintained at scale of 1 per man throughout the year. They	

Instructions regarding War Diaries and Intelligence Summaries are contained in F. S. Regs., Part II. and the Staff Manual respectively. Title pages will be prepared in manuscript.

WAR DIARY
or
INTELLIGENCE SUMMARY.
(Erase heading not required.)

Army Form C. 2118.

Place	Date	Hour	Summary of Events and Information	Remarks and references to Appendices
			wired for 3,000 to complete them.	
Westoutre	22/9/17		N.Z. Divl Artillery moved to me & lorry & AOC personnel reported to me for duty in assisting to ordnance then R.A. 2 lorry loads of stores brought with them for issue. Advised HQ N.Z. Div Arty of my location & requested them to notify units to draw. Staff Capt N.Z. Div Arty informed me 1 Brigade, the D.A.C. & T.M.Bs were stationed round about Hazebrouck & asked me to arrange to send stores for these units out to Hazebrouck for refilling. Arranged this for 23rd inst. AA & QMG does not wish new S.D. Clothing awaiting issue to units to be issued to them before the battle unless they urgently require it, to avoid waste. Ade was instructed to inform QMs of units of this & to retain any clothing & [illegible] not urgently required. Received 10 Vickers AA Mountings per Corps & obtained distribution from DMGO. Divn now complete with all necessary stores except pistols, field glasses & compasses which have not been available at Base for a long period.	

A5834 Wt. W4973/M687 750,000 8/16 D. D. & L. Ltd. Forms/C.2118/13.

Instructions regarding War Diaries and Intelligence Summaries are contained in F. S. Regs., Part II. and the Staff Manual respectively. Title pages will be prepared in manuscript.

WAR DIARY
or
INTELLIGENCE SUMMARY.
(Erase heading not required.)

Army Form C. 2118.

Place	Date	Hour	Summary of Events and Information	Remarks and references to Appendices
Westoutre	23/9/17		Corps have ordered the Ordnance Stores of the 23rd, 33rd + 39th Divns to be changed round in a triangular move to suit the situation as regards supplying of their respective units. Before I can move the agreement of the D.A.D.O.S. of the other two Divisions in conjunction with the agreement between the Q branches of the 3 Divns. 25th inst decided upon as most convenient. When the 3000 water Bottles complete with carriers & slings are received 500 are to be handed over to 21st Divn & 1000 to 39th who have asked 10th Corps for them. The balance to be kept in reserve. Trucks arriving every other day regularly at Ordnance Railhead under dom "A". Sent stores out	
" "	24/9/17		to refilling points arranged for 100th + 98th Brigade. Units did not all [illegible] well & lorry had to deliver other Trucks containing waterbottles & a truck of pontoons for 212 Field Coy arrived unexpectedly at Bailleul our supply Railhead. Collected the water bottles & sent them direct to 39th Div Store at Dezon Camp M.12.c.6.5 Sheet 28 near La Clytte to save transport tomorrow when I take over this Store from DADOS 39th Divn. Also sent over all anti-gas appliances to new store. DADOS 23rd Div moved 2 loads of his stores to my store in Westoutre preparatory to taking over [after] tomorrow. Collected 600 Trench shelters & [illegible] of poles from Area Commdt La Clytte & delivered to 98th + 100th Brigades.	transport line; to-morrow when
Dezon Camp M.12.C.6.3 Sheet 28	25/9/17		Moved in 3 journeys to Store in Dezon Camp. N.Z artillery personnel & stores also moved with me. Sent a lorry to collect the last 30 pr crates for water tins from OO 10th Corps Tps. Lorry sent to Hazebrouck with stores for N.Z Artillery Units & to collect 10 Vickers A-A. Sights.	
" "	26/9/17		Divn in action. Some units collected from stores. General Routine work.	

[illegible signature]

A5834 Wt. W4973/M687 750,000 8/16 D. D. & L. Ltd. Forms/C.2118/13.

Instructions regarding War Diaries and Intelligence Summaries are contained in F. S. Regs., Part II. and the Staff Manual respectively. Title Pages will be prepared in manuscript.

WAR DIARY
or
INTELLIGENCE SUMMARY
(Erase heading not required.)

Army Form C. 2118.

Place	Date	Hour	Summary of Events and Information	Remarks and references to Appendices
Dezon Camp M.15 C.6.3 Sheet 28	27/9/17		Sent out 12 M.G. Barrels and 35 Belts 250 rds & 26 Boxes Belt very urgently required by 100th M.G. Coy to their transport lines at Dickebusch by car, having first drawn the Belts & Boxes from O.O. 10th Corps Tps under Corps authority. Visited Staff Capt 100th Bde to find out any urgent requirements of 100th Bde who are heavily engaged at present. He has no news at all. 2nd A & SH wired for 4 Lewis Guns complete. Wired for them to O.C. Store & drew them ~~same day~~ & issued to unit direct by lorry. Visited DADOS 23rd Div & 39th to see which Div was taking over my store tomorrow on move of Div as Div came out of line & immediate move to back area ordered.	
Blaringhem	28/9/17		Loaded truck arranged for with RTO Reninghelst with 18,000 Vest woollen recently received of Winter Clothing indent not yet required for issue. DADOS 37th Div took over store at Dezon Camp. Moved to Blaringhem leaving my own Artillery personnel & stores for issues to continue pending their move to another Div in forward area. Wired 1st NZ Div to collect their Arty personnel & Stores to-day as Corps have retransferred NZ Arty back to their own Div. Notified my own Artillery moved to 21st Div. Sent lorry back to Dezon Camp to take my Arty personnel & remaining stores to DADOS 21st Div at Steenvoorde. DADOS 37th Div has agreed to take over balance of Salvage packed up & labelled ready for despatch to Base as owing to sudden order of move I was unable to clear the last lot before moving.	

2449 Wt. W14957/M90 750,000 1/16 J.B.C. & A. Forms/C.2118/12.

Instructions regarding War Diaries and Intelligence Summaries are contained in F. S. Regs., Part II. and the Staff Manual respectively. Title Pages will be prepared in manuscript.

WAR DIARY
or
INTELLIGENCE SUMMARY

(Erase heading not required.)

Army Form C. 2118.

Place	Date	Hour	Summary of Events and Information	Remarks and references to Appendices
Blaringhem	29/9/17		Opened Stores office & shops. Lorries sent back to [illegible] Camp to clear balance of Stores. Truck of 15 bales clothing loaded yesterday at [illegible] has arrived. Cleared same & dump along store, no Clothing Exchange being found as yet. General Routine work. Further recent demands for Lewis & Vickers Guns received to replace losses in action. Losses of technical stores & guns believed very heavy. Saw AA & QMG re refitting of Divn. He informed me Divn must be refitted by 4th prox. ready to go back to line on 5th prox if necessary.	
"	30/9/17		Went & saw QMs of all Bns, MG Coys & Bde HQs by car & obtained approximate requirements of SD clothing, boots, Technical Stores, Lewis & Vickers guns to complete to establishment in replacement of losses & destroyed. I intend going to Base Calais in car with 3 lorries tomorrow to obtain immediately all Stores & Clothing required by the Divn. The ordinary bulk programme of supply is too slow to enable refitting to be completed by 4th. Losses in recent action very heavy in technical equipment & Lewis Guns of which 66 are required. [illegible] Store further. Demands cancelled 2nd Army & I was instructed to demand on Base further. This was exactly [illegible]	Important

[illegible] Capt.
DADOS
33 Div

2449 Wt. W14957/M90 750,000 1/16 J.B.C. & A. Forms/C.2118/12.

11 SECRET

Instructions regarding War Diaries and Intelligence Summaries are contained in F. S. Regs., Part II. and the Staff Manual respectively. Title Pages will be prepared in manuscript.

WAR DIARY
or
INTELLIGENCE SUMMARY
(Erase heading not required.)

DADOS 33rd Div

October 1917

Vol 24

Army Form C. 2118.

Place	Date	Hour	Summary of Events and Information	Remarks and references to Appendices
BLARINGHEM	1/10/17		Went to Calais by car & met my 3 lorries at the Ordnance Depot. After some discussion the OO agreed to issue me all stores bulk & detail (demanded on consolidated DADOS indent) which I required at once for refitting as far as items were available. Took IOs to various groups & arranged to draw the stores by lorry in the afternoon. 3 loads brought from Base & 3 more loads remaining which includes 6 Lewis & 6 Vickers Guns complete. Asked Base not to send these by rail owing to length of time it would take to obtain them. This system of obtaining stores from Base is very inconvenient to Base as it causes dislocation in the daily routine. It was only carried out owing to extreme urgency. ~~[illegible]~~ All bulk clothing & Boots demanded & practically all technical stores demanded were available & were issued to units.	
	2/10/17		The SD clothing & Boots obtained from Base when added to the SD clothing & Boots still outstanding from Base but much delayed owing to reconsignments is sufficient to completely re-equip the Division. Saw GOC in evening & informed him situation as regards the re-equipping. He considers the losses of technical stores such as Machine Guns, Binoculars, compasses, wirecutters in recent action very excessive. Referred this matter to AA & QMG who will see GOC. Issue proceeding to units as quickly as possible. Sent 3 lorries to Calais to collect Machine Guns & balance of stores.	

2449 Wt. W14957/M90 750,000 1/16 J.B.C. & A. Forms/C.2118/12.

Instructions regarding War Diaries and Intelligence Summaries are contained in F. S. Regs., Part II. and the Staff Manual respectively. Title Pages will be prepared in manuscript.

WAR DIARY
or
INTELLIGENCE SUMMARY
(Erase heading not required.)

Army Form C. 2118.

Place	Date	Hour	Summary of Events and Information	Remarks and references to Appendices
Blaringhem	3/10/17		Light ordnance workshops allotted to Divn have moved & the nearest shop is at Strazeele which is much too far for units to send their vehicles. ADOS authorised me to inspect & condemn vehicles where necessary. G.O.C. is very anxious that all vehicles should be painted without delay. Wired for 10 cwt Paint S.C. and 6 cwt Paint for Steel Helmets. ~~Stock of~~	
	4/10/17		Stock of serviceable rifles in Divl Armourers shop becoming low 50 at least required from Railhead to make up reserve. Arranged to move to Wizernes tomorrow as Divn HQ are moving there. Sent stores drawn from Railhead direct there with a W.O. to obtain a store from the Billeting Officer. Division is going into Training area.	
Wizernes	5/10/17		Moved all stores except salvage & armourers shop to Wizernes. Informed at 1 pm that Divn had been ordered to return to here to-morrow. Opened office temporarily in Wizernes but not store. Suspended all issues from Base by urgent wire & phoned R.T.O. at Railhead - Steenbecque till 8th inst to hold & then reconsign all trucks received for us to Steenwerck the new Railhead from 8th onwards. Arranged with R.T.O. to load up a truck of Anti-gas appliances [illegible] and other reserve stores also load [illegible] off loaded at Railhead to-day. Went by car to Bailleul [illegible] & obtained a store from Town Major returned to [illegible]	

Army Form C. 2118.

Instructions regarding War Diaries and Intelligence Summaries are contained in F. S. Regs., Part II. and the Staff Manual respectively. Title pages will be prepared in manuscript.

WAR DIARY
or
INTELLIGENCE SUMMARY.
(Erase heading not required.)

Place	Date	Hour	Summary of Events and Information	Remarks and references to Appendices
Bailleul	6/10/17		Sent on 2 lorries with office + stores leaving 1 lorry to clear Salvage direct from Blaringhem to Railhead. The usual large amount of Salvage has been returned by units on moving out. Shoemakers + Armourers shop left at Lozerres to be collected by 2 lorries on return from Bailleul 1st lorry after completing removal of Salvage from Blaringhem. Went by train from Lozerres at 5 pm + arrived at Bailleul very late about 9.30 p.m. Visited offices + Stores + found situation satisfactory. Lorries returned very late to Lozerres + not expected till early morning. Advised of dispatch of 10,500 Blankets (1st Blanket) from Stoneport. By 3 Field Coys + Pioneers now with 21st Div. are returning to 8th Corps + rejoining Div. on 7th inst. Stores I have for issue to them retained.	
Bailleul	7/10/17		Opened Store for issues. General Routine work. 4 Bns 30? 95th Bde + 10? 19th detached from Div. for duty with 10th + Anzac Corps near Ypres. Arranged to ordnance them direct to save complication as their move is only temporary. Notified Corps concerned.	
" "	8/10/17		4 Trucks Blankets received at Railhead. Arranged with 19th + 100th Bde to deliver their Blankets immediately by lorry from Railhead. 98th Bde units not available + their Blankets were put into Store to be drawn by units on return to the Div. Number of blankets demanded not sufficient to complete 1st Blanket (less Arty) Demanded another 1,500 to complete. Also demanded 1500 for Pioneers + Field Coys as 21st Div. had not made provision for them.	

A5834 Wt. W4973/M687 750,000 8/16 D. D. & L. Ltd. Forms/C.2118/13.

Army Form C. 2118.

Instructions regarding War Diaries and Intelligence Summaries are contained in F. S. Regs., Part II. and the Staff Manual respectively. Title Pages will be prepared in manuscript.

WAR DIARY
or
INTELLIGENCE SUMMARY

(Erase heading not required.)

Place	Date	Hour	Summary of Events and Information	Remarks and references to Appendices
Bailleul	9/10/17		Dvl HQ moved to Ravelsberg Camp about 2 miles east of Bailleul. Visited DADOS Dn whose store at a farm near above camp. I am taking over. Accommodation rather limited & yard & road leading to store in bad state although a large amount of road material & labour had been expended on it. A small amount of area stores will be handed over to us. Arranged to move 10th inst.	
S.17.c.7.1 Sheet 28	10/10/17.		Moved to farm near Ravelsberg S17.c.7.1. Sheet 28. Move difficult & prolonged owing to receipt of over 20 tons of stores due to suspension of issues during preceding move from Wizernes. Armourers' ~~[illegible]~~ shop left at Bailleul to continue urgent work until 11th inst when they can be moved to new store.	
" "	11/10/17		Until today no lorry has been available to collect remaining personnel & shop equipment from Wizernes. Lorry borrowed from Corps for this purpose & sent off today. Moved Armourers & opened their shop in new store. General Routine work.	
" "	12/10/17		Q & DADOS has been [illegible] issue of Horse Rugs & Stewart Clippers. Latter received to-day per OC 2nd Army Tps. 20 Machines & 60 Spare Heads. This is total Divl Allotment. Indent for this number cancelled on Base. No authority yet given for demanding Horse Rugs. Clipping to be commenced on 15th. Requirements of Lamps F.S. Soyer's stove communicated to [illegible] Corps "Q". 1250 of former & 47 of latter 3 in possession	

2449 Wt. W14957/M90 750,000 1/16 J.B.C. & A. Forms/C.2118/12.

Instructions regarding War Diaries and Intelligence Summaries are contained in F. S. Regs., Part II. and the Staff Manual respectively. Title pages will be prepared in manuscript.

WAR DIARY
or
INTELLIGENCE SUMMARY.
(Erase heading not required.)

Army Form C. 2118.

Place	Date	Hour	Summary of Events and Information	Remarks and references to Appendices
S. 17. C. 7.1	13/10/17		Visited O.O. 5th Corps Tps. He has 200 prs Gum Boots available & pas orders to issue to me if required in part satisfaction of the 800 asked for by "Q". 4000 Tin Discs numbered consecutively 1 – 2000 in duplicate required for use in scheme for exchange of ankle for Gum Boots & vice-versa. Tin to be obtained from Supply Dumps & cut up & stamped by Armourers. To enable clipping to be commenced 160 Rugs are wanted by 15th inst (morning). Asked A.D.O.S. for these & he instructed 30th Divn to hand over 160 to me if available. 30th Div ord informed me they would be available 14/10.	Capt. A.A.D.O.S.
" "	14/10/17		Collected 160 Horse Rugs & sent to Clipping Shed. Question of attached personnel taken up with D.A.A.G. who has withdrawn two Employment Coy men from me for Salvage work in forward area. Fatigue work in Armourers shops has therefore to be done by a skilled & highly paid N.C.O. & this is not economical. Tables & forms urgently required for Camps. Paid bill for 60 Tables which had been purchased by A.D.O.S. 8th Corps for use in their area previous to our taking it over. 2nd Army have given authority for the purchase by Divns of 12 Table & 24 forms additional to those already provided by L.P.	
" "	15/10/17		General Routine work. 2 American officers attached to Div for instruction in Salvage work being sent to me for instruction in Salvage from an Ordnance point of view & to see method of supplies of Ordnance to units in the Field.	Capt. W. H. Dawson.

A5834 Wt. W4973/M687 750,000 8/16 D. D. & L. Ltd. Forms/C.2118/13.

SECRET

Instructions regarding War Diaries and Intelligence Summaries are contained in F. S. Regs., Part II. and the Staff Manual respectively. Title Pages will be prepared in manuscript.

WAR DIARY
or
INTELLIGENCE SUMMARY

(Erase heading not required.)

Army Form C. 2118.

33rd Division
D.A.D.O.S.

1st Sheet

Place	Date	Hour	Summary of Events and Information	Remarks and references to Appendices
Ravelsberg	16/10/17		Went on leave to England. Demanded 800 Blankets from Base to complete	
	-"-		1st Issue. Sent lorry to 14th Division to collect stores for 3 Field Coys + Pioneers	
	-"-		who were attached to 14th Division and afterwards moved to 33rd Division –	
	-"-		Sent urgent hastener to Base for supply of Rugs horse as non-arrival	
	-"-		was holding up clipping in Division –	
	17/10/17		Lorry containing stores for 3 Field Coys + Pioneers arrived from 14th Division –	
	18/10/17		Received notification from D.D.O.S. 2nd Army that 18 pdr No. 300 issued to	
	-"-		B/46 of 14th Divl Arty was a short life piece and if not in action it	
	-"-		could be exchanged. Staff Capt Div Arty replied that gun was in action	
	-"-		and that he proposed keeping it until unserviceable.	
	-"-		Demanded 4.5" piece for D/46 to replace one condemned for wear, by I.O.M	
	19/10/17		Send 2nd Hastener for Rugs horse to Base. Borrowed 260 Rugs from 30th Divn	
	-"-		Made provision for a quantity of special stores to equip Gum Boot Store	
	-"-		Received 4.5" carriage for D/47 – 14th Divl Arty.	
	20/10/17		Received 17,700 Blankets (2nd Issue) from Base. Asked Corps for a further	
	-"-		allotment of 10 Chaff Cutters –	

2449 Wt. W14957/M90 750,000 1/16 J.B.C. & A. Forms/C.2118/12.

SECRET

Instructions regarding War Diaries and Intelligence Summaries are contained in F. S. Regs., Part II. and the Staff Manual respectively. Title Pages will be prepared in manuscript.

WAR DIARY
or
INTELLIGENCE SUMMARY
(Erase heading not required.)

Army Form C. 2118.

33rd Division
D.A.D.O.S.

Place	Date	Hour	Summary of Events and Information	Remarks and references to Appendices
Ravelsberg	21/10/17		Received 5000 Rugs horse and sent on consignment to Divisional	
	-"-		Clipping Depot. Received 10000 Woollen Drawers and put them into Divl	
	-"-		Clo Ex. Sent down demand for Jerkins. S/S. Coats etc to Base	
	22/10/17		Received 351 pairs Gum Boots from 8th Corps Troops. Demanded 18pdr carriage	
	-"-		for A/47. 14th Divl. Arty to replace one destroyed. shellfire. Visited Clipping	
	-"-		Depot and arranged for Armourer to overhaul machines daily. Moved	
	-"-		Divl. Armourers shop & personnel to Neuve Eglise.	
	23/10/17		Received 1000 pairs Gum Boots from D.A.D.O.S. 30th Division. Drew Carrier for No7	
	-"-		Dial Sight from 2nd Army. H.M Workshop	
	24/10/17		Demanded 500 Waterproof Bags for carrying Socks. made local purchases etc.	
	25/10/17		Drew 2. Carriers for No7 Dial Sights from 2nd Army. H.M. Workshops.	
	26/10/17		Issues of 1st + 2nd Blanket to all Battalions in Division, completed. Went to 2nd Army	
	-"-		School Sniping to draw rifles with telescopic sights, Nil available, all drawn previous	
	-"-		day by D.D.O.S 2nd Army. Arranged to loan D.A.D.O.S 14th Divl 500 Rugs horse	
			for use of 33rd Divl. Arty, attached to 14th Divl.	
	27/10/17		Returned from Leave & resumed duty.	
	28/10/17		Visited Divl Armourers shop which was established at Neuve Eglise during my absence on leave.	
			Owing to inability to give constant supervision to this shop, ~~[illegible]~~ being detached from 8 Corps	
			I do not think the work turned out is satisfactory. It would be advisable to change the personnel & shop. General Routine work	

2449 Wt. W14957/M90 750,000 1/16 J.B.C. & A. Forms/C.2118/12.

Instructions regarding War Diaries and Intelligence Summaries are contained in F. S. Regs., Part II. and the Staff Manual respectively. Title Pages will be prepared in manuscript.

WAR DIARY
or
INTELLIGENCE SUMMARY
(Erase heading not required.)

Army Form C. 2118.

Place	Date	Hour	Summary of Events and Information	Remarks and references to Appendices
RAVELSBERG 5.17.c.7.1 Sheet 28	29/10/17		Visited my representative who is attached to D.A.D.O.S. 31st Div to assist in supply of ordnance to 33rd Div Arty. Found him working under difficulties due to bad state of ground on which his store was situated & of the road leading up to it & also due to large quantity of winter clothing additional to the ordinary Bulk which has to be dealt with by himself & 2 men. He also has experienced difficulty in obtaining his proper proportion of Bulk Stores as indented separately for 33 Div Arty Units for convenience in distribution. Found out how issue of winter clothing stood to 33 Div Arty. Issues of both Bulk & Detail Stores is now satisfactory & all units are well equipped. Proceeded afterwards to 2nd Army Sniping School & drew 2 Rifles with Tel. Sights for 2 Battalions & later to 2nd Army H.M. Workshops & drew a Carrier No 7 Dial Sight No 1 for issue in satisfaction of a long outstanding indent of D/147 Bde 14 Div Arty.	
	30/10/17		The Div Clipping Shed have several Stewart machines which require repair or replacement of parts. The wear on these machines is very great owing to pressure of work. An Armourer Sgt attends every day to inspect the machines & reports to this Office daily any fresh parts which require replacing. Demand 2 complete machines to replace 2 rendered unserviceable both in head & in the standard. All Stores required for the Right Sector Gum Boot Store ready for issue except 50 [illegible] Boots but these can be borrowed from Area Comdt Stock & replaced when those on demand are received. 6250 Leather Jerkins received. To save dumping made immediate arrangements with Staff Capt of 98th & 100th Brigades to take 3000 & 500 respectively to complete Battalions who were able to take them. Sent 4 lorry loads out & delivered to units. Remainder stores	

Army Form C. 2118.

Instructions regarding War Diaries and Intelligence Summaries are contained in F. S. Regs., Part II. and the Staff Manual respectively. Title Pages will be prepared in manuscript.

WAR DIARY
or
INTELLIGENCE SUMMARY

(Erase heading not required.)

Place	Date	Hour	Summary of Events and Information	Remarks and references to Appendices
	30/10/7		Lorry sent to Bde Depot [illegible] to collect 500 Bags, waterproof for carrying dry socks to line [illegible] required by Bde going into line to-night	
RAILSBERG S17.c.7.1 Sheet 28	31/10/7		Sent 3 lorries at 5.30pm to STINKING farm with all stores required for opening Right Sector Gum Boot Stores, 15 washing bowls, wooden slats, Braziers, Soyers Stoves, H.F. Containers, soap etc & Gumboots. also metal discs numbered 1-500 in duplicate for use in exchange of Gumboots for ankleboots handed in & vice-versa.	
			General Routine work. Visited 3 Bdes & discussed their immediate requirements if any. The 100 Bags W.P. issued to 19th Bde are sufficient to carry 3000 prs dry socks. Informed Bdes that a proportion of Fur Coats were being issued with the Leather Jerkins. G.O.C. 100th Bde wishes to obtain the correct proportion of Jerkins to Fur Coats & also wishes this proportion to be issued to each Bn in his Bde. 19th Bde prefer 2½ Bns to be equipped with Jerkins & 1½ with furcoats so as not to mix them except in the case of one Battalion. To ensure each Bde receives the same proportion of Fur Coats to Jerkins it will be necessary to withdraw 500 from 98th Bde & issue 500 Fur Coats in lieu. Arranged this through 'Q'.	

[signature] Capt.
D.A.A.G.
33rd Divn.

2449 Wt. W14957/M90 750,000 1/16 J.B.C. & A. Forms/C.2118/12.

Army Form C. 2118.

Instructions regarding War Diaries and Intelligence Summaries are contained in F. S. Regs., Part II. and the Staff Manual respectively. Title Pages will be prepared in manuscript.

WAR DIARY
or
INTELLIGENCE SUMMARY
(Erase heading not required.)

SECRET.

November 1917 D.A.D.O.S. 33rd Division

Vol 25

Place	Date	Hour	Summary of Events and Information	Remarks and references to Appendices
RAVELSBERG S.17.c.7.1 Sheet 28	1/11/17		Collected Jerkins from R.S.W.S.(?) — these were left by Bns of 98th Bde before moving to Ypres for detached duty & are to be replaced with fur coats on Bns rejoining Divn. Issued these Jerkins to complete 100th Bde. General Routine work.	
	2/11/17		General Routine work.	
	3/11/17		33rd Div Arty moved from 21st Divn to 33rd Divn. The D.A. are moving into rest area about Bavinchove N.(?) S of Cassel. Awaited arrival of my AOC personnel & Lorry from Ordnance 21st Divn.	
	4/11/17		General Routine work. Informed move of 33rd Div Arty to all concerned.	
	5/11/17		AOC Personnel for Div Arty & Lorry with remaining stores arrived & reported for duty. Sent lorry back to D.A.D.O.S. 21st Divn to collect balance of stores due to 33rd Div Arty units. Refilling at suitable place in 33rd D.A. area will have to be arranged on alternate days owing to distance from my store to this area — about 30 kilometres.	
	6/11/17		Visited Staff Capt & CRA 33rd DA at their HQ at Château Les Noppe(?) on main Cassel–St Omer Road & fixed up refilling point for 8th inst at 11 a.m. for all R.A. units. This temporary arrangement for supply will hold pending final move of R.A. much further back. When this occurs 33rd RA must be moved by 2nd Army to a Divn in back area for administration. Interviewed O.C. of RHB(?) Brigade & DAC & C.R.A. & noted their most urgent needs — Paint for camouflage of all vehicles & guns & paint for Steel Helmets most urgently reqd. Informed ADOS of arrangements made for supply.	

2449 Wt. W14957/M90 750,000 1/16 J.B.C. & A. Forms/C.2118/12.

Instructions regarding War Diaries and Intelligence Summaries are contained in F. S. Regs., Part II. and the Staff Manual respectively. Title Pages will be prepared in manuscript.

WAR DIARY
or
INTELLIGENCE SUMMARY
(Erase heading not required.)

Army Form C. 2118.

Place	Date	Hour	Summary of Events and Information	Remarks and references to Appendices
RAVELSBERG S.17.c.7.1. Sheet 28	7/11/17.		A.D.O.S. informed me my R.A. had made a complaint to 8th Corps R.A. on Ordnance Supply. He asked me to investigate. I did so & could find no cause for it, so visited A.D.O.S. & informed him of this & that all units had recently had all their demands for bulk completed in full & a fair quantity of detail while with 21st Divn. Also arrangements made for ordnance supply while R.A. were temporary in middle area was agreed to by Staff Capt. Rang up Staff Capt R.A. on the matter. He made no complaint whatever but only asked Corps R.A. to what Division he would be attached.	
			General Routine work. Some stores received for 33 Div Arty units in my track [?] so move order has taken effect quickly & without any hitch	
	8/11/17		2 lorry loads stores sent to refilling point for R.A. units. Asked A.D.O.S. to arrange with 2nd Army for ordnancing of 33 Div Arty when they move to Tilques area in a few days time. Discussed salvage methods with A.D.O.S. & disposal of area stores & possible ordnance dumps which could be taken over by me on move of Divn to Ypres sector in 3 weeks time. No ordnance store in Ypres. Most advanced store is at Brandhoek & at present used by 2nd Can Divn. Also a store is required in Merris area when Divn moves thence temporarily before going to Ypres at end of month. Visited Merris & [illegible] possible stores & informed Camp Commandant of them.	

2449 Wt. W14957/M90 750,000 1/16 J.B.C. & A. Forms/C.2118/12.

Army Form C. 2118.

Instructions regarding War Diaries and Intelligence Summaries are contained in F. S. Regs., Part II. and the Staff Manual respectively. Title Pages will be prepared in manuscript.

WAR DIARY
or
INTELLIGENCE SUMMARY
(Erase heading not required.)

Place	Date	Hour	Summary of Events and Information	Remarks and references to Appendices
Sheet 28	9/11/17		Arranged next refilling for R.A. same place & time as yesterday on 10th inst. A.A.D.O.S. 8th Corps visited H.Q. RA to investigate the complaint previously mentioned – Found no cause & situation satisfactory. General Routine work	
	10/11/17		D.A.D.O.S. 5th Australian Div visited office. Shewed him over Store workshops, etc., to give him an idea of the accomodation as he may possibly take over from me on 1st Anzac Corps relieving 8th Corps in this area. Received instructions from 2nd Army re disposal of area stores on the Division relieving another. Arranged another refilling for R.A. same time & place on 12th inst.	
[illegible] S.17.C.7.1.	11/11/17		Informed by G that on Brigades moving to Hemsdock area Div H.Q. will remain in present position. No need for Store in Hemsdock. 95th Bde move into Hems area 17th inst 19th on 14th inst & 100th to Laere area on 16th. Owing to distance of units from Store when these moves occur refilling by Brigades will be necessary. Found one Field Ambulance was returning all Slings for Stretchers in their possession. Asked A.D.M.S. to state if Slings were used by any F.Amb or not. If not I would request that issue of them be discontinued. However all the F.A.s use them so no action necessary.	

2449 Wt. W14957/M90 750,000 1/16 J.B.C. & A. Forms/C.2118/12.

Instructions regarding War Diaries and Intelligence Summaries are contained in F. S. Regs., Part II. and the Staff Manual respectively. Title Pages will be prepared in manuscript.

WAR DIARY
or
INTELLIGENCE SUMMARY
(Erase heading not required.)

Army Form C. 2118.

Place	Date	Hour	Summary of Events and Information	Remarks and references to Appendices
RAVELSBERG S.17.c.7.3. Sheet 28	12/11/17		98th Bde moved to Nerris area. Bde HQ in Nerris. arranged refilling point at Bde HQ on 13th inst. Div moves to Ypres on 16 inst. my store will be at Brandhoek. I take over from 2nd Can Div there. Railhead from 14th inclusive is Hoogedoorne. To take stock of all area & reserve stores with a view to keeping records & for handing over purposes. Only balance of 2000 prs Trousers S.D. 100 Yukon packs & 500 W.P. Ration Bags to be taken out of area on Div move.	
	13/11/17		Visited proposed store at Brandhoek. Found out 5th Canadian Div had relieved the 2nd Can Div to-day. No accommodation at all except Bde Qrs office & very small Armourers shop. Lorries cannot draw up to store off road. A quantity of R.E. material & Timber Felt & Revet. boards will be needed to construct suitable accommodation before sending stores to the dump. Shall be able to take over store on 17th inst.	
	14/11/17		Wired Ordnance I Anzac Corps to inform me which Australian Divn would take over my store. [illegible] there [illegible] moved 33rd Div Art complete to [illegible] 5th Div in instruction from HQ	

Instructions regarding War Diaries and Intelligence Summaries are contained in F. S. Regs., Part II. and the Staff Manual respectively. Title Pages will be prepared in manuscript.

WAR DIARY
or
INTELLIGENCE SUMMARY
(Erase heading not required.)

Army Form C. 2118.

Place	Date	Hour	Summary of Events and Information	Remarks and references to Appendices
RAVELSBERG Sheet 28 S.17.c.7.7	15/11/17		I'd 5th Div wired that they could not administer 33rd Div Arty after 16th only to move. Wired them to suspend issues from Base as I had already moved the D.A. to them. Stores for 33rd Div Arty sent to new refilling point before Templeux – about 60 kilometres run as 33 DA have now moved further back. This is last refilling as my A.O.C. personnel lorry + remaining stores will be sent to 5th Div at Ouilles-les-Alquines tomorrow. Put 19th Bde at Strazeele to draw from Base. Except for 14 Div Arty suspended issues. Asked A.D.O.S. to whom 14 Div Arty should [illegible] attached, be moved. He replied – 5th Australian Div. Issued move orders accordingly.	
	16/11/17		→ A.O.C. personnel of both 33rd D.A. + 14 D.A. sent to their respective destinations. Last truck of stores from Base received. No further issues to units can be made owing to move of Divn – 19 + 98th Brigades move today + tomorrow to Ypres area. 100th Bde moves to Locre. Drew load of R.E. material ready for sending to new [illegible] tomorrow before stores are sent up on 17th. Issued orders for move of stores, shops + personnel on 17th + 18th.	

2449 Wt. W14957/M90 750,000 1/16 J.B.C. & A. Forms/C.2118/12.

Army Form C. 2118.

Instructions regarding War Diaries and Intelligence Summaries are contained in F. S. Regs., Part II. and the Staff Manual respectively. Title Pages will be prepared in manuscript.

WAR DIARY
or
INTELLIGENCE SUMMARY
(Erase heading not required.)

Place	Date	Hour	Summary of Events and Information	Remarks and references to Appendices
RAKELSBERG	17/11/17		Sent lorry with R.E. material, W.P. Covers & Marquees early in morning with a W.O. & working party of Shoemakers etc to commence building a store. At other times sent later with stores & personnel so as to clear store for the 2nd Australian Div Ordnance who sent 2 lorries with stores to-day. Sent 5 loads to new store in all, leaving 1 lorry for Armourers shop next day & 2 for office remaining stores & cookhouse. Arranged with [illegible] for 4 G.S. wagons in morning to collect 300 Horse Rugs remaining on hand at Clipping Shed & to take to new store any stores which could not be taken by lorry. Went by car to new store & took over from D.A.D.O.S. 4th Can Div. Supervised checking of area stores being left by 4th Canadians. Took over indents & small quantity of stores for 2nd Canadian Divl Arty who have been moved to me for administration.	
BRAAKHOEK H 7 C central Sheet 28	18/11/17		Moved office, cookhouse & remaining stores to H 7 C central & opened store workshops (Boot & armourers) & office at B'Sch. Div H.Q. H.7.C. 8.5. Reported to [illegible] quantities of area stores taken over. Armourers shop accommodation very small so arranged to pitch a Marquee next to shop & allot half of it to Armourers for storage & cleaning purposes. Reviewed 2nd Can Div Arty indents & statement of outstanding guns etc. Found no action had been taken by 2nd Can Ordnance on indents for over a week apparently owing to their own move to 1st Army & consequent suspension of issues from Calais Base. Took immediate action on indents & wired for a gun for 15th Batt 5th Bde. C.F.A. A quantity of stores including Horseshoes sent over by lorry from 2nd Can Ordnance to issue to their artillery. No distribution [illegible] given for the Horse shoes. Obtained this from Staff Capt 2nd Can D.A.	

C.F. 2449 Wt. W14957/M90 750,000 1/16 J.B.C. & A. Forms/C.2118/12.

WAR DIARY
or
INTELLIGENCE SUMMARY
(Erase heading not required.)

Army Form C. 2118.

Instructions regarding War Diaries and Intelligence Summaries are contained in F. S. Regs., Part II. and the Staff Manual respectively. Title Pages will be prepared in manuscript.

Place	Date	Hour	Summary of Events and Information	Remarks and references to Appendices
BRANDHOEK H.Q. Central Sheet 28.	19/11/17		General Routine work putting stone marker & sorting out the miscellaneous heap of packsaddles, water bottles, gum boots, wire cutters etc left by 4th Can Divn. Base were wired on 18th re issue of ... to arrive Railhead, now Vlamertinghe today, no trace received.	
" "	20/11/17		~~...~~ Being informed by AD 4th Can. Div. that a reserve of 10 complete Lewis guns for emergency issues during recent operation was maintained at Bde. HQ. Made enquiries as to numbers now held by Bde in line i.e. 98th Bde. They reported 5 in possession. Issued instructions as to replacement of guns from this reserve. Received urgent demands for Latrine Buckets & demanded 100 for the area.	
" "	21/11/17		Large quantities of Salvage received from units, the bulk of this had been left in Camps by Canadian troops they relieved. Consulted 'Q' as to area stores at present in possession which are not reqd by units as ADOS 8th Corps had requested this information. 5000 water bottles with slings & carriers not required ~~...~~ also 160 Yukon Packs reported. Although further stores may not be required ~~...~~, a detail of these cannot be forwarded until Divnl requirements are fully seen.	
" "	22/11/17		200 sets Tent bottoms received from Base via ODS Corps Troops & drawn direct from Railhead. Total number of sets available approx 400. These will be issued(?) for dentage(?) accommodation being erected in area East of Ypres. General Routine work.	

2449 Wt. W14957/M90 750,000 1/16 J.B.C. & A. Forms/C.2118/12.

Instructions regarding War Diaries and Intelligence Summaries are contained in F. S. Regs., Part II. and the Staff Manual respectively. Title Pages will be prepared in manuscript.

WAR DIARY
or
INTELLIGENCE SUMMARY
(Erase heading not required.)

Army Form C. 2118.

Place	Date	Hour	Summary of Events and Information	Remarks and references to Appendices
BRANDHOEK H7 Central Sheet 28.	23/11/17		Issued 102 sets Tent bottoms to each of 2 Camps just East of Ypres off the Ypres – Potyze Road. 100 anti-gas blankets urgently required by DGS. The 100 on demand since 17th reached arrived from Base. [illegible] 100 from O.O. [illegible] Corps Troops. asked [illegible] for 6 forage stores on loan. urgently required	
" "	24/11/17		Informed 2nd Can Div Arty moving to-day to 1st Army to rejoin their Div. Issued move orders accordingly. Staff Capt asked for an immediate issue of nosebags to enable horses to be fed whole on the march. Wired to 4 Can Ord [illegible] having no return as regards demand for 2 Can Div & my own bulk demands not yet being due. The Artillery have run short of nosebags. Issued all nosebags ~~[illegible]~~ in my stores ~~although~~ appropriated for my own units. Latter demands will be carried forward another week as they are in a better position than 2nd Can Div Arty. ~~[illegible]~~	
" "	25/11/17		2nd Can DA have a good many 18 pdrs, 4.5 Hows & Carriages outstanding. As however the DOS 10 & 56 [illegible] have the carriages awaiting for the guns & the guns waiting for carriages, I wired Base & repeated to Army & Corps not to transfer outstandings for guns etc to 2nd Can DA but to continue issue to me to enable DOS to complete guns for pool. Outstanding Bulk for 2nd Can DA considered cancelled on change of Base & DADOS 2nd Can Div [illegible] statement of cancelled requirements [illegible] Home Base.	

2449 Wt. W14957/M90 750,000 1/16 J.B.C. & A. Forms/C.2118/12.

Instructions regarding War Diaries and Intelligence Summaries are contained in F. S. Regs., Part II. and the Staff Manual respectively. Title pages will be prepared in manuscript.

WAR DIARY
or
INTELLIGENCE SUMMARY.
(Erase heading not required.)

Army Form C. 2118.

Place	Date	Hour	Summary of Events and Information	Remarks and references to Appendices
Brandhoek H.7 C [illegible] Sheet 28	28/11/17		DMGO letter received giving instructions for taking census of all guns in possession & required to complete batteries, through Para 1 287. Census to be taken at noon 28th inst & no issues from Base will be made between midnight 27th inst & midnight 28th & no guns will be taken in or sent out by IsOO of Ordnance Workshops or by OO of Gun Parks. Attended conference at ADOS's office with Staff Capt 18 Corps RA, OO 8th Corps Troops, DADOS 8th Div & IOOs 10 & 56 workshops when best methods for securing accurate returns to clear up present complications were considered. Decided that each DADOS & OO CT should obtain information as to exact number of guns actually with every battery administered by him at 12 noon direct from Staff Capt RA of the group containing these batteries by conferring with him as soon after 12 noon on 28th inst as possible. This also ensures exact agreement between statements of AODs & RA. A copy of the report from each Ordnance officer will be sent to Base DMGO GHQ, DOS & DDOS Army by last D.R.L.S. evening of 28th. The 'B' form of this report gives requirements to complete to establishment & as all indents prior to 28th inst will be ~~all~~ cancelled on that date this 'B' form will act as an indent off which issues will be made to complete batteries. Information as to guns under repair or awaiting carriages will be obtained by DADOS OS in consultation with IsOO on 28th.	

A5834 Wt. W4973/M687 750,000 8/16 D. D. & L. Ltd. Forms/C.2118/13.

Instructions regarding War Diaries and Intelligence Summaries are contained in F. S. Regs., Part II. and the Staff Manual respectively. Title pages will be prepared in manuscript.

WAR DIARY
or
INTELLIGENCE SUMMARY.
(Erase heading not required.)

Army Form C. 2118.

Place	Date	Hour	Summary of Events and Information	Remarks and references to Appendices
Brandhoek H.7.c central Sheet 28	27/11/17		Issued Packsaddlery to Brigade going into line 18/19th & lot for balances. Collected 36 Air Cylinders for Stromboss Horns from OO 8th Corps T.Ps for DSO ~~&~~ & 700 T.S. Lamps & 6½ Lamps R.R. which is in satisfaction of our Divl requirements given as 800 T.S. & 200 Lamps R.R by 'G'. General Routine work.	
" "	28/11/17		The stock of 1½" & 1" Illuminating Pistols has gradually accumulated by receipts from Salvage, duplicate issues from Base, allotments from previous Corps until present stock is too large for requirements of Divn. Informed ADOS 25 1½" Pistols were surplus & available for issues to other Divns or return to Base. Instructions re Census of Guns contained in OC RL's letter & decided upon at ADOS Conference 26th carried out satisfactorily. For purposes of this return I dealt with 4 RFA Bdes which are 8th C.T. units but are depending on Divl front, & signed the report for OO 8th Corps Troops to prevent confusion in covering letter from Base. My own RA were ~~are~~ with 5th now 58th Divn in back area. ADOS obtained their statements from O/C 33rd RA & forwarded them himself to agree with the Corps RA statement.	
" "	29/11/17.		General Routine work. Considerable quantity of repair work & on bicycles ~~& Lewis [illegible]~~ & guns carried out in Armourers shop, a good many made up from salvage [illegible]	
" "	30/11/17		General Routine work.	

A.M.E. Beavan. Capt. DADOS 33rd Divn.

A5834 Wt. W4973/M687 750,000 8/16 D. D. & L. Ltd. Forms/C.2118/13.

SECRET

Army Form C. 2118.

Instructions regarding War Diaries and Intelligence Summaries are contained in F. S. Regs., Part II. and the Staff Manual respectively. Title Pages will be prepared in manuscript.

WAR DIARY or ~~INTELLIGENCE SUMMARY~~

(Erase heading not required.)

December 1917 ~~D A D O S~~ 33rd Div.

Vol 26

Place	Date	Hour	Summary of Events and Information	Remarks and references to Appendices
BRANDHOEK H. 7. c. central Sheet 28	1/12/17		Visited A.D.O.S. 8th Corps & discussed various questions. General Routine work	
	2/12/17		Wired one 58th Divn to move 33rd Div Arty Tons as I am informed by Staff Capt 33 RA that they are moving up to rejoin Divn. Also wired ADOS 8th Divn to send any lorry & AOC personnel to rejoin me as soon as possible bringing any remaining stores for 33 D Arty with them.	
	3/12/17		33rd Div Arty rejoined 33rd Divn. Issued move orders to all concerned. General Routine work.	
	4/12/17		Lorry & A.O.C. personnel arrived from Nesles-les-Alequin (58th Div HQ) There are 3 more loads of Stores to be collected from latter as Ballents moved at very short notice & Stores could not be issued before moving. 2 lorries to be sent in morning to collect remainder. Owing to lack of accomodation a Store will have to be built for 33rd Div Arty Stores. Indented on CRE for timber & chose site for new store.	
	5/12/17		General Routine work. New Store constructed & issues proceeding to units of 33 Div Arty.	

2449 Wt. W14957/M90 750,000 1/16 J.B.C. & A. Forms/C.2118/12.

Army Form C. 2118.

WAR DIARY
or
INTELLIGENCE SUMMARY
(Erase heading not required.)

Instructions regarding War Diaries and Intelligence Summaries are contained in F. S. Regs., Part II. and the Staff Manual respectively. Title Pages will be prepared in manuscript.

Place	Date	Hour	Summary of Events and Information	Remarks and references to Appendices
~~Sheet 28~~ H 7 c central	6/12/17		General Routine work. During Bombing Raid by hostile aeroplanes 2 bombs dropped in vicinity of store & lorry park - one dropping near store wounded 5 O.R. - 3 seriously - one dropping on lorry park killed 2 lorry drivers & wounded 1 slightly. No lights were shewn on my camp or on lorry park. Only 2 A.O.C. casualties occurred. Reported matter to A.D.O.S. who applied to 2nd Army for a replacement for 39th AOC Det.	
	7/12/17		Obtained 34 German rifles from 8th Corps Salvage Dump Vlamertinghe & found 9 were fit for re-issue to Corps School for instructional purposes under authy of recent A.R.O. Reported this to A.D.O.S. & asked for disposal. General Routine work.	
	8/12/17		Received 1 Vickers Gun for 39th Div M.G. Coy & 1 Lewis Gun for 5th Scottish Rifles from Base as M.G. Store is not to make issue to formations in 1st Corps. ~~[illegible]~~ asked R.T.O. Vlamertinghe to arrange with Traffic Hazebrouck for supply of 18 Flat trucks as soon as possible to take surplus vehicles on re-organization of D.A.C (No 3 Sec) to Base. Latter arranged trucks to go and ~~R.T.O. [illegible]~~ 1 Cart Maltese 18 Wagon GS & 132 Sets Harness. 2 sets S.D. Harness despatched to Base & report sent accordingly to A.D.O.S.	
	~~[illegible]~~ 9/12/17 ~~[illegible]~~		Visited DADOS 39 Div at Steenvoorde re replacement of the NCO i/c 39 Div Arty stores who was wounded on 6th inst. He will send another NCO to the Div & hand over the 39 Arty as soon as he arrives from Base. Took note of accommodation of store, workshop & office in Steenvoorde with a view to taking over on 11th 12th & 13th. 4 - 4.5 Hows received from Base off my form 18 (Census return) of 28/11/17. Reported receipt to [illegible]	
	10/12/17		Recd information that Div HQ moves to Steenvoorde on 13th & 2 Bdes moving 11th & 12th inst to that area. Suspended issues on Base except to 33rd & 39th Div Artys who are not moving & will be transferred to relieving Div i.e. 50th. 4 - 4.5 Hows on [illegible] collected from Railhead by 4 D/186 Bde. [illegible]	

2449 Wt. W14957/M90 750,000 1/16 J.B.C. & A. Forms/C.2118/12.

Instructions regarding War Diaries and Intelligence Summaries are contained in F. S. Regs., Part II. and the Staff Manual respectively. Title Pages will be prepared in manuscript.

WAR DIARY
or
INTELLIGENCE SUMMARY
(Erase heading not required.)

Army Form C. 2118.

Place	Date	Hour	Summary of Events and Information	Remarks and references to Appendices
H.7. C. central Sheet 28			Railhead for 6-Day inclusive changes for Wamerlinghe to Poperinghe	
	11/12/17		As 39th Ordnance have now moved from Steenvoorde I sent Armourers & Shoemakers shop equipment & Armourers personnel to ~~[illegible]~~ latter town to take over premises & open their shop. Gave orders for stock taking of all gear & tentage stores for reserve with a view to handing over to relieving Divn. Obtained decision from Q. as to what area & stores in order to Divl establishment of Yukon Packs & Bags [illegible] for Ration should be taken to back area by arrangement with 50th Divn. On commencement of ADOS in Steenvoorde area has no area & stores in it whatever. Transferred 33rd & 39 Artillery any 3 Field Coys RE & Pioneers to 50th Divn to enable base to divert stores to correct destination before all are [illegible]. ~~[illegible]~~ arranged for all salvage to be sent to railhead [illegible] to be handed over.	
	12/12/17		Sent all Stores, Bde WOs & DADOS office to Steenvoorde with instructions to open store & offices ready for arrival of Divn tomorrow. Gave instructions for store of surrounding camp to be cleared up & all dumps of area store to be [illegible] for checking & handing over. Wrote out hand over file for DADOS 50th Div giving all necessary information respecting accomodation of stores, workshops & billets in present camp, area store to be handed over & outstanding questions concerning 33rd & 39th Div. Artys so that no delay may occur through lack of information for his predecessor. DADOS 50th Div sent an NCO & some men his Armourers shop personnel & tentage & covers which he is giving [illegible] & change for that handed over in situ to present store to take over. Arranged for a WO to return from Steenvoorde tomorrow to check & hand over all stores & accomodation to representative of 50th Div Ordnance.	

Instructions regarding War Diaries and Intelligence Summaries are contained in F. S. Regs., Part II. and the Staff Manual respectively. Title Pages will be prepared in manuscript.

WAR DIARY
or
INTELLIGENCE SUMMARY

(Erase heading not required.)

Army Form C. 2118.

Place	Date	Hour	Summary of Events and Information	Remarks and references to Appendices
Steenvoorde	13/12/17		Div H.Q. moved to Steenvoorde. Went there myself by car at 8 a.m. after being notified earlier of the fire which broke out at Div H.Q. in Ramparts, Ypres, involving the loss of practically all officers' clothing & kit & O.R. men's blankets & kit. Arranged with D.D.S.&T. to draw 100 blankets this morning for issue to officers & men of Div H.Q. who all arrive in Steenvoorde deficient of them owing to above mentioned fire. Wired Officers Clothing Depots at Bailleul & St Omer to inform me what stocks of Jackets S.D. Officers [illegible] are immediately available as a large demand for latter may be expected from Officers of Div H.Q. Issued fire orders & orders affecting discipline while in Steenvoorde to H.Q. Detachment & attached personnel & fixed up billets, cookhouse & salvage dump. Arranged for necessary number of fire buckets to be made by Armourers & painted. Sack brought from old store split up ready for issue to units on coming to store to draw. 100th Bde returned to forward area for work on advanced [illegible]. Bde H.Q. at [illegible].	
	14/12/17		Wrote Staff Capt 98th Bde to arrange a programme for sending in Lewis Guns of [illegible] Battalions to Div Armourers shop for overhaul at rate of 4 per day – to commence on 17 inst. Asked Staff Capt 100th Bde to inform me if he wished any special refitting of ordnance [illegible] as most of Bde units are in forward area. All have however left their Q.M.s' stores & transport in this area near Winnezeele so that they can easily draw from my store in Steenvoorde. 19th & 98th Bdes asking for area [illegible] drying Boots & Lamps to be issued to units for use in billets. Sent urgent demand to Base for 1000 [illegible] Boots & 300 [illegible]	

2449 Wt. W14957/M90 750,000 1/16 J.B.C. & A. Forms/C.2118/12.

Instructions regarding War Diaries and Intelligence Summaries are contained in F. S. Regs., Part II. and the Staff Manual respectively. Title Pages will be prepared in manuscript.

WAR DIARY
or
INTELLIGENCE SUMMARY
(Erase heading not required.)

Army Form C. 2118.

Place	Date	Hour	Summary of Events and Information	Remarks and references to Appendices
Steenvoorde	15/12/17		Visited 6 C.C.S.s near Poperinghe at request of A.D.O.S to advise + report on [illegible] of their [illegible] which is an urgent + important matter. A report was made by DADOS 39th Div's on 6th inst. + a further report of progress is now required. Found progress satisfactory in most cases but one very slow. Gave advise + urged completion without delay. All C.C.S.s have good supply of material or can obtain it at once from O.O. 8th Corps Tps. Reported accordingly to A.D.O.S. Baths Officer requests weekly supply of soap. Arranged this + made immediate issue from surplus stock. Issued 160 lamps F.S. to 15th Div depot stock + 16 to Baths Officer + requested G. to apply for a further issue of 300 for the area. Truck of stores received from B.A.O.S. including Gas alarm rattles + 500 L.G. Magazines to meet outstanding demands on coming out of line.	
	16/12/17.		Received 7,500 New Patt Containers for S.B.R.s from Base + handed over to Div Gas Officer for issue to complete whole Div with this pattern container in replacement of old Black pattern. 1,000 of Div'l reserve of new patt. containers were issued to 33rd Div Arty [illegible] Div'n leaving forward area to complete them. [illegible] 7,500 will be put into stock to complete reserves. General Routine work	

2449 Wt. W14957/M90 750,000 1/16 J.B.C. & A. Forms/C.2118/12.

Instructions regarding War Diaries and Intelligence Summaries are contained in F. S. Regs., Part II. and the Staff Manual respectively. Title Pages will be prepared in manuscript.

WAR DIARY
or
INTELLIGENCE SUMMARY
(Erase heading not required.)

Army Form C. 2118.

Place	Date	Hour	Summary of Events and Information	Remarks and references to Appendices
	17/12/17		Wrote 20th R. Fus. to investigate why the Lewis Gun returned by them to Div Armourers shop was in a rusty & neglected condition. Reported to A.D.O.S. present position of supply of Compasses Mag. Prismatic. None now outstanding. Sent 850 pr worn out Boots to D.A.D.O.S. 14 Div for issue to troops in forward area for use in billets while their own boots are being dried after coming out of line. All worn out boots are being collected for this service & not sent to Base. General Routine work. The outstanding demand for a Lewis Gun for [illegible] R.E. made up from salvaged gun & parts recd from Base yesterday in Armourers shop Div is now completed. 3 Vickers Guns issued to M.G. Coys to complete all outstanding demands. These guns were sent for repair after salving in forward area & were in a very faulty state. Question of issue of worn out boots for billets to own units taken up with [illegible] & 'Q' office.	
	18/12/17		Hastened Drawers woollen 5,000 & Gloves woollen 16,000 still not received & very urgently required. Lewis Gun made up in Armourers shop for issue to 16 [illegible]. General Routine work. Balance of Leather Jerkins required to complete Signals, M.G. Coys, T.M.Bs. Field Coys & H.Q. R.E. received. Those demanded for Field Coys ~~[illegible]~~ in the surplus of issue to these 3 units has been made by D.A.D.O.S. 50th Divn. out of surplus from issues to 33 Div H.Qs. asked latter by letter if this could be effected.	
	19/12/17		Visited the following units & Bde H.Qs by car & reviewed indents where possible & found out what stores they urgently need which are outstanding. Gloves woollen are urgently reqd by all units. Troughs are very short of aprons kilt & want outstandings hastened. Visited 2 Army School of Sniping at Mont des Cats & handed in rifle & 5 [illegible] still received	

[signature]

2449 Wt. W14957/M90 750,000 1/16 J.B.C. & A. Forms/C.2118/12.

Army Form C. 2118.

WAR DIARY
or
INTELLIGENCE SUMMARY
(Erase heading not required.)

Instructions regarding War Diaries and Intelligence Summaries are contained in F. S. Regs., Part II. and the Staff Manual respectively. Title Pages will be prepared in manuscript.

Place	Date	Hour	Summary of Events and Information	Remarks and references to Appendices
STEENVOORDE			from salvage & handed in by units. Drew 4 new Rifles off outstanding indents. Units visited 245 M.S. Coy. 98th M.G. Coy. 98 Bde H.Q. 2nd A & S.H. 1st Middlesex. 1st Queens. H.L.I. 100th Bde H.Q. 64 & 158 A.F.A. Bde with Amn Cols moved	
	20/12/17		to me for supply by O.O. & Corps Tps. Customers move to all concerned. As Base report no outstanding indents with them for winter clothing & formations have reported outstanding demands urgently reqd and 2nd Army have arranged to send along to Base to draw all items urgently required to avoid further delay. Reported stores worsted & sweaters as still outstanding & urgently reqd. Spoke O.O. & Corps Troops re transfer of outstanding indents of 64 & 158 A.F.A. Bde moved to me yesterday, also what quantity of stores they had for transfer. Arranged for my lorry collecting for Corps Salvage Dump tomorrow to call at O.O. & C.T. & collect all stores on hand for these Brigades. Arranged office & store personnel for dealing with indents & stores for these 2 Bdes. Difficult to arrange this owing to present reduction in Staff (A.O.C.) 1 N.C.O. & 2 men away with 50th Div & 1 W.O. lent to O.O. & Corps Tps. Informed A.D.O.S. of difficulty & asked for an extra storeman	
	21/12/17		Reviewed outstanding requirements of grouped M.G. Coys with A.A. & Q.M.G. Group as established when in line & checked present outstanding indents of individual M.G. Coys with this list — deleted therefrom all items [illegible] demanded on former to avoid duplication. On receipt of same D.O.S. will distribute to Coys to complete them.	

2449 Wt. W14957/M90 750,000 1/16 J.B.C. & A. Forms/C.2118/12.

Instructions regarding War Diaries and Intelligence Summaries are contained in F. S. Regs., Part II. and the Staff Manual respectively. Title Pages will be prepared in manuscript.

WAR DIARY
or
INTELLIGENCE SUMMARY

(Erase heading not required.)

Army Form C. 2118.

Place	Date	Hour	Summary of Events and Information	Remarks and references to Appendices
STEENVOORDE	21/12/17		DADOS 50th warned that my Field Coys were now complete with Jerkins. Instructed Bde wos to complete all remaining units of Div not provided for in original demand from surplus 700 received by me for my Field Coys. All demands for Jerkins for re-inforcements can also be met. Valued items of AOD supply, destroyed in fire at Adv Div HQ on 13th met for purposes of Court of Enquiry. Attended conference of all Staff Officers of Div HQ at 'A' Mess with G.O.C. Subject dealt with — Avoidance of friction between Staff & units.	
	22/12/17		Visited ADOS & discussed procedure re issue of Area stores. They are not to be issued to Div'l units but in bulk to Area Commandants & ADOS informed of distribution by areas. As 8th Div Arty are moving to Steenvoorde area to-day they will be administered temporarily by me. 1st Div sending AOC personnel comp. stores there to assist until 8th Div move up into line on 27th about. Visited DADOS 50th Div at my late store, Brandhoek to ensure 33rd Div Arty were being properly administered. Found everything satisfactory. My representative with 33rd Div Arty requires another 120 Jerkins leather to complete all. [illegible] them from my surplus. DADOS 50th Div has [illegible] a further 30 [illegible] containers issued them in forward area [illegible]	

2449 Wt. W14957/M90 750,000 1/16 J.B.C. & A. Forms/C.2118/12.

Instructions regarding War Diaries and Intelligence Summaries are contained in F. S. Regs., Part II. and the Staff Manual respectively. Title Pages will be prepared in manuscript.

WAR DIARY
or
INTELLIGENCE SUMMARY.

(Erase heading not required.)

Army Form C. 2118.

Place	Date	Hour	Summary of Events and Information	Remarks and references to Appendices
Steenvoorde	22/12/17		Visited O.O. 8th Corps Troops & obtained particulars of any outstanding guns & carriages [illegible] Batteries of 158 & 64 A.F.A. Bdes recently transferred to us. Only 1 18 pdr carr for C/64 outstanding. To go to 10 & 56 Workshops on receipt for No 5 Gun Park. My W.O. sent to O.O. 8th Corps Troops is quickly learning the procedure in that office which is different to work of a Bde W.O.	
	23/12/17.		4000 Gloves woollen recd from Base so long need not now be sent [illegible] 2nd Army to Base as arranged. 5000 Socks received to make up [illegible] reserve allowing for present clothing being issued to [illegible] exchange & units to replace losses only. 3000 drawers woollen received as part issue of 5000 demanded a month ago & handed over to Bath Officer. Sent return to [illegible] showing weight of stores carried by my 3 lorries for 10 days only. This is required for comparison by 8th Corps. General routine work. 15 Lewis Guns sent in by 4 Suffolks for overhaul.	
	24/12/17		General routine work. W.O. & 4 men [illegible] 8th Div Arty reported for duty with lorry & stores from 14th Divn. Arranged with Town Major for a suitable store for them. Wired [illegible] to instruct all Batteries etc to draw from me & submit indents to me till further notice. 2700 [illegible] received as reinforcement from 2nd 14th Divn [illegible]	

2449 Wt. W14957/M90 750,000 1/16 J.B.C. & A. Forms/C.2118/12.

Instructions regarding War Diaries and Intelligence Summaries are contained in F. S. Regs., Part II. and the Staff Manual respectively. Title Pages will be prepared in manuscript.

WAR DIARY
or
INTELLIGENCE SUMMARY
(Erase heading not required.)

Army Form C. 2118.

Place	Date	Hour	Summary of Events and Information	Remarks and references to Appendices
Steenvoorde	25/12/17		Shop closed & only issue made from stores as no units had come to draw. General Routine work in office. Wired D.O.S. [illegible] re issue of [illegible] & [illegible] arrange for fitting [illegible] [illegible] issue [illegible]	
	26/12/17		Shop reopened & normal routine work resumed. [illegible] A.H. & [illegible] 8 Lewis Guns for overhaul in a very rusty & dirty state showing great neglect on part of their Armourer. Matter being brought to notice of G.O.C. for action as a great many spares have become unserviceable through the neglect. Armourer Workshop making out full report on condition. 64 Vickers A.A. sights correct pattern received from Base Hd Qrs.	
	27/12/17		Visited No 3 Can. C.C.S. & found [illegible] of Tentage completed. General Routine work. Notified A.H.Q. that no Vickers A.A. sights would be required owing to receipt of sufficient from Base to complete the [illegible] deficient in [illegible]. Instructed latter to indent for numbers req'd to complete & to return any of incorrect pattern to my store for return to Base. Reviewed all outstanding detail indents of 19th Bde & 248 [illegible] & Supply Column. Very few items outstanding. Hastened those outstanding over a month. Pistols Webley & [illegible] are most difficult items to obtain. Reported neglected condition of 7 Lewis Guns ~~[illegible]~~ A & S.H. handed in for overhaul to [illegible] Office for investigation.	

2449 Wt. W14957/M90 750,000 1/16 J.B.C. & A. Forms/C.2118/12.

Instructions regarding War Diaries and Intelligence Summaries are contained in F. S. Regs., Part II. and the Staff Manual respectively. Title Pages will be prepared in manuscript.

WAR DIARY
or
INTELLIGENCE SUMMARY
(Erase heading not required.)

Army Form C. 2118.

Place	Date	Hour	Summary of Events and Information	Remarks and references to Appendices
Steenvoorde	28/12/17		~~Routine~~ General Routine work. Lorry sent to No 5 Gun Park to collect Lewis & Vickers A.A. Mountings & Sights & to deliver latter to 5th & 51st Div ordnance according to instructions from A.D.O.S. 15 Lewis Sights allotted to this Div brought back by lorry. Distributed 5 per Bde on instructions from G. Reported receipt of 64 A.A. Sights Vickers to DADOS & instructions re Corps indent for numbers of correct pattern required. Issue will then be made to complete them.	
	29/12/17		Visited all units of 00 Bde & reviewed outstanding indents & took note of any special requirements of units & suffer detail items outstanding. Revolvers are the worst item nearly all units & especially 1st Slap having outstandings of over a month old. Hastening action has already been taken with Corps & Base without result. Informed G. Office & DADOS that the allotments of Lewis & 4 Vickers A.A. Sights will not be required as I have more than sufficient in store to complete all deficiencies.	

2449 Wt. W14957/M90 750,000 1/16 J.B.C. & A. Forms/C.2118/12.

Instructions regarding War Diaries and Intelligence Summaries are contained in F. S. Regs., Part II. and the Staff Manual respectively. Title Pages will be prepared in manuscript.

WAR DIARY
or
INTELLIGENCE SUMMARY
(Erase heading not required.)

Army Form C. 2118.

Place	Date	Hour	Summary of Events and Information	Remarks and references to Appendices
STEENVOORDE	30/12/17		6,200 Muzzle Protectors No 3 received from Base; they complete all outstanding demands on Base & is more than sufficient to meet present requirements of units to complete to 1 per rifle. Have asked 150 White Scouts for patrolling in snow by wire to A.D.O.S. as G.O.C. particularly wishes same to be complete before going into line in view of continuance of snowy weather. 16 Lewis guns with spares received from 2nd Worcesters for overhaul in Divl Armourers Shop.	
	31/12/17		General Routine work. Monthly returns to Corps despatched except "comparative statement of Bulk issues & receipts". Demanded one 3" T.M complete less Bedplate & spares for 100 T.M.B to replace one rendered unserviceable thro' premature in barrel while demonstrating anti-aircraft firing. Repeated indent by wire to No 5 Gun Park as method of demanding T.Ms now follows that for guns as regards Gun Park.	

A.M. Bevan Capt
D.A.D.O.S.
33rd Divn

2449 Wt. W14957/M90 750,000 1/16 J.B.C. & A. Forms/C.2118/12.

No 33 Div Supply Col

Return of casualties for month of December 1917

	Killed	Wounded	Gas
Personnel.	2.	1.	–

Vehicles — Several slightly damaged by shrapnel.

SECRET

WAR DIARY
or
~~INTELLIGENCE SUMMARY~~
(Erase heading not required.)

Army Form C. 2118.

Instructions regarding War Diaries and Intelligence Summaries are contained in F. S. Regs., Part II. and the Staff Manual respectively. Title Pages will be prepared in manuscript.

D.A.D.O.S. 33rd Divn
January 1918.
Vol 27

Place	Date	Hour	Summary of Events and Information	Remarks and references to Appendices
Steenvoorde	1/1/18		General Routine work. Issues from Base suspended except stores for 64th A.F.A. Bde & 8th Div Arty, in view of forthcoming move of Divn to forward area.	
	2/1/18		D.A.D.O.S. 50th Div called to arrange details of relief between Ord 50th Div & Ord 33rd Divn & inspected my stores, offices, shops, billets etc in Steenvoorde. As one of his Infty Bdes is moving into this area on 3rd & one of my Bdes is moving up into forward area same date he suggested we start our moves on 3rd to be completed by 4th inst. & also suggested that to economise transport we use each others lorries on 3rd to take each others stores to new stores i.e. 33rd to Brandhoek & 50th to Steenvoorde on return journeys. As there are three lorries from each Divn on one trip out & home will transfer 6 loads of each others stores & 'dead' journeys will be avoided. Agreed with these proposals & arranged accordingly. Shops instructed to close & pack up ready for moving on 3rd inst.	
	3/1/18		Moved 8th Div Arty to 8th Divn & arranged to send lorry personnel to [illegible] 4th inst. Visited store at Brandhoek & saw D.A.D.O.S. 50 Div re various matters re area & trench stores, re his handing over in the store, transfers of his & my Artillery & M.G. outstanding guns etc. Inspected his store & arranged allotment of accomodation to suit my own system of working. Moved [illegible] of shops personnel & stores to Brandhoek [illegible] on 4th & prepared handing over file for D.A.D.O.S. 50 [illegible]	[illegible] D.A.D.O.S. 33 Div[illegible]

Army Form C. 2118.

WAR DIARY
or
INTELLIGENCE SUMMARY
(Erase heading not required.)

Instructions regarding War Diaries and Intelligence Summaries are contained in F. S. Regs., Part II. and the Staff Manual respectively. Title Pages will be prepared in manuscript.

Place	Date	Hour	Summary of Events and Information	Remarks and references to Appendices
BRANDHOEK H.7.C.6.7. Sheet 28	4/1/18		Moved to store at Rear Div H.Q. Brandhoek H.7.C.8.5. Shops opened & work commenced. 2 tons of stores for Artillery units recently attached but now moved to 50th Div & 8th Div received at Railhead. Instructed 9th H.L.I. to send the balance of their Lewis Guns to Armourers shop for overhaul before Bde goes into line. Confirmed move of 50th Div Arty to me for administration. WO & clerk & storeman & lorry left with me by DADOS 50th Div to assist in latter. Opened issues again from Base.	
	5/1/18.		General Routine work. Sent stores for 66 A.F.A. Bde & 8th Div Arty received yesterday off units landing. Bulk demands to 30th Div & 8th Div, by lorry.	respectively
	6/1/18		Drew 1,000 prs Thigh Gum Boots from O.O. 4th Army Troops No 1 at Caestre on Ordnance 8th Corps authority. These are urgently required in anticipation of thaw. General routine work.	
	7/1/18.		1000 water tins urgently reqd to replace lost & other left in forward area & taken away by 50th Div units. ADOS arranged for this number to be drawn from 8th Corps Salvage Dump. Salvage Dump would not issue without written statement of the authority & [illegible] officer [illegible] & arranged to collect & return all petrol tins & receive at future for handing over to M.S. General Routine work.	

2449 Wt. W14957/M90 750,000 1/16 J.B.C. & A. Forms/C.2118/12.

Instructions regarding War Diaries and Intelligence Summaries are contained in F. S. Regs., Part II. and the Staff Manual respectively. Title Pages will be prepared in manuscript.

WAR DIARY
or
INTELLIGENCE SUMMARY
(Erase heading not required.)

Army Form C. 2118.

Place	Date	Hour	Summary of Events and Information	Remarks and references to Appendices
BRANDHOEK H.7.c.6.7. Sheet 28.	8/1/18.		Demanded 500 water tins from Base to replace wastage. Visited D.A.D. Div H.Q. Ypres. Saw Div Salvage Officer. He collects ammunition mainly. Any clothing & equipment salvaged he is sending to my dump. No necessity for me to collect. Found 101st Field Amb had returned a MK V water cart less draught pole to Salvage Dump. Asked unit if the cart was salvaged by them. Unit replied – found in Prison Ypres on taking over from 50th Div. Asked Salvage Officer to return it to Railhead for despatch to Base for over haul.	
	9/1/18		Received 25 Steel Helmets fitted with new & improved pattern Chain visor. Shewed one to SOC & asked GSO1 for distribution for trial. Issued 6 new pattern Hot Food Containers to 100th Bde (Infantry) for trial. These are similar to a petrol tin but have double walls enclosing asbestos for heat retention. These containers are provided with a large opening for stew etc. Blankets urgently reqd for reinforcements arriving with one only.	
	10/1/18		Visited Cassel – Officers Clothing Depot & DDOS 2nd Army Tps to obtain some Blankets if possible. None available! Obtained some for immediate requirements from surplus stock with 8th Divn. General & Routine work.	

2449 Wt. W14957/M90 750,000 1/16 J.B.C. & A. Forms/C.2118/12.

Instructions regarding War Diaries and Intelligence Summaries are contained in F. S. Regs., Part II. and the Staff Manual respectively. Title Pages will be prepared in manuscript.

WAR DIARY
or
INTELLIGENCE SUMMARY
(Erase heading not required.)

Army Form C. 2118.

Place	Date	Hour	Summary of Events and Information	Remarks and references to Appendices
BRANDHOEK H.7.C 6.7 Sheet 28	11/1/18.		Store visited by A.D.O.S. 8th Corps & inspected. Attended as President of an Interviewing committee of Officers at H.Q. 1/4 East Yorks Regt Winnezeele. Only 40% of the N.C.Os & men shewn on nominal rolls attended. Completed the Registration forms & despatched them to H.Q. 8th Corps "A".	
	12/1/18		Report received from A.D.O.S. on condition of store. Replied giving explanations & shewing disciplinary action taken in cases of minor offences on part of 2 men of A.O.C. Detachment. Camp was in a very wet & muddy state at time of ADOS inspection owing to sudden thaw & difficulties of working greatly increased thereby.	
	13/1/18.	Suspended issues to 50th Div Arty [?]	Tried to arrange with D.A.D.O.S. 29th Divn to administer 50th Div Arty for a few days as latter are moving into back area in advance of their own Divn. 29th replied that they were moving forward themselves so could not administer. Informed 50 Div accordingly & latter asked me to retain his personnel & stores for a few days until he was ready to receive them in back area. Agreed. A proportion of the 30,000 Frost cogs demanded urgently by me for 50th Div Arty received from Base. CRA 50th Divn will draw from D.A.D.O.S. 50th Div on way to back area so these cogs will have to be collected by DADOS 50 Div as thaw precautions are on & I have no car available to-day	

2449 Wt. W14957/M90 750,000 1/16 J.B.C. & A. Forms/C.2118/12.

WAR DIARY
or
INTELLIGENCE SUMMARY
(Erase heading not required.)

Army Form C. 2118.

Instructions regarding War Diaries and Intelligence Summaries are contained in F. S. Regs., Part II. and the Staff Manual respectively. Title Pages will be prepared in manuscript.

Place	Date	Hour	Summary of Events and Information	Remarks and references to Appendices
BRANDHOEK	14/1/18.		Moved 50th Div. Artillery to 50th Div. Demanded 100 tubs washing from Base to replace lost & unserviceable in camps in forward area. On arrival arranged to issue to Area Commandant East of Ypres area. Moved 446 Field Coy ~~fr~~ to 50th Div & confirmed move of 7 Field Coy from 50th Div to 33rd Div.	
	15/1/18		General Routine work. Visited ADV HQ & saw DAQMG & AA & QMG. 18 Soyer stoves are urgently required in connection with special ~~kitchens~~ for feeding 3 Battalions in support line. Arranged to order & supply 12.	
	16/1/18		General Routine Work. Visited A.D.O.S. office & stated urgency for issue of these 12 Stoves. Corps are very short of them, so many having already been issued into Corps area. I have asked for an additional 1000 prs Thigh Gum Boots.	
	17/1/18.		Demanded a quantity of tentage as a great increase of same required for 19 Field Amb (Div Rest Station) to replace others damaged by recent gale & by accidental fire. Before demanding I issued Marquees as far as possible from stock taken over from 50th Div. 4th Army have approved issue of 200 blankets as 3rd blanket for elderly men in Div. These will be sent up [illegible]	

2449 Wt. W14957/M90 750,000 1/16 J.B.C. & A. Forms/C.2118/12.

Instructions regarding War Diaries and Intelligence Summaries are contained in F. S. Regs., Part II. and the Staff Manual respectively. Title Pages will be prepared in manuscript.

WAR DIARY
or
INTELLIGENCE SUMMARY

(Erase heading not required.)

Army Form C. 2118.

Place	Date	Hour	Summary of Events and Information	Remarks and references to Appendices
	18/1/18		General Routine Work.	
	19/1/18		General Routine work.	
	20/1/18		Moved 7" + 4.7" Teloscopes, H.Q. 50th D.L. + 7th D.L.I. Pioneers to 50th Divn + arranged to re consign stores [illegible] received after this onto 50th Divn. Drew 300 prs Thigh Gum Boots from O.O. 8th Corps Tps. This is in satisfaction of Q's demand for 1000 prs. No more available in Corps. Visited DDOS 4th Army on personal matters. 7 Lewis AA Mtgs (4 Army Pattern) received from O.O. 8th Corps Tps. These are Trench stores	
	21/1/18		Recd 14 Lewis AA Sights + 5 Mountings (4 Army Pattern) from No 5 Gun Park by Car. Distribution of these has been given by "G". Referred demand from 1st Middlesex for Lewis AA Mountings for their 8 guns in continuous use for AA work to S.S.O. 2. Latter approved issue of the additional 7, drawn from O.O. 8th Corps Tps, to the Pioneers to be handed over as Trench stores on relief	
	22/1/18.		Issued a Lewis Gun from Salved Stock in Armourers shop to 5th Scottish to replace one rendered "U" through shell fire. Reported issue to Army [illegible]	

2449 Wt. W14957/M90 750,000 1/16 J.B.C. & A. Forms/C.2118/12.

Army Form C. 2118.

Instructions regarding War Diaries and Intelligence Summaries are contained in F. S. Regs., Part II. and the Staff Manual respectively. Title Pages will be prepared in manuscript.

WAR DIARY
or
INTELLIGENCE SUMMARY
(Erase heading not required.)

Place	Date	Hour	Summary of Events and Information	Remarks and references to Appendices
BRANDHOEK H.7.c.6.7. Sheet 28	23/1/18		Visited D.A.D.O.S. 4th Army. Went to Coudekerque Branche near Dunkirk & arranged with M. Vandersluys for 25 converted Petrol Tins as per approved pattern for use as Hot-food containers to be finished & ready for collection on 26th inst. Under original contract made by A.D.O.S. 8th Corps 100 are to be completed by end of January & another 100 by 10th of February. Hastened [illegible] owing to pressing need of these containers in the line. Demanded 18 pdr gun for C/162 to replace piece condemned under C.O.O.'s authority. Collected 25 Tables, 50 forms & 70 Lamps Barrack Hanging from O.O. 8th Corps Tps.	
	24/1/18		Collected 400 Petrol tins for use as water tins by lorry from 8th Corps Salvage Dump. Poperinghe. These will be held in stock & issued to replace wastage. Submitted application for replacement of A.O.W.O. 98th Bde who has gone sick with debility & it is essential to complete establishment of my Detachment. Recommended present Sergt-Clerk for promotion to fill above vacancy.	
	25/1/18		Completed valuation of Chaffcutters privately owned in possession of 33rd Div Artys. & forward statement of same to A.D.O.S. 8th Corps. Collected 2 Rifles fitted with telescopic sights for 2nd Army Sniping School; 1 for 5 [illegible] & 1 for 1st [illegible]. General Routine work. Asked S.M.T.O. for 4 lorries on 28th for moving [illegible]	

2449 Wt. W14957/M90 750,000 1/16 J.B.C. & A. Forms/C.2118/12.

Instructions regarding War Diaries and Intelligence Summaries are contained in F. S. Regs., Part II. and the Staff Manual respectively. Title pages will be prepared in manuscript.

WAR DIARY
or
INTELLIGENCE SUMMARY.
(Erase heading not required.)

Army Form C. 2118.

Place	Date	Hour	Summary of Events and Information	Remarks and references to Appendices
BRANDHOEK H.7.c.6.7. Sheet 28	25/1/18	cont.	Wired DADOS 50th Div to arrange use of my 4 lorries to convey his stores here on 29th & return journey on condition I use his to complete my move thus economising transport. Latter replied "agreed". Arranged to visit him at WIZERNES on 27th inst. Gave instructions for Salvage Dump to cease receipts to enable large accumulation to be cleared before 28th inst & instructed Shops to close on 27th ready for moving 28th inst.	
	26/1/18.		General Routine work. Demand 18 pdr piece for B/162 condemned for damage by shell fire.	
	27/1/18.		Visited DADOS 50th Div at WIZERNES, inspected his Store, shops, offices & billeting accomodation – all very good indeed especially the Store. Arranged details of move with him. First loads for both ends to start simultaneously on 28th & return on 29th with each others stores & complete move by evening of 29th. Had Store shops thoroughly cleaned & area stores arranged for easy checking. Prepared list of all area & trench stores to be handed over	

Instructions regarding War Diaries and Intelligence Summaries are contained in F. S. Regs., Part II. and the Staff Manual respectively. Title pages will be prepared in manuscript.

WAR DIARY
or
INTELLIGENCE SUMMARY.
(Erase heading not required.)

Army Form C. 2118.

Place	Date	Hour	Summary of Events and Information	Remarks and references to Appendices
BRANDHOEK H7.C.6.7 Sheet 28	28/1/18		Four lorries of 38th Supply Col reported & were despatched with Armourers Boot shops - equipment & personnel & all Bulk stores received yesterday & main portion of Divl reserve stores. Four lorries arranged by SMTO 8th Corps. which should have reported 8 a.m. did not report until 1 p.m. They were surplus to original programme but were used for a trip to WIZERNES & return 29th with 50% Divl stores to avoid using Divl lorries on dead runs on 29th. 2 lorries lent one to Gas Officer & 1 to Camp Commandant. Arranged for 2 only of my own lorries to return first thing 29th to H7C6.7 to collect office, cookhouse remaining stores & personnel & to complete move. Re-opened issues from 30th inst.	
WIZERNES	29/1/18		Completed move - shops re-opened ready for work.	
" "	30/1/18		General Routine work. Arranged programme for overhaul & fitting of new bolt-catches to Lewis guns of 2 Bns 100th Bde & 4 Bns of 19th Bde whose guns have not been recently overhauled. Programme commences 31st inst. Arranged programme for Refilling of 38th Div Arty in Thiembronne area which is too far away for Batteries to draw from my store. Reviewed issues & new returns of unserviceable underclothing since last balance was made of Nov 11th 1917.	

A6945 Wt. W11422/M1160 350,000 12/16 D. D. & L. Forms/C./2118/14.

Army Form C. 2118.

Instructions regarding War Diaries and Intelligence Summaries are contained in F. S. Regs., Part II. and the Staff Manual respectively. Title pages will be prepared in manuscript.

WAR DIARY
or
INTELLIGENCE SUMMARY.
(Erase heading not required.)

Place	Date	Hour	Summary of Events and Information	Remarks and references to Appendices
WIZERNES.	31/1/18		General Routine work. Bdes units & Div Tps drawing from ~~new~~ store. Completed revision of outstanding Detail Indents of whole Divn & Bde Coys & NCO. i/c Artillery instructed what action to take on those over one month old. Dues out are very small at present time. Handed over Impment a/cs after balancing & important notes for action to my Chief Clerk before proceeding on leave to U.K. to-morrow.	
			A. W. McGowan Capt D.A.D.O.S. 33rd Division	

A6945 Wt. W11422/M1160 350,000 12/16 D. D. & L. Forms/C./2118/14.

SECRET

Instructions regarding War Diaries and Intelligence Summaries are contained in F. S. Regs., Part II. and the Staff Manual respectively. Title pages will be prepared in manuscript.

WAR DIARY
or
INTELLIGENCE SUMMARY.
(Erase heading not required.)

SECRET

D.A.D.O.S. 33rd DIVISION

Army Form C. 2118.

FEBUARY. 1918

1st Sheet

Vol 28

Place	Date	Hour	Summary of Events and Information	Remarks and references to Appendices
WIZERNES	Feby 1st		Capt. A.M.E. Beavan. A.O.D. proceeded to England on 14 days leave. Got in communication with ADOS as to date of issue of 4000 paillasses urgently required by men in rest area who were sleeping on stone floors. Question put up to Army. Vehicles arrived at Railhead and drawn by B Echelon D.A.C. 18th Midds (Pioneers) + A/156 Bde R.F.A.	
	2nd		Arranged with O.C. 20th R Fus. to take in all his Technical Stores and to have same carefully checked by a responsible person prior to despatch to Base. Saw R.O.O. St Omer for fixing a date for a truck to convey 20th R Fus equipment to Base. G.O.C. 33rd Div. Arty came to Office and requested that a quantity of Paint of various colours be demanded as early as possible to enable guns + carriage to be suitably painted whilst Arty are in rest.	
	3rd		Received information from AA + QMG that 2nd R Wel Fus were being transferred from 33rd to 38th Division, gave necessary orders to Store Staff as to supplying of Bulk to Battalion and despatch to new	

A6945 Wt. W11422/M1160 350,000 12/16 D. D. & L. Forms/C./2118/14.

SECRET

Instructions regarding War Diaries and Intelligence Summaries are contained in F. S. Regs., Part II. and the Staff Manual respectively. Title pages will be prepared in manuscript.

WAR DIARY
or
INTELLIGENCE SUMMARY.
(Erase heading not required.)

D.A.D.O.S.
33rd DIVISION

Army Form C. 2118.

2nd Sheet

Place	Date	Hour	Summary of Events and Information	Remarks and references to Appendices
WIZERNES	Feby		news.	
	3.		Formation of incomplete detail indents and statement of bulk out-standings. Arranged with S/Capt. 98th Bde to refill at BOISDENGHEM.	
	4th		Moved 2nd R.W.Fus. to 38th DIVISION. Cancelled all outstanding dues out of 20th R.Fus. on Base.	
	5th		Moved 2 Sections of 11th – 222nd Field Coy RE from 33rd Divn to O.O. 4th Army Troops No 3. Issued Training stores to 3 Brigades. Made arrangements with Divl DADOS to re-call Arm S/s Humpage, Crump & Sullivan into Armourers Shop owing to large amount of work involved by conversion of Lewis Guns.	
	6th		Sent lorry to 5th Ord Gun Park with 16 Lewis Guns & component parts which had been returned by 20th R.Fus. under instructions contained in 4th Army (D.D.O.S) letter S.O./1 d/d 31/1/18. Demanded a further 500 Bayonet fighting sacks by wire from Base. Arranged with Corps for a further supply of 30 Lamps [illegible] for billets of 19th Bde	
	7th		Arranged for Lewis Guns of 1st Middx to be sent in to Armourers Shop for overhaul & alteration of Butt Catches. Also for Lewis Guns of 1st Middlesex	

SECRET

Instructions regarding War Diaries and Intelligence Summaries are contained in F. S. Regs., Part II. and the Staff Manual respectively. Title pages will be prepared in manuscript.

D.A.D.O.S.
33rd DIVISION

Army Form C. 2118.

WAR DIARY
or
INTELLIGENCE SUMMARY.
(Erase heading not required.)

3rd Sheet.

Place	Date	Hour	Summary of Events and Information	Remarks and references to Appendices
WIZERNES	8/2		Arranged with Staff Captain 19th Infty Bde to review outstanding indent with Q.Ms of units. Received quantity of paint from Base for 33rd Divl Arty and arranged with S/Capt for distribution to Batteries.	
	9/2		Put further bulk demand on Base for Paint to enable Divl Arty to carry on with painting gun & carriages. Received information from 2nd Cav C.C.S. that T/S/Cdr Lobb J.R. AOC had been evacuated to Base and informed ADOS 8th Corps of fact with a view to obtaining his relief. Moved 2 Sec of 212th Field Coy R.E. to 4th Army Tps No 3.	
	10/2		Wired S/Capt 33rd Div Arty as to whether How Batteries were in possession of "Mat gun wheel" as O.O. 8th Corps Tps had some for issue. Sent lorry out to C.C.S. at St Omer to collect rifles and bayonets for completion of reserve of these items in Divl Armourers Shop. Collected 5 Lewis & 18 Vickers A.A. Sight from O.O. 8th Corps Tps. and issued according to distribution given by "G"	
	11/2		Collected 24 Steel helmets with visors from B'des for re-issue to 8th Divn for trial.	

A6945 Wt. W11422/M1160 350,000 12/16 D. D. & L. Forms/C./2118/14.

SECRET

Instructions regarding War Diaries and Intelligence Summaries are contained in F. S. Regs., Part II. and the Staff Manual respectively. Title pages will be prepared in manuscript.

WAR DIARY
or
INTELLIGENCE SUMMARY.
(Erase heading not required.)

D.A.D.O.S.
33rd DIVISION

Army Form C. 2118.

4th Sheet

Place	Date	Hour	Summary of Events and Information	Remarks and references to Appendices
WIZERNES	12/7/18		General Routine work	
	13/7/18		General Routine work	
	14/7/18		Sent an Armourer to Salvage Dump, Vlamertinghe to collect 30 German Rifles & 600 Rounds of German Amm with a view to making as many as possible serviceable for instructional purposes in this Div. Moved 4th Suffolk Regt to 58th Div as a Pioneer Bn. Moved 262 Rly Construction Coy to 50th Div as by time Stores are drawn from BASE the 50th Div will be in back area having relieved this Div. Under such circumstances [illegible] ‖ Demanded an 18 pdr gun for B/162 to replace No 6176 [illegible]	
	15/7/18		Demanded 5000 socks from Base to increase reserve to meet requirements of a 2 Bde front.	
	16/7/18		Capt A.H. Shearman A.O.D. returned from leave. Spoke to D.M.G. [illegible] on phone re avoidance of duplication of indents by submitting all future demands for MG Coys under heading of Div MG Bn which, though not officially formed, is being administered as one unit & as far as [illegible] regards that the O.C. of the Bn should visit my office to clear up questions arising from that change & to revise outstanding indents.	

A6945 Wt. W11422/M1160 350,000 12/16 D. D. & L. Forms/C./2118/14.

Instructions regarding War Diaries and Intelligence Summaries are contained in F. S. Regs., Part II. and the Staff Manual respectively. Title pages will be prepared in manuscript.

WAR DIARY
or
INTELLIGENCE SUMMARY.
(Erase heading not required.)

Army Form C. 2118.

Place	Date	Hour	Summary of Events and Information	Remarks and references to Appendices
WIZERNES	17/2/18		Altered last refilling for R.A from Tuesday to Monday as Batteries are moving on first mentioned day. Arranged a similar change in refilling for 95th Bde group. Received truck of general stores from Base. Suspended issues till further notice in view of forthcoming move of Div commencing 20th inst & finishing 23rd inst.	
	18/2/18.		General Routine work. Practically all stores in dump issued to units & no more stores expected from Base till move is completed. 16 Lewis Guns of 1st Middlesex Regt overhauled & butts & safety catches altered. Armourer Sgt Shop reported 8 of these guns were in a very neglected condition & extensive repairs were required. List of deficiencies in spare part bags very large. Forwarded his report to Div H.Q. for disciplinary action. The Bn had previously demurred at sending in their guns on the ground that they were in good order & did not therefore require overhaul.	

A6945 Wt. W11422/M1160 350,000 12/16 D. D. & L. Forms/C./2118/14.

Instructions regarding War Diaries and Intelligence Summaries are contained in F. S. Regs., Part II. and the Staff Manual respectively. Title pages will be prepared in manuscript.

WAR DIARY
or
INTELLIGENCE SUMMARY.
(Erase heading not required.)

Army Form C. 2118.

Place	Date	Hour	Summary of Events and Information	Remarks and references to Appendices
WIZERNES.	19/3/16		attended Lecture at Hazebrouck by O.O. Calais on "Economy in Government stores". Subject treated under following headings ① Restriction of demands to actual requirements – Officers signing an indent also sign a certificate to this effect. Demands never queried by Base if demands are covered by Mob tables G.R.O.s etc hence necessity for strict observance of the certificate to avoid shortage of supply to other units as stocks are governed by output at home & shipping available. ② Misapplication of stores – causes great waste & has same affect as ①. ③ Return of all unserviceable irreparable stores, past further use at the front, in whatever condition they may be, to Base where facilities exist for the repair & utilisation of every variety of ordnance stores. Particularly applies to unserviceable clothing which is very valuable for the wool it contains & rags fetch a very high price. Only 45% of total issues to troops are ultimately recovered – hence great wastage occurring.	

W 5942 Wt. W11422/M1160 350,000 12/16 D. D. & L. Forms/C.2118/14.

Instructions regarding War Diaries and Intelligence Summaries are contained in F. S. Regs., Part II. and the Staff Manual respectively. Title pages will be prepared in manuscript.

Army Form C. 2118.

WAR DIARY

or

INTELLIGENCE SUMMARY.

(*Erase heading not required.*)

Place	Date	Hour	Summary of Events and Information	Remarks and references to Appendices
WIZERNES	19/7/18		Statistics given & samples of repair & recovery work at Base shewn. Saw Chief Clerk, ADOS 5th Div & arranged details of relief commencing 21st inst & finishing noon 23rd inst. 4 lorries asked for on 22nd & all other [illegible] to GHQ.	
	20/7/18.		[illegible] emphasising need for great economy in expenditure of lubricants of all sorts & calling for suggestions as to how this may best be effected. Submitted a letter to ADOS [illegible] embodying suggestions from experience gained in issues to this Divn & gave a tabulated statement of average weekly issue of each variety of lubricant & expendable stores generally i.e. soap, [illegible], dubbin etc to various types of units. Stated extent to which these average issues might be cut down without detriment to units efficiency, to effect a considerable saving & requested that this new scale should be made compulsory, safeguards against shortage in emergencies being provided by the holding of reserves in [illegible] stores.	
			General routine work. All salvage sorted & packed & despatched to Base. All units were warned on 18th inst to send any more salvage [illegible] … form a heap & all surplus … sent to Base.	

Instructions regarding War Diaries and Intelligence Summaries are contained in F. S. Regs., Part II. and the Staff Manual respectively. Title pages will be prepared in manuscript.

WAR DIARY
or
INTELLIGENCE SUMMARY.
(Erase heading not required.)

Army Form C. 2118.

Place	Date	Hour	Summary of Events and Information	Remarks and references to Appendices
WIZERNES	20/2/18		Moved C/162 Bde RFA to 004 Army Tps No 3, while attached to 2nd Army Arty School.	
	21/2/18		Armourers & Shoemakers' shops packed up & ready for move by lorry to Brandhoek this afternoon – four lorries being sent down by 50th Div with their shops & personnel & same lorries will be used to take my shops & personnel to forward area.	
	22/2/18		Despatched 2 lorry loads of stores to Brandhoek using my own lorries. These lorries will return tonight with balance of stores of 50th Div Co & will be available 23rd for completing my move to forward area. Re-opened issues from Base from 23rd inclusive. 3 loads of stores & personnel of 50th Div [illegible] arrived mid-day. These lorries will be available for our use on 23rd. Reported receipt of 29 Lewis Guns for A.A. defence for Bns Field Coys & RFA Batteries to D.O.S. [order] 4 Army & 8th Corps. Packed up ready for moving first thing on 23rd inst.	
Brandhoek H.7.c.6.7 Sheet 28	23/2/18		Completed move to BRANDHOEK. Opened shops – Checked area & trench stores handed over by DADOS 50 Div. General routine work.	

A6945 Wt. W11422/M1160 350,000 12/16 D. D. & L. Forms/C./2118/14.

Instructions regarding War Diaries and Intelligence Summaries are contained in F. S. Regs., Part II. and the Staff Manual respectively. Title pages will be prepared in manuscript.

WAR DIARY
or
INTELLIGENCE SUMMARY.
(Erase heading not required.)

Army Form C. 2118.

Place	Date	Hour	Summary of Events and Information	Remarks and references to Appendices
BAPAUME (?)	24/2/18		General Routine work – Large quantity of stores received for [illegible] to previous suspension of issues. Hastened 156 & 162 Bde RFA for statement	
	25/2/18		of Telescopes Sighting surplus to 3 per Battery (18 pdr) & position of the surplus to my store. This information is required by Q for report to Corps by 25th inst. Units were written further several days previously	
	25/2/18		also published authorising increase of Lewis Guns for A A defence on scale of 2 per Bde & 1 per Battery of R.F.A. The first issue of L.G. for these purposes (39) completed. Instructed H.Q. [illegible] to return the picketing gear etc rendered surplus by reduction in [illegible] Table equipment under GRO 3411. Indents received for X/33 TMB for 15 6" Newton Mortars to complete to establishment of 6 per Battery. M.T.M.Bs are now re-organized on basis of 2 6" Newton Batteries per Div the H.T.M.B (V Battery) being broken up & absorbed in the new Corps Heavy T.M.Bs armed with 9.45" Mortars. Q asked HQ RA to report how many 2" Mortars they wish to retain for the present as auxiliary to the 6" when received	
	26/2/18		Cancelled all outstanding & [illegible] indents of V & X & Z/33 T.M. Bs & took Bulk [illegible] [illegible] & [illegible] [illegible] to [illegible]. Informed [illegible] of [illegible] [illegible] [illegible] [illegible] [illegible] [illegible] reorganization	X V/33 XYV/33 TMBs

A6945 Wt. W11422/M1160 350,000 12/16 D. D. & L. Forms/C.2118/14.

Army Form C. 2118.

WAR DIARY
or
INTELLIGENCE SUMMARY.
(*Erase heading not required.*)

Instructions regarding War Diaries and Intelligence Summaries are contained in F. S. Regs., Part II. and the Staff Manual respectively. Title pages will be prepared in manuscript.

Place	Date	Hour	Summary of Events and Information	Remarks and references to Appendices
[illegible] Sheet 28 H 7 c 6 7	26/3/18	cont.	Reported to A.D.O.S. 8th Corps all Telescopes Sighting No 4 surplus with 33rd Div Arty now withdrawn i.e. 5 in all. Visited "Q" & discussed various questions. 4 Syringes urgently required by Burial Officer for spraying dead horses previous to burial. Wired Ordnance 8th Corps for authority to obtain from Base – also for 50 Washing Boards urgently required for trench foot hut at Seine Camp.	[illegible] Capt A.A.D.O.S. 33 Div
	27/3/18		162nd Bde R.F.A. now report 4 more Telescopes Sighting surplus to scale & returned them to my store. Reported this to "Q" for action with units & to A.D.O.S. for information & amendment of previous report. Local Purchase in morning – Bought large Brass Bell for use as Gas Alarm in large system of dugouts at Crest Farm. Drew 2 Rifles fitted with Tel. Sights from 2nd Army S.T.S. [illegible] at Mont des Cats. With the 4 returned by 20th R Fus on Saturday I have now sufficient to satisfy all outstanding demands for replacements.	
	28/3/18		All [illegible] returns to Corps [illegible] Submitted [illegible] for 11 6" New [illegible] to [illegible] complete [illegible] 6 each. Visited "Q" & discussed various matters with [illegible] Officers Bath House to be established at [illegible] [illegible]	P.T.O.

A6945 Wt. W11422/M1160 350,000 12/16 D. D. & L. Forms/C./2118/14.

to wire layer stores req to complete work 30 authorised. Asked
ADOS if issue would be made by OO & Corps [illegible]
[illegible] on Base? 2000 towels obtained 1000 from Base & 1000
from Corps & issued to Baths Officer for trench feet treatment
huts & baths at Ypres to enable men to be supplied with clean
towels on coming out of line in exchange for dirty which will be
washed at Laundry, Blendecques.

D. A. D. O. S. 33RD DIVISION

SECRET.

Army Form C. 2118.

WAR DIARY
or
~~INTELLIGENCE SUMMARY.~~
(Erase heading not required.)

MARCH 1918

Instructions regarding War Diaries and Intelligence Summaries are contained in F. S. Regs., Part II. and the Staff Manual respectively. Title pages will be prepared in manuscript.

Place	Date	Hour	Summary of Events and Information	Remarks and references to Appendices
BRANDHOEK H.7.C.6.7. SHEET 28.			Demanded 23 Lewis Guns (2 extra per Bn + 1 per Battery less C/162 (with 4 A.T. No 3) for 1024 Gun Parts – also 5 Hotchkiss Guns (1 per Train H.Q. Coy + 1 for 2 3 0 Emp Coy (?))	
	1/3/18.		All indents outstanding over 2 months old are to-day considered cancelled.	
			Reviewed these cancelled indents & noted if re-demands had been submitted by units as an indication that the stores were still required. Revised D.A.D.O.S indents over 2 months old & submitted redemands in 3 2	
			cases only viz. Covers Ejector 1 per Lewis Gun + 8 Lights Luminous for L.G.s	
			Remainder now cancelled. 50 prs Hedging Gloves urgently required by 19th Bde Pioneer Coy for use in large amount of wiring work now in	
			progress – authorised scale of 48 per Bn not sufficient to meet requirements ~~[illegible]~~ wired O.O. 8 C.T. asking how many had in store. 50 required.	
	2/3/18		Received D.O.S letter thro A.D.O.S emphasizing urgent necessity for economy in demands for Gun & Machine Gun parts in view of existing shortage of raw material & manufacturing difficulties & laying down the precautions ~~[illegible]~~ to be adopted both to prevent over provision by Bases & over issues to units by causing the return of all "U" stores before replacement action on latter was already taken in letter to H.Q. 33 R.A. a few days ago.	
			Submitted draft for D.R.O. on economy in M.G. parts urging units to consider advisability of not carrying spares in limbers & of attempting any but most minor repairs in the lines as loss of spares & damage to guns may result.	

A6945 Wt. W11422/M1160 350,000 12/16 D. D. & L. Forms/C.2118/14.

Instructions regarding War Diaries and Intelligence Summaries are contained in F. S. Regs., Part II. and the Staff Manual respectively. Title pages will be prepared in manuscript.

WAR DIARY
or
INTELLIGENCE SUMMARY.
(*Erase heading not required.*)

Army Form C. 2118.

Place	Date	Hour	Summary of Events and Information	Remarks and references to Appendices
BRANDHOEK Sheet 28 H.7.c.6.7	3/3/18	(cont)	Sent return to A.Q.s showing position at noon of day of supply of Lewis & Hotchkiss Guns for A.A. defence - Showed the 29 Guns demanded under 4th A.Q. [illegible]	7 & 3 as received
			Complete Travelling Kitchen required by 4th Kings Liverpool to replace one condemned. Wired Ordce 8th Corps to state if one available in Army. Meanwhile reorganization of Pioneer Bn is completed & one W.T. is now surplus with them. Wired unit to state if fit for re-issue - They replied - "requires overhaul". Instructed them to send it to D.O.M. [illegible] for repair & wired latter to issue direct to 4th Kings on completion - notified 4th Kings of this arrangement & cancelled my wire to 8th Corps. Informed Q of this absorption of one surplus W.T.	
			Transferred one surplus & serviceable water cart from 33rd M.G. Bn who are being organized for 4 M.G. Coys, to 4th Kings to replace one condemned by D.O.M. & informed Q of this absorption.	
	3/3/18		Received copy of 4th Army letter re "G" giving detail of deficiencies & surpluses in transport & horses arising from formation of 33 M.G. Bn. Asked M.G. Bn to notify date of disposal of surpluses to enable me to arrange for trucks with R.O.O.	
			Sent statement of surplus Lewis Guns, Vehicles & Harness to be [illegible] on reorganization on 3 Coy basis to units & asked them to explain deficiencies in comparison with list submitted by them & also to return [illegible] after [illegible]	

A6945 Wt. W11422/M1160 350,000 12/16 D. D. & L. Forms/C/2118/14.

Instructions regarding War Diaries and Intelligence Summaries are contained in F. S. Regs., Part II. and the Staff Manual respectively. Title pages will be prepared in manuscript.

WAR DIARY
or
INTELLIGENCE SUMMARY.
(Erase heading not required.)

Army Form C. 2118.

Place	Date	Hour	Summary of Events and Information	Remarks and references to Appendices
BRANDHOEK Sheet 28 H.7.c.6.7	3/3/18	cont	Notification received from Gun Park that 11. 6" Newton Mortars complete but without spares etc were available. Wired SMTO. 8th Corps for 2 lorries on 5/3/18 to collect them. 12. 2" Mortars + equipment returned by DTMO. These are to be sent to Base & list of items returned to be reported to ADOS 8th Corps. 8 Lewis Guns for 2 A.I.S.A. + 8 from 4th Kings fitted with Ball Catches in Armourers Shop.	
	4/3/18		Wired for 1 Lewis Gun less magazines + spare part bag for 4th Kings to replace 1 destroyed by shell fire. General Routine work.	
	5/3/18		Attended conference of DDOS & ADOS 8th Corps office. Wired 33 MTB to return surplus vehicle 1 water cart + 3 Mess carts to ROO Hazebrouck. Received Lewis Gun for 4th Kings from No 4 Gun Park. 48 Altered Butts for Lewis Guns received from 4th Army Heavy Mobile Workshop. These are fitted with oil bottles + swivels for sling + a front band fitted with swivel for attachment to front casing of the gun. Issued with 1 alt butt. 48 old pattern butts are to be withdrawn on issue of the new butts + returned to 4th A.H.M.W. for alteration + re-issue + so on till all butts with Bn are exchanged. 4th Army want information	

A6945 Wt. W11422/M1160 350,000 12/16 D. D. & L. Forms/C./2118/14.

P.T.O

4/3/16 (Cont) Wrote to AA + QMG stating that at 8th Corps Conference today it was notified that the DDOS 4th Army wished precautions to be adopted to ensure the safe storage from the present of any stores now held by DADOS which are not required for immediate issue & which could not be moved quickly in the event of the enemy breaking thro' our defences. He is providing a store in Acheux for such stores. Gave suggested disposal of all area & Divl stores not required & asked the AA & QMG's to approve or amend according to the present requirements of the Div while in the line.

Instructions regarding War Diaries and Intelligence Summaries are contained in F. S. Regs., Part II, and the Staff Manual respectively. Title pages will be prepared in manuscript.

WAR DIARY
or
INTELLIGENCE SUMMARY.
(*Erase heading not required.*)

Army Form C. 2118.

Place	Date	Hour	Summary of Events and Information	Remarks and references to Appendices
BRANDHOEK H.7.c.6.7. Sheet 28	5/3/18	cont	as to number of sets of Packsaddlery G.S. in possession of units surplus to establishment with a view to withdrawing those if so [illegible] to form reserve at Army HQ for special operations. Reviewed my records of issues & receipts & find 430 sets unaccounted for ie this number should be with units if latter have not handed them over at various times or lost & rendered them unserviceable. Wired 3 Bdes & H.A. Sec of D.A.C. asking the former to return [illegible] Packsaddlery & report sets now in possession. ~~[illegible]~~ Received 28 Lewis Guns for AA defence of [illegible] demand submitted to No 4 Gun Park under 4th A.R.O. 1507 the first demand under ARO 1743 having been completed last month. Informed Corps & Army. 2 A & S H have lost 1 wagon limbered G.S. 2 sets H.P.D G.S. 3 wheels & 4 wagon covers by shell fire. Wired A.D.O.S. asking if vehicle was available within Army – He replied "No". Wired Base for vehicle harness, wheels & covers as all are urgently required.	

A6945 Wt. W11422/M1160 350,000 12/16 D. D. & L. Forms/C./2118/14.

Instructions regarding War Diaries and Intelligence Summaries are contained in F. S. Regs., Part II. and the Staff Manual respectively. Title pages will be prepared in manuscript.

WAR DIARY
or
INTELLIGENCE SUMMARY.
(Erase heading not required.)

Army Form C. 2118.

Place	Date	Hour	Summary of Events and Information	Remarks and references to Appendices
BRANDHOEK Sheet 28 H.7.c.6.7	6/3/18.		Wired S.M.T.O. for lorry to collect load of tables, forms & lamps for R.R. & B.H. for 8th Corps Troops, Poperinghe on 7th, these stores have been allotted by 8th Corps for use in newly erected Reading Rooms in square, YPRES & on Saville Road between Ypres & Potijze. Wired 19th Bde to instruct their 3 Bns. to draw 16 new pattern Lewis Gun Batts from my Store – fit them & the [illegible] Bands & return the old pattern Batts to me as soon as possible as 4th Army H.M.W. are in urgent need of these batts for conversion – 19th Bde is now in Reserve. Visited Staff Captains of 100th Bde & 98th Bde at Potijze to talk over various questions & to get to know any special requirements they may have – Informed them I had 40 Washing Bowls & 26 Tables F.S. for issue if required & took up question of large deficiencies between Mess Tins issued & those returned to me in accordance with a D.R.O. of 18th February. Reported latter to Q & gave statements of issues & returns during January & February.	

Army Form C. 2118.

Instructions regarding War Diaries and Intelligence Summaries are contained in F. S. Regs., Part II. and the Staff Manual respectively. Title pages will be prepared in manuscript.

WAR DIARY
or
INTELLIGENCE SUMMARY.
(Erase heading not required.)

Place	Date	Hour	Summary of Events and Information	Remarks and references to Appendices
BRANDHOEK Sheet 28 H.7.c.6.7	6/3/18 cont.		11. 6" Newton Mortars, complete less certain components not at present available, received from No 4 Gun Park for X & Y/33 M.T.M. Bs. Reported receipt to Army & Corps & phoned D.T.M.O. to arrange collection.	
	7/3/18.		Received authority from A.D.O.S. 8th Corps for Divl. Baths Officer to draw 3,500 sets underclothing (less socks) from O.O. 8th Corps Troops. Wired O.O.E.C.T. to wire me when available for collection & notified Baths Officer. This issue will obviate any further issues from Base this month to maintain stock for Baths. Issued surplus 5,000 socks from my reserve (doubled) during this tour in line, to Baths Officer to maintain his stock as no socks are available from Corps. Sent supplementary Bulk wire for Horse & Mule shoes for 33rd H.G. Bde after the issuing of latter's indent, received too late for Bulk, & sent from stock as far as possible. Indents recently submitted by this unit very excessive & incorrect – took up matter with them & the whole to be carefully checked by my W.O. & remarks & latter given instructions for future guidance.	R.M.

A.D.S.S. Wt. W11422/M1160 350,000 12/16 D. D. & L. Forms/C.2118/14.

Instructions regarding War Diaries and Intelligence Summaries are contained in F. S. Regs., Part II. and the Staff Manual respectively. Title pages will be prepared in manuscript.

WAR DIARY
or
INTELLIGENCE SUMMARY.
(Erase heading not required.)

Army Form C. 2118.

Place	Date	Hour	Summary of Events and Information	Remarks and references to Appendices
BRANDHOEK Sheet 28 H.7.c.6.7	8/3/18.		1 Water Cart & only 2 Officers Mess Carts returned to Railhead by 2nd M.G. Bn as surplus for return to Calais Base. Inspected wheels & found them serviceable & complete.	
			2 G.S. Wagons returned by 18th Middlesex Pioneers as surplus to Railhead – all correct! Exchanged a Lewis Gun of 18 Middlesex, condemned for wear, for a serviceable gun salved & repaired in Armourers Shop. Informed [illegible] Corps. The condemned gun which is suitable for instructional purposes sent per G.S.O. II to [illegible] Corps Reinforcement Camp at [illegible] to complete them with 3 – one having been lost by them some weeks ago. All 2" Mortar Equipment carefully checked – contents of all Boxes Spare Parts & tools being examined – 12 Mortars – 15 4 per [illegible] M.T.M. Bn.	
	9/3/18		Returned 2" T.M. Equipment to Railhead for despatch to Base in accordance with instructions from G.H.Q. List of all stores returned typed & sent to A.D.O.S. Corps. Pioneers returned their surplus stores & Lewis Guns as far as available – all carefully checked – Lewis Guns to be sent to No 4 Gun Park.	

A6945 Wt. W11422/M1160 350,000 12/16 D. D. & L. Forms/C./2118/14.

Instructions regarding War Diaries and Intelligence Summaries are contained in F. S. Regs., Part II, and the Staff Manual respectively. Title pages will be prepared in manuscript.

WAR DIARY
or
INTELLIGENCE SUMMARY.
(Erase heading not required.)

Army Form C. 2118.

Place	Date	Hour	Summary of Events and Information	Remarks and references to Appendices
BRANDHOEK H.7.C.6.7. Sheet 28	9/3/18	Cont.	1 Wagon Limbered G.S. & Harness, 6 Belts etc. wired for for 2/A A & S H received. Wired Unit to draw vehicle from Railhead & balance from my store. Wired for a Carriage 18 pdr (& spring recuperator) for A/156 to replace one condemned by I.O.M. for broken Trail. Demanded 1 extra Hotchkiss Gun for 33 [illegible] A.D.O.S. 8th Corps informed me they are to be treated as an A.S.C. Coy under 4th A.R.O. 1801.	
	10/3/18		Visited M. Vanderslups, Marine Engineer, at Oudekerque Branche re a bill for alteration of 192 Petrol tins into Hot food Containers completed by him. Received authority by wire from A.D.O.S. 8th Corps to submit indents on No 4 Gun Park for Dial Sights No 7 to complete 33 Div Arty to 1 per gun and How & 1 spare per Battery. Wired 33 Div Arty for numbers required by each Battery. Complaint received by "G" from 98 Bde to the effect that certain Lewis Guns in possession of their units, which had been originally salved & repaired in Armourer Shop, were unreliable in action. Replied to "G" [illegible] such guns issued & [illegible] serviceable & in all respects equal to new & that [illegible]	[illegible]

A6945 Wt. W11422/M1160 350,000 12/16 D. D. & L. Forms/C./2118/14.

Instructions regarding War Diaries and Intelligence Summaries are contained in F. S. Regs., Part II. and the Staff Manual respectively. Title pages will be prepared in manuscript.

WAR DIARY
or
INTELLIGENCE SUMMARY.
(Erase heading not required.)

Army Form C. 2118.

Place	Date	Hour	Summary of Events and Information	Remarks and references to Appendices
BRANDHOEK H.7.c.6.7 Sheet 28			6. Hotchkiss Machine Guns received from No 4 Gun Park [illegible] Surplus Store on re-organization of 18 Middlesex Pioneers,	[illegible] Supply & Supply Col.
	11/3/18		Checked & packed ready for despatch to Base. Received list of items returned with Field Store which should have been returned & found units' explanation of discrepancies satisfactory. Reported return of 2 [illegible] by above unit to Base to A.D.O.S. 8th Corps & to 33 Div Q. Visited Nos 2, 3 & 4 Coy 33rd Div Train & SHA Sec 33 DAC & inspected Q.M.'s stores with regard to amount of stock held permanently by these units. Found stock small & consistent with requirements for emergencies. Got to know any special requirements of units for Ordnance Store — no complaints as to supply of stores.	
	13/3/18		Visited "Q" & discussed correspondence with 33 [illegible] re excessive demands for [illegible] Clothing from Batteries & D.A.C. during previous 3 months. "Q" want details of issue during last 3 months to Batteries & D.A.C. Arranged for these to be supplied. Sent list of surplus Stores, [illegible] Lewis Guns & Vehicles returned by 18 Middlesex Pioneers to A.D.O.S. 8 Corps. Also sent list of 2" T.M. & 9.45 T.M. equipment returned by [illegible] T.M.B.s [illegible] 9.45 [illegible] 2" T.M.s [illegible] Sent to A.D.O.S. 8 Corps.	

A6945 Wt. W11422/M1160 350,000 12/16 D. D. & L. Forms/C./2118/14.

Instructions regarding War Diaries and Intelligence Summaries are contained in F. S. Regs., Part II, and the Staff Manual respectively. Title pages will be prepared in manuscript.

WAR DIARY
or
INTELLIGENCE SUMMARY.
(Erase heading not required.)

Army Form C. 2118.

Place	Date	Hour	Summary of Events and Information	Remarks and references to Appendices
BRANDHOEK H.7.c.6.7. Sheet 28.	12/3/18 cont:-		Demanded 18 pdr gun for C/156 Bde to replace one condemned - "Shell fire" by I.O.M.	
	13/3/18		General Routine work. Sent details of issues of SD Clothing & Mess Tins to 33rd Div Arty Batteries & D.A.C. Sections during last 5 months commencing 1st Oct. 1917, to "G" for action as issues are very excessive compared with Army averages. Issued 2 Carriers No 7 Dial Sight, [illegible] from C.O. 8th Corps Tps. as arranged yesterday by A.D.O.S. 8th Corps. These are to complete deficiencies in B/162 & B/156 equipment of carriers. Demanded 3 Dial Sights from No 4 Gun Park to complete C/156, A/162 & B/162 to scale of 1 per gun & 1 spare per Battery as per wire from A.D.O.S. 8th Corps S. Issued 1 Hotchkiss M Gun to each of Div Train Coys. 1 awaiting issue to each of [illegible] Employment Coy & 33 Sap. Col.	
	14/3/18.		1500 Small Box Respirators wired for from Base. Very urgently reqd by D.G.O. to complete Reserve. Demanded 4.5" How for D/162 to replace No 63113 condemned Shell fire. Inspected 2 limb. R.E. wagons just issued to 156 & 162 Bde R.F.A. Signal Sections to complete new Establishment. These were transferred from Depots [illegible] & were in bad state of repair - Instructed units to send them to I.O.M. [illegible] for overhaul & repair I.O.M.	

A6945 Wt. W11422/M1160 350,000 12/16 D. D. & L. Forms/C./2118/14.

Instructions regarding War Diaries and Intelligence Summaries are contained in F. S. Regs., Part II. and the Staff Manual respectively. Title pages will be prepared in manuscript.

WAR DIARY
or
INTELLIGENCE SUMMARY.
(Erase heading not required.)

Army Form C. 2118.

Place	Date	Hour	Summary of Events and Information	Remarks and references to Appendices
BRANDHOEK Sheet 28 H.7.C.6.7.	14/3/18	cont.	Demanded 17 bicycles from Base on instruction from 'Q' + authority of DADOS 8th Corps to complete Div'l [illegible] to new establishment of 33. None available with 2 surplus Bn transports attached to Divn as stated in QMG's letter re formation of MG Bn. Demanded 10 Soyer Stoves by wire from Base to complete Div'l Scale of 50 in replacement of deficiencies + unserviceable.	
	15/3/18.		Visited M. Vandesteene at Oudezeele-Brouck near [illegible] to get Bill for Hot Food Containers amended. Left new bills with DADOS 8th Corps for necessary authority for the transaction to be given by him. Informed him that areas [illegible] my 'Q' had decided were [illegible] + obtained disposal from him to send them to Base. Also informed him that Div'l Stores i.e. 530 [illegible] Packs + Bayonet Frogs, Socks etc 'Q' wanted Stored at Calais for safe custody in event of break through by Enemy. Returned Salvaged No 1 Dial Sight + Carrier No 1 to 4th HMW near Poperinghe for repair + return to stock.	

A6945 Wt. W11422/M1160 350,000 12/16 D. D. & L. Forms/C.2118/14.

Instructions regarding War Diaries and Intelligence Summaries are contained in F. S. Regs., Part II. and the Staff Manual respectively. Title pages will be prepared in manuscript.

WAR DIARY
or
INTELLIGENCE SUMMARY.
(Erase heading not required.)

Army Form C. 2118.

Place	Date	Hour	Summary of Events and Information	Remarks and references to Appendices
BRANDHOEK H. 7. C. 6. 7. Sheet 28.			Informed Base + DDOS of amalgamation of 33rd Div Supply Colm with 33rd A.S.B. to form 33rd Div M.T. Coy + instructed Base to amend outstanding indents accordingly.	
	16/3/18.		General Routine work. Improvements in my Dump effected – tarring of Nissen Huts – ablution houses built + equipped. Saw AA + QMG re storage of Divl Stores not at present required + suggested sharing store used by 29th Div DADOS in Poperinghe for storing his stores not required for immediate use, instead of the 4th Army Store at Caestre as arranged by DDOS 4th Army. He agreed to this arrangement as being more convenient if stores are urgently required when Div is in the line, + as saving in man power by use 29th Divl guard already at Poperinghe. Arranged accordingly with DADOS 29th Divn.	
	17/3/18.		Wired for 1 wagon limber R.E. body from Base – not available in Army. Also demanded Body of G.S. for M.G. Bn – Visited ADOS 8th Corps + OO 8th Corps Tps. Wired SMTO 8th Corps for 1 lorry to report at latter's Store 18th inst to draw G Chaff cutters allotted to Divn as area stores for distribution to units not in possession of one on establishment. Reported receipt of 4.5" How Carriage for.	

A6945 Wt. W11422/M1169 350,000 12/16 D. D. & L. Forms/C./2118/14.

Instructions regarding War Diaries and Intelligence Summaries are contained in F. S. Regs., Part II. and the Staff Manual respectively. Title pages will be prepared in manuscript.

WAR DIARY
or
INTELLIGENCE SUMMARY.
(Erase heading not required.)

Army Form C. 2118.

Place	Date	Hour	Summary of Events and Information	Remarks and references to Appendices
BRANDHOEK H.7.C.6.7.	18/3/18	Cont.	On instructions from A.D.O.S. & notification from 33rd Div M.T. Coy – moved latter unit to O.O. 8th Corps Tps for administration. A.D.O.S. visited Stores & office. The Hotchkiss Gun drawn for 33rd Div Sup Col is now surplus as 33rd Div M.T. Coy have drawn one from O.O. 8th Corps Tps being now a Corps Troops unit. Informed A.D.O.S. & turned No 4 Gun Park to collect. Demanded 3 Lewis & 3 Hotchkiss Guns complete from [illegible] for 33 D.A.C for A.A. defence. Under Q.M.G. authority received from A.D.O.S. General Routine Work	
	19/3/18		General Routine work. Authority for demand of Lewis & Hotchkiss Guns for A.A. defence for 33rd D.A.C amended to read Lewis Guns only – Cancelled demand for Hotchkiss on No 4 Gun Park. Queried heavy demand of for Horse & Mule Shoes from 162 Bde as latter have already been issued with double the Army monthly average issue per month. Unit reduced demand accordingly. Received 3 Lewis Guns for A.A. defence for 33rd DAC	
	20/3/18		Drew Tables, forms & Lamps R.R. for O.O. 8th Corps Tps on authority of A.D.O.S. for issue to [illegible] Bde R.F.A. [illegible] General Routine Work.	

A6945 Wt. W11422/M1160 350,000 12/16 D. D. & L. Forms/C./2118/14.

Army Form C. 2118.

Instructions regarding War Diaries and Intelligence Summaries are contained in F. S. Regs., Part II. and the Staff Manual respectively. Title pages will be prepared in manuscript.

WAR DIARY
or
INTELLIGENCE SUMMARY.
(Erase heading not required.)

Place	Date	Hour	Summary of Events and Information	Remarks and references to Appendices
BRANDHOEK H.7.c.6.7. Sheet 28	21/3/18		General Routine Work. Ruling as to issue of Khaki Drill Clothing for Cooks received from Base. Class 'W' SD Jackets to be issued in lieu of frocks Khaki Drill on cons instructions from D.O.S. Forwarded to 'Q' with reference to complaint received from G.O.C. 19th Bde on Cooks Clothing issued to units to effect that part worn SD Jackets cannot be washed. Visited Advanced H.Q. Prepared list of Gun Park stores in stock for submission to ADOS tomorrow – being the first of a fortnightly return of this nature. Stock of MG parts has been reduced to requirements of Armourers shop for overhauls of units Lewis & Vickers guns periodically to avoid delay in obtaining parts for G.P.	
	22/3/18.		Visited St Omer for local Purchase – saw ADOS 8th Corps & discussed various Ordnance matters of common interest. General Routine work. 4000 water bottles for emergency use in line allotted to Div by 8th Corps – arranged to collect & issue them to forward Div Ammn Dumps.	

A6945 Wt. W11422/M1160 350,000 12/16 D. D. & L. Forms/C./2118/14.

WAR DIARY
or
INTELLIGENCE SUMMARY.
(Erase heading not required.)

Place	Date	Hour	Summary of Events and Information	Remarks and references to Appendices
BRANDHOEK	23/3/18.		Question of deficiencies in components & accessories of the travelling kitchen of 20th R Fus as taken over by 20 MG Bn taken up with 19th Bde H.Q. ~~[illegible]~~ Arranged for the return to Base of the 3rd Surplus Officers Mess Cart belonging to 33 MG Bn. This had been temporarily retained by 98th Bde without authority. The matter was previously reported to Div HQ for action.	
			General Routine work.	
	24/3/18.		Issued a Lewis Gun to 1st Middlesex from salvaged stock in Armourers Shop to replace one rendered unserviceable in line by hostile shell fire. General Routine work.	
	25/3/18.		A Battalion of each of 98th & 19th Infty Bde sent rifles to Divl Armourers shop for repair. This work should be done by the Armourer attached to each Bde HQ under Divl arrangements. Reported the matter to the Bde HQ concerned for investigation & action to prevent this occurrence in future. Reviewed outstanding indents for all technical stores e.g. Binoculars, Wirecutters, periscopes etc. & found outstandings very small & none more than 10 days old. Submitted draft for letter to Brigades, [illegible]	

WAR DIARY
or
INTELLIGENCE SUMMARY.
(Erase heading not required.)

Instructions regarding War Diaries and Intelligence Summaries are contained in F. S. Regs., Part II. and the Staff Manual respectively. Title pages will be prepared in manuscript.

Army Form C. 2118.

Place	Date	Hour	Summary of Events and Information	Remarks and references to Appendices
BERTHEN			on the preparation of programmes by the Reserve Brigade in Brand hoek area for the overhaul of Lewis Guns of Battalions at rate of 16 per every 2 days. This will enable all guns in Divn to be again overhauled & spares completed while Divn is in line & in preparation for any battle the Divn may be called upon to fight in case of emergency. My Chief Clerk returns from one months leave.	
	26/3/18		Gun Park No 2 wired me to return all Mark I Lewis Gun Butts to Assistant Inspector of Armourers. Wired Gun Park that 36 were available for collection by them. Demanded one Pontoon wagon for 11th Field Coy to replace one condemned by I.O.M. Visited Sub Depot of O.O. 2nd Army Troops at Caestre & arranged with the NCO i/c for the storage of Yukon packs, Socks, Bayonet fighting etc not required by the Divn which I have already been given [illegible] [illegible] 12 [illegible] Store at CAESTRE. Wired [illegible] to [illegible] Corps for a lorry on 28th to take these stores to CAESTRE.	

A6945 Wt. W11422/M1160 350,000 12/16 D. D. & L. Forms/C./2118/14.

Instructions regarding War Diaries and Intelligence Summaries are contained in F. S. Regs., Part II. and the Staff Manual respectively. Title pages will be prepared in manuscript.

WAR DIARY
or
INTELLIGENCE SUMMARY.
(Erase heading not required.)

Army Form C. 2118.

Place	Date	Hour	Summary of Events and Information	Remarks and references to Appendices
BRANDHOEK H.7.C.6.7. Sheet 28	27/3/18		General Routine work. Had all Tentage in store on my establishment kitchens ready for use in case of a move. Detachment warned to hand in any surplus kit & arranged for all stores not required by Divn to be returned to Base or sent to CAESTRE for safe custody.	
	28/3/18		Returned cash to Field Cashier in order to reduce cash in hand to minimum at end of financial year on March 31st. Visited DADOS 8th Corps. Army Commander has refused to sanction issue of 4,000 water bottles to this Divn for reserve water at Bde H.Q. Informed "Q" of this decision. General Routine work.	
	29/3/18		General Routine work. Wrote to "Q" asking if Armourers & Boot Shops should be closed, personnel returned to their units & tools & equipment stored in the event of the Divn moving to take part in present battle in view of probable shortage of lorries & general consideration of mobility.	

A6945 Wt. W11422/M1160 350,000 12/16 D. D. & L. Forms/C./2118/14.

Instructions regarding War Diaries and Intelligence Summaries are contained in F. S. Regs., Part II. and the Staff Manual respectively. Title pages will be prepared in manuscript.

WAR DIARY
or
INTELLIGENCE SUMMARY.
(Erase heading not required.)

Army Form C. 2118.

Place	Date	Hour	Summary of Events and Information	Remarks and references to Appendices
BRANDHOEK Sheet 28 H.7.c.6.7	30/3/18		General Routine Work. End of month returns prepared & despatched to D.A.D.O.S. 8th Corps.	
	31/3/18		Visited Adv. Div. H.Q. & discussed various matters with D.A.Q.M.G. Received decision from "Q" to the effect that Armourers & Boot Shops were to be kept open & if shortage of transport occurred they were to be left at Div. Store in Poperinghe until they could be collected again. Received information that 19th Infantry Bde were moving to 3rd Army area at 3 pm to-day. Thereupon visited D.A.D.O.S. 8th Corps to obtain instructions as to disposal of area stores at present in my store in the event of early move of Div. which latter he confirmed from 8th Corps "Q". Returned to my store & gave orders for the disposal of all stores not required & all area stores. Suspended issues from Base.	

[signature] Major A.O.D.
D.A.D.O.S. 33rd Divn.

A6945 Wt. W11422/M1160 350,000 12/16 D. D. & L. Forms/C./2118/14.

Army Form C. 2118.

WAR DIARY
~~or~~
~~INTELLIGENCE~~ SUMMARY.
(*Erase heading not required.*)

Instructions regarding War Diaries and Intelligence Summaries are contained in F. S. Regs., Part II, and the Staff Manual respectively. Title pages will be prepared in manuscript.

SECRET

APRIL 1918

DADOS 33rd Divn

Vol 30

Place	Date	Hour	Summary of Events and Information	Remarks and references to Appendices
19 BRANDHOEK Sheet 28. H.7. c. 6.7	1/4/18		All Surplus area Stores sent to O.O. 8th Corps Troops. Last Truck received prior to move of Divn cleared yesterday & stores practically all issued except to 19th Bde units who moved yesterday to 17th Corps. ADOS 8th Corps decided that if necessary (ie if length of time elapsing between departure of 19th Bde & the Divn taking them over again exceeds a few days) the Bde WO & storeman with company outstanding stores should be sent on to Divl administering the Bde for temporary duty. Visited "Q" but could get no definite information re move of Division beyond date 15. 5th & 6th inst which will be quite a short one in first instance. Arranged to move Stores & shops [struck through, illegible] to be near [struck through, illegible] new Divn H.Q. & arranged to accompany Camp Commandant on his billeting trip to-morrow to fix up accommodation etc. Reviewed outstanding Technical Stores due to all units & also outstanding detail indents of 19 Bde. Found to be very small.	

A6945 Wt. W11422/M1160 350,000 12/16 D. D. & L. Forms/C./2118/14.

Instructions regarding War Diaries and Intelligence Summaries are contained in F. S. Regs., Part II. and the Staff Manual respectively. Title pages will be prepared in manuscript.

WAR DIARY
or
INTELLIGENCE SUMMARY.
(Erase heading not required.)

Army Form C. 2118.

Place	Date	Hour	Summary of Events and Information	Remarks and references to Appendices
BRANDHOEK. H. 7. C. 6. 7. Sheet 28	2/4/18.		Visited DADOS 59 Div at PROVEN & arranged details of taking over from him about 5th. Gave him information respecting my stores, area stores to be handed over, disposition of units transport, Railhead etc. On return [illegible] was informed move to Coalhove & PROVEN area cancelled. — Div HQ moving from Ypres to Brandhoek on 5th inst. & 2 Bdes will be accommodated [illegible] about latter for entrainment on 6th inst. [illegible] Received additional area stores, returned by Trench Foot Treatment depots for collection to 00 8th Corps Troops tomorrow.	
	3/4/18.		Cleared all Salvage to Railhead — Received wire from Ordnance 7 Corps to the effect that 19th Bde could be moved to 4th Div for ordnance if desired. Issued wire orders accordingly notifying Havre & Rouen Bases as 3rd Army formations are supplied by letter. Cancelled outstanding indents of whole Div (less Artillery) on Calais & re-demanded on HAVRE & ROUEN as instructions have been received from [illegible] 2nd Army for transfer of all outstanding indents from Northern to Southern Bases on move of Divs to 3rd Army [illegible]	

A6945 Wt. W1422/M1160 35,000 12/16 D. D. & L. Forms/C./2118/14.

Instructions regarding War Diaries and Intelligence Summaries are contained in F. S. Regs., Part II. and the Staff Manual respectively. Title pages will be prepared in manuscript.

WAR DIARY
or
INTELLIGENCE SUMMARY.
(Erase heading not required.)

Army Form C. 2118.

Place	Date	Hour	Summary of Events and Information	Remarks and references to Appendices
BRANDHOEK H.7.c.6.7 Sheet 28	4/4/18		Visited 'Q' & attended Conference re forthcoming move arrangements. The 2nd Blanket per man to be taken off all remaining units in Corps (less R.A.) before move to 3rd Army. Arranged detail of scheme with OC Div MT Coy & issued instructions to all units re collecting bundling & stacking of blankets at their camps on 5th inst 10 a.m. ready for collection by my lorries. 14 lorries detailed & an R.O.C. man sent with each lorry collecting from more than one unit (i.e. small units) to give receipt & check blankets from each unit. Saw R.O.O. Poperinghe re taking over the returned blankets as they cannot be loaded direct into trucks at railhead owing to shortage of trucks & congestion on railways. R.O.O. arranged to store the blankets at Poperinghe. Notified each unit of time my lorries would collect from them. General Routine work	

A6945 Wt. W1142/M1160 350,000 12/16 D. D. & L. Forms/C./2118/14.

Instructions regarding War Diaries and Intelligence Summaries are contained in F. S. Regs., Part II. and the Staff Manual respectively. Title pages will be prepared in manuscript.

WAR DIARY
or
INTELLIGENCE SUMMARY.
(*Erase heading not required.*)

Army Form C. 2118.

Place	Date	Hour	Summary of Events and Information	Remarks and references to Appendices
BRANDHOEK H.7.c.6.7. Sheet 28	5/4/18		Blanket collection completed satisfactorily 10,464 Blankets collected in all – reported to Q & AADOS. SADOS 59 Div moved into portion of my store vacated by me. Arranged details of handing over including list of area stores (only packs and long & short feathers) Arranged with 33rd M.T. Coy to let me have my 4 lorries this afternoon & loaded up 3 of them (2 with anti-gas appliances) ready for departure first thing on 6th inst. – Destination not yet known definitely. Arranged with Camp Commandant to find a store & office at new Div H.Q. for me. Wired Havre & Rouen that I am prepared to receive stores at new Railhead on 8th inst. Cancelled outstanding indents for Rifles with Telescopic Sights at 2nd Army School of Sniping & arranged to re-demand from 5th Army School on arrival in new area.	
	6/4/18		Destination for lorries is HAUTEVILLE near Avesnes-le-Comte. Despatched 4 lorries – 1 Yukon Packs, M.G. stores, Lewis [illegible], Ammunition & 2 Gas stores	

A6945 Wt. W11422/M1160 350,000 12/16 D. D. & L. Forms/C./2118/14.

Army Form C. 2118.

WAR DIARY
or
INTELLIGENCE SUMMARY.
(Erase heading not required.)

Instructions regarding War Diaries and Intelligence Summaries are contained in F. S. Regs., Par. II. and the Staff Manual respectively. Title pages will be prepared in manuscript.

Place	Date	Hour	Summary of Events and Information	Remarks and references to Appendices
HAUTEVILLE	6/4/18	59th Div. [illegible] 3rd Army	Moved 33rd [illegible] Arty. to ~~59~~ 33rd Div. — I cancelled move later as it was decided Arty would move with the Div to 3rd Army. Arranged for collection & handing over on 7th of their 2nd Blanket [illegible] ~~[illegible]~~ under the former ~~[illegible]~~ decision. My Arty personnel & lorry therefore left with 59th D.A.D.O.S.	
	7/4/18	[illegible] 2nd Army [illegible] 3rd Army	Requested D.A.D.O.S. 4th Div to move 19th Infty Bde back to me as I am not able to administer them on their rejoining Div. Sent lorry to collect my personnel & remaining stores. Opened store & shops in HAUTEVILLE & prepared to receive stores [illegible] at Railhead	
	8/4/18	Div [illegible] in 3rd Army	Div now administered by 6th Corps. — 17 Corps having been transferred to 2nd Army for administration. [illegible] 19th Bde moved to 33 Div by 4th Div.	
	9/4/18		[illegible] the Lewis Guns of 5th Scottish Rifles on [illegible] programme of periodic overhauls. Orders issued for move of Div to 6th Corps area (Div HQ [illegible] at Conteville near Saulty). Made arrangements for move in morning. Havre & Calais Bases both asked to state action taken on the various Bulk Indents I have submitted & re-submitted to them according to changes of Base or changes of formation.	
	10/4/18	Div now in 2nd Army	Sent lorry to Conteville with Shoemakers shop & [illegible] to enable additional accommodation to be erected at new store & went myself with Camp Commandant to find new stores. Lorry offloaded & store shops & billets allotted. On return to HAUTEVILLE found move cancelled	

A6945 Wt. W11422/M1160 350,000 12/16 D. D. & L. Forms/C./2118/14.

Instructions regarding War Diaries and Intelligence Summaries are contained in F. S. Regs., Par. II. and the Staff Manual respectively. Title pages will be prepared in manuscript.

WAR DIARY
or
INTELLIGENCE SUMMARY.
(*Erase heading not required.*)

Army Form C. 2118.

Place	Date	Hour	Summary of Events and Information	Remarks and references to Appendices
HAUTEVILLE			and 2nd order 1 hours notice to move elsewhere in view of development of enemy offensive on Portuguese front in 2nd Army. Sent lorry in afternoon to collect shoemakers etc from [illegible]. No stores yet received from either Base. Orders received at 6 pm to move in 1 hours time to Caestre & await further orders there. Men entraining & transport ~~pro~~ following by road to new area.	
CAESTRE Station	11/4/18		Arrived at Caestre 4. a.m. to used vacant shed belonging to O.O. 2nd Army troops in Railhead yard. Store & approaches very convenient but I can only remain temporarily. Selected alternative site on Eecke Road near the Station to obtained permission of Area Commandant to pitch tentage there. Truck received for me at Railhead TINQUES in last area. Instructed R.O. to reconsign as I cannot clear owing to distances & lack of available transport. Visited "C" in METEREN. [illegible] can be arranged at present as Div'l transport has not arrived & units do not require any [illegible]	
	12/4/18.		owing to rapid advance of enemy towards METEREN & Strazeele. Orders given for me to move at evening to Godewaersvelde near Station No 2. [illegible] now moved to WATTEN. Arranged the [illegible] & proceeded to HQ of 100th Bde, in lines, at Ravelsberg Camp with [illegible] & delivered Magazine	[illegible]

A6945 Wt. W11422/M1160 35,000 12/16 D. D. & L. Forms/C./2118/14.

WAR DIARY
or
INTELLIGENCE SUMMARY.
(*Erase heading not required.*)

Army Form C. 2118.

Instructions regarding War Diaries and Intelligence Summaries are contained in F. S. Regs., Part II. and the Staff Manual respectively. Title pages will be prepared in manuscript.

Place	Date	Hour	Summary of Events and Information	Remarks and references to Appendices
Store & Office GODEWAERSVELDE R.7.a.21. Sheet 27	12/4/18		to G.O.C. 100th Bde. Suspended all issues from Base except Vehicles.	
	13/4/18		Opened Stores but not Shops owing to possible early move. 33rd Div Arty moved by 59th Div to 33rd Div. Could not collect my personnel & Stores from 59th Div Store owing to lack of transport. 3 Tons of stores, mainly detail wagon parts received. Sent 2 lorries out with Bde W.O.s to try & find units transport for the few locations obtainable from "Q" & deliver detail stores & any flannelette rifle rag & dubbin they require from stock. Visited "Q" Rear on hill at Fontaine near to Mont des Cats.	
	14/4/18		All ~~p~~ recent moves of Rear Div H.Q. done by my lorries owing to shortage of transport with M.T. Coy during present emergency. Sent 98th Bde W.O. out with lorry to deliver wheels to his Train Coy, Bde H.Q. & Field Coy & to endeavour to salvage packs & greatcoats dumped by his Bde in forward area (Meteren & Mont Noir) & now in danger of capture by enemy on his rapid advance. 1 load of Blankets cleared from latter village under heavy shell fire both there & en [illegible] where salvage work was unsuccessful owing to Shelling. Moved office to Rear H.Q. (about 1 mile) from Stores. Demanded 14 Vickers guns for 33 M.G.Bn to replace destroyed by shell fire also demanded 2 Lewis Guns for 1st Cameronians for similar reason.	

A6945 Wt. W11422/M1160 350,000 12/16 D. D. & L. Forms/C./2118/14.

Instructions regarding War Diaries and Intelligence Summaries are contained in F. S. Regs., Par. II. and the Staff Manual respectively. Title pages will be prepared in manuscript.

WAR DIARY
or
INTELLIGENCE SUMMARY.
(Erase heading not required.)

Army Form C. 2118.

Place	Date	Hour	Summary of Events and Information	Remarks and references to Appendices
Store – GODEWAERSVELDE R.7.a.2.1 (Sheet 27)	14/4/18		Received urgent wire from SOC 19th Bde for 40 Vickers Gun Barrels, 2 Vickers Guns. Collected 17 Barrels (total stock) + 4 Boxes Spare parts Vickers filled reqd by ~~H~~ M.G.Bn. attached to 19th Bde from my store & endeavoured to deliver to 19th Bde H.Q. by midnight but was unable to get there owing to car breakdown. Returned with difficulty to Rear Div H.Q. & arranged to go out again early in morning. Bde H.Q. in Farm near Meteren. Sent priority wires to Gun Park for the 2 Vickers Guns 100 Barrels Vickers Gun ~~[illegible]~~ 1A, 800 Lewis Gun Magazines + 500 Belts M.G. to meet immediate requirements in line & despatched 2 lorries at midnight to No 2 Gun Park at WATTEN to draw & return immediately.	
Office. R.14.c.8.4 Sheet 27	15/4/18		Delivered 4 Boxes. SP filled to 19th Bde H.Q. early in morning – road & vicinity of Bde H.Qs heavily shelled. The 17 Barrels not required as 9th Corps, having reserve stock of guns & barrels delivered direct to 19th Bde yesterday evening & no cancellation of requirements was forwarded to me. 14 Vickers Guns for M.G.Bn and 2 L.Gs for Cameronians received from Gun Park. Also 200 Lewis Gun Magazines previously demanded. Delivered 200 Lewis Gun Magazines by car to H.Q. Composite Bde commanded by General Armitage, at La Manche by midnight. Delivered 50 Magazines to the 2 L.Gs	

A6945 Wt. W11422/M1160 350,000 12/16 D. D. & L. Forms/C./2118/14.

Instructions regarding War Diaries and Intelligence Summaries are contained in F. S. Regs., Part II. and the Staff Manual respectively. Title pages will be prepared in manuscript.

WAR DIARY
or
INTELLIGENCE SUMMARY.
(Erase heading not required.)

Army Form C. 2118.

Place	Date	Hour	Summary of Events and Information	Remarks and references to Appendices
GODEWAERSVELDE R. 7. c. 2. 1 Sheet 27	15/4/18 cont.		for 1st Camerons to 19th Bde Transport officers at Noote Boom. Demanded 14 Lewis Guns for 9th H.L.I. & issued the 14 Lewis Guns plus 2 others drawn from Gun Park & rendered surplus by action of 9th Corps Ordnance to H.C.S. Bn delivering by car & lorry with a number of Belts & Boxes to Transport [illegible] near Berthen. Packed up offices & Store & moved former ~~[illegible]~~ to Abeele with Rear D.W. H.Q. at 8 p.m. No accommodation arranged there so sent lorry & personnel back to store for night. Remained myself at Abeele to be in liaison with "Q". One lorry sent with 200 L.G. Magazines & balance of load filled up with as much S.A. Ammn as possible (collected from S.A.A. Sec by order of "Q") to deliver half of each to one Bn in La Bassee Farm about ½ mile N of METEREN and one Bn near 4 Fils Aymon about same distance N.E of METEREN. Load had to be delivered to-night to ensure guns being kept in action. a/S/Cdr Wheeler A.O.C. sent in charge of lorry & after 3 attempts by different routes to reach these units (in support line) he succeeded in delivering whole to one of them who arranged to hand over half to the other.	2 pneumatic lamps failed owing to lamp [illegible] [illegible] [illegible] 16/4/18 [illegible] sent [illegible]

A6945 Wt. W11422/M1160 350,000 12/16 D. D. & L. Forms/C./2118/14.

Instructions regarding War Diaries and Intelligence Summaries are contained in F. S. Regs., Part II. and the Staff Manual respectively. Title pages will be prepared in manuscript.

WAR DIARY
or
INTELLIGENCE SUMMARY.
(Erase heading not required.)

Army Form C. 2118.

Place	Date	Hour	Summary of Events and Information	Remarks and references to Appendices
ABEELE (Sheet 27 L. 25. D. 8. 0.)	16/4/18.		Demanded 13 Lewis Guns for 1st Queens to replace destroyed by shell fire.	
			Moved Store to Aerodrome on Abeele – Steenvoorde road about ¼ mile from former – Rear Div HQ in adjoining aerodrome. Wired for 2000 sets SD Clothing 3000 greatcoats, 1000 prs Boots, 1000 ground sheets & 1000 sets web equipment [illegible]	
	17/4/18		Opened issues from Base and demanded 1 Lewis Gun for 5 Scottish Rifles [illegible]. Armourer & Boot shop equipment remain all together as stay in present location may be very short.	
	18/4/18		Sent 3 lorries to Base Depot, Calais first thing in morning to collect SD Clothing, Greatcoats, Groundsheets, Equipment & Boots demanded by wire for refitting Bdes. 2 Bdes have lost practically all their greatcoats & packs containing groundsheets & necessaries. Demanded 1000 sets of latter to meet estimated demands. One lorry sent to HAUTEVILLE to collect salvage personnel & balance of stores left there prior to recent operations. Lorries returned from Base late at night – all stores except greatcoats available & collected.	
	19/4/18.		Railhead still Ebblinghem – Trucks received & stores split up for issue. A few units O.M.S. called at Store. 1" Signal Pistols & Bicycle outer covers urgently required by Composite unit – also Flannelette & oil & Field Dressings.	

A6945 Wt. W11422/M1160 350,000 12/16 D. D. & L. Forms/C./2118/14.

Instructions regarding War Diaries and Intelligence Summaries are contained in F. S. Regs., Part II. and the Staff Manual respectively. Title pages will be prepared in manuscript.

WAR DIARY
or
INTELLIGENCE SUMMARY.
(Erase heading not required.)

Army Form C. 2118.

Place	Date	Hour	Summary of Events and Information	Remarks and references to Appendices
ABEELE. L. 25. D. 8. 0. Sheet 27			Base have cancelled all indents dated prior to 14th inst on account of confusion caused by new stores having been returned in large quantities by formations. Sent up all requirements less a few Outer covers & the 1" Pistols which I could not obtain locally from other Ordnance stores, by car to Sergt Armitage at Adv. Div H.Q. No 1" Pistols available at Base.	[illegible]
	20/4/18		Sent lorry to Hoppenbosch Railhead to collect 800 blankets if available & deliver to 100th Bde, who are coming out of line tonight, at Convent, Mont des Cats. Done & another 720 blankets collected & dumped at Store ready to meet emergency requirements of units coming out of line. Asked DADOS 9th Corps to whom 33 Div Arty are to be transferred on Div moving to 8 Corps Area. Replied – 9 Corps troops. Issued move orders accordingly. Moved Portage & some stores to site of new store at TROIS. ROIS Q.26.a.9.8.	
	~~21/4/18~~		~~Moved to TROIS. ROIS [illegible]~~. To avoid double handling of large stock of repaying Clothing etc. arranged to deliver a lorry load of miscellaneous Bulk to each Bde area. (100th & 98th) Units instructed to attend refilling point & lorry indents for actual requirements – all previous demands for Clothing Boots & [illegible] & equipment considered cancelled to avoid confusion. Done & lorries returned to aerodrome ready for completion of move to TROIS. ROIS 21/4/18.	

A6945 Wt. W11422/M1160 350,000 12/16 D. D. & L. Forms/C./2118/14.

Army Form C. 2118.

Instructions regarding War Diaries and Intelligence Summaries are contained in F. S. Regs., Part II. and the Staff Manual respectively. Title pages will be prepared in manuscript.

WAR DIARY
or
INTELLIGENCE SUMMARY.
(Erase heading not required.)

Place	Date	Hour	Summary of Events and Information	Remarks and references to Appendices
TROIS ROIS Sheet 27 Q.26.a.9.8.	20/4/18		Completed move to TROIS ROIS. Sent lorries to collect blankets and packs of 98th + 100th Bdes + convey to the respective HQs of these Bdes. Saw Staff Capt 100 Bde + asked him to hasten units to submit indents for technical equipment at once.	
do	21/4/18		Completed move to TROIS ROIS. Refitted 19th, 98th + 100th Bdes with miscellaneous stores urgently reqd. Also collected + delivered 12 lorry loads of 19 Bde Blankets + Packs from dump at St. Sylvestre-Cappel with 6 borrowed lorries.	
do	22/4/18		Move of 33 Div Arty to 9th Corps Troops cancelled by latter. Issued amendment to my original move order substituting 22nd Corps Troops for 9th Corps Troops. 1 lorry detached with my personnel with 22nd Corps Troops on transfer from 9th Corps Troops.	
do	22/4/18		Demanded 13 Lewis Guns for 4th Kings, 19 for 2nd Worcesters, 11 for 16 [illegible] + 4 Vickers Guns for 33 M.G. Bn. Spare parts + magazines not demanded unless complete guns demanded. Supplementary bulk indent submitted for actual requirements of spares + magazines after verification by unit made out. Statement of outstanding indents received + outstanding for important technical stores	

A6945 Wt. W11422/M1160 350,000 12/16 D. D. & L. Forms/C./2118/14.

Instructions regarding War Diaries and Intelligence Summaries are contained in F. S. Regs., Part II. and the Staff Manual respectively. Title pages will be prepared in manuscript.

Army Form C. 2118.

WAR DIARY
or
INTELLIGENCE SUMMARY.
(Erase heading not required.)

Place	Date	Hour	Summary of Events and Information	Remarks and references to Appendices
Trpt - Ref. Sheet 27 O.26.a.9.8.			Sent General Hastmer to Base for outstanding Technical Stores. Wrote all units	
	23/4/18		of 98th Bde & urged submission of all indents to cover refitting. Demanded	
			6 3" T.Ms complete for 98 T.M.B to replace lost – unit left similar	
			number near Strazeele & could not recover them.	
	24/4/18		Instructions received from 2nd Army for withdrawal of Winter Clothing	
			commencing immediately with Jerkins, Fur Coats & Gloves of all sorts	
			Drafted instructions to all units for publication by 'Q' for the	
			conditioning & stacking in Bde Dump of items previously	
			mentioned, for collection by lorry & despatch to Railhead	
			of the Serviceable & Repairable articles, & the Surveying Army	
			Stores of the unserviceable & its ultimate disposal. All Lewis Guns	
			on demand received & issued direct by lorry to units.	
			Demand 1 Lewis Gun for 5th Scottish Rifles & 2 for 1st Middlesex Regt.	
	25/4/18		Sent 1 lorry to Calais Base to collect all available detail Stores	
			of important nature & proceeded ~~to~~ lorry myself in car & arranged	
			with O.O. Field Indents for immediate issue as far as available	
			Told O.O. Issues to suspend loading of trucks tomorrow as I was sending	
			3 lorries to collect all bulky details urgently reqd to save delay.	

Instructions regarding War Diaries and Intelligence Summaries are contained in F. S. Regs., Part II. and the Staff Manual respectively. Title pages will be prepared in manuscript.

WAR DIARY
or
INTELLIGENCE SUMMARY.
(Erase heading not required.)

Army Form C. 2118.

Place	Date	Hour	Summary of Events and Information	Remarks and references to Appendices
[illegible] Sheet 27	25/4/18		Arranged refilling for 3 Bdes in afternoon. As units are ~~[illegible]~~ under short notice to move they cannot send transport to my store to collect so refilling by lorry will be arranged as often as necessitated by quantities of stores received daily & urgency. 6. 3" T.Ms received from No 2 Gun Park & issued to 98th T.M.B.	
[illegible] 8.26.0.9	26/4/18		4 Vickers guns received & issued to M.G. Bn. Sent 3 lorries to Base Calais to collect Bulk & detail stores urgently required – lorries returned late in evening with all stores except Bicycles which were for [illegible].	
	27/4/18		Hastened 50 Bags Spare parts for Lewis Guns outstanding from No 2 Gun Park by wire.	
	27/4/		Wired ADOS 8th Corps reporting shortage of Pistols Webley at Base – 203 due to Bdes & 65 (total establishment) for M.G. Bn. Requested that priority of issue may be given for latter as completion is very necessary for them most of all others. Arranged transfer of [illegible] Wagon surplus with 1st Queens Regt to No 33 Coy [illegible] Train to complete deficiency in that which was [illegible]	[illegible] Base

A6945 Wt. W11422/M1160 350,000 12/16 D. D. & L. Forms/C./2118/14.

Instructions regarding War Diaries and Intelligence Summaries are contained in F. S. Regs., Par. II. and the Staff Manual respectively. Title pages will be prepared in manuscript.

WAR DIARY
or
INTELLIGENCE SUMMARY.
(Erase heading not required.)

Army Form C. 2118.

Place	Date	Hour	Summary of Events and Information	Remarks and references to Appendices
Sheet 7 TPO E8 – R.E. 0.26. F.9.8	27/4/18	cont	2nd Army wired authority for completion of M.G. Bns to scale of 32 Belts M.G. per Gun i.e. increase of 16 per Gun, to be issued by Gun Park. This increase will exhaust all supplies in France & England & this fact was impressed on O.C. 33 M.G. Bn. Demanded 1064 to complete less 250 already in stock available for issue.	
	28/4/18		Hastened 31 Clinometers Field Mk V for 33 M.G. Bn – very urgently reqd to complete – wired 2nd Army S.O.S. School to ask if any rifles with Telescopic Sights or 1914 pattern Rifles in use were available for issue of my outstanding indents for 23. Sent 2nd General Hastener to Base for important technical stores outstanding. Visited 19 Bde H.Q. & their Bns & saw Q.M's re refitting. Explained that delay in completion of their technical Equipment as compared with the other Bdes was due to their indents being received later. Refitting of Bdes carried out.	
	29/4/18.		Sent 2nd Hastener to No 2 Gun Park for outstanding Spare Part Bags for Lewis Guns. Gun Park promised to send 25 in part soon as possible. Sent list of Clothing, Blankets, Equipment & important technical	

A6945 Wt. W11422/M1160 350,000 12/16 D. D. & L. Forms/C.2118/14.

Instructions regarding War Diaries and Intelligence Summaries are contained in F. S. Regs., Part II. and the Staff Manual respectively. Title pages will be prepared in manuscript.

WAR DIARY
or
INTELLIGENCE SUMMARY.
(Erase heading not required.)

Army Form C. 2118.

Place	Date	Hour	Summary of Events and Information	Remarks and references to Appendices
TROIS ROIS Sheet 27 D.26 a.9.8	29/4/18		Stores lost by units of Divn in recent battle to A.D.O.S. for transmission to D.O.S. G.H.Q. for provision purposes. General Routine work. Packed up & gave instructions for move of stores & office etc to Blaringhem & clearance of 11 tons stores from Railhead later to-day. Divn H.Q. moved to Blaringhem but 1 hour after move commenced orders were received cancelling move & ordering return to TROIS ROIS - office loaded lorry already loaded for moving & opened store again & resumed routine work. Refitted 3 Bde in afternoon & thereby reduced stock in view of another move.	
	30/4/18		General Routine work. Bdes again refitted with stores received to-day. More technical stores received including 18 bicycles. Prepared to move on 1st proximo to Blaringhem. Sent urgent demand to Base for Greatcoats, Boots & necessaries reqd to complete refitting of re-inforcements for which indents only recently received.	

[signature] Major
32nd Div DADOS

A6945 Wt. W11422/M1160 350,000 12/16 D. D. & L. Forms/C./2118/14.

Instructions regarding War Diaries and Intelligence Summaries are contained in F. S. Regs., Part II. and the Staff Manual respectively. Title pages will be prepared in manuscript.

MAY 1918

WAR DIARY
or
~~INTELLIGENCE SUMMARY.~~
(*Erase heading not required.*)

SECRET

D.A.D.O.S. 33 Div.

No C 31

Army Form C. 2118.

Place	Date	Hour	Summary of Events and Information	Remarks and references to Appendices
TROIS ROIS.	1/5/18		Moved to BLARINGHEM – Divn still administered by 8th Corps. Experienced great difficulty in obtaining a site for stores & workshops owing to ~~number~~ lack of vacant fields in the village – obtained portion of a field by private arrangement with owner. The ~~[illegible]~~ recognised DADOS store in village reserved by 8th Corps for another Divns Surplus Kit Stores – Demanded 6 Lewis Guns complete for 18 Middlesex Pioneers to complete to 12.	OHS 5003 (OC) 23/4/18
BLARINGHEM	2/5/18		98th Bde moved to Busseboom area – Divn moving tomorrow to Winnezeele area. Large quantity of stores received to-day including bicycles. ~~[illegible]~~ Sent lorries out to 19th & 100th Bde present areas to deliver as many detail stores as possible direct to units so as to reduce bulk of stores to be moved & to complete units equipment before going into line.	
WINNEZEELE J.11.c.4.5 Sheet 27	3/5/18		Moved to Winnezeele & obtained location of Rear Div HQ from Report Centre at Area Commdts office. Established store just outside village in corner of large meadow – Pitched tentage among avenue of large trees to obtain camouflage against hostile aircraft. Rear Div HQ about 200yds away in a farm. Divn now administered by 22nd Corps.	
" "	4/5/18		[illegible] distance of stores from units transports (situated about L.14 Sheet 27) refilling daily will be necessary. Arranged with Bdes accordingly.	

A6945 Wt. W11422/M1160 350,000 12/16 D. D. & L. Forms/C.2118/14.

Instructions regarding War Diaries and Intelligence Summaries are contained in F. S. Regs., Part II. and the Staff Manual respectively. Title pages will be prepared in manuscript.

WAR DIARY
or
INTELLIGENCE SUMMARY.
(Erase heading not required.)

Army Form C. 2118.

Place	Date	Hour	Summary of Events and Information	Remarks and references to Appendices
J.H.C. 4.5	4/5/18	cont.	190 98th Bde refil L.14. cent. sheet 27 3 pm 5th inst. Reconnoitred the location & found it suitable if lorry circuits remain unchanged by 2nd Army. Received 6 Lewis Guns complete for 18th Middlesex Pioneers. Unit refused to take half the magazines owing to lack of transport for carrying them. ~~[illegible]~~ Took magazines into stock & issued off other outstanding indents.	
J.H.C. 4.5	5/5/18		Unable to send lorries to refilling as arranged owing to break down of lorries. Delivered as far as possible to units transport direct. Demanded 960 No 36 Rifle Grenade Dischargers by wire from Base under QMG authority 10002/10 (Q.C.2) dated 7/5/18. This is to complete Bns to 96 per Bn - original issue was on scale of 8 per Bn but most of these have been lost or overused "U." Visited AA & QMG 22 Corps & arranged to ordnance my own artillery again, 33 A at present with 22 Corps Troops. Confirmed move of all units 33 A except X & Y/33 who are with 41st Div as far as I know. My A.O.C. personnel with balance of stores & lorry returned & opened store with me.	

A6945 Wt. W11422/M1160 350,000 12/16 D. D. & L. Forms/C./2118/14.

Instructions regarding War Diaries and Intelligence Summaries are contained in F. S. Regs., Part II. and the Staff Manual respectively. Title pages will be prepared in manuscript.

WAR DIARY
or
INTELLIGENCE SUMMARY.
(*Erase heading not required.*)

Army Form C. 2118.

Place	Date	Hour	Summary of Events and Information	Remarks and references to Appendices
J. 11. C. 4. 5. Sheet 27	6/5/18		Arranged to supply 30th Composite Bde attached to us during operations with any Machine Gun stores & other technical stores urgently required whilst DADOS 30th Div. effect arrangement as he is in back area. × Issued 4 Lewis Guns, made up from salvage in my Armourers Shop, to above unit. Refilled 100th Bde.	
	7/5/18		Refilled 19 & 98th Bdes. General Routine work.	
	8/5/18		Demanded 18 pdr gun for B/162 replace condemned & an 18 pdr carriage for B/156 for same reason. General Routine work. Refilled 100th Bde. including Pioneers & 33rd M.G. Bn.	
	9/5/18		Sent lorry to Base, Calais to collect the 960 Grenade Dischargers very urgently required for use in line. Saved [illegible] time by forward of lorry. Received 18 pdr gun from No 2 Gun Park [illegible] for issue to B/162. Refilled 19 & 98th Bdes.	
	10/5/18		Collected 8,000 Blankets from 3 Bdes & other units from pre-arranged dumps at their transport lines with help of 2 additional lorries from [illegible] M.T. Coy & loaded them over to RO Bergues for despatch to Paris. Demanded 1 Vickers Gun for 33 MG Bn to replace destroyed by shell fire	

A6945 Wt. W11422/M1160 350,000 12/16 D. D. & L. Forms/C.2118/14.

Army Form C. 2118.

Instructions regarding War Diaries and Intelligence Summaries are contained in F. S. Regs., Part II. and the Staff Manual respectively. Title pages will be prepared in manuscript.

WAR DIARY
or
INTELLIGENCE SUMMARY.
(Erase heading not required.)

Place	Date	Hour	Summary of Events and Information	Remarks and references to Appendices
	10/5/18	cont	Demanded 4 6" Newton T Ms for X & Y/33 T.M.B by arrangement with D T M O & H Q R A Arty. All the 12 T Ms held by X & Y/33 were returned to No 2 Gun Park on 21/4/18 as not being required then. 4 are now required in case of emergency. Reviewed question of outstanding technical equipment of D T M Batteries & reported to "Q" that all indents were complete except 3 over 2 months old which were cancelled & not re-submitted by units. Demanded 18 pdr Carriage for B/162 replace destroyed by shell fire 1 18 pdr " " C/162 not repairable in 3 days. Demanded 5 Lewis Guns for 1st Cameronians to replace destroyed by shell fire.	
T. Wilson Capt Edgell	11/5/18.		Received 4 6" T.Ms from No 2 Gun Park & issued to D T M O. Received 18 pdr carriage for B/156. Visited 19th Bde H Q & all units of the Bde to obtain their refitting requirements on coming out of line into reserve. Requirements very small. 2 Bns have salved as many guns as they lost so none are required except by 1st Cameronians.	

A6945 Wt. W11422/M1160 350,000 12/16 D. D. & L. Forms/C.2118/14.

Instructions regarding War Diaries and Intelligence Summaries are contained in F. S. Regs., Part II, and the Staff Manual respectively. Title pages will be prepared in manuscript.

WAR DIARY
or
INTELLIGENCE SUMMARY.
(Erase heading not required.)

Army Form C. 2118.

Place	Date	Hour	Summary of Events and Information	Remarks and references to Appendices
T. 14. C. 4. 5 (Sheet 27)	12/5/18.		Received 5 Lewis Guns for 1st Cameronians. Arranged to return surplus M.G. parts to No 2 Gun Park. Only stocks of Barrels & Magazines now held for immediate issue. Division transferred to 2nd Corps ~~[illegible]~~ without changing areas. General Routine work.	
	13/5/18		Received 18 pdr Carriage for C/162. General Routine work.	
	~~14/5/18~~		Visited various C.C.S to obtain all available Revolvers taken from Casualties – only 10 obtained in all.	
	14/5/18.		One Lewis Gun made up from Salvage & issued to 4th Kings Liverpools to replace gun condemned.	
	15/5/18.		500 S.B.Rs of various sizes demanded a week ago not received today as expected in spite of two hasteners. Owing to urgency of requirement sent lorry to Base to collect them. Found delay due to error in labelling the cases at Base.	
	14/5/18		Demanded 4 Vickers Guns for 33rd M.G. Bn – 3 condemned & 1 destroyed by shell fire. also demanded 2 Lewis Guns for AA work for A/156 to replace losses to enemy.	
	15/5/18.		Demanded sufficient New Pattern Butts to complete all Lewis Guns with old pattern butts in possession of units. Demanded 2 Lewis Guns for 2nd A & S.H to replace lost to enemy	

Army Form C. 2118.

WAR DIARY
or
INTELLIGENCE SUMMARY.
(Erase heading not required.)

Instructions regarding War Diaries and Intelligence Summaries are contained in F. S. Regs., Part II. and the Staff Manual respectively. Title pages will be prepared in manuscript.

Place	Date	Hour	Summary of Events and Information	Remarks and references to Appendices
J.11.c.4.5	16/5/18.		Received 2 Lewis Guns for A/15 B, 2 for 2nd A & SA & 4 Vickers for 33rd M.G.Bn. General Routine work.	
"	17/5/18.		Demanded 1 Lewis Gun for D/15 B. destroyed by shell fire. General Routine work. Received instructions from ADOS 2nd Corps to send a representative to ROUSBRUGGE Railhead on 18th to take in & give receipts for any winter Clothing returned by units of 33rd Div in accordance with a CRO being published to-day. 1 Lewis Gun received for D/15 B.	
"	18/5/18.		~~Demanded 18 pdr for A/15 B (condemned).~~ Sent representative to ROUSBRUGGE, no winter Clothing returned by units. Forwarded my views on a proposed new system of keeping Bulk records of issues & receipts by Brigade WOs for checking purposes.	
"	19/5/18.		Visited ADOS & OO 2nd Corps troops re further allotment of leather & cotton Gloves for Anti-gas protection of R.A. personnel to scale of 6 per gun of leather & 12 per cotton. A part issue has already been drawn fr OO 2nd Corps Tps & issued. Discussed the new Bulk record system – ADOS will arrange conference of DADOS & OO CT at his office to discuss the system & report to DDOS 2nd Army. Demanded 200 fly traps to meet units requirements authorised by ADMS.	

A6945 Wt. W11422/M1160 350,000 12/16 D. D. & L. Forms/C./2118/14.

Instructions regarding War Diaries and Intelligence Summaries are contained in F. S. Regs., Part II. and the Staff Manual respectively. Title pages will be prepared in manuscript.

WAR DIARY
or
INTELLIGENCE SUMMARY.
(Erase heading not required.)

Army Form C. 2118.

Place	Date	Hour	Summary of Events and Information	Remarks and references to Appendices
T. 11. C. 4. 5 Sheet 57	19/5/18		Published circular letter to all formations 33 Divn giving instructions for the immediate return of winter clothing still in possession, in accordance with CRO recently published. Woollen drawers & vests will not be returned to Railhead but withdrawn through the Baths & the woollen drawers replaced by cotton, the stock of which has been received & issued in bulk to Div Baths.	
	20/5/18.		Demanded a further 500 yds Butter Muslin to meet urgent requirements due to spell of hot weather. General Routine work. Sent a representative to ROUSBRUGGE Railhead to take in winter clothing. 6 men of 18th Middlesex	
	21/5/18		Pioneers & an NCO of 2nd Worcesters - employed by me - sent to their Base Depots for examination by Medical Board for reclassification as ADMS has classified them "B". They can only be obtained again for work through the 23rd Employment Coy - application made by 33 Div HQ to Base Depots for the return of the NCO & 5 of the men to Employ. Coy & so [illegible] on my recommendation that they were very suitable for work in my store	

A6945 Wt. W11422/M1160 350,000 12/16 D. D. & L. Forms/C./2118/14.

Army Form C. 2118.

Instructions regarding War Diaries and Intelligence Summaries are contained in F. S. Regs., Par. II. and the Staff Manual respectively. Title pages will be prepared in manuscript.

WAR DIARY
or
INTELLIGENCE SUMMARY.
(*Erase heading not required.*)

Place	Date	Hour	Summary of Events and Information	Remarks and references to Appendices
[illegible]	21/5/18		Received 18pdr gun for A/156.	
	22/5/18		Demanded 36 Lewis Guns complete to bring Battalions up to scale X i.e. 20 guns per Bn exclusive of A.A. Guns. Authority Q.M.G. OB 1515 9/5/18. Demand to complete to scale E i.e. 24 per Bn may be submitted Guns 3rd when Sqn is ready to receive them.	
	23/5/18		General Routine work.	
	24/5/18		Despatched 0/4490 T/Sub Condr Webb. AOC to England for training in an R.A.F. Cadet unit for a commission in general list for duty with R.A.F. Notified D.A.O.S. 2nd Army & A.A.O.S. 2nd Corps. asked for replacement for this W.O. (19th Bde). 36 Lewis guns received & handed over to Armourers shop for stripping, easing & alteration of safety catches & Butt catches & replacement of old pattern Bolts where necessary, before issue to Bns as complaints have in some cases been received that new guns are very tight in the body & difficulty in stripping & stripping is experienced.	

A6945 Wt. W11422/M1160 350,000 12/16 D. D. & L. Forms/C.2118/14.

Army Form C. 2118.

Instructions regarding War Diaries and Intelligence Summaries are contained in F. S. Regs., Par. II. and the Staff Manual respectively. Title pages will be prepared in manuscript.

WAR DIARY
or
INTELLIGENCE SUMMARY.
(Erase heading not required.)

Place	Date	Hour	Summary of Events and Information	Remarks and references to Appendices
T. 11. C. 4. 5. Sheet 27	26/5/18		Rear Divl H.Q. moved forward to location adjacent to ADs H.Q. I remain in present location to take charge of the buildings & sites for 33rd Divn in case Divl H.Q. wishes to return here at any time. Moved my office into the farm & occupied some of the standing tents.	
	26/5/18		Demanded 3 German M.Gs (heavy 08 pattern) for instructional purposes to replace those previously issued to Divn but returned at various times. Visited ADs H.Q.	
	27/5/18		& went on in car to 98th Bde in Dirty Bucket & Border Camps. Saw Staff Capt & Quartermasters of the 3 Bns & asked if their equipment was in good order & if any outstanding stores were urgently required — no complaints. Proceeded to 19th Bde & saw Staff Capt & the Brigadier. Bde very well supplied with stores & no complaints.	
	27/5/18.		General Routine work. Visitor "Q", Field Cashier & Camp Commandant & DCSO in afternoon. Raised question of difficulty with car for my use & asked for same more frequently to enable me to visit units.	

A6945 Wt.W11422/M1160 350,000 12/16 D. D. & L. Forms/C./2118/14.

Instructions regarding War Diaries and Intelligence Summaries are contained in F. S. Regs., Part II. and the Staff Manual respectively. Title pages will be prepared in manuscript.

WAR DIARY
or
INTELLIGENCE SUMMARY.
(*Erase heading not required.*)

Army Form C. 2118.

Place	Date	Hour	Summary of Events and Information	Remarks and references to Appendices
[illegible]	27/5/18		Ordnance Refilling point for 3 Bdes. moved to L.19.c.7.0 owing to	[illegible] traffic
	28/5/18		General end of month Routine work. D.A.D.O.S. demands 6 complete Stokes Hows to replace unserviceable. Reason for demand not understood so referred indent to him for explanation – Authority exists for 20 per month of Hows so would not seem applicable to Btys in reserve & rest billets. Reqd nos of Guns How & Carriages in possession of 33rd Div Arty not reqd by A.A.O.s this month as information already given earlier in month – no amendments thereto received from Batteries so presume still correct as automatically amended by condemnation & replacement issues from I.O.M. & Gun Park respectively.	
	29/5/18.		Visited 9th HLI, 16th KRRC & saw C.Os & C.Q.M.S of these Bns re outstanding demands – they had no complaints re supply of stores except kilt aprons for 9 HLI which have been outstanding 3 weeks & repeatedly hastened. Base replied to-day "not available". Visited also 4 Coy Train & S.A.A. Sec D.A.C. saw Staff Capt 100th Bde. Everything satisfactory.	

A6945 Wt. W11422/M1160 350,000 12/16 D. D. & L. Forms/C.2118/14.

Army Form C. 2118.

Instructions regarding War Diaries and Intelligence Summaries are contained in F. S. Regs., Part II. and the Staff Manual respectively. Title pages will be prepared in manuscript.

WAR DIARY
or
INTELLIGENCE SUMMARY.
(Erase heading not required.)

Place	Date	Hour	Summary of Events and Information	Remarks and references to Appendices
T. 11. C. 4. 5. Sheet 57	30/5/18		General Routine Work. Reported receipt of 18 pdr gun with [illegible] for C/162 from 10/15 workshops & issued [illegible] 11/12 workshops	
	31/5/18.		Visited 162 Bde H.Q. A B & C/162, H.Q. R.A + H.Q. & A B C & D/156 to ascertain any urgent requirements before Div Arty goes into action in a few days time – all batteries well equipped – Several complain of bad quality of the repaired harness & saddlery now being issued from Base. I think this complaint is mainly due to units disliking the appearance of repaired harness as by suitable treatment with lubricants supplied & care & lining with Collar & Serge Saddlers roughness in Breastcollars can be obviated. It is obvious that here & there badly repaired items may be issued owing to the lack of the rigid inspection which is instituted in Peace time; thro active service conditions – Hastened Indicators Fuze bars of which 32 are outstanding to Batteries – these are urgently required & supply is very slow & controlled. Requested a part issue to 33 Div Arty at least. Also hastened outstanding Baskets Ammunition 18 pdr.	

A6945 Wt. W11422/M1160 350,000 12/16 D. D. & L. Forms/C.2118/14.

Instructions regarding War Diaries and Intelligence Summaries are contained in F. S. Regs., Part II, and the Staff Manual respectively. Title pages will be prepared in manuscript.

Army Form C. 2118.

WAR DIARY
or
INTELLIGENCE SUMMARY.
(Erase heading not required.)

Place	Date	Hour	Summary of Events and Information	Remarks and references to Appendices
	31/5/18		From discussion with Battery Commanders I found that the frequent heavy demand for Head Collars received from Batteries is due to the loss of them from Battery equipment through being sent away with sick horses to M.V.S. & never returned to the Battery although the MVS is provided with 100 Stable head Collars for the purpose of sending sick horses to Base with them. All leather head collars should therefore be returned to units. Took up the matter with DDVS with a view to rectification.	
			[illegible] Major DADVS 33rd Divn	
			31/5/18	

A6945 Wt. W11422/M1160 350,000 12/16 D. D. & L. Forms/C./2118/14.

Instructions regarding War Diaries and Intelligence Summaries are contained in F. S. Regs., Part II. and the Staff Manual respectively. Title pages will be prepared in manuscript.

WAR DIARY
or
INTELLIGENCE SUMMARY.
(Erase heading not required.)

SECRET

DADOS 33rd Div.

JUNE. 1918

Vol 32

Army Form C. 2118.

Place	Date	Hour	Summary of Events and Information	Remarks and references to Appendices
J. 11. C. 4.5 Sheet 27	1/6/18		General Routine Work. Base issued a Trav. Kitchen Body to 5th S. R. which DOH immediately condemned as U/S.	
	2/6/18		Bulk Return completed, checked & sent to ADOS. Issues of New Tins particularly high. Issued instructions to Bde WOs to watch future demands & bring to my notice any discrepancies for investigation. Excessive issues last month probably due to heavy losses in April not being made up till May owing to delay in submission of indents for equipment & accessories refitting by units. Other issues normal. 3 light German M.Gs collected from 2nd A.T. No 3 & issued 1 per Bde for instruction.	
	3/6/18		Demanded 36 Lewis Guns complete under Authy O.B. 1215 (GHQ. Q letter) dated 9/5/18 to complete Bns to scale E. 16 to 24 each.	
			General Routine Work. Visited Q. Issued 2 long & 2 short pattern expendable Belt Boxes to M.G. Bn for trial & report. Ordinary tools belts issued with Boxes.	
	4/6/18		No 2 Gun Park wired authority to draw these guns – Arranged to send lorries to fetch first opportunity when available. Issued 4 Boxes Belt MGs A.H. Vickers to M.G. Bn for trial & report.	
	5/6/18		General Routine Work. Visited Q & QM 1st Queens & 1st Cameronians 19th Bde. Visited 5th S.R. & inspected the U/S K.T. condemned by DOH & found it unfit for use. A new one was wired for & complaint & report forwarded to Base. Instructed unit to send U/S body to R.H.Q.	
	6/6/18		Received 36 Lewis Guns from Gun Park. Guns inspected, tested & spare parts checked. List of deficiencies made out for demanding by units. All Magazines tested. Issues to units to be made at refilling points. Q informed of receipt.	

A6945 Wt. W11422/M1160 350,000 12/16 D. D. & L. Forms/C./2118/14.

Instructions regarding War Diaries and Intelligence Summaries are contained in F. S. Regs., Part II. and the Staff Manual respectively. Title pages will be prepared in manuscript.

WAR DIARY
or
INTELLIGENCE SUMMARY.
(Erase heading not required.)

Army Form C. 2118.

Place	Date	Hour	Summary of Events and Information	Remarks and references to Appendices
	6/6/18		Demanded 18 pdr Carriage with No 7 Dial Sight for A/156 to replace destroyed by shell fire. Issued 3 Monkey Puzzle adjustable Lewis AA Mountings one to each Bde for trial & report to "Q" in due course.	
	7/6/18		General Routine work. Visited "Q".	
T. 11. C. 4. 5. Sheet 27	8/6/18		Received 1 Cart Cable Light from Base without indent for 33 Div Signals in part completion of establishment of 2 Cable Carts. As demand were reversed with Limb GS or RE wagons in lieu of these Cable Carts they cannot now return one on receipt of the Cable Cart. Reported this to A.A.O.S. A further 3 Monkey Puzzle AA Mtgs received & issued 1 per Bde. On instruction from "Q", after consultation with A.A. & QMG & DGSO, & reference to A.A.O.S, I demanded 1000 suits of SD clothing as part of Corps Reserve of SD clothing. These suits are for issue thro' Div Baths to men whose clothing has been contaminated with Yellow Cross Gas at a moment's notice to avoid the men becoming casualties. Visited "Q".	
	9/6/18		General Routine work.	

A6945 Wt. W11422/M1160 350,000 12/16 D. D. & L. Forms/C./2118/14.

Instructions regarding War Diaries and Intelligence Summaries are contained in F. S. Regs., Part II. and the Staff Manual respectively. Title pages will be prepared in manuscript.

WAR DIARY
or
INTELLIGENCE SUMMARY.
(Erase heading not required.)

Army Form C. 2118.

Place	Date	Hour	Summary of Events and Information	Remarks and references to Appendices
	10/6/18		A further 24 Golf Bag Lewis Gun carriers allotted by Corps & issued 8 per Bde. These bring that issued up to 114. Very few Bags carrying L.G. replaced by the new Golf Bag carriers yet returned by Bns – Reported to "Q" for action.	
	11/6/18.		Issued a Lewis gun, made serviceable from Salvage in Armourers Shop, to 1st Cameronians to replace one destroyed by Shell fire. 18pdr Carriage issued to A/156 thro' 11/20 MW	
J. 11. C. 4. 5 Sheet 27	12/6/18		Demanded 18pdr gun for C/162 to replace one condemned for scoring by I.O.M. Lieut. G. Smith A.O.D. reported for instruction in duties of a DADOS. Report on his suitability to be sent to AADOS 2nd Corps on 26th inst.	
	13/6/18.	[illegible]	General Routine work. "Q" phoned instructions to obtain 24 knobkerries 60 prs Mk V wirecutters & 300 Armbands distinguishing White for a Raid – must be issued to 19th Bde by tomorrow afternoon at latest. Asked AADOS for first two items – no knobkerries available within Army – may be obtainable at Base. 60 prs wirecutters can be drawn from No 2 Gun Park on authority of DDOS 2nd Army – White Armbands in stock. Wired OO Calais asking if 24 knobkerries were available for drawing by car. Base replied "available".	
	14/6/18		Went by car to Base, obtaining authority of DDOS 2nd Army on way to collect by car & duly collected 24 knobkerries. Collected the 60 prs wirecutters on return journey. Issued by car to 19th Bde H.Q. in afternoon.	

Army Form C. 2118.

Instructions regarding War Diaries and Intelligence Summaries are contained in F. S. Regs., Part II. and the Staff Manual respectively. Title pages will be prepared in manuscript.

WAR DIARY
or
INTELLIGENCE SUMMARY.
(Erase heading not required.)

Place	Date	Hour	Summary of Events and Information	Remarks and references to Appendices
J. 11. C. 4. 5.	14/6/18		A further 49 Golf Bag Lewis Gun Covers received & issued equally to 3 Bdes. 6 Pawls stop Magazine & 6 Feed arms ~~[illegible]~~ MkII pieces of guns to take	Mark II
			95 round Magazines, issued to each of 3 Bdes for trial & report	on
			their suitability for use with the ordinary MG magazines!	
	15/6/18		2nd Army S.O.S. School informed me that 20 Rifles with Tel Sights demanded on units indents for their Bns, which have been outstanding over 3 months are now available. Drew 11 of these (all immediately available). Wrote to Bdes asking for statements of numbers of Rifles with Tel Sights as distinct from Rifles 1914 Pattern in possession of each Bn as the outstanding indents are now no criterion of the situation. Bns are entitled to 5 Rifles with T/S & 3 1914 Pattern Rifles – The latter are already in possession	
	16/6/18.		~~[illegible]~~ 18 pdr gun for "C"/162 Bde issued thro' M/2 workshops to unit. Visited QM Stores of 100th Bde Bns & saw QMs & also QM of 1st Cameronians. No stores urgently required & very little outstanding. Went on to 19th Bde H.Q. & saw Staff Capt as to any refitting required on coming out of line into ~~Reserve~~ Reserve for a few days – no appreciable losses reported & no special action necessary. Saw [illegible] & G.O.C.	

Instructions regarding War Diaries and Intelligence Summaries are contained in F. S. Regs., Part II. and the Staff Manual respectively. Title pages will be prepared in manuscript.

WAR DIARY
or
INTELLIGENCE SUMMARY.
(Erase heading not required.)

Army Form C. 2118.

Place	Date	Hour	Summary of Events and Information	Remarks and references to Appendices
	17/6/18		Received pair of hand horse-clippers fitted with new pattern permanent guard for the teeth – for trial & report – introduced to obviate damage to teeth by frequent loss of the loose leather guard previously fitted. Sent the pair to D.A.D.V.S.	
J. 11. C. 4. 5. Sheet 27	18/6/18		Bayonet fighting sacks required for training purposes by reserve Bde – Demanded 100 urgently from D.A.D.O.S. General Routine work.	
	19/6/18		Demanded 18 pdr Carriage for B/162 to replace one destroyed by shellfire. Visited 98 Bde 'B' Echelon & saw Q.Ms of 3 Rgts – took up question of excessive demands for clothing by 4th Kings Liverpools during past 4 months – Q.M. promised to watch demands more carefully. (a report giving monthly issues to the Bn was sent to them thro' "Q" a few days ago). Proceeded to "Q" & thence to Div Salvage Dump at International Corner (A9.a.2.4 sheet 28)	
	20/6/18		General Routine work.	
	21/6/18		Demanded a Vickers gun complete for 33 M.G. Bn to replace one destroyed by shellfire. Visited "Q". General Routine work.	

Army Form C. 2118.

WAR DIARY
or
INTELLIGENCE SUMMARY.
(Erase heading not required.)

Instructions regarding War Diaries and Intelligence Summaries are contained in F. S. Regs., Par. II. and the Staff Manual respectively. Title pages will be prepared in manuscript.

Place	Date	Hour	Summary of Events and Information	Remarks and references to Appendices
	22/6/18		Made application to CRE for 20 tons Stone for repair of bad patch of road outside my store which gives considerable trouble to lorries in wet weather. DAA Roads regretted impossible to supply owing to shortage of material.	
			Demanded 18 pdr gun with B.M. for B/156 to replace one condemned for scoring. ~~3 Heavy German M.Gs~~	
J. 11. C. 4. 5. Sheet 27	23/6/18		3 Heavy German Machine Guns received from Base & issued 1 to each Inf Bde for instructional purposes. Visited Railhead Hopoutre for Lt Smith to see offloading & checking of contents of Truck with Way Bill. Inspected 24 15 ? Cart Cable light which had arrived at Railhead for units – all new vehicles. Proceeded to II Corps Railhead Rousbrugge via Dunkirk & Bray Dunes – Obtained list of F S Boots & Blankets recently returned there by units 33rd Divn. 18 pdr Carriage for B/162 issued there 11/12 OM to Battery. Vickers gun for 33 M G Bn received from No 2 Gun Park. Drove 33 M.T. Coy on way to Railhead – Supply of ordnance quite satisfactory	

A6945 Wt. W11422/M1160 350,000 12/16 D. D. & L. Forms/C. 2118/14.

Instructions regarding War Diaries and Intelligence Summaries are contained in F. S. Regs., Part II. and the Staff Manual respectively. Title pages will be prepared in manuscript.

WAR DIARY
or
INTELLIGENCE SUMMARY.
(Erase heading not required.)

Army Form C. 2118.

Place	Date	Hour	Summary of Events and Information	Remarks and references to Appendices
			Recd + issued 4 feet 3 inch Cordage to each L.T.M.B for manufacture of slings for getting mortars more quickly into action. Army authority obtained for issue.	
	24/6/18		Demanded 72 Lewis Guns from No 2 Gun Park to complete Bdes to Scale "G" on instructions from A.A.O.S under authority OB1215. of 9/5/18.	
			A second Cart Cable light issued to 33 Divl Signal Coy.	
			Reported to AAOS that no wagon limbered G.S or R.E was available for return in place of this vehicle for reasons given on issue of previous Cable Cart. Signals establishment of vehicles now complete. Demanded 18 pdr gun for B/162 to replace condemned for scoring. 8 Clinometer lists received from Base for issue to 33rd M.G. Bn for trial & report.	
J. 11. C. 4. 5. Sheet 27	~~24/6~~			
"	25/6/18.		Demanded Base Plate for 3" Stokes Mortar for 98 T.M.B by wire to replace destroyed by shell fire. General Routine together. Visited "C" [illegible]	
"	26/6/18.		+ watches 98 & 19 Bde refilling en route. Saw D.D.O.S who agreed to immediate issue of 73 more [illegible] No refilling for 100 Bde to-day as no stores available for issue this afternoon - notified all concerned. Next refilling follows fixed programme i.e. on Friday 28th.	
	27/6/18.		Sent 3 lorries to No 2 Gun Park, Watten to collect 72 complete Lewis Guns after notifying A.A.O.S & No 2 Gun Park of our decision to draw & issue to units immediately. 18 pdr guns for B/162 + B/156 issued to Batteries.	

WAR DIARY
or
INTELLIGENCE SUMMARY.
(Erase heading not required.)

Instructions regarding War Diaries and Intelligence Summaries are contained in F. S. Regs., Part II. and the Staff Manual respectively. Title pages will be prepared in manuscript.

Army Form C. 2118.

Place	Date	Hour	Summary of Events and Information	Remarks and references to Appendices
	28/6/18	Forwarded another complaint from M [illegible] to ADOS re Batteries of 41 D. Supplying [illegible] [illegible] [illegible] instructions	Lorries returned with 72 guns complete less certain deficiencies in each set which will be made up when received from Base without further indents. All guns inspected, cased & components & spares checked by Armourers & all Magazines tested. Issues will be made at subsequent refillings. Demanded 18 pdr gun for C/156 to replace one condemned for scoring. Letter received from QMG notifying that the issue of BMs with all guns by Gun Park, whether required or not will be discontinued for pieces below 6" calibre & asking formations to suspend return to Gun Park of all surplus serviceable BMs due from Units [illegible] Is O.M. In two cases have BMs been issued when not required wrote Bg [illegible] concerned to report the return of surplus BMs to I.O.M for transmission to Gun Park.	
	29/6/18.		General Routine work. Reported to ADOS Truck Nos & date of arrival of Bulk Clothing Trucks from Vadrona showing the delay as compared with other Trucks. This covers the past fortnight. End of month returns sent to ADOS.	

Instructions regarding War Diaries and Intelligence Summaries are contained in F. S. Regs., Part II. and the Staff Manual respectively. Title pages will be prepared in manuscript.

WAR DIARY
or
INTELLIGENCE SUMMARY.
(*Erase heading not required.*)

Army Form C. 2118.

Place	Date	Hour	Summary of Events and Information	Remarks and references to Appendices
	29/6/18		Informed A.D.O.S. I could attend Course on Ammunition commencing 7/7/18 at No 19 Ord Depot. My "Q" agrees & suggested Lieut Smith remain with me & act for me while on this Course to give him experience of the work of a D.A.D.O.S.	
	30/6/18		H.Q. 19th Corps have taken over Wanquetin area & require the site of my present store for their O.O. Corps Troops & therefore want me to move quickly. Reported this to my "Q" who are taking up matter with II Corps "Q". Meanwhile allowed O.O. 19th Corps Troops to occupy a portion of my site as an emergency arrangement & visited D.W. H.Q. to obtain another site near the latter and is convenient for Railhead & for units to draw direct. General Routine work. Forwarded to H.Q. 33 D.A. list of surplus H & S returned by Nos 1 & 2 Sec 33 D.A.C. on reduction of lead horses in D.A. by 96 & asked for explanation of deficiency in No 1 Sec's return.	

30/6/18

[signature] Major A.O.D.
D.A.D.O.S.
33 Divn

A6945 Wt. W11422/M1160 350,000 12/16 D. D. & L. Forms/C./2118/14.

SECRET

Army Form C. 2118.

Instructions regarding War Diaries and Intelligence Summaries are contained in F. S. Regs., Par. II. and the Staff Manual respectively. Title pages will be prepared in manuscript.

WAR DIARY or ~~INTELLIGENCE SUMMARY.~~

(*Erase heading not required.*)

July 1918 D.A.D.O.S. 33 Div

Vol 33

Place	Date	Hour	Summary of Events and Information	Remarks and references to Appendices
J.11. c. 4.5.	1/7/18		Calais Base opens issues from Vendroux to-day on new Bulk programme (3 issues weekly still but differently grouped). Arranged to watch date of arrival of trucks at Railhead as 24 hours delay will probably occur now & refilling date must be altered if this is so. General Routine work. Gave orders to Store for to prepare for a move between to-day & date of arrival of next truck by issuing all stores as far as possible & packing up where possible.	
" "	2/7/18		18 pdr gun for B/156 received by Workshops from Gun Park. 1 Lewis Gun salved & made serviceable in Armourers Shop issued to C/156 to complete estab. of A-A guns. Completed inspection & adjustment of 72 Lewis Guns & issued last 24 of them to 100th Bde. Orders received from Div HQ to move to new site.	
Store F17.C.5.0. Office F.22 Central	3/7/18		Moved Store to F17. c. 5. 0 & Office to Div HQ at F22 cent. (Both Sheet 27) Cancelled refilling arrangements. Notified all concerned change of location. Opened Workshops & Salvage Dump. Location of mobile workshops for repair of guns & vehicles of the Div changed by A.A.O.S. to No 9 & 10. Asked 'Q' to amend Administrative orders accordingly.	

A6945 Wt. W11422/M1160 350,000 12/16 D. D. & L. Forms/C. 2118/14.

Instructions regarding War Diaries and Intelligence Summaries are contained in F. S. Regs., Par. II. and the Staff Manual respectively. Title pages will be prepared in manuscript.

WAR DIARY
or
INTELLIGENCE SUMMARY.
(Erase heading not required.)

Army Form C. 2118.

Place	Date	Hour	Summary of Events and Information	Remarks and references to Appendices
Stores F17.C.5.0 Office F17 Cent	4/7/18		Demanded 4.5in How. for D/156 replace condemned ... Brigade asked for refilling to be continued to save Horse Transport of their Amm. Agreed. General Routine work.	
" "	5/7/18		Arranged refilling programme onto different days ~~[illegible]~~ but at same locations. Change in days necessitated by change in days of receipt of stores from D.A.D.O.S. No refilling required for Artillery as they are all very close to store & can draw direct. Obtained special passes for A.M. for lorries to go against arrows on traffic maps to save mileage when refilling.	
" "	6/7/18		Proceeded to No 9 Ordnance Depot for short Ammunition Course as arranged by D.A.D.O.S. Handed over to Lieut. G. Smith A.O.D. who I arranged with D.A.D.O.S. should remain with him indefinitely until sent elsewhere for duty by D.O.S. This is a good opportunity for this officer to acquire practical experience of Div'l Ordnance work. Collected 9 Reflectors with Telescopic Sights for 2nd Army S.O.S. School (now at Bournonville) to complete my outstanding indent. These should complete all Battalions to 5 each.	

A6945 Wt. W11422/M1160 350,000 12/16 D. D. & L. Forms/C.2118/14.

Instructions regarding War Diaries and Intelligence Summaries are contained in F. S. Regs., Par. II, and the Staff Manual respectively. Title pages will be prepared in manuscript.

WAR DIARY
or
INTELLIGENCE SUMMARY.
(Erase heading not required.)

Army Form C. 2118.

Place	Date	Hour	Summary of Events and Information	Remarks and references to Appendices
			Reported to "Q" that the 72 Lewis Guns recently received were [illegible] at light [illegible] & other defects which required 3 days work in Armourers Shop to rectify - DOC forwarded	Complaint to 2nd Army(?)
Stores	7/7/18		Demanded 3 in Stokes Mortar Complete for 108 T.M.B. replace	
F.17.C.5.0			destroyed shell fire. Also Lewis Gun for C/156 for same reason	
Office			Demanded 1 Vickers gun for instructional purposes - for 38th	
F.22.Cent.			M.G.Bn under authority O.B. 407/6 dated 4/7/18.	
			4 lbs Luminous Paint + 50 Knobkerries, authorised by GHQ(?)	
			for issue for raid purposes, received from Base.	
	8/7/18		6 Officers + 213 ORs of "Queens", to leave the line 6 days(?) to	
			proceed to Paris for ceremonial "parade" on 14th July - "Q"	
			ordered their refitting with new clothing & equipment where	
			necessary, at once - Clothing to be obtained from reserve stock	
			in Div(?) Baths & other items from stock at Stores or Salvage	
			Personally attended refitting during the night - as size	
			roll could be obtained in advance owing to the party	
			being in the line till last moment. Refitting as far as possible	
			completed by 6.30 am 9/7/18. 4.5 in How received for D/156	
			by IOM from Gun Park. Demanded 18 pdr Gun for C/162	
			to replace [illegible].	

A6945 Wt. W11422/M1160 350,000 12/16 D. D. & L. Forms/C./2118/14.

Army Form C. 2118.

Instructions regarding War Diaries and Intelligence Summaries are contained in F. S. Regs., Part II. and the Staff Manual respectively. Title pages will be prepared in manuscript.

WAR DIARY
or
INTELLIGENCE SUMMARY.
(Erase heading not required.)

Place	Date	Hour	Summary of Events and Information	Remarks and references to Appendices
Stone F.17.C.5.0 Office E.22 Central Sheet 27	9/7/18		~~[struck out]~~ 18 pdr Carriages for C/162 Bde to replace damaged by shell fire. Received 3" Stokes Mortar for 100th T.M.B. Demanded 7 more Rifles with Telescopic Sights to complete Bde. Refitting of party of 1st Cheam completed as far as stocks permitted by 6.30 am. Reported deficiencies to ADOS who arranged for these to be made up at Etaples Base en route for Paris.	
" "	10/7/18		Received Lewis Gun for C/156 Bde. [illegible] 50 [illegible] & 4 lbs luminous paint sent to Ridge Dump (Div Ammn Dump) ready for immediate issue. Visited 212 Field Coy by car. 2 lorries sent to Bathing officer — no others being available — Purchased 2 rat traps for 33 Divl Reception Camp on instructions from "Q". Base asked for consolidated demand for overseas chevrons. Wrote them to return detail indents already submitted. Demanded 5,000 red & 25,000 Blue — estimated requirements. Draft for DRO instructing all units to indent for numbers they are entitled to wear, at once.	

A6945 Wt. W11422/M1160 350,000 12/16 D. D. & L. Forms/C./2118/14.

Instructions regarding War Diaries and Intelligence Summaries are contained in F. S. Regs., Part II. and the Staff Manual respectively. Title pages will be prepared in manuscript.

WAR DIARY
or
INTELLIGENCE SUMMARY.
(Erase heading not required.)

Army Form C. 2118.

Place	Date	Hour	Summary of Events and Information	Remarks and references to Appendices
Stores F.17.C.5.0 Offices F.22.Cent.	11/7/18		Demanded 4·5" How for D/156 replace condemned for wear. Received Vickers Gun for 33rd M.G. Bn for instructional purposes. General Routine work.	
	12/7/18.		Took up the return of Surplus Lead Harness from Artillery Bdes DAC section with Staff Capt. RA as the return is proceeding too slowly. Hasteners sent to all Batteries. DAC satisfactory. 300 numbered Raid discs (in duplicate) sent to Ridge Dump & 100 to 19th Bde. ADOS visited office & Stores.	
" "	13/7/18		18 pdr & carriage for C/162 received by Workshops for repair. Visited 2nd Salvage Dump, St Sixte. Fair amount of useful repairable stores ready for collection – arranged to send lorry in a few days time when more had accumulated.	
" "	14/7/18		Replied to memo from ADOS re complaint sent in by "Q" on condition of last 72 new Lewis guns received from Gun Park, [illegible]. 6 Fly Sprayers sent to Ridge Dump for accessibility to units in forward area. General Routine work.	
" "	15/7/18		4·5" How. for D/156 Bde received by Workshops. Drew 40 large and small belt boxes to carry the extra stock of belts held by 33rd Bn – No British Boxes available	

A6945 Wt. W11422/M1160 350,000 12/16 D. D. & L. Forms/C.2118/14.

Army Form C. 2118.

WAR DIARY
or
INTELLIGENCE SUMMARY.
(Erase heading not required.)

Instructions regarding War Diaries and Intelligence Summaries are contained in F. S. Regs., Part II. and the Staff Manual respectively. Title pages will be prepared in manuscript.

Place	Date	Hour	Summary of Events and Information	Remarks and references to Appendices
Stores F.F.J. C.S.O. Offices F.22 Central.	15/7/18 Cont.		Informed by 'Q' that an American Mechanic would be sent to Div'l Armourers shop for one week's instruction in construction & repair of the Lewis Gun & English Rifle (short) & that this Armourer would be succeeded by an Armourer each week until 5 weeks from 16th inst. Arranged for their instruction in the Shop. Div'l Reception Camp cannot draw stores demanded by them owing to distance. No use sending by A.M.F.O. owing to delay & uncertainty of delivery. As Watten very near No 2 Gun Park at Watten arranged for G.P. lorry when delivering to my stores to collect any stores for Reception Camp & take to Watten. Instructed Reception Camp to call frequently & collect from No 2 Gun Park.	
" "	16/7/18		Instruction received for A.D.O.S. to visit Corps Salvage Dump frequently – now open at Proven – Rifles & Equipment always available in considerable quantity. Sent lorry to collect 78 prs Boots after arranging this with C.S.O. Demanded 3in Stokes Mortar	
" "	[illegible]		for 19th T.M.B. replace condemned by I.O.M. Received 12 Special packs for carrying Lewis Guns & members for issue 4 per Brigade for trial	

A6945 Wt. W11422/M1160 350,000 12/16 D. D. & L. Forms/C.2118/14.

Instructions regarding War Diaries and Intelligence Summaries are contained in F. S. Regs., Par. II. and the Staff Manual respectively. Title pages will be prepared in manuscript.

WAR DIARY
or
INTELLIGENCE SUMMARY.
(*Erase heading not required.*)

Army Form C. 2118.

Place	Date	Hour	Summary of Events and Information	Remarks and references to Appendices
Store F.17.C.50 Office F.22.Cent	17/7/18		General Routine work. Demanded 4'5in How Carriage for D/162 replace destroyed shellfire. also 18 pdr Carriage for C/162 for same reason.	
	18/7/18		Received 3in Stokes Mortar for 19th TMB less Base plate. Issued a Lewis Gun to 1st Middlesex Regt to replace unserviceable, from one salved repaired in Armourers Shop. ADOS asked how many more Mats Gun Wheel were required by 33rd Div Arty to complete to 2 per 4'5in How – Staff Capt RA replied "Nil" in possession & "Nil required" not being of any use – A.A.O.S. informed accordingly. Visited 19 Bde Rear H.Q.	
" "	19/7/18		Demanded 16 Lewis Guns complete for 33 Div Arty to increase establishment of Batteries from 2 to 4 for AA work. General Routine work	
" "	20/7/18		~~[illegible]~~ General Routine work	
			Lt Smith A.O.D. proceeded on leave to U.K.	
" "	21/7/18		16 Lewis Guns received for 33 Div Arty – Handed over to Armourers shops for stripping, inspection & easing where necessary. – Corresponding number of Magazines tested before issue. General Routine work	
" "	22/7/18.		18 pdr Carriage for C/166 received also 4'5in How Carriage for D/162 Major Beavan. A.O.D. returned from Ammunition Course & took over	

A6945 Wt. W11422/M1160 350,000 12/16 D. D. & L. Forms/C./2118/14.

Instructions regarding War Diaries and Intelligence Summaries are contained in F. S. Regs., Part II. and the Staff Manual respectively. Title pages will be prepared in manuscript.

WAR DIARY
or
INTELLIGENCE SUMMARY.
(Erase heading not required.)

Army Form C. 2118.

Place	Date	Hour	Summary of Events and Information	Remarks and references to Appendices
S/OR. F.T.C.S.O Office F.22 cent.	22/7/18	Cont	5000 red & 5000 Blue Over Seas Service Chevrons received from Base. Discussed question of issue to units with Q. Decide not to commence issues till sufficient has been received to complete all requirements – to avoid complaints.	
" "	23/7/18		General Routine work. Reviewed situation as regards return of lead & covers in lieu of remaining lead to wheel Harness by R.F.A Batteries. Not yet completed owing to misunderstandings by Batteries – Reported matter to Staff Capt R.A.	Shortage of Soap at Base reported to [illegible]
" "	24/7/18		Visited 100th Bde HQ, who came out of line early this morning. Informed Staff Capt reasons for delay in issuing TM Mounting & Traversing handles to 100 T.M.B. – Promised issue at next refilling. Reported Soap Shortage. Proceeded to visit 98th Bde Bns & 100th Bde Bns – Saw all QMs & took notes of any special or urgent requirements – no complaints & situation generally satisfactory.	
" "	25/7/18		General Routine work.	
" "	26/7/18		Visited Corps Salvage Dump & brought back some Reparable Boots & Bicycle parts. Arranged to send weekly equipment OS & Leather &c to Corps Salvage instead of to Base as heretofore. Visited ADOS office – ADOS not in. 1 Vickers Gun demanded	33 M.G. [illegible] replaced

A6945 Wt. W11422/M1160 350,000 12/16 D. D. & L. Forms/C. 2118/14.

Instructions regarding War Diaries and Intelligence Summaries are contained in F. S. Regs., Part II. and the Staff Manual respectively. Title pages will be prepared in manuscript.

WAR DIARY
or
INTELLIGENCE SUMMARY.
(*Erase heading not required.*)

Army Form C. 2118.

Place	Date	Hour	Summary of Events and Information	Remarks and references to Appendices
	27/7/18		General Routine work.	
Stores	27/7/18		Visited QMs of 19th Bde & M.G. Bn. Everything satisfactory.	
F.M.C.S.O.			Received 2 complete sets Temple Grenade Throwers – Reported	
Office			to G & asked for instructions.	
F22 Central	29/7/18.		Visited AAOS & ~~[illegible]~~ took samples of defective Battery for Lucas Daylight Signalling Lamp as received from Base & of Heads for Side Drums as received from Base by 4th Kings – AAOS will take these complaints to DDOS for action. 2 previous complaints re these Batteries & Drum heads have been made to Base direct. Discussed question of amount of transport required to move my store, shops & office in the event of a sudden move due to enemy offensive. Shops to be sent to back area when attack is imminent. I can move balance on 4 lorries (including any gas reserves).	
" "	30/7/18		General Routine work – Temple Grenade throwers allotted to 19th Bde for trial. – Ordered repainting of all Tentage at Store.	

Instructions regarding War Diaries and Intelligence Summaries are contained in F. S. Regs., Par. II. and the Staff Manual respectively. Title pages will be prepared in manuscript.

WAR DIARY
or
INTELLIGENCE SUMMARY.
(Erase heading not required.)

Army Form C. 2118.

Place	Date	Hour	Summary of Events and Information	Remarks and references to Appendices
Stone F.17.C.50 Office F.22 cent. Sheet 27	31/7/18		General Routine work - end of month returns despatched to ADOS. Visited Div Salvage Dump & Salvage Officer - Inspected Dump & instructed S.O. to set aside certain Bicycles, gum boots, Lewis gun magazines etc for collection by my lorry tomorrow. Tin discs for contact aeroplane signalling by troops in forward area to be held in reserve & only issued on instructions from S.O.C. in event of an offensive. Collected the weeks requirements of web Equipment from Corps Salvage Dump - a few items not available & carried forward to Base for supply - This latter occurrence causes delay in issue to the disadvantage of obtaining stores from Corps Salvage Dumps.	
			11	
			[illegible] Major DADOS 33rd Divn	

A6945 Wt. W11422/M1160 350,000 12/16 D. D. & L. Forms/C./2118/14.

SECRET

WAR DIARY
or
~~INTELLIGENCE SUMMARY.~~
(Erase heading not required.)

Army Form C. 2118.

Instructions regarding War Diaries and Intelligence Summaries are contained in F. S. Regs., Part II. and the Staff Manual respectively. Title pages will be prepared in manuscript.

August 1918 — D.A.D.O.S. 33rd Div — Vol. 34

Place	Date	Hour	Summary of Events and Information	Remarks and references to Appendices
Office F.22 cent. Stores F.17.C.5.0	1/8/18		General Routine work. Demanded 12 Lewis Guns complete, 4 for each Field Coy special authority by G.H.Q. as line equipment, not A.A.	
" "	2/8/18		Visited 18th Middlesex (Pioneers), 212 & 222 Field Coys. A & B Echelons of each. 222 Field Coy complained of poor condition of repaired Harness & Saddlery issued to them. Asked them to submit a formal complaint giving full particulars of issue, etc. [illegible] complaints & equipment [illegible] in each case. Received 12 Lewis Guns for 3 Field Coys from No 2 Gun Park.	
" "	3/8/18		General Routine work.	
" "	4/8/18		General Routine work	
" "	5/8/18		Attended Conference at A.D.O.S. office, of D.A.D.O.S. in Corps. Discussed best methods of keeping strict check on returns of all 'wornout' stores as against issues of new stores. D.O.S. wishes this to be done & on no account are 'wornout' stores in exchange [illegible] to be returned to Salvage organisations as otherwise this check would be difficult to maintain. Decided it is impossible to check return of every item with present Staff but a percentage check could be kept — taking say one indent per Bde per day for a fairly large quantity of stores such as H.S., Textiles, Iron & Steel goods, of which the 'wornout' article has a high produce value &, where issue has been made, watching the return of an equal number of u/s articles. Units to be [illegible] if [illegible] & then if not returned reporting the matter to [illegible] for disciplinary action. Each Bde wo & NCO who [illegible] to keep a [illegible]	

D. D. & L., London, E.C. (A10366) Wt W5300/P713 750,000 2/18 Sch. 52 Forms/C2118/16

Instructions regarding War Diaries and Intelligence Summaries are contained in F. S. Regs., Part II. and the Staff Manual respectively. Title pages will be prepared in manuscript.

WAR DIARY
or
INTELLIGENCE SUMMARY.
(*Erase heading not required.*)

Army Form C. 2118.

Place	Date	Hour	Summary of Events and Information	Remarks and references to Appendices
Office F.22.central Stores F.17.C.5.0.			for this purpose & to submit it to me weekly for checking & instructions as to action to be taken with any unit. Discussed details as to personnel to be added to ordnance establishments of Div & Corps Troops for as fatigue men cooks, orderlies, sorters of incoming stores, etc. Decided on 12 in all as necessary for these services, including 2 cooks & an orderly for D.A.D.O.S. offices. 4 for dealing with returned stores & 4 fatigue men & 1 Sanitary man. A.A.O.S. will put this suggestion forward to D.D.O.S. Question of substitution of a 15 cwt Box Car for 1.3 ton lorry with D.A.D.O.S. [illegible] on account of greater economy in personnel, [illegible] running costs & greater speed of collection & delivery of small loads without decrease in carrying capacity per unit of time. Owing to shortage of yellow soap at Base A.A.O.S. has arranged to purchase up to £100 on D.O.S. authority for each Div. if required, at 4 [illegible] per kilo.	7
	6/8/16		Asked A.A.O.S. to purchase £100 worth yellow soap & for O.O. 2nd Corps Troops to pay the bill & deliver the soap. Done & receipt given to O.O. C.T. to support his Imprest a/c. Made enquiries as to possibility of buying soap for next week's issue at a cheaper price. Found it could be obtained in Bergues at 3.25 per kilo. General Routine work.	

D. D. & L., London, E.C.
(A10266) Wt W5300/P713 750,000 2/15 Sch. 52 Forms/C2118/16

Army Form C. 2118.

Instructions regarding War Diaries and Intelligence Summaries are contained in F. S. Regs., Part II. and the Staff Manual respectively. Title pages will be prepared in manuscript.

WAR DIARY
or
INTELLIGENCE SUMMARY.
(Erase heading not required.)

Place	Date	Hour	Summary of Events and Information	Remarks and references to Appendices
	7/8/18		Asked "C" to impress on all units that "worn out" Ordnance stores must be returned to D.A.D.O.S. store & not to Salvage. This was done at Quartermasters conference to-day & published in the minutes of the latter. My Bde W.O.s instructed to bring to notice of units' representatives when issuing stores to them. Sent out circular letters to Bdes, M.G. Bn & Pioneers, Field Coys & Bde H.Q.s calling attention to instructions re-condemning, bundling & labelling articles of worn out S.D. clothing with unit's name before handing them into my store ~~as~~ as given in D.R.O.s & ~~to~~ to the instructions in A.R.O.s re ~~demanding~~ demanding new clothing only to replace articles actually "worn out."	
	8/8/18		Instructed N.C.O. i/c Receipt to carefully examine all S.D. clothing returned by units & bring to my notice any not "worn out." ~~Such~~ articles will be re-issued to unit & the matter reported to "C".	
	~~8/8/18~~		18 pdrs demanded for B/162. condemned for inaccuracy. 2 Vickers Guns demanded for 33rd M.G. Bn replace condemned by armourers.	
	9/8/18		General Routine work. 2 Vickers Guns received for 33rd M.G. Bn.	

D. D. & L., London, E.C.
(A10266) Wt W5300/P713 750,000 2/18 Sch. 52 Forms/C2118/16

WAR DIARY
or
INTELLIGENCE SUMMARY.
(*Erase heading not required.*)

Army Form C. 2118.

Instructions regarding War Diaries and Intelligence Summaries are contained in F. S. Regs., Part II. and the Staff Manual respectively. Title pages will be prepared in manuscript.

Place	Date	Hour	Summary of Events and Information	Remarks and references to Appendices
	9/8/18	cont	Purchased 192 kilos "Sunlight" Soap in Bergues & collected it by lorry. With part issue sent up from Base & patent cloths for use in a few days time, a full weekly supply is available.	
	10/8/18		Orders received from A.D.O.S. 2nd Corps for Lieut. G. Smith A.O.D. to proceed to D.A.D.O.S. 1st Army for duty. Salved Lewis Gun issued from Armourers Shop to 1st Queens to replace one lost to enemy.	
	11/8/18		Lieut. G. Smith left for 1st Army. Departure reported by wire to D.D.O.S. 1st & 2nd Armies & 2nd Corps & by post to D.O.S. G.H.Q. General Routine work.	
	13/8/18		~~[illegible]~~ 18 pdr received at workshops for B/162. Returned 2 sample sets of Triple Grenade throwers issued to 19th Bde for trial. W.O. 2nd Corps troops. Made up 400 tin tallies 100 each of 4 different shapes for 2nd Corps Laundry. Demanded 3in Stokes Mortar for 98th T.M.B. to replace u/s. Damaged one returned – apparently damage due to premature – wrote and asked if a report had been sent to [illegible] H.Q. Retained u/s Barrel in case it is required for inspection by A.D.O.S.	

Instructions regarding War Diaries and Intelligence Summaries are contained in F. S. Regs., Part II. and the Staff Manual respectively. Title pages will be prepared in manuscript.

WAR DIARY
or
INTELLIGENCE SUMMARY.
(Erase heading not required.)

Army Form C. 2118.

Place	Date	Hour	Summary of Events and Information	Remarks and references to Appendices
Store F.17.C.5.0	13/8/18		General Routine work.	
Office F.22 C.4.4	14/8/18		Hastened issue of S.B.R.s required by Divl Gas Officer to complete Divl Reserves.	
" "	15/8/18		Visited all Bn Q.Ms, in view of imminent move of Divn as to refitting requirements. Only 4 Bns require larger amount of S.D. Clothing than usual weekly demands. Technical equipment practically complete.	
" "	16/8/18		Suspended issues from Base till further orders. Demanded Lewis Gun for C/162 to replace one destroyed by shell fire. Arranged that refitting for Brigades in present area & fixed last day for accepting Ordnance Stores as 19th inst. If all stores are drawn by units before move I can move complete in my 4 lorries less Anti-gas reserve which I am arranging to transport on 21st inst.	
" "	17/8/18		D.O.O. of 30th American Divn visited me. Shewed him accomodation at my present Store & Office as he will take same over when Divn is relieved by his Divn in line.	

Army Form C. 2118.

Instructions regarding War Diaries and Intelligence Summaries are contained in F. S. Regs., Part II. and the Staff Manual respectively. Title pages will be prepared in manuscript.

WAR DIARY
or
INTELLIGENCE SUMMARY.
(Erase heading not required.)

Place	Date	Hour	Summary of Events and Information	Remarks and references to Appendices
Sheet F.22 cent. Sheet 17.C.5.0	18/8/18.		On instruction from A.D.O.S 2nd Corps, moved 33 Div Arty to O.O. 2nd Corps Troops for advance. Informed latter I would attach a W.O., storeman & fatigue man & a lorry to him to administer 33 Div. Arty. Received Demi Sam for C/162. Opened issues for Div. Cos R.A from 22nd inst.	
" "	19/8/18		Sent complaint to C.O.O. Calais respecting a number of repaired boots sent up in a recent consignment which were found unfit for issue to troops either thro' being odd or badly repaired. Returned the defective boots to Base labelled for special examination. This is the 3rd occasion on which defective repaired boots have been issued by Base. A complaint was sent in first case verbally. Visited D.A.D.O.S 14th Div in Eperlecques & arranged to take over his store on 20th.	
Sheet Stone EPERLECQUES	20/8/18.		Moved store equipment, reserves, & offices & personnel to EPERLECQUES in one trip. ~~C.O.O. took over as 14th Div shops~~ Opened store & shops. Div administered by 7th Corps but under orders of 2nd Corps for Tactical purposes.	

D. D. & L., London, E.C. (A10266) Wt W5300/P713 750,000 2/18 Sch. 52 Forms/C2118/16

Instructions regarding War Diaries and Intelligence Summaries are contained in F. S. Regs., Part II. and the Staff Manual respectively. Title pages will be prepared in manuscript.

WAR DIARY
or
INTELLIGENCE SUMMARY.
(Erase heading not required.)

Army Form C. 2118.

Place	Date	Hour	Summary of Events and Information	Remarks and references to Appendices
Office stores EPERLECQUES	20/8/18 cont.		Forwarded complaint fm 9 H.L.I. re issue of too large size kilts for those demanded by unit, thus detracting from smart appearance of the Battalion. Large size waist measurements for a given length are now available issued by Base. Asked if these could be rectified by Base or if question should be put up to G.H.Q. for taking up with the manufacturers.	
" "	21/8/18.		Arranged to refit 19th Bde who are billetted in Recques area about 15 kilometres from my stores. Instructed other units to draw direct from my store. Submitted draft for Administrative Orders to this effect & gave location & No. of Ordnance workshops for repair of vehicles (No 30 light mob. worksh).	
" "	22/8/18.		Wrote Staff Capts of Bdes to arrange a programme for Bdes to send in Lewis Guns on their charge which require overhaul to 2nd Armourers Shop at rate of 12 per week each Bde — too many Guns now in Bdes to attempt to overhaul some here. General Routine work.	

D. D. & L., London, E.C.
(A10266) Wt W5300/P713 750,000 2/18 Sch. 52 Forms/C2118/16

Instructions regarding War Diaries and Intelligence Summaries are contained in F. S. Regs., Part II. and the Staff Manual respectively. Title pages will be prepared in manuscript.

WAR DIARY
or
INTELLIGENCE SUMMARY.
(Erase heading not required.)

Army Form C. 2118.

Place	Date	Hour	Summary of Events and Information	Remarks and references to Appendices
Office & Stores EPERLECQUES	23/8/18.		Demanded 5000 Socks for Div'l Clothing Exchange to replace Nos stock. First demand since April last. ~~[illegible]~~ A Visited Staff Capt 19th Bde - Pots tureens urgently required by the Bdes. Went to Calais for local purchases.	
" "	24/8/18.		Red bunting urgently required by 98th Bde for musketry ranges. Asked 33rd "G" to obtain from Corps Training if possible - Cannot buy & Army authority required in order to obtain from Base. 4th Kings & 1st Middlesex require a large tarpaulin for use as a bath - owing to distance from Div'l Baths. Asked A.D.O.S. 7th Corps if these could be issued from stock held by O.O. 7th Corps troops if any. Also asked A.D.O.S if any fire buckets were available with O.O. Corps troops without obtaining from Base with consequent delay - 100th Bde urgently requires one for their area.	
" "	25/8/18.		Visited [illegible] Purchase medal Ribbon for presentation by G.O.C. none in stock & none available with A.D.O.S or at E.F.C. Canteens.	

D. D. & L., London, E.C. (A10266) W1 W5300/P713 750,000 2/18 Sch. 52 Forms/C2118/16

Instructions regarding War Diaries and Intelligence Summaries are contained in F. S. Regs., Part II. and the Staff Manual respectively. Title pages will be prepared in manuscript.

WAR DIARY
or
INTELLIGENCE SUMMARY.
(Erase heading not required.)

Army Form C. 2118.

Place	Date	Hour	Summary of Events and Information	Remarks and references to Appendices
Office & Stores	25/8/18.		Collected 10 yds red bunting authorised for issue by 2nd Army from O.O. 2nd Army Troops No 1, for rifle ranges. Received warning order to "Stand by" at 10 p.m.	
EPERLECQUES " "	26/8/18.		Warning order received that Divn may move at any hour to another Army. Later – date of move given as 27th after 6 a.m. Cleared all Returned Stores to Railhead & sent lorries to all units in 19 & 98th Bde to collect O/S stores to save time. Packed up Shops & Stores ready for move. Informed Divn moving to 3rd Army by train night 27/28. Decided to load up	
	27th		~~[illegible]~~ & move off early on 28th inst to Saulty. Stores Armourers & Boot Shop equipment & a portion of the Anti-gas Reserve in Divl Dump of Stores (to enable use to move on 4 lorries in use [illegible])	
" "	27/8/18		Informed Northern & Southern Bases & O.O. and 2nd & 3rd Armies, etc. of move of Divn from 2nd to 3rd Army to enable outstanding indents (detail) to be transferred to Havre & Rouen by Calais. Redemanded all outstanding Bals (cancelled by Calais) on Havre & Rouen. Redemanded outstandings at No 2 Gun Park, on No 3 Gun Park. Returned 2 Heavy Pattern & 3 Light German M.Gs to O.O. 2nd Corps Troops & O.O. 2nd Army Troops No 3 respectively. One Heavy gun has previously been returned to O.O. 2nd Corps Troops – Reported these transactions to A.D.O.S. 2 Corps. Decided to leave Armourers & Boot Shop equipment at stores until it is seen what the Divn is to do. Then collect & open up.	

D. D. & L., London, E.C.
(A10266) Wt W5300/P713 750,000 2/18 Sch. 52 Forms/C2118/16

Instructions regarding War Diaries and Intelligence Summaries are contained in F. S. Regs., Part II. and the Staff Manual respectively. Title pages will be prepared in manuscript.

WAR DIARY
or
INTELLIGENCE SUMMARY.
(*Erase heading not required.*)

Army Form C. 2118.

Place	Date	Hour	Summary of Events and Information	Remarks and references to Appendices
Saulty.	28/8/18.		Moved office & stores & all personnel to Saulty & opened in the village. Railhead is Frevent from 29th inst.	
" "	29/8/18.		Opened issues from both Bases. Obtained location of Ordnance Workshops from ADOS 17th Corps – No 23 & 27 light at X.3.d.8.8. Sheet 51C. Asked 'Q' to publish latter in D.R.Os. As this weeks oil grease & flannelette was returned to Base owing to inability to carry it owing to sudden move, decided to complete units requirements from reserve stock. Arranged with Bdes to send these stores out to supply refilling points at 10 am on 30th – all Bdes a good distance behind Saulty. Asked CRE to instruct 3 Field Coys to each return 4 bicycles under a recent GRO. – 2 to be issued to X & Y/32 T.M.B on return of 33 Div Arty & balance to be sent to ~~[illegible] 3rd Army Troops~~ Base.	
" "	30/8/18.		Refitted 3 Brigades & collected some worn out clothing & stores. 'Q' decided to have workshops opened here. General Rawlins Visited ADOS 17 Corps to obtain 18 Silver Vases urgently required for presentation by GOC tomorrow – none available but obtained them from ADOS 6th Corps.	

D. D. & L., London, E.C. (A10266) Wt W5300/P713 750,000 2/18 Sch. 52 Forms/C2118/16

Army Form C. 2118.

WAR DIARY

~~or~~

~~INTELLIGENCE~~ SUMMARY.

(Erase heading not required.)

Instructions regarding War Diaries and Intelligence Summaries are contained in F. S. Regs., Part II. and the Staff Manual respectively. Title pages will be prepared in manuscript.

Place	Date	Hour	Summary of Events and Information	Remarks and references to Appendices
Saulty.	31/8/18.		Sent 2 Armourers to 2nd A & S H + 1/9 H.L.I. to inspect Arms, Lewis Guns + Bicycles + effect any repairs required. Sent 1 Armourer also to Pioneers. Sent 2 lorries to [illegible] to collect Armourers + Boot Shops + balance of Anti-gas Reserve now urgently required owing to recent heavy issues to units by D.G.O. General Routine work. 3000 more Tin Discs very urgently required for ~~Aeroplane~~ Ground Signalling by advancing Troops to Aeroplanes. Collected Tin from Dumps + prepared to make them up as rapidly as possible tomorrow when Armourers Shop can be opened.	

31/8/18

[illegible signature] Major
D.A.D.O.S.
33 Div.

D. D. & L., London, E.C.
(A10266) Wt W5300/P713 750,000 2/18 Sch. 52 Forms/C2118/16

17

Instructions regarding War Diaries and Intelligence Summaries are contained in F. S. Regs., Part II. and the Staff Manual respectively. Title pages will be prepared in manuscript.

WAR DIARY
or
~~INTELLIGENCE SUMMARY.~~
(Erase heading not required.)

Army Form C. 2118.

SECRET
DADOS 33 Divn
September 1918

Place	Date	Hour	Summary of Events and Information	Remarks and references to Appendices
Saulty	1/9/18		Opened Armourers & Boot Shop - 4 Lewis + 1 Vickers Gun received for repair + a good many bicycles. Most urgent work being the making of 3000 tin discs, set whole shop on to this work till completed. Confirmed arrival of 33 Div Arty from O.O. 2 Corps Troops + sent a lorry to HOUT-KERQUE to collect my personnel + Stores + return with them to Saulty. Havre wired that they could not despatch Stores to us owing to truck shortage + asked if any other formation was using our Railhead - wired them 3rd Army Troops No 1 using & that they may issue our Stores in latters' truck to save trucks. Wire sent to Rouen 29th ult re [illegible] issue, never answered by them. Asked Signals to investigate as delay has caused inconvenience to all concerned. Wired ADOS 17 Corps for authority to draw 50 Yukon Packs urgently reqd by Bdes.	
"	2/9/18		Demanded 4.5" How for D/156, condemned for wear. Demanded 18 pdr gun for B/162, condemned for scoring. Drew 50 Yukon Packs from O.O. 17 Corps Troops & issued 12 to each Infty Bde - Retained balance in store. Sent ~~[illegible]~~ Stores withdrawn as surplus under a recent SRO, from 33 M.G. Bn to Railhead for despatch to Base. Took into stock previously all items which were [illegible]	

D. D. & L., London, E.C. (A10266) Wt W5300/P713 750,000 2/18 Sch. 52 Forms/C2118/16

Army Form C. 2118.

WAR DIARY
or
INTELLIGENCE SUMMARY.
(Erase heading not required.)

Instructions regarding War Diaries and Intelligence Summaries are contained in F. S. Regs., Part II. and the Staff Manual respectively. Title pages will be prepared in manuscript.

Place	Date	Hour	Summary of Events and Information	Remarks and references to Appendices
Lucheux.	3/9/18		Moved to Lucheux & opened stores, office & shops. No stores received at Railhead altho' truck notified as due to-day. All units notified of change of my location - all are located close enough to store to draw direct except Artillery whom I arranged to refill on same days as before at Rebreuvitte commencing when stores are available - delay in receipt of RA stores may be expected owing to recent change of Base. 4.5in How for B/156 & 18pdr. for B/162 issued by Gun Park to 2 Corps O.M.W.(L) for fitting as the carriages of the pieces condemned in 2 Corps by 9/10 O.M.W.(L) have been brought from 2 Corps by Batteries & taken to 23/27. Notified all concerned of this arrangement.	23/27 2 Corps to 23/27
" "	4/9/18		Very heavy demands received for Cardigan Waistcoats from nearly all units following instructions from "Q" to complete establishment. 4000 approximately required. Took matter up with each unit whose demand was excessive & asked for explanation of deficiencies. Many units imagine these garments are a winter issue only. Drew attention to Summer Scale of Clothing where Cardigans are included. Men throw them away in hot weather or the units dump them & they are lost to the Service & probably to the Public. Asked "Q" to make it clear to all units that the Establishment of these garments must be kept up all the year round & if not required during Summer months they may be stored by units in D.O.'s Store until required in the winter. 3 weeks demands for Boots received in full.	

D. D. & L., London, E.C.
(A10266) Wt W5300/P713 750,000 2/18 Sch. 52 Forms/C2118/16

Instructions regarding War Diaries and Intelligence Summaries are contained in F. S. Regs., Part II. and the Staff Manual respectively. Title pages will be prepared in manuscript.

WAR DIARY
or
INTELLIGENCE SUMMARY.
(Erase heading not required.)

Army Form C. 2118.

Place	Date	Hour	Summary of Events and Information	Remarks and references to Appendices
Lucheux.	5/9/18		100th Bde demanded a quantity of various coloured buntings for making up into flags for special Training Scheme involving Tanks. Asked 'G' to wire 3rd Army ~~for~~ to authorize issue from ~~the~~ stocks within Army if available or ~~[illegible]~~ local Purchase owing to urgency. 'G' ordered immediate purchase out of Canteen funds if Army authority not obtained. Rang up ADOS. on phone & found OO 17th Corps Troops had a small stock of red, blue, yellow & black but no green or white. Collected 3 yds of each colour available by car in evening from OO 17th C.T. Used white towelling in lieu of white calico & surplus green curtains from Chateau in lieu of green bunting. Handed parcel of coloured cloths required to Signals for despatch by first DR on 6th. 100th Bde will make up the flags in Regtl Tailors shops. Visited Doullens in afternoon & found location of Officers' Clothing Depot adjacent to OO 3rd Army Troops No 2. Good stock of most items available for issue. Published location in notices to next issue of DDOS & advised Officers to obtain their requirements from the Depot instead of indenting on me in order to save delay. Demanded new Barrel for 3" Stokes Mortar for 98th TMB replace [illegible] & altered slot in traversing screw of the mortar to take new pattern handle recently issued from 12 Inc. in Armourers shop.	

(A10266) W. W5300/P713 750,000 2/18 Sch. 52 Forms/C2118/16 "D. D. & L., London, E.C.

Instructions regarding War Diaries and Intelligence Summaries are contained in F. S. Regs., Part II. and the Staff Manual respectively. Title pages will be prepared in manuscript.

WAR DIARY
or
INTELLIGENCE SUMMARY.
(Erase heading not required.)

Army Form C. 2118.

Place	Date	Hour	Summary of Events and Information	Remarks and references to Appendices
Lucheux	6/9/18		5 tons oil, grease & camp equipment etc received from Havre Base. This is first truck received from the Base since leaving 2nd Corps. General Routine work.	
" "	7/9/18.		The system of marking units' bicycles (with open & secret serial numbers) for checking the holding of unauthorized cycles, which ADOS 17 Corps asked me to adopt, not approved by G.O.C. & therefore no action taken in the matter. The present system in force records Registered Nos of each Cycle which comes into shop for repair & so keeps a check on manner in which units treat their bicycles. Last month's Bulk Return amended, using actual strengths of men & horses as given by 'Q' & not approx. strengths as ADOS requires the former method of obtaining issues & returns per 1000 men & horses.	
" "	8/9/18		General Routine work. ADOS 17 Corps arranged for units of this Division while in back area to send vehicles & guns for repair to 3rd Army Heavy Mobile Workshop, Auxi-le-Chateau as Corps workshops are well forward & too far from Divl. area. This arrangement published in D.R.O.s.	

Army Form C. 2118.

Instructions regarding War Diaries and Intelligence Summaries are contained in F. S. Regs., Part II. and the Staff Manual respectively. Title pages will be prepared in manuscript.

WAR DIARY
or
INTELLIGENCE SUMMARY.

(Erase heading not required.)

Place	Date	Hour	Summary of Events and Information	Remarks and references to Appendices
Louchaux	8/9/18	cont.	G.R.O. published authorising issue of 2 types of ankle Boots Class A for M.T. & mounted men, Class B for Infantry & dismounted men. The former are of lighter construction as regards protection of the sole. Had a R.O. published instructing units to state separately in indents numbers of each class required, in future. Asked A.D.O.S. for 200 washing Bowls for Div^l area. Area Commandants have none - O.C. 17 C.T. has a few, but if O will arrange [illegible] of numbers required for each area he will try & get them from Base without delay & issue to area commandants thro' O.C. 17. C.T. 1 Serviceable Lewis Gun demanded for 33 Div^l Reception Camp for training purposes - 2 additional D.P. guns will be authorised later.	
" "	9/9/18.		Ten bicycles returned by 3 Field Coys instead of 12 (4 per coy) as ordered by GOC's letter. Two field Coys have each one deficient & hence only 3 can be withdrawn from them. 2 issued to [illegible] T.M. Bns on scale of 1 each to complete establishment.	

D. D. & L., London, E.C. (A10266) Wt W5300/P713 750,000 2/18 Sch. 52 Forms/C2118/16

Army Form C. 2118.

WAR DIARY
or
INTELLIGENCE SUMMARY.
(Erase heading not required.)

Instructions regarding War Diaries and Intelligence Summaries are contained in F. S. Regs., Part II. and the Staff Manual respectively. Title pages will be prepared in manuscript.

Place	Date	Hour	Summary of Events and Information	Remarks and references to Appendices
Lucheux	9/9/18	cont	No 4 by Train hastened issue of horse shoes - 3 weeks demands outstanding owing to moves change of base & [illegible] shortages all operating together. Base have notified despatch of horseshoes yesterday.	
" "	10/9/18		Visited 3rd Army H.M.W. & returned to them a salvaged No 7 Dial Sight for repair & taking into stock - also visited 33. M.T. Coy & managed to obtain 6. 5/8" Copper tubes 7 7/8" long for cutting up into rings for soldering on to Condenser tubes of Vickers Guns behind union screw to prevent latter slipping off. 16 Condenser tubes sent in to Div Armourers Shop by 33 M.G. Bn for this alteration to be made. No copper tubing of suitable dimensions obtainable from Base or Ordnance workshops.	
Lucheux	11/9/18		General Routine work. 18 pdr gun demanded for B/156. U/s thro' [illegible]	
" "	12/9/18		Obtained a further supply of coloured cloth for 15 Bde for special training purposes. Demanded 18 pdr for B/156. U/s thro' [illegible]. General Routine work.	
" "	13/9/18		Wrote to Train re [illegible] in need of horse shoes - 19 boxes outstanding. Wired [illegible] for information where any surplus shoes could be obtained. [illegible] some at Corps Salvage [illegible]. Orders received for [illegible] to move to 5 Corps area [illegible] stores on hand and handed over any stores belonging to 17 Corps to D.O.O. 17 Corps Troops. Arranged to move 3 lorry loads of Store equipment tentage etc & personnel to Beaulencourt on Bapaume - Le Transloy Road on 14th. Railhead will be at Bapaume on 15-9-18.	

Army Form C. 2118.

WAR DIARY
or
INTELLIGENCE SUMMARY.
(Erase heading not required.)

Instructions regarding War Diaries and Intelligence Summaries are contained in F. S. Regs., Part II. and the Staff Manual respectively. Title pages will be prepared in manuscript.

Place	Date	Hour	Summary of Events and Information	Remarks and references to Appendices
Lucheux	14/9/18.		One lorry sent to Sw HQ to take advanced party of carpenters & R.E. material to new Sw HQ, Le Meillard, to build a Sw HQ. 19th Bde proceeded to new area by bus, to go immediately into line. Sent as much Returned advance as possible to Railhead, then loaded up 3 lorries with Ordnance - stores & advanced party under a W.O. & sent them to Beaulencourt. Proceeded there by car in afternoon & selected a site for stores after some difficulty owing to concentration of troops there. On way to new area called at ADOS 5th Corps office & found out particulars of location of workshops [illegible], ads. Gun Park, etc. Remained at Rear Sw HQ, Les Boeufs for the night pending arrival of balance of my offices & personnel on 15th.	
Store - Beaulencourt office - Les Boeufs	15/9/18		Lorry remaining at Lucheux night of 14th cleared balance of Returned stores to Railhead, Frévent. 3 extra lorries from 33 M.T. Coy reported at Lucheux at 9 a.m. My own lorry cleared 3 tons Clothing from Frévent & the four lorries then loaded up with all remaining office gear, kit, Ordnance, & shops, & personnel & proceeded to Beaulencourt & Les Boeufs where my office was opened in afternoon. Anti-gas stores & personnel cleared from Lucheux to Les Boeufs on one of the above lorries. 18 pdr gun demanded for C/156. [illegible]	

D. D. & L., London, E.C.
(A10266) Wt W5300/P713 750,000 2/18 Sch. 52 Forms/C2118/16

Instructions regarding War Diaries and Intelligence Summaries are contained in F. S. Regs., Part II. and the Staff Manual respectively. Title pages will be prepared in manuscript.

WAR DIARY
or
INTELLIGENCE SUMMARY.
(Erase heading not required.)

Army Form C. 2118.

Place	Date	Hour	Summary of Events and Information	Remarks and references to Appendices
Beaulencourt, Les Boeufs	16/9/18		Arranged with Bdes to send stores to supply refilling points daily, unless cancelled when stores are not available. Units must send a limber each to these refilling points as very little stores can be taken on supply wagons in addition to supplies. Adv. Gen H.Q. at Le Mesnil. Visited AA & QMG & informed them of arrangements made for refilling. Obtained location of 19/46 am. w(L) both present & future in case of any further advance. - Published same in [illegible] administrative arrangements. Demands for M Gun & T.M. are now wired to advanced Gun Park who issue without any authority in case of M.G.s - no report to Rear Gun Park necessary except for Field Guns & Howitzers	
Office O.34.c.5.9 (Sheet 57.C) Stores Beaulencourt	17/9/18.		Brigades unable to collect stores from refilling points to-day owing to sudden advance of transport. Sent lorries to 98th & 100th Bde transport lines near Lechelle & Equancourt, respectively & delivered to units Ordnance stores. Moved office to Rear Div. H.Q. between Rocquigny & Le Mesnil. 19th Bde could not accept any stores owing to operations.	
Office " O.34.c.5.9 Stores O.34.d.1.9	18/9/18		Issued small quantities of urgently required stores to 19th Bde units on supply wagons at supply refilling point. Moved store & shops to Rocquigny Railhead. O.34.d.1.9. Early in morning as Railhead changed to Rocquigny to-day. Train arrived very late - not available for offloading till 8 pm. Store very conveniently situated as regards clearing Railhead. Refitted 98th & 100th Bdes. at their transport lines. 2 18 pdrs for B/15 b received at [illegible] to [illegible] [illegible] advanced Gun Park 5 Vickers Guns [illegible] complete with tripods etc & spares demanded from Adv. Gun Park	

D. D. & L., London, E.C.
(A10266) Wt W5300/P713 750,000 2/15 Sch. 52 Forms/C2118/16

Instructions regarding War Diaries and Intelligence Summaries are contained in F. S. Regs., Part II. and the Staff Manual respectively. Title pages will be prepared in manuscript.

WAR DIARY
or
INTELLIGENCE SUMMARY.
(Erase heading not required.)

Army Form C. 2118.

Place	Date	Hour	Summary of Events and Information	Remarks and references to Appendices
Office O.34.c.5.9 Stores O.34.d.1.9.	19/9/18		Arranged to refit Brigade units at their transport lines in future & published this arrangement in new Administrative Orders. Units other than Bde units & Field Ambulances can more conveniently draw direct from my stores so instructions issued to them to do so regularly. One 18 pdr for C/15th received at workshops for fitting. 5 Vickers guns received from Adv Gun Park & issued by lorry to M.G. Bn.	
"	20/9/18.		Visited O.O. 3rd Army Troops No 4 at Auxi-le-Château & collected 12 Hurricane Lamps by car: urgently required for use in dugouts by 15th Bde H.Q.	
"	"		in line. Lamps drawn on 3rd Army authority. Also visited 3rd Army Heavy Mobile Workshops and arranged with them to send repaired 18 pdr gun & carriage for C/15th to my Railhead to save sending along separ. Gun urgently required having been left with I.O.M. a week ago when in back area. Found a 4.5" How of D/15th not yet completed owing to inability of I.O.M. to obtain a new piston rod from Gun Park or Base. This How has been in shops since 9th inst. On my return wired Ordnance 5th Corps asking if this How. could be condemned on the grounds of inability to repair within a reasonable time under C.O.O's authority. Reported situation to 33rd Div. Arty. Also visited No 3 Gun Park re certain gun stores outstanding.	
"	21/9/18.		One Vickers gun demanded for M.G. Bn & one 3" Stokes Mortar complete for 15th T.M.B. Adv. Gun Park delivers M.G.s & T.M.s about noon on day following date of demand.	
"	"		M.G. Bn involved in heavy fighting in present attack & casualties in guns may be heavy. Arranged to send out guns immediately on receipt by lorry or by car in case of single guns or barrels. Heavy demands for replacement of barrels expected.	

D. D. & L., London, E.C. (A10266) Wt W5300/P713 750,000 6/18 Sch. 52 Forms/C2118/16

Instructions regarding War Diaries and Intelligence Summaries are contained in F. S. Regs., Part II. and the Staff Manual respectively. Title pages will be prepared in manuscript.

WAR DIARY
or
INTELLIGENCE SUMMARY.

(Erase heading not required.)

Army Form C. 2118.

Place	Date	Hour	Summary of Events and Information	Remarks and references to Appendices
Office O.34c.5.9 Store O.34.d.1.9	21/9/18 Cont.		Demanded 30 barrels for Vickers M.G. by priority wire to meet anticipated demands on warning from G. Visited Advanced Gun Park at Behucourt re supply of these barrels. Found all M.G. components other than complete or single guns are held at Rear Gun Park & forwarded daily to ADOS R for issue. Asked ADOS to obtain & issue without delay. Refilled 19 Bde at Transport lines as units can now accept all stores on coming out of line.	
	~~21/9~~		Refilling now quite regular at Bde Transport lines, including Field Coys. Barrel of 3" Stokes Mortar sent in by 98 Bde T.M.B. as U/S & replacement demanded. Barrel only very slightly dented by shell fire near muzzle, but sufficient to prevent the bomb from sliding down easily. Sent Barrel to 19/46 O.M.W for repair & return for re-issue without delay. 19/46 O.M.W now completely moved from Senlis to O.35.d.5.2. Informed G & RA of change of location.	
" "	22/9/18.		1 Vickers gun received & issued by car to M.G. Bn. Authority received to draw 9,000 leather jerkins from O.O. V Corps troops for issue to Infantry to complete to one per man. Wired Bdes to inform me when they could accept. Arranged to draw these 3000 at a time as required by Bdes. 1 Vickers gun recd & 2 more demanded.	

D. D. & L., London, E.C. (A10266) Wt W5300/P713 750,000 2/18 Sch. 52 Forms/C2118/16

Army Form C. 2118.

Instructions regarding War Diaries and Intelligence Summaries are contained in F. S. Regs., Par. II. and the Staff Manual respectively. Title pages will be prepared in manuscript.

WAR DIARY
or
INTELLIGENCE SUMMARY.
(Erase heading not required.)

Place	Date	Hour	Summary of Events and Information	Remarks and references to Appendices
Office	23/9/18.		Drew 500 Suits S.D. Clothing for 00 V Corps troops as Div[l] Anti-gas Reserve	
O. 34 C. 5. 9.			Issued 30 suits to an Artillery Battery to replace badly gassed	
Stores			clothing. Sent 200 suits to Div[l] Clothing Exchange for convenience	
O. 35. A. 1. 9.			in issue. Received 3 Vickers guns for M.G. B[n]. Demanded 1 Vickers	
			gun + one 3" Stokes Mortars complete for 19 T.M.B. One 3"	
			Stokes Mortar received for 19th T.M.B. Demand 4·5" How Carriage	
			for D/156.	
" "	24/9/18.		5th Scottish Rifles' Clothing in very bad state owing to damage by	
" "			wire in recent actions. Unit demanded 100 Jackets + 500 prs	
			Trousers – latter demand considered very excessive + reported	
			to "Q" for decision as to issue. A.A.+Q.M.G. immediately visited	
			B[n] to find out reason for this demand – meanwhile issued	
			100 Jackets + 250 Trousers from anti-gas reserve + demanded	
			replacement thro' A.D.O.S. 5th Corps. – "Q" approved issue	
			of 250 Trousers. One Vickers gun received + issued to M.G. B[n]. 18 complete	
			Lewis guns demanded for 1st Cameronians, 12 for 1st Queens + 16 (10 complete	
			+ 6 guns only) for 2nd A. + S. H. Also demand another Vickers gun for 33 M.G. B[n].	

A6945 Wt. W11422/M1160 350,000 12/16 D. D. & L. Forms/C./2118/14.

Instructions regarding War Diaries and Intelligence Summaries are contained in F. S. Regs., Part II. and the Staff Manual respectively. Title pages will be prepared in manuscript.

WAR DIARY
or
INTELLIGENCE SUMMARY.
(Erase heading not required.)

Army Form C. 2118.

Place	Date	Hour	Summary of Events and Information	Remarks and references to Appendices
Offices Le Mesnil Stores 035 d.1.9	25/9/18		Office moved to Rear Div H.Q. at Le Mesnil which Adv Div H.Q. vacated ~~moving~~ forward to Equancourt. Stores kept at Rocquigny where Railhead remains there. Demanded 5000 Rat Pins, 2500 remnant buttons & a quantity of cart line for repair of Vintages in Div. Area, some of which ~~is~~ is unusable but serviceable as regards material. 4 Lewis Guns received from Gun Park	
	~~26/9/18~~		~~24 Hurricane Lamps urgently required~~ for 1st Queens + 6 Guns only issued from Salvage. 4 Vickers Guns demanded for 33 M.G. Bn and 3 Lewis Guns for 2nd A & S.H. 4.5" How Carriage for D/156 delivered to Ordnance Workshops by Gun Park. 4.5" How demanded for D/156 Bde also 18 pdr carriage for B/156.	
" "	26/9/18.		24 Hurricane Lamps urgently required for forward area dumps.	
" "			None available at Corps. Asked Q to obtain Army Authority for issue ~~[illegible]~~. Army authority given to Base to issue to me without indent. 300 expendable belts for Vickers M.G. available at O.O. V Corps Troops. These are for issue to M.G. Bn for trial & report. 700 Shovels very urgently required by 19th Bde to complete mobile Reserves of Bde H.Q. & Bns which were left in line during last battle — none available in R.E. Parks — wired Base for 700 to be despatched first truck.	

A6945 Wt. W11422/M1160 350,000 12/16 D. D. & L. Forms/C./2118/14.

Army Form C. 2118.

Instructions regarding War Diaries and Intelligence Summaries are contained in F. S. Regs., Part II. and the Staff Manual respectively. Title pages will be prepared in manuscript.

WAR DIARY
or
INTELLIGENCE SUMMARY.
(Erase heading not required.)

Place	Date	Hour	Summary of Events and Information	Remarks and references to Appendices
Office Le Mesnil Store	26/9/18 cont		3" Stokes Mortar complete received for 19 T.M.B also 18 Lewis Guns for 1st Cams. 3 Lewis Guns only issued to 2nd Worcesters from Salvage + 2 to 5th Scottish Rifles. 5 Vickers gun received for M.G. Bn + 16 Lewis guns for 2nd A&SH.	
O.35. d.1.9	27/9/18		3 Lewis guns received for 2nd A&SH. Visited QMs of 100th Bde at Advance Refilling point - All urgent requirements completed. Collect as many shovels as possible from Corps Salvage Dump & sent them to Advanced Hd Qrs Dump at Heudecourt.	
" "	28/9/18.		Visited QMs of all 19th & 98th Bde. Units & found out some urgent requirements of Boots & SD Clothing which were at once completed from stock. Establishment of Lewis & Vickers guns now complete. Authority given by 5th Corps "Q" to draw 12 Tarpaulins for Corps Amn Dump Ls Bangles. Reviewed outstanding detail indents of 100th + 19th Bdes. Very few items outstanding over a month & all such outstandings covered by Base report as supply below demand. Certain demands for perches & Draught Poles being urgent & outstanding over 2 weeks hastened by wire - all outstanding vehicle demands & bathing [illegible] hastened by wire + 3 Wagons [illegible] demanded by wire for BAA sec to replace destroyed by shell fire.	

A6945 Wt. W11422/M1160 350,000 12/16 D. D. & L. Forms/C. 2118/14.

Instructions regarding War Diaries and Intelligence Summaries are contained in F. S. Regs., Part II. and the Staff Manual respectively. Title pages will be prepared in manuscript.

WAR DIARY
or
INTELLIGENCE SUMMARY.
(Erase heading not required.)

Army Form C. 2118.

Place	Date	Hour	Summary of Events and Information	Remarks and references to Appendices
	28/9/18 cont.		One Lewis Gun issued from Salvage to 16 K.R.R.C. 18 pdr carriage for B/156 and 4.5" How for D/156 received at 19/46 Ordnance Workshops from Gun Park.	
Officer Ston EQUANCOURT	29/9/18.		Visited [illegible] in morning & received orders to move store & office to Equancourt as whole Divn is moving forward in view of advance in present sector. Railhead will be at Fins, 1 kilometre in front of Equancourt tomorrow. Moved main portion of [illegible] & all remaining stores to Equancourt. Collected & delivered 12 tarpaulins to adv Divl Dump for convenience in drawing by R.A.	
			19 Lewis Guns demanded for 9th H.L.I.	
" "	30/9/18.		19 Lewis Guns received for 9th H.L.I. & 4 Vickers for M.G. Bn – all delivered by lorry to units transport as they are very urgently required [illegible]. Completed move of offices & personnel to Equancourt. 100 Hot food containers & 400 Braziers received in addition to general stores – Visited new Railhead at Fins to see if lorries could be brought up to trucks easily [illegible] all in order. Store situated in same group of buildings as clothing exchange & Divl kit store. [signature] Major DADOS 33 Divn	

A6945 Wt. W11422/M1160 350,000 12/16 D. D. & L. Forms/C.2118/14.

19

SECRET

WAR DIARY
or
INTELLIGENCE SUMMARY.
(*Erase heading not required.*)

D.A.D.O.S. 33rd Divn

October 1918.

Vol 36

Army Form C. 2118.

Instructions regarding War Diaries and Intelligence Summaries are contained in F. S. Regs., Part II. and the Staff Manual respectively. Title pages will be prepared in manuscript.

Place	Date	Hour	Summary of Events and Information	Remarks and references to Appendices
EQUANCOURT.	1/10/18		General Routine Work. 3 Vickers Guns received & issued to 33rd M.G. Bn. Arranged refitting for 19, 98 & 100th Bdes at their transport lines ~~19 100th [illegible]~~ near Railton Crossroads.	
"	2/10/18		Visited 98th Bde Transport lines & saw QMs re submission at once of indents for refitting. Owing to Bdes having orders to move forward shortly units are unable to accept any quantity of stores & requested that all available stores such as clothing should be handed over to their representative at Divl Stores EQUANCOURT	
"	3/10/18		98th Bde transport moved to Targelle Ravine between Villers Guislain & Honnecourt. Visited Transport & reconnoitred route for refitting. Honnecourt. Refitted 100th Bde & 98th. 19th Bde have moved over the Canal at Honnecourt. Arranged to refit them tomorrow at ~~[illegible]~~ Quarry between Honnecourt & La Terrière as they could not accept to-day. Demanded 18 pdr guns for ~~[illegible]~~ A/156th Bde ~~[illegible]~~ condemned for scoring.	
"	~~4/10/18~~ 4/10/18		Blankets received at Railhead & stored at Equancourt 11,900 until units can accept a scale of 1 per man. Demanded 18 pdr guns for B & C/156 Bdes – Both condemned for scoring ~~[illegible]~~	

D. D. & L., London, E.C. (A10265) Wt W5300/P713 750,000 2/18 Sch. 52 Forms/C2118/16

Instructions regarding War Diaries and Intelligence Summaries are contained in F. S. Regs., Part II. and the Staff Manual respectively. Title pages will be prepared in manuscript.

WAR DIARY
or
INTELLIGENCE SUMMARY.
(Erase heading not required.)

Army Form C. 2118.

Place	Date	Hour	Summary of Events and Information	Remarks and references to Appendices
EQUANCOURT.	4/10/18 cont.		General Routine work. ~~[illegible]~~ Over 100 German Light & Heavy M.G.s salved around Villers Guislain by my Armourers, others & rest not taken & reported to [illegible] & A.D.O.S. 5th Corps.	
"	5/10/18.		Artillery waggon lines now excessively far from my Stores. Arranged refilling for them at A.R.P. on Honnecourt – La Terrière road tomorrow. Refilled 100th Bde at Railton.	
"	6/10/18.		Received 18 pdr guns for A/156, B/156 & C/156 Bde. A number of Lewis guns salved & made serviceable & issued as follows to replace losses & unserviceable. 2nd Worcesters 4, 1st Middlesex 5, 16th K.R.R.C. 2. General Routine work.	
"	7/10/18.		Advance towards Le Cateau in progress. Impossible to issue any Stores for the present. Arranged to keep stores in present location while Railhead remains at Fins & accumulate Stores & clothing for refitting in a few days time.	
"	8/10/18		Rear Div H.Q. moved forward to 18 c. G. 1. (near Railton) Advanced H.Q. to Villers Outreaux – stayed there & then proceeded to factory on Clary – Bertry road.	

D. D. & L., London, E.C.
(A10266) Wt W5300/P713 750,000 2/18 Sch. 52 Forms/C2118/16

Instructions regarding War Diaries and Intelligence Summaries are contained in F. S. Regs., Part II. and the Staff Manual respectively. Title pages will be prepared in manuscript.

WAR DIARY
or
INTELLIGENCE SUMMARY.
(*Erase heading not required.*)

Army Form C. 2118.

Place	Date	Hour	Summary of Events and Information	Remarks and references to Appendices
Equancourt	9/10/18		Rear Divn HQ followed Advanced HQ to Villers Outreaux & thence to Clary. My office now out of communication with Divn HQ & Signals. Instructions from 'Q' were to remain at Equancourt till further notice.	
"	10/10/18.		Went with 2 lorries with urgent stores for Artillery to Villers Outreaux & thence to Clary - arranged with Staff Capt RA for Batteries & DAC to draw from his ARP at Bertry at 4 pm to-day. Sent the lorry on there with W.O. & storeman to deliver stores to units & return on completion to Equancourt after collecting our rations from Sorel? court. Visited all Bdes transport & saw QMs re their urgent requirements & possibility of accepting any stores. Found all units' baggage wagons with Divnl train during the advance thence they cannot accept any quantity of stores yet. Delivered small quantities of urgent technical stores, & Lewis guns to	

D. D. & L., London, E.C. (A10266) Wt W5300/P713 750,000 2/15 Sch. 52 Forms/C2118/16

Army Form C. 2118.

WAR DIARY
or
INTELLIGENCE SUMMARY.
(Erase heading not required.)

Instructions regarding War Diaries and Intelligence Summaries are contained in F. S. Regs., Part II. and the Staff Manual respectively. Title pages will be prepared in manuscript.

Place	Date	Hour	Summary of Events and Information	Remarks and references to Appendices
Equancourt	10/10/18		100th Bde Transport in Clary. Returned in one of my empty lorries as no car available. Saw "Q" & represented that I could not carry on so far away from Div HQ & obtained permission to move my store to Clary tomorrow, maintaining the present store at Equancourt for any stores not immediately required & for staging stores drawn from Railhead at Fins. 1 lorry & Railhead personnel, Armourers & Boot shop to remain at Equancourt for present.	
Clary	11/10/18.		Moved office, store & all personnel except as detailed above to School at Clary. All units can easily draw direct from new store. Left Arm S.M. i/c Armourers shop in charge of all stores & personnel at Equancourt.	
"	12/10/18.		Chose suitable shops for Armourers & Shoemakers in Clary – Armourers shop very good indeed, having top light.	

D. D. & L., London, E.C. (A10266) W1 W5300/P713 750,000 2/18 Sch. 52 Forms/C2118/16

Instructions regarding War Diaries and Intelligence Summaries are contained in F. S. Regs., Part II. and the Staff Manual respectively. Title pages will be prepared in manuscript.

WAR DIARY
or
INTELLIGENCE SUMMARY.
(Erase heading not required.)

Army Form C. 2118.

Place	Date	Hour	Summary of Events and Information	Remarks and references to Appendices
Clary	13/10/18		4 Lewis guns made up from Salvage & issued to 1st Middlesex. Moved Armourers Shop & Shoemakers shop to Clary & opened them for work. Refitting indents coming in. Got up 2000 sets SR Clothing from Ord Store Egnancourt & issued to all units at once. All indents for Technical & Battle Stores marked "Very urgent, Refit" & dispatched to Base without delay.	
" "	14/10/18.		1 Lewis Gun issued to 4th Kings Liverpools. Demanded 18 pdr gun for B/162 ; condemned for scoring. General Routine work. O' sent a number of GS wagons & Pontoon wagons by road to Egnancourt to collect all ~~[illegible]~~ blankets which are required immediately units come out of line tomorrow. Lorries unable to do the work quickly enough owing to limited number & amount of ordnance stores to be moved up. Went to Egnancourt by car to meet this horse transport there tomorrow & arrange loading & allocation to each unit according to actual strength.	

A6945 Wt. W11422/M1160 350,000 12/16 D. D. & L. Forms/C./2118/14.

Army Form C. 2118.

Instructions regarding War Diaries and Intelligence Summaries are contained in F. S. Regs., Part II. and the Staff Manual respectively. Title pages will be prepared in manuscript.

WAR DIARY
or
INTELLIGENCE SUMMARY.
(Erase heading not required.)

Place	Date	Hour	Summary of Events and Information	Remarks and references to Appendices
Clary	15/10/18.		All wagons loaded with correct numbers of blankets & sent to report to units in Clary area. Arranged to store balance of blankets surplus to total requirements in my store at Clary. ~~As Railhead is moving~~ 12 Lewis Guns made up from Salvage surplus ... requirements & returned to 9th H.L.I.	
" "	16/10/18.		As Railhead is moving to Masnières arranged to clear balance of my stores from ~~Clary~~ Equancourt & store all at Clary. Demanded 18 pdr carriage for B/162 to replace one destroyed by shell fire. Received 18 pdr gun for D/162	
" "	17/10/18.		11 Lewis Guns issued to 9th H.L.I. from Salvage & 9 to 2nd A. & S.H. General Routine work. Brought most of units ordnance stores left in Kurt Dumps at Equancourt up to Clary & handed them over to them.	
" "	18/10/18.		General Routine work.	
" "	19/10/18.		Issued 2 Lewis Guns to 9th H.L.I. from Salvage. General Routine work.	
"	20/10/18.		Demanded 18 pdr for B/136. Condemned for Scomp. Received 18 pdr carriage for B/162. Demanded 18 pdr for A/162 - Scomp.	

A6945 Wt. W11422/M1160 350,000 12/16 D. D. & L. Forms/C./2118/14.

Army Form C. 2118.

Instructions regarding War Diaries and Intelligence Summaries are contained in F. S. Regs., Part II. and the Staff Manual respectively. Title pages will be prepared in manuscript.

WAR DIARY
or
INTELLIGENCE SUMMARY.
(Erase heading not required.)

Place	Date	Hour	Summary of Events and Information	Remarks and references to Appendices
Clary.	20/10/18	Cont.	1 Vickers gun issued for Salvage to M.G. Bn.	
			Received Divl Reserve of Frost Caps – 5,000 sets – proportion of 3/8" + 1/2". Visited Divl Store & my own store at Equancourt with DAQMG to see how many loads of units stores & my own still remained to be cleared! DAQMG then arranged to lend me extra lorries to clear everything tomorrow. Visited Railhead [?] with a view to obtaining a truck for surplus vehicles & stores [?], while Railhead is temporarily at [?] owing to explosion of a mine between there & Masnières [?]. Arranged this satisfactorily. Refitting practically completed.	
" "	21/10/18.		18 pdr guns demanded for A/156 & C/156 – Scoring [?] + 18 pdr [?] Carriage for A/162 – Wear – General Routine Work.	
" "	22/10/18.		Received Winter Clothing from Base – Coats S.D. lined, 10,000 Woollen Gloves & 8,000 fingerless. [?] in store for ~~immediate~~ issue as soon as units can accept – Division now in line & advancing again. Divl H.Q. moved to Troisvilles [?].	

A6945 Wt. W11422/M1160 350,000 12/16 D. D. & L. Forms/C./2118/14.

Instructions regarding War Diaries and Intelligence Summaries are contained in F. S. Regs., Part II. and the Staff Manual respectively. Title pages will be prepared in manuscript.

Army Form C. 2118.

WAR DIARY
or
INTELLIGENCE SUMMARY.
(Erase heading not required.)

Place	Date	Hour	Summary of Events and Information	Remarks and references to Appendices
Clary	23/10/18.		18pdr guns received for A/162, A/156, C/156 + 18pdr carriage for A/162. Received ~~4~~4,000 woollen vests + ~~3~~4,000 pr woollen drawers ~~fr~~ from Base off original demand for 15,000 + 27,000 respectively. Put into Clothing Exchange at Clary direct for issue when Divn comes out of line.	
Forest.	24/10/18.		Divl HQ moved to Forest early - moved office + stores drawn from Railhead last night + some Ordnance personnel + Bde WOs offices, cookhouse etc to Forest in morning. One hour after opening office - heavy shelling of village occurred + one shell burst in office wounding 2 Private clerks seriously + Chief Clerk slightly. One Bde WO + 2 attached men wounded by shell bursting in field next to office where stores were to have been issued. Disposed of casualties - Both WOs returned to duty - others evacuated - Phoned to ADOS 5th Corps for reinforcements + reported casualties to all concerned. Moved stores + [illegible] just outside village + covered over with [illegible] for night.	

WAR DIARY
or
INTELLIGENCE SUMMARY.
(Erase heading not required.)

Army Form C. 2118.

Instructions regarding War Diaries and Intelligence Summaries are contained in F. S. Regs., Part II. and the Staff Manual respectively. Title pages will be prepared in manuscript.

Place	Date	Hour	Summary of Events and Information	Remarks and references to Appendices
Office Troisvilles Store Clary	25/10/18		Divn relieved & moving to Troisvilles – Montay & Forest. DWHQ [illegible] & 1 Bde in each. Moved stores [illegible] back to Clary & opened old store again. Opened office in Troisvilles. Went to Clary 7am in car & detailed 6 lorries from M.T. Coy to take blankets & greatcoats from Bulk Dumps in Clary to Bdes at Troisvilles, Montay & Forest – Completed delivery by 4 pm.	
" "	26/10/18		General Routine work. Returns of office records sorted out & office re-established – Brought Sergt Clerk from [illegible] Bde store at Clary into office to run Payments Repairing & Bulk pending arrival & training of reinforcements. Winter Clothing split up ready for issue to units & refitting again commenced.	
" "	27/10/18		General Routine work.	
" "	28/10/18		Received 500 Bags W P for Div – authorised under same SHQ authority as was given last winter. Reported receipt to G for distribution.	

Instructions regarding War Diaries and Intelligence Summaries are contained in F. S. Regs., Part II. and the Staff Manual respectively. Title pages will be prepared in manuscript.

WAR DIARY
or
INTELLIGENCE SUMMARY.
(Erase heading not required.)

Army Form C. 2118.

Place	Date	Hour	Summary of Events and Information	Remarks and references to Appendices
Office:- Troisvilles	29/10/18		General Routine work	
Elm C:- Clary	30/10/18		Following Lewis guns received from Gun Park. 9 for 1st Middlesex, 6 for 5th Scottish, 8 for 4th Kings Liverpools 6 for 1st Queens & 2 for 1st Cameronians. 18 pdr gun & carriage received for A/162. 1 Lewis gun demanded for 5th Scottish Rifles.	
" "	31/10/18		18 pdr carriage for C/162 demanded to replace one condemned for Base Repair. 5 Vickers Guns issued to M.G. Bn to replace losses & u/s from Salvage. 7 Lewis guns issued to 4th Kings Liverpools & 1 to 9 H.L.I. from Salvage. Replying indents for urgent technical stores received from units & passed to Base at once for immediate supply. Found suitable store, shops & billets at Troisvilles & moved stores etc up from Clary.	

[signature] Major
D.A.D.O.S.
33 Div

D. D. & L., London, E.C.
(A10266) Wt W5300/P713 750,000 2/18 Sch. 52 Forms/C2118/16

SECRET

D.A.D.O.S. 33rd Divn

Army Form C. 2118.

Instructions regarding War Diaries and Intelligence Summaries are contained in F. S. Regs., Part II. and the Staff Manual respectively. Title pages will be prepared in manuscript.

WAR DIARY
or
~~INTELLIGENCE SUMMARY.~~
(Erase heading not required.)

November 1918.

Vol 37

Place	Date	Hour	Summary of Events and Information	Remarks and references to Appendices
Troisvilles	1/11/18	–	General Routine Work. Hastened issue of S.D. Clothing from Base – Very urgently required for refitting. Demanded 4.5 Body Amm. Wagon for D/156 to replace one condemned by I.O.M.	
" "	2/11/18	–	Refilling discontinued as units are near enough to draw from stores & lorries are fully occupied in clearing Railhead owing to uncertainty in arrivals of trains at Railhead – normally CAUDRY but usual at Cambrai Annexe or Ville as an emergency owing to enemy mines blowing up.	
" "	3/11/18		Hastened units of 100th & 98th Bdes to remove stores awaiting issue to them at my store in view of imminent move into line. Demanded 2. 18pdr Amm. Wagons for A/156 to replace condemned.	
" "	4/11/18		Received 3 Vickers Guns for 33 M.G.Bn. but unit could not draw them before moving forward. Moved office with Div. H.Q. to Forest. Store remains at Troisvilles for present. Took 3 Vickers Guns & a quantity of urgently required 3" T.M. parts for 100 & 98 T.M.Bs. with office & wired units to draw from there before 10 a.m. 5th inst	

A6945 Wt. W11422/M1160 350,000 12/16 D. D. & L. Forms/C./2118/14.

Instructions regarding War Diaries and Intelligence Summaries are contained in F. S. Regs., Part II. and the Staff Manual respectively. Title pages will be prepared in manuscript.

WAR DIARY
or
INTELLIGENCE SUMMARY.
(Erase heading not required.)

Army Form C. 2118.

Place	Date	Hour	Summary of Events and Information	Remarks and references to Appendices
Office:- Forest Stores:- Troisvilles	5/11/18		Moved office to Englefontaine & opened it in P.O. Office owing to lack of other accomodation. Adv DWHQ moved on immediately to Les Grandes Patures in the Centre of the Forêt de Mormal owing to rapid advance of our front line. No issues can be made at present so arranged to accumulate stores as received from Base at Troisvilles & have them ready for issue immediately locations are settled & units can accept.	
Office Englefontaine Stores Troisville	6/11/18		Moved office to SARBARAS on the Eastern Edge of the Forêt de Mormal - on arrival at Les Grandes Patures found Adv H.Q. had moved forward & Rear H.Q. moving in a few hours. Very limited accomodation in SARBARAS & traffic route very bad & congested. Could not return lorry from SARBARAS to Englefontaine owing to traffic conditions - Useless to attempt to bring stores up nearer than Les Grandes Patures for present.	

(A9175) Wt W2358/P360 600,000 12/17 D. D. & L. Sch. 52a. Forms/C2118/15.

Instructions regarding War Diaries and Intelligence Summaries are contained in F. S. Regs., Part II. and the Staff Manual respectively. Title pages will be prepared in manuscript.

WAR DIARY
or
INTELLIGENCE SUMMARY.
(Erase heading not required.)

Army Form C. 2118.

Place	Date	Hour	Summary of Events and Information	Remarks and references to Appendices
Cont:-	6/10/18		After considerable searching in Englefontaine found a suitable building for a Blanket & Greatcoat Store for 'Q'. Reported its location to 'Q' & arranged with Area Commandant to reserve it.	
Office:- SARBARAS Store Troisvilles	7/10/18		Visited store at Troisvilles by car & arranged removal of 19, 98 & 100 Bde Blankets & Greatcoats from Troisvilles, Montay & Forest respectively to Englefontaine by my own lorries as far as possible. 'Q' asked V Corps for 5 additional lorries to assist. The 19 Bde Blankets etc all moved to Englefontaine by [illegible] 22 hours to-day. General Routine work otherwise. No issues of Stores made yet.	
" "	8/10/18		Saw 'Q' & found Div. is being relieved at once. – Hence Blankets & Greatcoats are required to be issued to-morrow night. 'Q' informed 'Q' 10 lorries would be required from V Corps to collect & deliver 3 Bdes' Blankets & Greatcoats to 21 wagons being sent by S.A.A. Sec. D.A.C. to a rendez-vous at Les Grandes Patures. The store at Englefontaine not, therefore, required now	

(A9475) Wt. W4355/P360 600,000 12/17 D. D. & L. Sch. 52a. Forms/C2118/15.

Army Form C. 2118.

Instructions regarding War Diaries and Intelligence Summaries are contained in F. S. Regs., Part II. and the Staff Manual respectively. Title pages will be prepared in manuscript.

WAR DIARY
or
INTELLIGENCE SUMMARY.
(Erase heading not required.)

Place	Date	Hour	Summary of Events and Information	Remarks and references to Appendices
Office	9/11/18		Met the lorries (7 of which arrived together) leaving 2 more to	
SARBARAS.			load up & come on later) at Les Grandes Pastures &	
Store			also the 21 wagons (7 per Bde) from S.A.A. Sec.	
Troisvilles			Obtained fatigue party from Bde Minimum Reserves &	
			transferred each units Blankets & Greatcoats to separate	
			wagons which moved off to units transport lines when	
			loaded. Three lorries sent back for another load as	
			there are 12 loads in all & not 10 as estimated.	
			Owing to lateness of arrival of the 2 lorries & these 3 latter	
			I arranged for them to deliver direct to units &	
			dismissed the 5 remaining S.S. wagons to avoid keeping	
			the animals & men waiting in the rain.	
			All Blankets & Greatcoats issued satisfactorily by	
			23 hours. Sent instructions to store to move to the	
			vacant store in Englefontaine as soon as possible.	
			Traffic still very congested on forward roads.	

WAR DIARY
or
INTELLIGENCE SUMMARY.
(*Erase heading not required.*)

Instructions regarding War Diaries and Intelligence Summaries are contained in F. S. Regs., Part II. and the Staff Manual respectively. Title pages will be prepared in manuscript.

Army Form C. 2118.

Place	Date	Hour	Summary of Events and Information	Remarks and references to Appendices
Office SARBARAS Store ~~[struck out]~~ TROISVILLES.	10/11/18.		more suitable store found by my Senior Bde W.O. who took it over for outgoing Train (38th) in Englefontaine. Arranged refilling for 3 Infty Bdes – R.A., M.G.Bn & Pioneers at the Supply Refilling point, Les Grandes Pâtures at 2 p.m. ~~[struck out]~~ all stores collected from Railhead (~~[struck out]~~ Truck 2 days late) sent direct to store at Englefontaine. 94 lorries returned to Troisvilles for refilling. Owing to amount of stores at Railhead lorries were about 1½ hours late but I reached the refilling point at 2 p.m & advised all units to wait. Only 1 Bde of R.A. attended refilling; the other Bde was moving.	
	11/11/18		Demanded an 18pdr. Amtn. wagon for C/156 to replace one destroyed by shell fire. Completed move of store to Englefontaine. Leaving Surplus Battle Stores, Stock of Blankets & Braziers & Hot Food Containers at Troisvilles i/c an N.C.O. to save transport. Refilled all units at new supply refilling point near SARBARAS at 3 p.m.	

(A9172) Wt. W2350/P560 600,000 12/17 D. D. & L. Sch. 52a. Forms/C2118/15.

Instructions regarding War Diaries and Intelligence Summaries are contained in F. S. Regs., Part II. and the Staff Manual respectively. Title pages will be prepared in manuscript.

WAR DIARY
or
INTELLIGENCE SUMMARY.
(Erase heading not required.)

Army Form C. 2118.

Place	Date	Hour	Summary of Events and Information	Remarks and references to Appendices
Office SARBARAS.	12/11/18		Moved office in afternoon to Berlaimont – reserved a good store there to which I propose to move stores on 14th inst. General Routine work. Wired all [illegible] asking if they had any surplus boots – very urgently req'd owing to [illegible]	
Store Englefontaine.	13/11/18		Proceeded on leave by car to Boulogne – Called at store & left instructions for the collection of 175 prs Ankle & F.S. Boots from D.A.D.O.S. 38th Div at Locquignol before 9 a.m. to-day.	
	14/11/18		Cleared Braziers from Troisvilles & Holford Containers & [illegible] to Railhead. Left Blankets Kitbags Frost Caps etc for removal to Maubeuge as Div is shortly moving there. Cancelled move of stores from Englefontaine to Berlaimont.	
	15/11/18		Demanded 10000 Blankets as 2nd issue. Authority G.M.G. 4041 (O.R.) ~~[illegible]~~. Made arrangements to have ~~[illegible]~~ Special Battle Stores returned by units to my office at Berlaimont under 'G' instructions, checked & sent to Railhead – also had Salvage removed to Englefontaine for sorting & despatch to Bases. 8 Lorry loads in all.	

D. D. & L., London, E.C.
(A10266) Wt W5300/P713 750,000 2/18 Sch. 52 Forms/C2118/16

Army Form C. 2118.

WAR DIARY
or
INTELLIGENCE SUMMARY.
(Erase heading not required.)

Instructions regarding War Diaries and Intelligence Summaries are contained in F. S. Regs., Part II. and the Staff Manual respectively. Title pages will be prepared in manuscript.

Place	Date	Hour	Summary of Events and Information	Remarks and references to Appendices
Office Berlaimont	16/11/18.		Sent 3 loads of Battle Stores to Englefontaine for sorting & despatch to Base.	
Store Englefontaine.	17/11/18		Moved offices from Berlaimont to Montigny & store to Brewery at O.18.B.4.3 Sheet 57B. on Clary–Bertry Road only 2 lorries available for these moves. All units can draw direct from new stores except R.A. M.G. Bn &	
Office Montigny Stores. O.18.B.4.3	Sht 57B.		Pioneers for the present.	
" "	18/11/18.		Railhead moved from Solesmes to Caudry. arranged to refill R.A. M.G. Bn & Pioneers at N.26.d.2.2.	
" "			(Locquignol) at 2 pm on 19th. Removed balance of stores from Englefontaine to Brewery. Asked G as to disposal of Armourers Shop in view of small amount of work now coming in & the difficulty of moving the shop on a long move backwards. No decision can be given until the Div. Commander returns from leave.	

D. D. & L., London, E.C.
(A10266) Wt W5300/P713 750,000 2/15 Sch. 52 Forms/C2118/16

Instructions regarding War Diaries and Intelligence Summaries are contained in F. S. Regs., Part II. and the Staff Manual respectively. Title pages will be prepared in manuscript.

WAR DIARY
or
INTELLIGENCE SUMMARY.
(Erase heading not required.)

Army Form C. 2118.

Place	Date	Hour	Summary of Events and Information	Remarks and references to Appendices
Offices Montigny Store O18.b.4.3.	19/11/18.		'Q' decided that the ~~[illegible]~~ Anti-gas Clothing authorised under SRO 5556 ~~[illegible]~~ not to be demanded. Visited old Store at Troisvilles & saw NCO left in charge of stores – all correct. Cleared Armourers Shop & all stores except Anti-gas reserve from Englefontaine. Refilled R.A. at all units attended & all stores issued.	
" "	20/11/18.		Drew stock of Blankets from Troisvilles & these together with some returned by units surplus to requirements owing to reduction in strength, totalled 1,400. Issued them to 8 Batteries of R.F.A. Cleared balance of Petrol tins & Braziers from Troisvilles to Railhead for despatch to BASE.	
" "	21/11/18.		2 Lorries sent to clear Anti-gas reserves & stores from Englefontaine to Montigny where D.G.O is located. A number of Picks & Shovels salved from a billet in Forest. Balance of stores cleared from Englefontaine to [illegible] at O18.b.4.3. All stores now centralised at [illegible].	

WAR DIARY
or
INTELLIGENCE SUMMARY.
(Erase heading not required.)

Army Form C. 2118.

Instructions regarding War Diaries and Intelligence Summaries are contained in F. S. Regs., Part II. and the Staff Manual respectively. Title pages will be prepared in manuscript.

Place	Date	Hour	Summary of Events and Information	Remarks and references to Appendices
Office Mentioned stores O.1.8.6.4.3.	22/11/18		Saw D.A.Q.M.G. re coming move to Corbie Area on 27th & 29th. Store instructed to dispose of any surplus stocks of stores in view of move.	
" "	23/11/18.		Suspended issues from both Bases. Received 5,000 Blankets and arranged issue to 19 & 98 Bdes.	
" "			Sent 2 lorries to Englefontaine under instructions from A.D.O.S. V Corps to collect 8 6 inch T.M. Sub Beds left by D.T.M.O. & deliver to No 3 Gun Park Cambrai.	
			Wire received from Q that 169 Bde R.H.A. has points 33 Div Arty - these points on charge	
" "	24/11/18.		Received notification from Q that move to Corbie Area had been put off until 1st & 3rd prox. Opened issues from Bases again up to 27th incl. Went to	
" "	25/11/18.		Fouilloy by D.O.S. Car to see store allotted to us. Found it far too small - it will be necessary to supplement accommodation with tentage. Received another 3,000 Blankets to complete demand & arranged issue to 100th Bde, M.G. Bn, Pioneers & Div troops. Despatched Div Anti-gas stores to Bases.	

D. D. & L., London, E.C.
(A10266) Wt W5300/P713 750,000 2/18 Sch. 52 Forms/C2118/16

Instructions regarding War Diaries and Intelligence Summaries are contained in F. S. Regs., Part II. and the Staff Manual respectively. Title pages will be prepared in manuscript.

WAR DIARY
or
INTELLIGENCE SUMMARY.
(Erase heading not required.)

Army Form C. 2118.

Place	Date	Hour	Summary of Events and Information	Remarks and references to Appendices
~~Office~~ Montigny Stores O.R. 6.4.3	26/11/18		Received information that No3. Gun Park will close down & all ~~demands~~ outstanding demands transferred to HAVRE for supply in future. Store instructed accordingly. Demanded a further 500 Blankets to complete Bn to 3 per man. This was necessary owing to Reception Camp taking the 1st blanket sent up with each Reinforcement from the man & returning it to Base. Had this stopped by Q. Railhead moved from CAUDRY to BERTRY. Re-opened issues from Bases owing to 'Q' informing me that move of Div was postponed indefinitely. Requested Bases to despatch stocks without delay as outstanding stores all urgently required.	
" "	27/11/18.		Drew SD Anti-gas Clothing ~~for~~ Reserve from Clothing [illegible] for issue owing to non-arrival of SD Clothing from Bases. Sizes found to be unsuitable in many cases & these were returned to Base.	

D. D. & L., London, E.C.
(A10266) Wt W5300/P713 750,000 2/18 Sch. 52 Forms/C2118/16

Instructions regarding War Diaries and Intelligence Summaries are contained in F. S. Regs., Part II. and the Staff Manual respectively. Title pages will be prepared in manuscript.

WAR DIARY
or
INTELLIGENCE SUMMARY.

(*Erase heading not required.*)

Army Form C. 2118.

Place	Date	Hour	Summary of Events and Information	Remarks and references to Appendices
Office Montigny Stores O.18.b.4.3	28/11/18.		General Routine work – Railhead moves from BERTRY to CAUDRY on 29th inst.	
	29/11/18.		Moved 169 Bde. R.F.A. from 5th Corps Troops to 38th Div for advance – all available stores & outstanding Bulk & detail indents forwarded by O.O. 5th Corps Troops. Redemanded outstanding Bulk. Hastened both Bases for stores. Last trucks received 18/11 from ROUEN & 28/11 from HAVRE. Bases replied delay due to serious truck shortage. Reported this to "Q" for action as all units are urging issue of outstanding stores. Corps replied no further action possible under present circumstances. All Units informed [illegible] predicament.	
Office SELVIGNY Stores O.18.b.4.3	30/11/18.		Moved office to SELVIGNY (Div H.Q.) Stores remains at O.18.d.4.3 to save labour & time in moving a short distance	

D. D. & L., London, E.C. (A10266) Wt W5300/P713 750,000 2/18 Sch. 52 Forms/C2118/16

Instructions regarding War Diaries and Intelligence Summaries are contained in F. S. Regs., Part II. and the Staff Manual respectively. Title pages will be prepared in manuscript.

WAR DIARY
or
INTELLIGENCE SUMMARY.
(Erase heading not required.)

Army Form C. 2118.

Place	Date	Hour	Summary of Events and Information	Remarks and references to Appendices
Cont.	30/11/18		Sent 3 lorries to [illegible] A.P. for moving.	
			[illegible signature] Major D.A.D.O.S. 33rd Div.	

D. D. & L., London, E.C.
(A10266) Wt W5300/P713 750,000 2/18 Sch. 52 Forms/C2118/16

SECRET

WAR DIARY

~~or~~

~~INTELLIGENCE SUMMARY.~~

(Erase heading not required.)

DADOS 33 Div

DECEMBER 1918.

Army Form C. 2118.

Instructions regarding War Diaries and Intelligence Summaries are contained in F. S. Regs., Part II. and the Staff Manual respectively. Title pages will be prepared in manuscript.

Place	Date	Hour	Summary of Events and Information	Remarks and references to Appendices
Office. SELVIGNY Store 018. b.4.3 Sheet	1/12/18.		Several weeks issues of stores, which have accumulated at Bases owing to truck shortage, received. All units can draw direct from present stores. All units short of Boots, Clothing & Horseshoes.	
" . " .	2/12/18		General Routine work. Div Reserves of stores for special operations i.e. Raid Dresses – Coloured Armbands & etc. returned to Base. Reserve of Socks handed over to Div Baths to stock to replace up	
" . " .	3/12/18.		Ditto. Div now moving to HORNOY area W of Amiens. 3 Fd Coys moved to that area to-day – Artillery will start to march there tomorrow arriving about 10th inst. Made special arrangements for issue of all available stores to Artillery units before they move. Large issue of Horseshoes made to carry them over the march.	
" . " .	4/12/18.		General Routine work. Visited store – Large quantity of technical & other detail Equipment has been returned by units on reduction of Establishment. Gave instruction for these to be checked, labelled & returned to Base without delay.	
" . " .	5/12/18.		Fd Coys wired hastening issue of stores due to them. These will have to be sent to them by lorry over 120 kilometres. Lorry situation does not admit of it. General Routine work.	

9 R 38

D. D. & L., London, E.C.
(A10266) Wt W5300/P713 750,000 2/18 Sch. 52 Forms/C2118/16

Instructions regarding War Diaries and Intelligence Summaries are contained in F. S. Regs., Part II. and the Staff Manual respectively. Title pages will be prepared in manuscript.

WAR DIARY
or
INTELLIGENCE SUMMARY.
(*Erase heading not required.*)

Army Form C. 2118.

Place	Date	Hour	Summary of Events and Information	Remarks and references to Appendices
Office. SELVIGNY Stores, O.18.b.4.3	6/12/18.		Major A.H.E. Beavan RAOC returned from leave to U.K.: Reviewed correspondence & ROs received & despatched during preceding fortnight – Decided to send lorry with Stores to Field Coys for ascertaining lorry situation to advantage. Issues suspended from both Base in view of forthcoming move of Div. to HORNOY area. Bdes will march – taking a week at least en route. I propose to move with Div HQ on 11th inst. & open issues immediately on arrival ~~in~~ new area so as to have stores available for units when they arrive.	
" "	7/12/18.		Lorries sent off to Field Coys with all stores available including those received from Base yesterday. General Routine work. Visited store & gave instructions for despatch of all remaining surplus stores, tentage no longer required & returned ordnance etc to Base at once.	
" "	8/12/18.		As the Artillery have now moved to new Area – no more stores can be issued to them here – 2 loads of stores available for them – arranged to send on one load of these stores by Bde Storeman to HORNOY – to open our new store there & be ready to issue to R.A. immediately they can accept stores. Lorry sent off 7. a.m. with instructions to return tomorrow 8th inst. to present store. If a second load can be so sent to new store before final move takes place – the final move can be made in 4 lorries.	

Instructions regarding War Diaries and Intelligence Summaries are contained in F. S. Regs., Part II. and the Staff Manual respectively. Title pages will be prepared in manuscript.

WAR DIARY
or
INTELLIGENCE SUMMARY.
(*Erase heading not required.*)

Army Form C. 2118.

Place	Date	Hour	Summary of Events and Information	Remarks and references to Appendices
Offices, SERVIGNY Store O.18.b.4.3.	9/12/18		General Routine work. All remaining Stores issued to Bdes etc before moving. Sent a second lorry with Artillery Stores to HORNOY - to offload & return here in time for moving off on morning of the 11th inst. After consulting 'C' - Closed Sword Armourers Shops & returned personnel.	
	10/12/18.		Prepared to move off 7.30 am with all four lorries (only 3 available as yet) by loading-up Stores + Offices ~~on~~ to-night.	
HORNOY SOMME	11/12/18		Proceeded to HORNOY by car & found storage accomodation allotted to me very limited & billets for men bad. 3 lorries arrived 7 pm. as 4th Lorry had not returned by this morning - left balance of stores & an NCO etc to load up 4th lorry on its return & proceed to HORNOY immediately. Railhead LONGPRE & 2 trucks advised as arriving there tomorrow.	
HORNOY. SOMME.	12/12/18		Found additional store for Artillery Stores in the village. No trucks arrived at Railhead. Ascertained our Supply Rhead does not officially open at Longpré till 17th inst - Divn being fed from reserve dump en route. To avoid delays asked D.A.A.R.T. Romescamps (Regulating Station) to forward all trucks from Bases to Longpré on any other Divl Supply Train.	
HORNOY SOMME	13/12/18.		One 18 pdr gun demanded for 379 Battery, 169 Bde A.F.A to replace one condemned for scoring. Demanded 13,000 Blankets from Base - 3rd Blanket per man. First requirements of Washing Bowls, Lanterns, Recreation Room Lamps, Paillasses & Marquees demanded by C from Corps 'C'.	

D. D. & L., London, E.C.
(A10266) Wt W5300/P713 750,000 2/18 Sch. 52 Forms/C2118/16

Instructions regarding War Diaries and Intelligence Summaries are contained in F. S. Regs., Part II. and the Staff Manual respectively. Title pages will be prepared in manuscript.

WAR DIARY
or
INTELLIGENCE SUMMARY.
(Erase heading not required.)

Army Form C. 2118.

Place	Date	Hour	Summary of Events and Information	Remarks and references to Appendices
HORNOY Somme	14/12/18		General Routine work. – No stores yet received from Base. One special issue of stores being made from Calais to all formations of 3rd Army in view of serious truck shortage. Instructions received from HAVRE & ROUEN to cancel certain Bulk outstandings & resubmit current weeks requirements only as previous weeks indents not yet issued had been restricted to Calais for special issue as above. Action taken accordingly. Bulk records very difficult to keep in order owing to continual non receipt & consequent carrying forward of demands & partial receipts at long intervals from Bases.	
HORNOY Somme	15/12/18.		Truck of Boots & Clothing & one of General Stores received from Calais. General Routine work.	
" " "	16/12/18.		General Routine work. Large quantity of Educational & Demobilization correspondence being received by personnel of R.A.O.C. expressly excluded from all demobilization provision for the present as Ordnance services must be maintained during demobilization. Informed Detachment of this ruling, giving explanations for it.	

D. D. & L., London, E.C.
(A10266) Wt W5300/P713 750,000 2/15 Sch. 52 Forms/C2118/16

Army Form C. 2118.

Instructions regarding War Diaries and Intelligence Summaries are contained in F. S. Regs., Part II. and the Staff Manual respectively. Title pages will be prepared in manuscript.

WAR DIARY
or
INTELLIGENCE SUMMARY.
(Erase heading not required.)

Place	Date	Hour	Summary of Events and Information	Remarks and references to Appendices
HORNOY Somme	17/11/18		Difficult to spare any personnel of RAOC for Education owing to pressure of work. Informed 'Q' of ability to send one NCO on an Agriculture Course. Railhead opened to-day - One truck received from HAVRE.	
HORNOY Somme	18/11/18		General Routine work. A Battery very short of Boots. Proposed to send a lorry to ROUEN to draw a special issue in view of non-arrival of 2 greatly overdue Trucks of Boots & clothing. Asked ADOS. V Corps for authority to do so. He informed me that OO V Corps Troops had just received a number of surplus Boots from O.O. 3rd Army Tps No 1. Cambrai. Asked my requirements, about 450 prs, to O.O. V Corps Troops & arranged to send lorry in morning. Arranged refilling of 98 & 100 Bdes at suitable location in their Bde areas for 19th inst & for 169 Bde A.F.A. & other RA units near them on 20th - also arranged 19 Bde refilling on 30th. Further refillings will depend on arrival of trucks from Bases & will be notified from day to day.	
	~~19/11~~	1 18pdr gun demanded for A/156 Bde R.F.A. to replace one condemned for scoring.		

Army Form C. 2118.

Instructions regarding War Diaries and Intelligence Summaries are contained in F. S. Regs., Part II. and the Staff Manual respectively. Title pages will be prepared in manuscript.

WAR DIARY
or
INTELLIGENCE SUMMARY.
(Erase heading not required.)

Place	Date	Hour	Summary of Events and Information	Remarks and references to Appendices
HORNOY. SOMME	19/12/18		400 prs Boots ankle received from Corps. Distributed these among Artillery units off current demands. Reduced current Bulk demand on Base accordingly. Large surpluses of stores arriving from HAVRE. All old outstanding completed up to date & several current demands complete & reduced on Base.	
	~~20/12/18~~		4.5 in How piece demanded for D/162 Bde RFA to replace one condemned for wear.	
" "	20/12/18		General Routine work. As units complained of distance which damaged vehicles have to be sent for repair (No 19/46 OME(L) are at DAOURS. 40 Kilos) arranged with A.D.O.S. for attendance of the 2 OME at a definite rendez-vous in this area to inspect all damaged vehicles at once & order those which are found fit to travel to be sent to the Shops & condemn those found unfit. Fixed 27th at 10.00 hours at Selincourt church as rendez-vous for Infantry Bde troops other than Artillery & 14.00 hours same date at Neuville church for Artillery units. Submitted these arrangements to A.D.O.S. & published them in administrative notes for the information & action of units.	
	~~21/12/18~~		18 pdr gun demanded for A/162 Bde RFA to replace one condemned for wear.	
	21/12/18		18 pdr gun demanded for 378 Battery, 169 Bde AFA to replace ~~[illegible]~~ condemned for wear.	
" "	22/12/18 23/12/18		General Routine work	
	24/12/18 25/12/18		3 trucks of Blankets arrived at R'head. Arranged with R.T.O for them to be cut off & held over for clearance under special arrangements on 26th	

D. D. & L., London, E.C.
(A10266) Wt W5300/P713 750,000 2/15 Sch. 52 Forms/C2118/16.

Instructions regarding War Diaries and Intelligence Summaries are contained in F. S. Regs., Part II. and the Staff Manual respectively. Title pages will be prepared in manuscript.

WAR DIARY
or
INTELLIGENCE SUMMARY.
(Erase heading not required.)

Army Form C. 2118.

Place	Date	Hour	Summary of Events and Information	Remarks and references to Appendices
HORNOY	26/12/18		Issued 6,500 Blankets direct from R'head to all units of 3 Inf Bde group by lorry – Each unit sent a representative to R'head to take over his blankets under instructions issued by me thro' "B" on 25th. Balance of Blankets advised as despatched 2 days ago – Expect these will arrive tomorrow but uncertain cannot therefore make any definite arrangements.	
" "	27/12/18.		Another 3 trucks of Blankets arrived – Arranged with R.T.O. to cut them off & hold over for clearance tomorrow – meanwhile made necessary transport arrangements with "Q" & arranged for attendance of representatives of all units other than Artillery & 3 Bde	
" "	28/12/18.		Delivered blankets to R.A. at prearranged rendez-vous & to balance of units under same arrangements as on 26th inst. All units now complete with 3rd Blanket per man. 2 18pdr guns demanded for 379 Battery, 169 Army Bde R.F.A. to replace others condemned for scoring by I.O.M.	
" "	29/12/18.		Field Coys left division for BUCHY nr ROUEN (11 Coy). HAVRE (212 Coy) & ST MARTIN EGLISE near DIEPPE (222 Coy). Moved them to Ordnance Base Depôts ROUEN, HAVRE & DIEPPE for supply & sent outstanding Bulk & detail indents to these Bases & informed units. All 3 Coys complained of bad state of their clothing & Boots – Issued them their outstanding boots at once as they were awaiting issue – S.D. clothing [illegible]	

D. D. & L., London, E.C.
(A10266) Wt W5300/P713 750,000 2/18 Sch. 52 Forms/C2118/16

Army Form C. 2118.

WAR DIARY
or
INTELLIGENCE SUMMARY.
(Erase heading not required.)

Instructions regarding War Diaries and Intelligence Summaries are contained in F. S. Regs., Part II. and the Staff Manual respectively. Title pages will be prepared in manuscript.

Place	Date	Hour	Summary of Events and Information	Remarks and references to Appendices
HORNOY Somme	30/12/18.		Sent to 33rd Corps troops for extra boots to meet requirements of all B[illegible]s of Bde who are moving to Bases in 3rd week. None available – wired A.D.O.S. for numbers required 250 of convenient sizes. He will ask D.D.O.S. to obtain them from within Army or from L of C as soon as possible.	
" "	31/12/18.		Complaints received of delay in issue of various classes of stores but chiefly Boots, ~~[illegible]~~ & Gunnery(?).. Explained to G + to Q.O.C that delay has arisen in certain cases thro' truck shortage at ROUEN during this month + latter half of last + to wrong consignment of Trucks of Boots & Clothing by Transportation authorities. All demands now supplied except current outstandings + small deficiencies carried forward from previous demands covering the whole month.	

[illegible signature] Major
D.A.D.O.S.
33rd Division

D. D. & L., London, E.C.
(A10266) Wt W5300/P713 750,000 2/18 Sch. 52 Forms/C2118/16

33rd. Division

"G"

War Diary for January herewith please

D. Wheal
Comdt.
9 DADOS

Ack.
9/2/19.

1/2/19

1 Sheet

Instructions regarding War Diaries and Intelligence Summaries are contained in F. S. Regs., Part II. and the Staff Manual respectively. Title pages will be prepared in manuscript.

WAR DIARY
or
INTELLIGENCE SUMMARY.
(Erase heading not required.)

SECRET

D.A.D.O.S.
33rd Division

Army Form C. 2118.

V 8 3

Place	Date	Hour	Summary of Events and Information	Remarks and references to Appendices
[illegible]	Jany 1st		arranged with 3 Field Coy RE to draw Ord Stores direct from O.O. Bases.	
	2nd		Moved 98th Bde from 33rd Divn to Ord Officer Havre for Ord Service	
			Moved 100th Bde — " — — " — — " — Dieppe	
			1st Queens included in 98th Infty Bde group.	
	3rd		Sent Bde W.O.s and staff to Havre and Dieppe to administer as regards Ord Supply. Same to return to DADOS on completion of duty.	
	5th		Arranged for refitting 19th Bde on 6th inst	
	6th		18th Middlesex Regt (Pioneers) less 1 Coy moved to No 13 Ord Depot for Ord supply	
	8th		2 18pdr Guns arrived at railhead for 379 Bty 169 Bde	
	9th		Sent urgent wire hastening to Calais for immediate supply of Ankle boots	
			— " — — " — — " — — " — — " — — " — — " — — " — Grinding	
	10th		33rd M. G. Btn moved for Ord Supplies as follows:- 1 Coy to 13 Ord Depot Stn O.O. 1 Coy to Rouen, 1 Coy to Havre and 1 Coy to Dieppe	
	13th		Whole question of Ankle Boot shortage put before ADOS 5th Corps with a view to supplies from Base being expedited.	

D. D. & L., London, E.C.
(A10266) W1 W5300/P713 750,000 2/18 Sch. 52 Forms/C2118/16.

SECRET 2nd Sheet

D.A.D.O.S.
33rd Division

Instructions regarding War Diaries and Intelligence Summaries are contained in F. S. Regs., Part II. and the Staff Manual respectively. Title pages will be prepared in manuscript.

WAR DIARY
or
INTELLIGENCE SUMMARY.
(Erase heading not required.)

Army Form C. 2118.

Place	Date	Hour	Summary of Events and Information	Remarks and references to Appendices
HORNOY	13/1/19		Div. Or 19th Bde and 2 Battalion moved to Rouen for Ord Supplies. No Bde W.O. sent owing to number of units left with Division for administration.	
			33rd Division moved to L of C. – now governed by D.D.O.S. (South). Division at Div Or moved to St Margarets Camp DIEPPE	
ANDRAINVILLE	14/1/19		moved DADOS Store and Office to ANDRAINVILLE. Local Sig Service and D.R.L.S. runs arranged there by Divl. Or	
	16/1/19		Arranged with Ord Calais for Ord Stores to be consigned to c/o RTO Oisemont. No Section number to be used.	
			Serious shortage of Boots Ankle and [illegible] reported to D.D.O.S. (S)	
	18/1/19		Moved 230th Employment Coy to Ord Dieppe for Ord Supplies.	
			Moved 3rd Field Survey Coy + 3rd O.R.A. Calibration Sec to 31st Divn.	
			Put down supplementary indent on Base for Boots Ankle.	
	19/1/19		Reported quantity of [illegible] surplus to Divl requirements to D.D.O.S. (S) for disposal.	
	[illegible]/1/19		Sent nominal roll of staff and list of units administered to D.D.O.S. (S)	
	20/1/19		Visited Abbeville for Local Purchase	
	21/1/19		Drew 426 pairs Ankle Boots + 500 pairs of ½ soles from ROUEN by lorry. This completes last weeks issue to R.A.	

D. D. & L., London, E.C.
(A10266) Wt W5300/P713 750,000 2/18 Sch. 52 Forms/C2118/16

SECRET · 3rd Sheet

Army Form C. 2118.

D.A.D.O.S

33rd Division

WAR DIARY
or
INTELLIGENCE SUMMARY.
(Erase heading not required.)

Instructions regarding War Diaries and Intelligence Summaries are contained in F. S. Regs., Part II, and the Staff Manual respectively. Title pages will be prepared in manuscript.

Place	Date	Hour	Summary of Events and Information	Remarks and references to Appendices
Andainville	22/1/19		Routine work.	
	23/1/19		Demanded 1 18pdr gun for B/156 condemned for scoring and 4 18pdr carriages condemned for extensive overhaul.	
			Demanded 18pdr gun and carriage for 376 Bty 169th Bde condemned for scoring + extensive overhaul	
	24/1/19		Demanded 18pdr gun and carriage for 378 Bty 169th Bde to replace other condemned for scoring and extensive overhaul. Major Amos Beavan R.A.O.C. DADOS proceeded to No 8 Convalescent ~~to~~ Home. CAP MARTIN for 3 weeks sick leave on authy of D.D.O.S. 3rd Army. D.D.O.S. (S) notified – approval given	
	25/1/19		General Routine work	
	26/1/19		Sent lorry with stores for 31st Division and 33rd Divl Recep Camp. 2 Trucks arrived from Calais, both had been broken open and contents pillaged. Report sent to C.O.O. Calais shewing deficiencies.	
	27/1/19		General Routine work	
	28/1/19		Wired Calais when supply of Ankle Boots might be expected. Units in bad way for Boots and also grindery to effect repairs.	

D. D. & L., London, E.C.
(A10266) Wt W5300/P713 750,000 2/15 Sch. 52 Forms/C2118/16

4th Sheet

— SECRET —

Army Form C. 2118.

WAR DIARY
or
INTELLIGENCE SUMMARY.
(Erase heading not required.)

DADOS 33rd Division

Instructions regarding War Diaries and Intelligence Summaries are contained in F. S. Regs., Part II. and the Staff Manual respectively. Title pages will be prepared in manuscript.

Place	Date	Hour	Summary of Events and Information	Remarks and references to Appendices
ANDAINVILLE	28/1/19		Demand 18 pdr gun + 2 18 pdr Carriages for C/156. condemned by I.O.M. 54 Ord Workshops (L)	
	29/1/19		Sent surplus Tentage to Base	
	30/1/19		Wired DADRT, Abbeville reference Truck No 55252 which left Calais on 22nd but has not yet turned up at Railhead.	
			Sent wire to DDOS (S) giving particulars of ankle Boots due from Base and asked for authority to draw direct from whichever Base had them available. On instruction from DDOS. sent wire to Calais to ask if any Boots on rail for Divn	
	31/1/19		Wired DDOS (S) to get on direct to Calais, hastening reply to my wire re Boots on rail. Demanded 2 18 pdr guns + 2 Carriages for A/156. all condemned by I.O.M. 54 Workshops (L)	

[signature] Major
D.A.D.O.S. 33rd Div

D. D. & L., London, E.C.
(A10266) Wt W5300/P713 750,000 2/18 Sch. 52 Forms/C2118/16

17

Instructions regarding War Diaries and Intelligence Summaries are contained in F. S. Regs., Part II. and the Staff Manual respectively. Title pages will be prepared in manuscript.

WAR DIARY
or
~~INTELLIGENCE SUMMARY.~~
(Erase heading not required.)

D.A.D.O.S. 33rd Divn Army Form C. 2118.

FEBUARY. 1919.

VR40

Place	Date	Hour	Summary of Events and Information	Remarks and references to Appendices
ANDAINVILLE SOMME.	1/2/19		Sent lorry to Rouen to obtain supply of Ankle Boots owing to urgent requirements of Divl Arty. and inability of Calais to meet demands. Cancelled Boots outstanding on Calais, authy D.D.O.S. (S) B/185 d/d 31/1/19	
	2/2/19		General Routine Work	
	3/2/19		Interviewed R.O.O. Oisemont with a view of to obtaining truck accommodation to convey surplus Harness & Saddlery, handed in by Divl Arty, to Base. Could not obtain trucks owing to congestion at Base.	
	4/2/19		Spoke to S/C. 33rd D.A. regarding move of 162 Bde as a to 17th Divn, owing to distance between Brigade and DADOS 17th Divn (MOLLIENS VIDAME) arranged to carry on supplying Ord to 162 Bde until further notice.	
	5/2/19 to 15/2/19		General Routine Work.	
	16/2/19		Closed Division al Shoemakers Shop - Insufficient work sent in to justify running of Shop.	
	17/2/19		Demanded Water Cart for No1 Coy Train to replace one "U"	
	18/2/19.		General Routine Work	

(A9175) Wt W2356/P360 600,000 12/17 D. D. & L. Sch. 52a. Forms/C2118/15.

Instructions regarding War Diaries and Intelligence Summaries are contained in F. S. Regs., Part II. and the Staff Manual respectively. Title pages will be prepared in manuscript.

WAR DIARY
or
INTELLIGENCE SUMMARY.
(Erase heading not required.)

Army Form C. 2118.

Place	Date	Hour	Summary of Events and Information	Remarks and references to Appendices
ANVANVILLE.	19/2/19.		Major. A. M. E. Bravan returned from No 8 Convalescent Home.	
	20/2/19.		General Routine work. Wrote H.Q. Sw Arty to ensure return of Watches, Binoculars & Compasses all at one time from every unit vide 9do 6228.	
	21/2/19.		General Routine work. Heavy indents for stores to complete Mob. Equipment have been received from RA. Wired 100th Bde H.Q. to say no relief could be sent for S/Cpl. Hoare who is due for leave. Suggested Base check units indents direct.	
	22/2/19.		Visited Sw H.Q at Varengeville near Dieppe by car. Stayed the night 22/23. Shewed indents received from RA units to DAQMG & pointed out the great delay in submission by units considering that instructions were issued just after the Nov 11th 1918 for indents to complete to be submitted by all units & also the large quantities of valuable stores demand. 'Q' instructed me to write to Staff Capt & point out these two things & ask for an investigation. Raised Question of retaining or returning releasable Employment Coy men at present attached to me. 'Q' ruled that these men should be returned to their unit for demobilisation & a working party obtained from the Artillery if necessary. Informed 'Q' that I had closed Sw Boot shop & asked for disposal of the 3 remaining Shoemakers. Camp Commandant Sw H.Q. may require the services of one of them for repairs of Sw H.Q units.	

(A9175) Wt W3358/P360 600,000 12/17 D. D. & L. Sch. 52a. Forms/C2118/15.

Instructions regarding War Diaries and Intelligence Summaries are contained in F. S. Regs., Part II. and the Staff Manual respectively. Title pages will be prepared in manuscript.

WAR DIARY
or
INTELLIGENCE SUMMARY.
(*Erase heading not required.*)

Army Form C. 2118.

Place	Date	Hour	Summary of Events and Information	Remarks and references to Appendices
ANDAINVILLE. SOMME.	23/3/19		Visited DDOS. L of C South at Pourville near Dieppe. Obtained information re relation of all officers, clerks & storemen, R.A.O.C. in Machinery of Demobilization. They are therefore all eligible for full bonus from 1st February. DDOS requires all demob particulars of Armourers in Divs from me as soon as possible. Arranged to get information from RAs at once. Informed DDOS that I could spare one Private Clerk from my staff owing to shortage of RAOC personnel in B.E.F. Gave full details of my present staff & how employed. Submitted question of sending RA indents to complete Establishment to Base for completion. DDOS suggests I obtain ruling from DAG 33 Div as instructions laid down in Demob. Instructions are that all units ordered to form a CADRE are to be made up to Establishment. The Ordnance cannot give a ruling themselves. Stayed in Dieppe overnight.	
	24/3/19.		Returned by car to Andainville. Forwarded batch of RA indents to Staff Capt. R.A. with letter asking for investigation & explanation of delay & for information as to which cadre strengths of any RA units have been reduced.	
	25/3/19.		Refused to accept bicycles surplus to units' requirements as no orders have yet been issued for their return & I cannot despatch them to Base at present time owing to congestion there.	

(A9475) Wt W2358/P560 600,000 12/17 D. D. & L. Sch. 52a. Forms/C2118/15.

Instructions regarding War Diaries and Intelligence Summaries are contained in F. S. Regs., Part II. and the Staff Manual respectively. Title pages will be prepared in manuscript.

WAR DIARY
or
INTELLIGENCE SUMMARY.
(Erase heading not required.)

Army Form C. 2118.

Place	Date	Hour	Summary of Events and Information	Remarks and references to Appendices
ANDAINVILLE	26/2/19.		Pte Bodycote, who was evacuated to C.C.S. in February & struck off my strength returned to me from C.C.S. I have already informed DADOS that a replacement for him was not necessary. Wrote DDOS & reported Pte Bodycote's return & requested that a storeman be taken from me instead of a clerk as my Sergt Clerk will be sent on leave shortly.	
	27/2/19.		General Routine work. Wrote RAO Oissemont(?) to ask if he could accept the large quantity of Binoculars, watches & Compasses returned by 33rd Div Arty for despatch to Base as Demob. Equipment. Sent all Demob. Harness & Saddlery returned during last fortnight to Hautbecq(?) as RAO has allotted me sufficient truck accommodation. Sent lorry with Shoemakers tools, Sewing machines & materials to Div H.Q. Vauchelles(?) & personnel for recreational purposes.	
	28/2/19.		Received reply from Staff Capt R.A. re indents submitted by RA units to effect that investigation is now very difficult, delay in submission of indents was due to orders being received for all RA stores to be handed in & then cancelled & to changes in personnel in batteries owing to demobilization. Batteries are reduced to Cadre 'B' plus personnel to look after 'X' Class horses & DAC to Cadre 'A'. Staff Capt. rang me up on phone re my [illegible] SRO 6341 not yet received by me, which lays down that RA units of Divs or L of C other than Regular RA need not be made up. Lorry returned from Dispersal(?)	

[signature] Major
DADOS 33rd Div
28/2/19

Instructions regarding War Diaries and Intelligence Summaries are contained in F. S. Regs., Part II. and the Staff Manual respectively. Title pages will be prepared in manuscript.

WAR DIARY
~~or~~
~~INTELLIGENCE SUMMARY.~~
(Erase heading not required.)

Army Form C. 2118.

DADOS. 33 Div
MARCH 1919.
Vol 41

Place	Date	Hour	Summary of Events and Information	Remarks and references to Appendices
ANDAINVILLE (Somme)	1/3/19.		Visited Abbeville by lorry taking mixed personnel (canteen) from Andainville for recreational purposes. Drew Imprest money from Base Cashier for pay of Detachment – made small local purchase of wire netting for meat-safe used in Detachment cookhouse. Passed Bill to CRO's for approval.	
	2/3/19.		General Routine work. A fire broke out in the thatch of cottage (Billet No 6) used as a billet & recreation room for the Detachment, at 18·30 hours. Extinguished it with loss of thatch only, with assistance of neighbouring units & French Civilian fire appliances in conjunction with my fire appliances. Asked H.Q. 33 Div Arty to convene a Court of Enquiry on 4th inst. Acted as interpreter between my personnel who were in the billet at the time & the Gendarmes attached to French Mission, 3rd Army, on a Procès Verbal taken immediately after the fire was extinguished. It is thought that the fire was due to the defective state of the Chimney Stack. No negligence occurred in the billet. No Government stores destroyed or damaged.	
	3/3/19.		Had sketch prepared of the cottage in duplicate shewing condition before & after the fire giving dimensions & details of chimney stack in relation to thatch.	

Instructions regarding War Diaries and Intelligence Summaries are contained in F. S. Regs., Part II. and the Staff Manual respectively. Title pages will be prepared in manuscript.

WAR DIARY
or
INTELLIGENCE SUMMARY.
(Erase heading not required.)

Army Form C. 2118.

Place	Date	Hour	Summary of Events and Information	Remarks and references to Appendices
	4/3/19.		Court of Enquiry sat at my Office. Finding cleared British troops from all blame. Outbreak attributed to defective state of chimney stack & therefore the fault of the owner who gave no warning to troops as to use of a fire in the fireplace – Evacuated the damaged billet.	
ANDAINVILLE.	5/3/19		General Routine work. CRE moved to [illegible] HQ Elrctat – Signal office at Andainville closed & my phone connected direct to [illegible] – made arrangements with Signal Master for D.R. [illegible] daily to call at my office for any OHS letters & for any wires to be sent over the phone to or from my offices. Took over premises vacated by Bath Officer near my stores & used it as a billet & recreation room for my Detachment. ROO requested that Binoculars etc returned to me be sent to Calais direct by lorry to ensure safety in transit. He can accept Bicycles for despatch to Base on certain days. Informed Staff Capt RA accordingly & asked him to notify units to return their surplus machines. ~~[illegible]~~ B3 M.T. Coy less one Section left this area & moved to unknown destination. Prepared move orders for them ~~[illegible]~~ but held them up pending receipt of information re destination of M.T. Coy from the remaining Section	

(A9175) Wt W2358/P360 600,000 12/17 D. D. & L. Sch. 52a Forms C2118/15

Instructions regarding War Diaries and Intelligence Summaries are contained in F. S. Regs., Part II. and the Staff Manual respectively. Title pages will be prepared in manuscript.

WAR DIARY
or
INTELLIGENCE SUMMARY.
(Erase heading not required.)

Army Form C. 2118.

Place	Date	Hour	Summary of Events and Information	Remarks and references to Appendices
	6/3/19		General Routine work. Wired 33 Div "Q" for destinations of 19th Fd Amb. 3 Coy Train CRE & 33 M.T. Coy less 1 section remaining with Artillery & asked by which Depots they would be Ordnanced.	
AUXI LE CHATEAU [ARDANVILLE]	7/3/19		43 M.V.S. moved to Abbeville to be absorbed into No 14 Veterinary Hospital. 19th Fd Amb & 3 Coy Train moved away to-day. Only 1 section of M T Coy & S.A.A. Section remain as Divnl Troops. Informed by wire that HQ RE & HQ Train are moving to Div HQ at [illegible] & will be ordnanced by Havre – 19th Fd Amb. No 3 Coy Train ~~[illegible]~~ move to Rouen & will be ordnanced by A.D.O.S. Rouen. 33 M.T. Coy less 1 section move to Havre & will be ordnanced by Havre. Issued move orders accordingly – Cancelled all outstanding for these units on Calais Base & instructed units to redemand requirements on new Bases.	Issued move orders for them.
	8/3/19.		Received orders for Major A.M.S. Beavan to report to C.O.O. Calais for duty. Conductor [illegible] Neal RAOC Chief Clerk will act in his absence. Handed over all records, Imprest a/c & War Diary to latter W.O.	
	9/3/19		General Routine work.	
	10/3/19		Major Beavan left for Calais by lorry taking load of valuable Technical Stores to Base.	A.M.S. Beavan Major DADOS

(A9475) Wt W2358/P360 600,000 12/17 D. D. & L. Sch. 52a Forms/C2118/15

Instructions regarding War Diaries and Intelligence Summaries are contained in F. S. Regs., Part II. and the Staff Manual respectively. Title pages will be prepared in manuscript.

WAR DIARY
or
INTELLIGENCE SUMMARY.
(Erase heading not required.)

Army Form C. 2118.

Place	Date	Hour	Summary of Events and Information	Remarks and references to Appendices
ANDAINVILLE	11/3/19		Took over acting position of DADOS 33rd Div. under supervision of D.D.O.S (S) on Major Beavan RAOC proceeding to Calais for duty. Authy DDOS (S) S/Con/754/A d/d 1/3/19.	
	12/3/19		Received 18 pdr carriages for following batteries, to replace others condemned by I.O.M. B/156 – 4, C/156 – 2, A/156 – 2, 376 Bty 169 Bde – 1, 378 Bty 169 Bde – 1.	
	13/3/19		General Routine Work	
	14/3/19		Informed Bases of disbandment of ~~33~~ 43rd Mobile Vet Sec, 33rd Div. Reception Camp and X + Y/33 TM Btys.	
	15/3/19		General Routine Work	
	19/3/19		—"— —"— —"—	
	20/3/19		Arranged with R.O.O. Croseman for a railway truck to convey returned bicycles to Base, got away 75.	
	21/3/19		General Routine Work	
	22/3/19		—"— —"— —"—	

A6945 Wt. W11422/M1160 350,000 12/16 D. D. & L. Forms/C./2118/14.

Instructions regarding War Diaries and Intelligence Summaries are contained in F. S. Regs., Part II. and the Staff Manual respectively. Title pages will be prepared in manuscript.

Army Form C. 2118.

WAR DIARY
or
INTELLIGENCE SUMMARY.
(*Erase heading not required.*)

Place	Date	Hour	Summary of Events and Information	Remarks and references to Appendices
ANDAINVILLE	23/3/19		Notified Bases of transfer of 10th Scottish Rifs from ~~7~~ 15th Divn to 33rd Divn	
	24/3/19		Asked DOO Calais if Demob. vouchers were being prepared in triplicate, as according to Demob Instructions, one copy is to be attached to Mob Table in possession of unit and one copy to the Mob Table in possession of OO Formation concerned, this would not permit a receipt being sent to Base under present system.	
	25/3/19		Cancelled all indents on Base as units have submitted Demob Indents to complete stores to Mob Table.	
	26/3/19		Received information that 17th ~~[illegible]~~ Worcestershire were transferred from 40th Division to 33rd Division	
	27/3/19 to 31/3/19		General Routine work in connection with Demobilization of 33rd Divl Arty and regimental work in connection with Det. R.A.O.C. and attached personnel	

H.Q. 33rd Divn 'Q' Branch

F. Wheal Condt
ADOS 33rd Divn
3/4/19.

(A9475) Wt W2356/P360 600,000 12/17 D. D. & L. Sch. 52a. Forms/C2118/15.

SECRET

Instructions regarding War Diaries and Intelligence Summaries are contained in F. S. Regs., Part II. and the Staff Manual respectively. Title pages will be prepared in manuscript.

WAR DIARY or INTELLIGENCE SUMMARY.

(Erase heading not required.)

D.A.D.O.S. 33rd DIVISION.

Army Form C. 2118.

APRIL 1919.

Vol 42

Place	Date	Hour	Summary of Events and Information	Remarks and references to Appendices
ANDAINVILLE (SOMME)	1/4/19		Demanded GS wagon for C/156 Bde to replace one condemned by I.O.M. No 8 Ord Depot.	
			Arranged disposal of a quantity of Primers percussion which were in possession of Divl Arty.	
	2/4/19		Demanded Wagon limbered RE for Signal Sub Sec of 162 Bde to replace one condemned by I.O.M. No 8 Ord Depot.	
			Hastened supply of Mineral Jelly on Base, now urgently required for preservation of gun park.	
	3/4/19		General Routine Work	
	4/4/19		Wagon GS demanded for 3 Sec DAC to replace one condemned by I.O.M.	
	5/4/19 – 10/4/19		General Routine Work.	
BLANGY	11/4/19		Moved Store and Office to Blangy (P.O.W. Camp)	
	12/4/19		General Routine Work.	

(A9175) Wt W2353/P360 600,000 12/17 D. D. & L. Sch. 52a. Forms/C2118/15.

SECRET

Instructions regarding War Diaries and Intelligence Summaries are contained in F. S. Regs., Part II. and the Staff Manual respectively. Title pages will be prepared in manuscript.

WAR DIARY
or
INTELLIGENCE SUMMARY.
(Erase heading not required.)

APRIL 1919 Army Form C. 2118.

DADOS 33rd Div Sheet (2)

Place	Date	Hour	Summary of Events and Information	Remarks and references to Appendices
	13/4/19		Oisemont closed as a Railhead. Got on to Traffic Abbeville to find out new Railhead. Experienced great difficulty owing to a number of new vehicles arriving at Oisemont and old vehicles being refused owing to closing of Railhead. R.O.O. orders old vehicles to be returned to Longpre. This course impossible owing to distance and shortage in horses. Wired Old Communications South if old vehicles could be parked at BLANGY and loaded up when Brigades entrain.	
	14/4/19		Hastened supply of mineral jelly.	
	15/4/19		Received 2 Barrels mineral jelly, arranged to hand over one barrel to each Brigade on Gun Park.	
	16/4/19		Wired Traffic Abbeville as to new Railhead, later heard from him that trucks would be arranged to Blangy	
	17/4/19		Arranged for all condemned vehicles to be parked with other vehicles at Blangy for loading up for despatch to Base. 2 remaining lorries withdrawn by M.T. Coy.	

SECRET

Instructions regarding War Diaries and Intelligence Summaries are contained in F. S. Regs., Part II. and the Staff Manual respectively. Title pages will be prepared in manuscript.

WAR DIARY
or
INTELLIGENCE SUMMARY.
(Erase heading not required.)

D.A.D.O.S. 33rd DIVISION.

APRIL 1919.

Army Form C. 2118.

Sheet 3

Place	Date	Hour	Summary of Events and Information	Remarks and references to Appendices
BLANGY	18/4/19		Arranged to issue Ankle Boots to personnel of Arty who are proceeding to Army of Occupation.	
	19/4/19		Received 14 Tons demobilization stores.	
	20/4/19		General Routine Work.	
	21/4/19		Received 5 Tons demobilization stores.	
	22/4/19		General Routine work.	
	23/4/19		Wired Traffic Abbeville for flats to load up condemned vehicles.	
	24/4/19		Considerable delay and inconvenience being caused owing to trucks being cut off at Oisemont. Wired Base to label to BLANGY sur BRESLE and also wired DADRT Abbeville to re-label any trucks passing thro.	
	25/4/19		Moved 156. 162. 169 Bde Sig Sub-Sections to Ord Base on these Sub-Sections rejoining 33rd Divl Signal Coy.	
	26/4/19		General Routine Work	
	27/4/19		-"- -"- -"-	
	28/4/19		Wired Traffic Abbeville for 10 ton van for Retd Ord. French are using all trucks that come loaded to get rid of produce.	

(A9175) Wt W2358/P360 600,000 12/17 D. D. & L. Sch. 52a. Forms/C2118/15.

— SECRET —

April 1919.

Army Form C. 2118.

Sheet 4

Instructions regarding War Diaries and Intelligence Summaries are contained in F. S. Regs., Part II. and the Staff Manual respectively. Title pages will be prepared in manuscript.

WAR DIARY or INTELLIGENCE SUMMARY.

(Erase heading not required.)

D.A.D.O.S. 33rd Divn.

Place	Date	Hour	Summary of Events and Information	Remarks and references to Appendices
BLANGY	29/4/19		General Routine Work	
	30/4/19		Received 3 Slats and loaded up all condemned vehicles for Base.	
			D. Wheal Condr. A/DADOS	
			33rd Divn. "G" Branch	

www.ingramcontent.com/pod-product-compliance
Lightning Source LLC
Chambersburg PA
CBHW080838010526
44114CB00017B/2328
9781474516457